T0212044

Communications
in Computer and Information Science   430

Juan M. Corchado   Javier Bajo
Jaroslaw Kozlak   Pawel Pawlewski
Jose M. Molina   Benoit Gaudou
Vicente Julian   Rainer Unland
Fernando Lopes   Kasper Hallenborg
Pedro García Teodoro (Eds.)

Highlights of Practical Applications of Heterogeneous Multi-Agent Systems

The PAAMS Collection

PAAMS 2014 International Workshops
Salamanca, Spain, June 4-6, 2014
Proceedings

 Springer

Volume Editors

Juan M. Corchado, Universidad de Salamanca, Spain
E-mail: corchado@usal.es

Javier Bajo, Universidad Politécnica de Madrid, Spain
E-mail: javier.bajo@upm.es

Jaroslaw Kozlak, AGH University of Science and Technology, Krakow, Poland
E-mail: kozlak@agh.edu.pl

Pawel Pawlewski, Poznan University of Technology, Poland
E-mail: pawel.pawlewski@put.poznan.pl

Jose M. Molina, Universidad Carlos III de Madrid, Spain
E-mail: molina@ia.uc3m.es

Benoit Gaudou, University of Toulouse, France
E-mail: benoit.gaudou@univ.tlse1.fr

Vicente Julian, Universidad Politécnica de Valencia, Spain
E-mail: vinglada@dsic.upv.es

Rainer Unland, Universität Duisburg-Essen, Germany
E-mail: rainer.unland@icb.uni-due.de

Fernando Lopes, Laboratório Nacional de Energia e Geologia (LNEG), Lisbon, Portugal
E-mail: fernando.lopes@lneg.pt

Kasper Hallenborg, University of Southern Denmark, Odense, Denmark
E-mail: hallenborg@mmmi.sdu.dk

Pedro García Teodoro, University of Granada, Spain
E-mail: pgteodor@ugr.es

ISSN 1865-0929   e-ISSN 1865-0937
ISBN 978-3-319-07766-6   e-ISBN 978-3-319-07767-3
DOI 10.1007/978-3-319-07767-3
Springer Cham Heidelberg New York Dordrecht London

Library of Congress Control Number: 2014939854

Typesetting: Camera-ready by author, data conversion by Scientific Publishing Services, Chennai, India

Printed on acid-free paper

Springer is part of Springer Science+Business Media (www.springer.com)

Preface

PAAMS workshops complement the regular program of the PAAMS conference with new or emerging trends of particular interest connected to multi-agent systems.

PAAMS, the International Conference on Practical Applications of Agents and Multi-Agent Systems, is an evolution of the International Workshop on Practical Applications of Agents and Multi-Agent Systems. PAAMS is an international yearly forum for presenting, discussing, and disseminating the latest developments and the most important outcomes related to real-world applications. It provides a unique opportunity to bring multi-disciplinary experts, academics, and practitioners together to exchange their experience in the development of agents and multi-agent systems.

This volume presents the papers that were accepted for the 2014 in the workshops: Workshop on Agent-Based Approaches for the Transportation Modeling and Optimization, Workshop on Agent-Based Modeling and Simulation of Complex Systems: Engineering and Applications, Workshop on Agents and Multi-agent Systems for AAL and e-HEALTH, Workshop on Agent-Based Solutions for Manufacturing and Supply Chain, Workshop on Intelligent Systems for Context-Based Information Fusion, Workshop on Multi-agent-Based Applications for Smart Grids and Sustainable Energy Systems, Workshop on Active Security through Multi-Agent Systems, Workshop on Intelligent Human–Agent Societies. Each paper submitted to the PAAMS workshops went through a stringent peer review by three members of the international committee of each workshop. From the 61 submissions received, 34 were selected for presentation at the conference.

We would like to thank all the contributing authors as well as the members of the Program Committees of the workshops and the Organizing Committee for their hard and highly valuable work. Their work helped contribute to the success of the PAAMS 2014 event. Thank you for your help, PAAMS 2014 would not exist without your contribution.

April 2014

Juan Manuel Corchado
Javier Bajo

Organization

Workshops

W1 – Workshop on Agent-Based Approaches for the Transportation Modeling and Optimization.
W2 – Workshop on Agent-Based Modeling and Simulation of Complex Systems: Engineering and Applications.
W3 – Workshop on Agents and Multi-agent Systems for AAL and e-HEALTH.
W4 – Workshop on Agent-Based Solutions for Manufacturing and Supply Chain.
W5 – Workshop on Intelligent Systems for Context-Based Information Fusion.
W6 – Workshop on Multi-agent Based Applications for Smart Grids and Sustainable Energy Systems.
W7 – Workshop on Active Security Through Multi-Agent Systems.
W8 – Workshop on Intelligent Human–Agent Societies.

Workshop on Agent-Based Approaches for the Transportation Modeling and Optimization

Program Committee Chairs

Jean-Michel Auberlet	IFSTTAR, France
Flavien Balbo	Université Paris-Dauphine, France
Jaroslaw Kozlak	AGH-UST, Poland

Program Committee

Emmanuelle Grislin-Le Strugeon	University of Valenciennes, France
Otthein Herzog	University of Bremen, Germany
Abder Koukam	UTBM, France
Jörg P. Müller	Clausthal University of Technology, Germany
Rudy Negenborn	Delft University of Technology, The Netherlands
Rosaldo Rossetti	University of Porto-LIACC/FEUP, Portugal
Nicolas Saunier	Polytechnique Montreal, Canada
Mahdi Zargayouna	IFSTTAR, France

Workshop on Agent-Based Modeling and Simulation of Complex Systems: Engineering and Applications

Program Committee Chairs

Alexis Drogoul	UMMISCO, IRD, UPMC, MSI-IFI, Vietnam
Benoit Gaudou	CNRS, IRIT, University of Toulouse, France
Patrick Taillandier	University of Rouen, France

Program Committee

Frédéric Migeon	University of Toulouse, France
Carole Adam	Joseph Fourier University, France
Frédéric Amblard	University of Toulouse, France
Julie Dugdale	Pierre-Mendes University, France
Ruben Fuentes	Universidad Complutense de Madrid, Spain
Franziska Klügl	Örebro University, Sweden
Serge Stinckwich	University of Caen, France
Sébastien Picault	University of Lille, France
Tom Holvoet	KU Leuven, Belgium
Christophe Lang	University of Franche-Comté, France
Christophe Le Page	CIRAD, France
Nicolas Marilleau	UMMISCO, France
Gildas Morvan	University of Artois, France
Victor Noel	University of Modena and Reggio Emilia, Italy

Workshop on Agents and Multi-agent Systems for AAL and e-HEALTH

Program Committee Chairs

Kasper Hallenborg	University of Southern Denmark, Denmark
Sylvain Giroux	University of Sherbrooke, Canada

Program Committee

Juan M. Corchado	University of Salamanca, Spain
Javier Bajo	Technical University of Madrid, Spain
Juan F. De Paz	University of Salamanca, Spain
Sara Rodríguez	University of Salamanca, Spain
Dante I. Tapia	University of Salamanca, Spain
Cristian I. Pinzón	Technical University of Panama, Panama
Sigeru Omatu	Osaka Institute of Technology, Japan
Paulo Novais	University of Minho, Portugal
Luis F. Castillo	University of Caldas, Colombia
Florentino Fernandez	University of Vigo, Spain
Belén Pérez Lancho	University of Salamanca, Spain
Jesús García Herrero	University Carlos III of Madrid, Spain

Workshop on Agent-Based Solutions for Manufacturing and Supply Chain

Program Committee Chairs

Pawel Pawlewski	Poznan University of Technology, Poland
Zbigniew J. Pasek	IMSE/University of Windsor, Canada

Program Committee

Paul-Eric Dossou	ICAM Vendee, France
Grzegorz Bocewicz	Koszalin University of Technology, Poland
Izabela E. Nielsen	Aalborg University, Denmark
Joanna Kolodziej	Cracow University of Technology, Poland
Peter Nielsen	Aalborg University, Denmark

Workshop on Intelligent systems for context-based information fusion Committee

Program Committee Chairs

José Manuel Molina	University Carlos III of Madrid, Spain
Juan M. Corchado	University of Salamanca, Spain
Nayat Sánchez Pi	Universidade Federal Fluminense, Brazil
Jesús García Herrero	University Carlos III of Madrid, Spain
Gabriel Villarrubia	University of Salamanca, Spain
Javier Bajo	Technical University of Madrid, Spain
Ana Cristina Bicharra García	Universidade Federal Fluminense, Brazil
Luis Marti	Pontificia Universidade Catolica, Brazil
James Liinas	State University of New York at Buffalo, USA

Program Committee

Juan F. De Paz	University of Salamanca, Spain
Sara Rodríguez	University of Salamanca, Spain
Fernando de la Prieta Pintado	University of Salamanca, Spain
Gabriel Villarrubia González	University of Salamanca, Spain
Antonio Juan Sánchez Martín	University of Salamanca, Spain
Miguel Angel Patricio	Universidad Carlos III, Spain
Antonio Berlanga	Universidad Carlos III, Spain
Lauro Snidaro	University of Udine, Italy
Eloi Bosse	Université Laval, Canada
Subrata Das	Machine Analytics, Inc., USA
Vicente Julian	Technical University of Valencia, Spain
Eugenio Oliveira	University of Porto, Portugal
Florentino Fdez-Riverola	University of Vigo, Spain
Masanori Akiyoshi	Osaka University, Japan

Luís Lima	Polytechnic of Porto, Portugal
Andrew Campbell	Dartmouth College, USA
Carlos Carrascosa	Technical University of Valencia, Spain
Eleni Mangina	University College Dublin, Ireland
Luís Correia	University of Lisbon, Portugal
Cristian Iván Pinzón Trejos	Universidad Tecnológica de Panamá, Panamá
Luiz André Paes Leme	Universidade Federal Fluminense, Brazil
José Viterbo Filho	Universidade Federal Fluminense, Brazil
Marley Velasco	Pontificia Universidade Catolica, Brazil

Workshop on Multi-agent-Based Applications for Smart Grids and Sustainable Energy Systems

Program Committee Chairs

Fernando Lopes	LNEG National Research Institute, Portugal
Rainer Unland	University of Duisburg-Essen, Germany

Steering Committee

Fernando Lopes	LNEG National Research Institute, Portugal
Giancarlo Fortino	Università della Calabria, Italy
Hugo Morais	Denmark Technical University, Denmark
Rainer Unland	University of Duisburg-Essen, Germany
Ryszard Kowalczyk	Swinburne University of Technology, Australia
Zita Vale	Polytechnic Institute of Porto, Portugal

Program Committee

Alberto Fernández	Universidad Rey Juan Carlos, Spain
Alberto Sardinha	Technical University of Lisbon, Portugal
Andreas Symeonidis	University of Thessaloniki, Greece
Anke Weidlich	Hochschule Offenburg, Germany
Benjamin Hirsch	Etisalat BT Innovation Centre, EBTIC, UAE
Bernhard Bauer	Universität Augsburg, Germany
Bo Nørregaard Jørgensen	Mærsk Mc-Kinney Møller Instituttet, Denmark
Carlos Ramos	Polytechnic Institute of Porto, Portugal
Christian Derksen	Universität Duisburg-Essen, Germany
Christoph Weber	Universität Duisburg-Essen, Germany
Costin Bădică	University of Craiova, Romania
David Sislak	Gerstner Laboratory, Czech Republic
Fabrice Saffre	British Telecom, UK
Frank Allgöwer	Universität Stuttgart, Germany
Georg Frey	Universität des Saarlandes, Germany
Hanno Hildmann	NEC Germany, Germany
Huib Aldewereld	Universiteit Utrecht, The Netherlands
Ingo J. Timm	JW Goethe-University Frankfurt, Germany

Jan Sudeikat	Hamburg Energie GmbH, Germany
Jan Treur	Vrije Universiteit Amsterdam, The Netherlands
John Collins	University of Minnesota, USA
Joseph Barjis	TU Delft, The Netherlands
Juan A. Rodríguez-Aguilar	IIIA, CSIC, Spain
Koen Hindriks	Delft University of Technology, The Netherlands
Lars Braubach	University of Hamburg, Germany
Lars Mönch	Fernuniversität Hagen, Germany
Laurent Vercouter	Graduate School of Engineering - Saint-Étienne, France
Marcin Paprzycki	Polish Academy of Sciences, Poland
Maria Ganzha	Polish Academy of Sciences, Poland
Massimiliano Giacomin	University of Brescia, Italy
Mathijs de Weerdt	TU Delft, The Netherlands
Matteo Vasirani	Universidad Rey Juan Carlos, Spain
Matthias Klusch	DFKI, Germany
Miguel Ángel López Carmona	University of Alcalá de Henares, Spain
Nir Oren	University of Aberdeen, UK
Olivier Boissier	ENS Mines Saint-Etienne, France
Ori Marom	Rotterdam School of Management, The Netherlands
Paolo Torroni	University of Bologna, Italy
Paulo Leitão	Polytechnic Institute of Bragança, Portugal
Paulo Novais	Universidade do Minho, Portugal
Peter Palensky	AIT Austrian Institute of Technology, Austria
Sascha Ossowski	Universidad Rey Juan Carlos, Spain
Sebastian Lehnhoff	University of Oldenburg, Germany
Stamatis Karnouskos	SAP, Germany
Steven Guan	Xian Jiatong-Liverpool University, China
Sudip Bhattacharjee	University of Connecticut, USA
Tiago Pinto	Polytechnic Institute of Porto, Portugal
Wamberto Vasconcelos	University of Aberdeen, UK
Wolfgang Ketter	Rotterdam School of Management, The Netherlands
Zakaria Maamar	Zayed University, UAE

Workshop on Workshop on Active Security Through Multi-Agent Systems

Program Committee Chairs

Pedro García Teodoro	University of Granada, Spain
Félix A. Barrio Juárez	Inteco, Spain
Javier Bajo	Technical University of Madrid, Spain

Program Committee

Aleksandar Kuzmanovic	University of Northwestern, IL, USA
Barbara Kordy	University of Luxembourg, Luxembourg
Danilo Mauro Bruschi	University of Milan, Italy
David W. Chadwick	University of Kent, UK
Davide Balzarotti	Eurecom, France
Federica Paci	University of Trento, Italy
Félix A. Barrio Juárez	Inteco, Spain
Flavio Lombardi	Roma Tre University, Italy
Gabriel Maciá Fernández	University of Granada, Spain
Jesús E. Díaz Verdejo	University of Granada, Spain
José Camacho Páez	University of Granada, Spain
Juan Manuel Estévez Tapiador	Universidad Carlos III de Madrid, Spain
Krzysztof Szczypiorski	Warsaw University of Technology, Poland
Lorenzo Cavallaro	Royal Holloway, University of London, UK
Matt Bishop	University of California, Davis, CA, USA
Miguel Soriano Ibáñez	Polytechnic University of Catalonia, Spain
Nicola Dragoni	Technical University of Denmark, Denmark
Nils Aschenbruck	University of Osnabrück, Germany
Simone Fischer-Hübner	Karlstad University, Sweden
Tarek M. Sobh	University of Bridgeport, CT, USA

Workshop on Intelligent Human–Agent Societies

Program Committee Chairs

Vicente Julian	Universitat Politècnica de València, Spain
Holguer Bilhart	University Rey Juan Carlos, Spain
Juan M. Corchado	University of Salamanca, Spain

Program Committee

Olivier Boissier	ENS Mines Saint-Etienne, France
Reyhan Aydogan	Delft University of Technology, The Netherlands
Sara Rodriguez	Universidad de Salamanca, Spain
Juan Antonio Rodriguez-Aguilar	CSIC-IIIA, Spain
Carles Sierra	CSIC-IIIA, Spain
Michael Ignaz Schumacher	University of Applied Sciences Western Switzerland, Switzerland
David Robertson	University of Edinburgh, UK
Kuldar Taveter	Tallinn University of Technology, Estonia
Matteo Vasirani	Ecole Polytechnique Federale de Lausanne, Switzerland

Jurgen Dunkel	Hannover University of Applied Sciences and Arts, Germany
Ramon Hermoso	University of Essex, UK
Victor Sanchez-Anguix	Universitat Politècnica de València, Spain
Javier Palanca	Universitat Politècnica de València, Spain
Stella Heras	Universitat Politècnica de València, Spain
Yves Demazeau	CNRS, France
Franco Zambonelli	University of Modena and Reggio Emilia, Italy

PAAMS 2014 Workshops Organizing Committee

Juan M. Corchado (Chair)	University of Salamanca, Spain
Javier Bajo (Co-chair)	Technical University of Madrid, Spain
Juan F. De Paz	University of Salamanca, Spain
Sara Rodríguez	University of Salamanca, Spain
Gabriel Villarrubia	University of Salamanca, Spain
Fernando de la Prieta Pintado	University of Salamanca, Spain
Davinia Carolina Zato Domínguez	University of Salamanca, Spain
Antonio Juan Sánchez Martín	University of Salamanca, Spain

PAAMS 2014 Sponsors

Table of Contents

Workshop on Agent-Based Modeling and Simulation of Complex Systems: Engineering and Applications

Practical Approach and Multi-agent Platform for Designing Real Time Adaptive Scheduling Systems 1
  Petr Skobelev, Denis Budaev, Vladimir Laruhin, Evgeny Levin, and Igor Mayorov

Multi-Agent Based Simulation of Environmental Pollution Issues: A Review 13
  Sabri Ghazi, Tarek Khadir, and Julie Dugdale

Agent-Based Modeling and Simulation for the Design of the Future European Air Traffic Management System: The Experience of CASSIOPEIA 22
  Martin Molina, Sergio Carrasco, and Jorge Martin

Risk Management in Construction Project Using Agent-Based Simulation 34
  Franck Taillandier and Patrick Taillandier

Workshop on Agents and Multi-agent Systems for AAL and e-HEALTH

Doubt Removal for Dependant People from Tablet Computer Usage Monitoring 44
  Clément Raïevsky, Annabelle Mercier, Damien Genthial, and Michel Occello

Development of Electrolarynx by Multi-agent Technology and Mobile Devices for Prosody Control 54
  Kenji Matsui, Kenta Kimura, Alberto Pérez, Sara Rodríguez, and Juan Manuel Corchado

A BDI Emotional Reasoning Engine for an Artificial Companion 66
  Carole Adam and Emiliano Lorini

Assessment of Agent Architectures for Telehealth 79
  Daniel Jørgensen, Kasper Hallenborg, and Yves Demazeau

Cognitive Architecture of an Agent for Human-Agent Dialogues 89
  Jayalakshmi Baskar and Helena Lindgren

A Different Approach in an AAL Ecosystem: A Mobile Assistant for
the Caregiver   101
    Angelo Costa, Oscar Gama, Paulo Novais, and Ricardo Simoes

RETRACTED CHAPTER: HomeCare, Elder People Monitoring System
and TV Communication.   111
    Victor Parra, Vivian López, and Mohd Saberi Mohamad

Workshop on Agent-Based Solutions for Manufacturing and Supply Chain

A Multi-Agent Approach to the Multi-Echelon Capacitated Vehicle
Routing Problem   121
    Paweł Sitek, Jarosław Wikarek, and Katarzyna Grzybowska

Mixing ABS and DES Approach to Modeling of a Delivery Process in
the Automotive Industry   133
    Jakub Borucki, Pawel Pawlewski, and Wojciech Chowanski

Agent Based Approach for Modeling Disturbances in Supply Chain   144
    Patycja Hoffa and Pawel Pawlewski

Combining Simulation and Multi-agent Systems for Solving Enterprise
Process Flows Constraints in an Enterprise Modeling Aided Tool   156
    Paul-Eric Dossou, Pawel Pawlewski, and Philip Mitchell

Workshop on Intelligent Systems for Context-Based Information Fusion + Agent-Based Approaches for the Transportation Modelling and Optimisation

A Proposal for Processing and Fusioning Multiple Information Sources
in Multimodal Dialog Systems   167
    David Griol, José Manuel Molina, and Jesús García-Herrero

PHuNAC Model: Creating Crowd Variation with the MBTI Personality
Mode   179
    Olfa Beltaief, Sameh El Hadouaj, and Khaled Ghedira

Ambient Intelligence: Applications and Privacy Policies   191
    Mar Lopez, Juanita Pedraza, Javier Carbo, and Jose M. Molina

High-Level Information Fusion for Risk and Accidents Prevention in
Pervasive Oil Industry Environments   202
    *Nayat Sanchez-Pi, Luis Martí, José Manuel Molina, and
    Ana Cristina Bicharra Garcia*

Workshop on Multi-agent Based Applications for Smart Grids and Sustainable Energy Systems

An Agent-Based Framework for Aggregation of Manageable Distributed
Energy Resources 214
    Anders Clausen, Yves Demazeau, and Bo Nørregaard Jørgensen

The Proper Role of Agents in Future Resilient Smart Grids 226
    Rune Gustavsson and Shahid Hussain

Symphony – Agent-Based Platform for Distributed Smart Grid
Experiments.. 238
    Michel A. Oey, Zulkuf Genc, Elizabeth Ogston, and
    Frances M.T. Brazier

Consensus in Smart Grids for Decentralized Energy Management 250
    Miguel Rebollo, Carlos Carrascosa, and Alberto Palomares

Elspot: Nord Pool Spot Integration in MASCEM Electricity Market
Simulator 262
    Ricardo Fernandes, Gabriel Santos, Isabel Praça, Tiago Pinto,
    Hugo Morais, Ivo F. Pereira, and Zita Vale

Particle Swarm Optimization of Electricity Market Negotiating Players
Portfolio 273
    Tiago Pinto, Zita Vale, Tiago M. Sousa, Tiago Sousa,
    Hugo Morais, and Isabel Praça

Bilateral Contracting in Multi-agent Energy Markets with Demand
Response 285
    Fernando Lopes, Hugo Algarvio, and Jorge Sousa

Risk Management and Bilateral Contracts in Multi-agent Electricity
Markets 297
    Hugo Algarvio and Fernando Lopes

Workshop on Active Security through Multi-agent Systems

Artificial Neural Networks in the Detection of Known and Unknown
DDoS Attacks: Proof-of-Concept 309
    Alan Saied, Richard E. Overill, and Tomasz Radzik

A Multiagent Self-healing System against Security Incidents
in MANETs.. 321
    Roberto Magán-Carrión, José Camacho-Páez, and
    Pedro García-Teodoro

An Agent-Based Cloud Platform for Security Services 333
Fernando De la Prieta, Luis Enrique Corredera,
Antonio J. Sánchez-Martin, and Yves Demazeau

Workshop in Intelligent Human-Agent Societies

An Architecture Proposal for Human-Agent Societies 344
Holger Billhardt, Vicente Julián, Juan Manuel Corchado, and
Alberto Fernández

Using Natural Interfaces for Human-Agent Immersion 358
Angel Sanchis, Vicente Julián, Juan Manuel Corchado,
Holger Billhardt, and Carlos Carrascosa

Understanding Decision Quality through Satisfaction 368
João Carneiro, Ricardo Santos, Goreti Marreiros, and Paulo Novais

Improving Intelligent Systems: Specialization 378
Jesús A. Román, Sara Rodríguez, and Juan Manuel Corchado

Retraction Note to: HomeCare, Elder People Monitoring System and TV
Communication.. C1
Victor Parra, Vivian López, and Mohd Saberi Mohamad

Author Index.. 387

Practical Approach and Multi-agent Platform for Designing Real Time Adaptive Scheduling Systems

Petr Skobelev[1], Denis Budaev[2], Vladimir Laruhin[2],
Evgeny Levin[2], and Igor Mayorov[2]

[1] Institute of the Control of Complex Systems of Russian Academy of Science
and Smart Solutions, Ltd, Russia, Samara
petr.skobelev@gmail.com
[2] Smart Solutions, Ltd, Russia, Samara
{Budaev,vl,levin,imayorov}@smartsolutions-123.ru

Abstract. The practical approach and multi-agent platform development for adaptive scheduling systems for real time resource management are considered. The approach is based on concept of demand and resource networks (DRN) where agents of demands and resources operate on virtual market and continuously trying to improve their individual values of satisfaction functions that reflects given multi-criteria objectives. To achieve the best possible results agents use the virtual money account that regulates their behavior and can increase by getting bonuses or decrease by penalties depending of their individual cost functions. The key rule of designed virtual market is that any agent that is searching for new better position in schedule must compensate losses for those conflicting agents who are able and agree to change their allocations to other resources after the initial agent request, with required amount of compensation determined in the process of re-allocations. This approach allows to balance many criteria for getting consensus between agents and adaptation of the schedules "on the fly" by events without any stop and restart of the system. The developed platform includes key classes of DRN agents and protocols of their negotiations and other components that help to develop the solution manage data and visualize results of scheduling. The platform provides rapid prototyping of multi-agent systems for real time resource management and helps to reduce man-efforts and time of development. The platform was applied for developing of multi-agent scheduling systems for managing resources in aircraft jet production, load balancing in computer grid networks and energy production in power-, gas- and heating networks.

Keywords: multi-agent technology, adaptive scheduling, distributed problem-solving, optimization, simulation, real-time.

1 Introduction

Modern enterprise resource management systems are basically characterized by the application of classical methodology and platforms of resource allocation, scheduling and optimization based on methods of linear and mixed programming, different heuristics, genetic algorithms and others [1,2,3].

J.M. Corchado et al. (Eds.): PAAMS 2014 Workshops, CCIS 430, pp. 1–12, 2014.
© Springer International Publishing Switzerland 2014

However, the increase in complexity, high uncertainty and dynamics of modern business as well as a number of other challenges of modern real time economics do not allow efficient use of traditional combinatorial mathematical and heuristic methods. In this regard, more and more scientists and engineers turn to multi-agent technologies [4,5,6], that give appropriate solutions based on methods of distributed problem solving with conflicts discovery and finding trade-offs by negotiations in order to achieve the balance of interests (consensus) of all parties involved.

However, in spite of significant progress in developing multi-agent solutions and technology, platforms and tools in last decade, the design process for multi-agent adaptive scheduling systems still remains to be very resource- and time-consuming.

In this paper we present practical approach to multi-agent platform for development of adaptive scheduling systems for real time resource management. The first part of the paper is focused on the concept of demand and resource networks (DRN) and methodology of adaptive resource scheduling based on individual satisfaction and cost functions for agents. It is shown that this approach allows to balance many criteria for getting consensus between agents and adaptation of the schedules "on the fly" by events without any stop and restart of the system. The second part of paper is focused on developed platform that includes key classes of DRN agents and protocols of their negotiations and other components helping to develop final solution, manage data and visualize the results of scheduling. The platform applied for developing of multi-agent scheduling systems for managing resources in aircraft jet production, load balancing in computer grid networks and energy production in power-, gas- and heating networks.

The first experience confirms that the platform provides rapid prototyping of multi-agent systems for real time resource management and helps to reduce man-efforts and time of development.

2   Brief Overview of Approaches to Resource Scheduling and Optimization

The serious issues of the centralized resource allocation, scheduling and optimization are already well known: combinatorial search is NP-hard and very time consuming, there are a number of individual constraints and preferences that cannot be taken into account, all conditions are changing very often and schedule become not adequate very quickly, etc.

That is why the distributed decision-making methods, and particularly, the ones based on multi-agent technologies, become more popular for practical applications.

One of the today areas of applying multi-agent technology is improving classical combinatorial algorithms by introducing methods of distributed problem solving, for example, for solving Distributed Constraint Optimization Problem (DCOP) [5]. Despite the fact that a centralized approach (top-down) keeps dominating in this area recently there has been developed a number of distributed models, methods and algorithms for solving scheduling and optimization problems with the use of multi-agent technologies. The examples are Asynchronous Distributed Constraint Optimization (ADOPT), Optimal Asynchronous Partial Overlay (OptAPO),

Distributed Pseudo-tree OPtimization (DPOP), Asynchronous BackTracking (ABT) [6,7,8], methods of swarm optimization (Particle Swarm Optimization) [9,10] and some others [11,12].

Another domain to use multi-agent systems for scheduling and optimization is based on the bio-inspired approach (bottom-up) that uses fundamental principles of self-organization and evolution that are similar to living organisms [13,14,15].

This approach from our point of view is very close to the methodology of complex adaptive systems [16,17] that may consider any solution of complex problem as "unstable equilibrium" formed as a consensus of many involved parties with conflicting interests and that is why can be more or less easily changed by new events.

Not only humans, but also any other physical and even abstract entities can take part in this process as parties. For example, for the factories it can be clients, orders, technological processes and its individual operations, machines, workers, materials, etc. These agents are working to get the best possible local solution. However, to get a better result some agents can fall into a conflict with other agents and have to find the compromise solution by negotiations and trade-offs, as people do it in real life.

This second area looks the most promising for the development of industrial multi-agent systems for real time resource management. In such systems, all orders and resources not known beforehand and can be changed in system runtime. Coming real-time events like new order coming, order cancellation, resource unavailability, delay in operations and others are results of real-time adaptive re-scheduling.

3   Suggested Approach to the Resource Management Problems Solution

3.1   Formal Problem Statement

The formalized problem statement for searching the consensus in DRN virtual market formulates as followed.

Let's assume that all agents of demands and resources have their own goals, criteria, preferences and constraints (for example, due date, cost, risk, priority, equipment type for execution, required worker qualification and other). The importance of each criteria can be represented by weight coefficients in a linear combination of criteria for the given situation in scheduling and can change during the schedule forming or execution.

Let's introduce the satisfaction function for each agent which will show deviation of the current value ("virtual value") of this function from the given ideal value by any of the criteria for the current step of finding scheduling solution for this agent.

Let each demand j has several individual criteria x_i and suggested ideal values x_{ij}^{id}. For each agent of demand j normalized bonus/penalty function is calculated by component i ("virtual value"), given for example as a linear function $f_{ij}^{task}(x_i\text{-}x_{ij}^{id})$. In most cases this function has bell form with maximum in the point of suggested ideal value. As a summary value of the result for each demand, the sum of virtual values for each criteria i with the given weight coefficients α_{ij}^{task} is estimated.

By the proper selection of signs and form of the function, the goal of each agent can be reformulated as an increase (maximizing) of virtual value y_j^{task} of demand j (upper index *task* means that the values belong to the demand agents):

$$y_j^{task} = \sum_i \alpha_{ij}^{task} \cdot f_{ij}^{task}(x_i - x_{ij}^{id}),$$

where $\forall j$ weight coefficients are normalized: $\sum_i \alpha_{ij}^{task} = 1$.

Similarly the problem of finding the states x_{ij}^* of agents of demands j, that maximize the total value of all orders can be formulated:

$$y^{task} = \sum_j \beta_j^{task} y_j^{task} = \sum_j \beta_j^{task} \sum_i \alpha_{ij}^{task} f_{ij}^{task}(x_i - x_{ij}^{id}) \tag{1}$$

$$y^{task^*} = \max_{x_i}(y^{task})$$

where β_j^{task} is demand weight that allows to set and dynamically change the priorities showing importance of criteria.

Similarly the value function can be given for the resources by criteria z_k, with bonus/penalty function $f_{kl}^{res}(z_k - z_{kl}^{id})$, weight α_{kl}^{res} of criterion k for resource l, and resource value β_l^{res} for the system (which is similar for weight for demand agents function):

$$y^{res} = \sum_l \beta_l^{res} \cdot y_l^{res} = \sum_l \beta_l^{res} \sum_k \alpha_{kl}^{res} \cdot f_{kl}^{res}(z_k - x_{kl}^{id}) \tag{2}$$

$$y^{res^*} = \max_{z_k}(y^{res})$$

$$z_k \in D^K , \ x_i \in D^I \ \forall i, k, I = Dim(D^I), K = Dim(D^K) \tag{3}$$

Variables x and z belong to some areas of the space of criteria for demands and resources, I and K are dimensions of the corresponding criteria spaces, upper index *res* means that the values belong to resource agents.

Thus in DS-network of resource and demands agents the optimization problem is formulated as solving (1)-(3). In other words, in suggested bottom-up methodology we have not just one global optimizer but many small optimizers which are able to negotiate and find trade-offs when they searching local optimums. It means that in practice we are focusing on balancing interests of DRN agents continuously looking for their consensus.

3.2   The Virtual Market Approach

The developed approach is based on concept of demand and resource networks (DRN) [18,19,20,21] where agents of demands and resources operate on virtual market (VM) with the use of their own budgets. Agents continuously try to improve their individual satisfaction functions which reflect given multi-criteria objectives, for example, service level, cost and time of delivery, risks.

The goal of the demand agent is to be scheduled and executed in time for the most suitable resource with obtaining the maximum profit and minimum of risks. The goal of the resource agent is to satisfy as much demands of the maximum price and to maximize its workload and profit. For example, order agents wants to complete the factory order exactly in time and with the minimum costs. Moreover, the equipment agents wants to use the machine with no down time or overloads, getting maintenance regularly, etc.

For getting position in the resulting schedule the DRN agents of demand and resources can take part in ongoing auctions on virtual market with different schemas or more complex negotiations on the basis of different modifications of Contract-net protocols, as a result of which the schedule becomes profitable for every participant and consensus is reached. Constant search of the options between these competing and cooperating agents allows you to find the solution of any complex problem as a dynamic network of agents of operations flexibly changed in real time.

The activity of agents depend on satisfaction function, bonus/penalty function and current budget allocated on specific accounts for money transfers (Fig. 1,2).

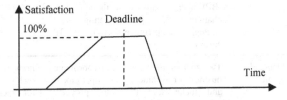

Fig. 1. Example of satisfaction function

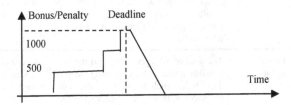

Fig. 2. Example of bonus/penalty cost function

To achieve the best possible results agents use the virtual money account that regulates their behavior and can be increased by getting bonuses or decreased by penalties depending of their individual cost functions. The key rule of the designed virtual market is that any agent which is searching for new better position in schedule must compensate losses for those conflicting agents who are able and agree to change their allocations to other resources after the initial agent request, with required amount of compensation determined in the process of re-allocations.

This approach allows to balance many criteria for getting consensus between agents and adaptation of the schedules "on the fly" by events without any stop and restart of the system.

Adaptive real time scheduling is considered as a critical part for supporting the whole resource management cycle. This includes reaction to events, resource allocation, scheduling and optimization (if there is available time), coordination of plans with the decision makers with the use of mobile devices, monitoring and control of plans execution and re-scheduling in case of growing gap between plans and reality.

3.3   Model of DRN for Real Time Resource Management

The generic model of DRN for real time resource management is presented in Table 1 where main classes of agents, their goals and tasks and key constraints are specified.

Table 1. Main classes of DRN agents

Agent Class	Type of Agent	Specification of agent behavior, main goals and tasks	Attributes, preferences and constraints
Order	Demand agent	The goal of order agent is to complete order in time, with maximum quality, minimal cost, delivery time and risk. Tasks include loading of business process, creation of business process (BP) agent, analysis of their results, changing BP agents settings and strategies, triggering proactivity of BP agents.	Service level, real and virtual money for order execution, given specifications for resources, deadline for order execution, risks.
Business process (technologic al process)	Demand agent	The goal of BP agent is to coordinate business or technical jobs (operations) and make sure they are properly scheduled. Tasks include decomposition of process into jobs (operations), creation of job agent, analysis of their results, changing settings and strategies for job agents, triggering proactivity of job agents.	Preferred time windows, real and virtual money for order execution, given specifications for resources, jobs interdependencies and deadlines.
Job	Demand agent	The goal of job agent is to find the best possible resource for executing the job. The tasks include finding the best resources with the given characteristics and getting agreement on allocating job to the free time slot or starting negotiations for solving conflicts with previously allocated jobs by shifting and moving the jobs between the resources, proactive improvement of the job state according to the situation.	Given characteristics of resources, real and virtual money for job execution, time and cost preferences, interconnections between jobs, deadlines.
Person for job execution	Resource agent	The goal of person agent is to maximize resource workload and utilization by the best orders and get bigger salary. The tasks include participating in matching and negotiations of jobs allocation, calculating dynamic price for jobs sharing costs between jobs, state analysis and proactive search of better jobs, overriding availability constraints when required, calculating salary and bonuses.	Availability (for example, 8-hour working day), key competencies and skills, current load and potential capacity, cost and risks.

Table 2. (*continued*)

Machine or tool for job execution	Resource agent	The goal of machine is to maximize resource workload and utilization by the best orders. The tasks are mainly same as for person but machine (tool) can be linked with person by competencies. One person can operate with a few machines or one machine can require a few persons.	Availability, maintenance regularity, load productivity, cost and risks, energy consumption.
Product (physical or abstract)	Resource agent	The goal of product agent is to get best characteristics in match with order specifications and requirements and product should be delivered in time with minimum costs and risks.	Domain-specific product requirements which are specified in order
Organization (team, department)	Resource agent	The goal is to manage the resource allocation considering the situation, for example, balance workload of the resources. The tasks include the resources switch on and off, resource workload monitoring, pre-selecting resource for allocation, discovering the "bottlenecks" in organization and generating recommendations, calculating KPIs for organization, managing resource strategies.	The list of resources, availability of resources and other preferences and constraints for organization.
Event	Supervisor agent	The goal is to manage the events queue. The tasks are input of the even into the system, activation of the required agents, collecting information on event processing, estimation of the result of event processing.	Event type, time of occurrence and time of input of event, time of event processing, value of event.
Resulting schedule	Supervisor agent	The goal is to fix the resulting schedule for users. The tasks include monitoring scheduling process and fixing the result in the case when it has reached the required level of quality, oscillations of solution reached the "plateau" with given delta-epsilon, the available time was exceeded or user intervened.	Level of solution quality, delta-epsilon for oscillation, the available time interval.

The concrete DRN model depends of application and may slightly differ for domain, for example, for transportation logistics, factory scheduling or project management.

When a new order for production arrives in the system, the agent of order, the agent of technological process and the agents of operations (Demand agents) are created. Agents of operations start negotiations with Resource agents to reconcile costs and buy time slots (intervals) of resources or to outbid time slots from conflicting agents of operations. Purchase of time slots is paid by virtual funds. These funds arrive into resources agents' virtual accounts and/or agents of operations (in case of compensations for losses during allocation changes to other resources).

Changes in the formed schedule are defined by certain type of penalty functions, by current values of satisfaction and by virtual funds of agents. If no external events occur, Demand agents constantly try to improve their satisfaction with the schedule, if there are sufficient virtual funds for improvement. If the schedule is stable within certain time period, it is transferred to Supervisor agent and becomes available to external use.

Adaptive planning in real time is done when new events reflecting the changes in the real world are received. The schedule should be corrected without stopping the system. The examples of the events can be the information on receiving a new order, cancelling the planned one, change of the resources and orders costs, change of the resource availability etc. Each event triggers its own basic protocol for the processing. For example, for the resource unavailability event its agent finds and activates all tasks that were allocated to this resource that starts the process of rescheduling to other resources. The establishing of new connections between the agents starts changes the conditions of operation for other agents and this process could be considered as an autocatalytic reaction in chemistry. This process of system self-organization can results in cardinal re-scheduling of total plan as the response for occurring events. The result is considered as obtained and system stops its operation in case when no agent have any possibilities to improve its condition, the time for search is over or user interrupted the process to start the manual scheduling rework.

Each agent can interact with the specific user that makes the decisions in manual mode if such mode of decision-making is set.

3.4   Microeconomics of the Virtual Market

Virtual market of the system supposes that demands to buy the services of the resources or other services of the system that, in their turn, have static or dynamic cost. To achieve these goals, all agents of DRN have their own financial accounts of "virtual money, that are used for dynamic calculation of options and money transfers for optimization of the schedule. Agents have their own virtual budgets, objective and bonus/penalty functions that are used for estimating the current state of the agents.

Dynamic cost of the resource depends on how the resource can be shared. For example, truck has certain cost, but it is distributed between its cargos with some planned profitability given in advance. As it is stated before, the agents can suggest each other compensations for shifts and reallocations, the sum of which is defined during negotiations between demands and resources.

If the cost of functioning is not covered by the obtained income, the resource can decide to switch off.

The main features of the suggested VM microeconomics:

–   demand agents have ideal and current values of objective functions, which are used to compute agent "satisfaction" by the current plan as deviation from ideal;

–   demand agents enter the system having money for achieving their objectives, including service level, costs and delivery time, etc;

–   there are dynamic values of weight coefficients of scalarized objective function which are linked with virtual money bonus or penalty functions, each criteria has its own coefficient of conversion to the virtual money;

- current virtual budget is used by agents to improve their local allocation of the demands and resources in the schedule;
- budget is spent by agent to improve criteria that currently has the worst value;
- agents iteratively improve their criteria to reach locally optimal values compensating the losses of other agents from their virtual budget.

Such approach gives also opportunity to introduce virtual taxes related to agents jobs planning and execution, cost of messaging between agents, etc. These VM mechanisms can be used for controlling process of self-organization of schedule to provide quality of schedule in given limitations of available time.

4   Multi-agent Platform for Developing Adaptive Scheduling Solutions

4.1   Brief Overview of Platform Functionality

Multi-agent platform is designed to automate developed methodology and increase quality and efficiency of development process for creating real time resource management systems for application in different problem domains. The developed multi-agent platform combines functionality of basic adaptive scheduler that can be easily modified for a new domain with simulation environment. This is useful for experiments with the different DRN models, methods and algorithms.

Functionality of the multi-agent platform provides possibility for end-users to specify initial network of resources, form sequence of events manually or automatically or load it from external files, make individual setting for all demands and resources, run simulations with different parameters and visualize process and results of experiments.

Example of one of the screens with user interface of the platform representing results of experiments discussed below is shown in Fig. 3. On Fig. 3 one can find the windows presenting resource network, Gantt chart with schedule of resources, orders and resources workload and satisfaction and some others.

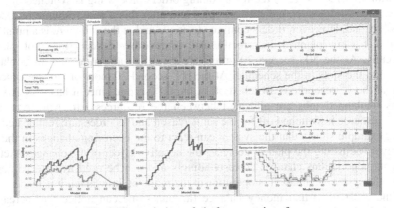

Fig. 3. General view of platform user interface

As a result of simulation a number of useful charts and diagrams can be visualized or exported in Excel files for future analysis:

– graph of network loading – shows how busy all resources are loaded;
– Gantt-chart – shows allocation of demands to resources in time;
– communication activity diagram – shows how many messages are generated in the platform at any moment of time;
– satisfaction of demand and resources and system as a whole – shows how level of satisfaction is changing during the process of simulations;
– orders execution – shows how good is execution of orders in time;
– resource utilization – shows how busy resources at different moment of time;
– log of messages – shows message exchange between selected agents in text of graphical view;
– log of decision making – presents results of decision making for selected agent;
– log of financial transactions – shows virtual money transfer between demand and resource agents.

The architecture of platform includes following components: initial scene editor, event generator, event queue for main classes of events, multi-agent world built as virtual market, basic classes of demand and resource agents and negotiation protocols, visual components for editing agents setting and visualization of results, export and import of data, logging and tracking of messages and agent financial transactions and other specific components.

These components can be easily adjusted for new domains and applications.

4.2   Examples of Experiments

Let's consider the platform operation with an example of the network shown above. Assume that there are two servers in computational grid network, that receive the flow of orders with requirement of due date of completion and given financial resources.

Free time slots number is decreasing in time and at the 20th second (unit of simulation time) a new resource for incoming orders processing is switched on. Then this resource is almost completely occupied and after this a new resource is added at the 28th second. However, orders continue to arrive and at the end there is a number of orders that were planned incorrectly and some other orders were not planned completely. At the 50th second 20 orders are cancelled and after that all unplanned orders find the slots in the schedule. At the 55th second 20 more orders are cancelled after that the 4th resource is switched off at the 60th second since it has very few jobs and its unplanned jobs are allocated between the resources left. After 5 seconds another resource is switched off for the same reason and its orders are reallocated too.

This example shows that the system can react to the occurring changes in the plan operatively adjusting the plan to decrease the negative effect of the changes. Activity of agents negotiations changes correspondingly and can be used to observe general state of the system and how it is operating at the moment, how much it is loaded, etc.

In the chart of virtual money balance (account) one can notice the increase of virtual balance of the resources that gain money by selling free slots to the orders.

The chart of deviation of system resource agents shows how system decreases deviation from the ideal even after introducing minor and major disturbances. For example, at the 40th second there was a big disturbance that was managed by the system during about 10 steps of simulation time.

Similar chart for orders agents also shows system ability to adaptation for the changes. Then, at the 42th second, a big disturbance occurred that resulted in major decrease of satisfaction (virtual profit), however the system could gain about the half of decrease and did it in rather short time. At the 46th second another disturbance was introduced that resulted in worsening the situation and after 3-4 seconds was reduced.

System load chart provides general information on changes in loading resources with orders. In the charts one can also observe the changes of the sum of objective function values for system agents. Adaptive reaction to the worsening of the situation can be noticed as the total system target improvement after another round of negotiations.

At the moment platform is already used for rapid prototyping of new multi-agent systems for resource management and was successfully applied for computational networks, project management, production planning, energy production in power-, gas- and heating networks and some other applications [22, 23, 24, 25]. The first experience shows that the developed platform allows to make fast development of the system comparing to traditional developments that is especially important for industrial commercial applications.

5   Conclusions

Multi-agent platform allows to make a step in implementing the advantages of multi-agent approach to scheduling and optimization of resources in real time. The further development of the platform supposes using of ontology editor for introducing new problem domains, generalization and advancing of virtual market mechanisms with self-regulation of agents and improving of results visualization.

The first applications of the platform were focused on smart aircraft jets production scheduling, smart project management, smart grid computing and others. The experience in the platform application shows significant possibilities for increasing the quality and efficiency of development process with the reducing the required labor, delivery time and costs for clients.

References

1. Leung, J.: Handbook of Scheduling: Algorithms, Models and Performance Analysis. CRC Computer and Information Science Series. Chapman & Hall (2004)
2. Voß, S.: Meta-heuristics: The state of the art. In: Nareyek, A. (ed.) ECAI-WS 2000. LNCS (LNAI), vol. 2148, pp. 1–23. Springer, Heidelberg (2001)
3. Rossi, F., van Beek, P., Walsh, T.: Handbook of Constraint Programming. Elsevier Science (2006)
4. Shoham, Y., Leyton-Brown, K.: Multi-Agent Systems: Algorithmic, Game-Theoretic, and Logical Foundations. Cambridge University Press, New York (2009)
5. Mailler, R., Lesser, V.: Solving distributed constraint optimization problems using cooperative mediation. In: 3rd Int. Joint Conf. on Autonomous Agents and Multiagent Systems (AAMAS 2004), pp. 438–445. IEEE Computer Society, New York (2004)

6. Meisels, A.: Distributed Search by Constrained. Springer (2008)
7. Petcu, A.: A class of Algorithms For Distributed Constraint. IOS Press (2009)
8. Yokoo, M.: Distributed Constraint Satisfaction: Foundation of Cooperation in Multi-agent Systems. Springer (2001)
9. Tasgetiren, M., Sevkli, M., Liang, Y., Yenisey, M.: Particle swarm optimization and differential evolution algorithms for job shop scheduling problem. International Journal of Operational Research 3(2), 120–135 (2006)
10. Mekni, S., Fayech, B., Ksouri, M.: TRIBES Optimization Algorithm Applied to the Flexible Job Shop Scheduling Problem. In: 10th IFAC Workshop on Intelligent Manufacturing Systems, Lisbon, Portugal, July 1-2, pp. 365–370 (2010)
11. Pinedo, M.: Scheduling: Theory, Algorithms, and Systems. Springer (2008)
12. Levner, E.: Multiprocessor Scheduling, Theory and Applications. I-TECH Education and Publishing (2007)
13. Bonabeau, E., Theraulaz, G.: Swarm Smarts. What computers are learning from them? Scientific American 282(3), 54–61 (2000)
14. Brussel, H., Wyns, J., Valckenaers, P., Bongaerts, L.: Reference architecture for holonic manufacturing systems: PROSA. Computer in Industry 37(3), 255–274 (1998)
15. Leitao, P., Vrba, P.: Recent Developments and Future Trends of Industrial Agents. In: Proc. of 5th Int. Conf. on Holonic and Multi-Agent systems in Manufacturing, France, Tolouse, pp. 15–28. Springer, Berlin (2011)
16. Prigogine, I., Stengers, I.: Order and Chaos: Man's dialogue with nature. Flamingo (1984)
17. Nicolis, G., Prigogine, I.: Exploring complexity: An introduction. W.H. Freeman, New York (1989)
18. Skobelev, P.: Open multi-agent systems for decision making support. Avtometriya, Journal of Siberian Branch of Russian Academy of Science 6, 45–61 (2002)
19. Skobelev, P., Vittikh, V.: Models of Self-organization for Designing Demand-Resource Networks, Automation and Control. Journal of Russian Academy of Science 1, 177–185 (2003)
20. Vittikh, V., Skobelev, P.: The compensation method of agents interactions for real time resource allocation. Avtometriya, Journal of Siberian Branch of Russian Academy of Science (2), 78–87 (2009)
21. Skobelev, P.: Multi-Agent Systems for Real Time Resource Allocation, Scheduling, Optimization and Controlling: Industrial Applications. In: Mařík, V., Vrba, P., Leitão, P. (eds.) HoloMAS 2011. LNCS, vol. 6867, pp. 1–14. Springer, Heidelberg (2011)
22. Madsen, B., Rzevski, G., Skobelev, P., Tsarev, A.: Real-time multi-agent forecasting & replenishment solution for LEGOs branded retail outlets. In: Proc. of 13th ACIS Int. Conf. on Software Engineering, Artificial Intelligence, Networking and Parallel/Distributed Computing (SNPD 2012), Kyoto, Japan, August 8-10, pp. 451–456 (2012)
23. Granichin, O., Skobelev, P., Lada, A., Mayorov, I., Tsarev, A.: Cargo transportation models analysis using multi-agent adaptive real-time truck scheduling system. In: Proceedings of the 5th Int. Conf. on Agents and Artificial Intelligence (ICAART 2013), Barcelona, Spain, February 15-18, vol. 2, pp. 244–249. SciTePress, Portugal (2013)
24. Goryachev, A., Kozhevnikov, S., Kolbova, E., Kuznetsov, O., Simonova, E., Skobelev, P., Tsarev, A., Shepilov, Y.: Smart Factory: Intelligent system for workshop resource allocation, scheduling, optimization and controlling in real time. In: Proc. of Int. Conf. Manufacturing 2012, Macao, China, vol. 630, pp. 508–513. Materials Research (2013)
25. Vittikh, V., Larukhin, V., Tsarev, A.: Actors, Holonic Enterprises, Ontologies and Multi-Agent Technology. In: Mařík, V., Lastra, J.L.M., Skobelev, P. (eds.) HoloMAS 2013. LNCS, vol. 8062, pp. 13–24. Springer, Heidelberg (2013)

Multi-Agent Based Simulation of Environmental Pollution Issues: A Review

Sabri Ghazi[1], Tarek Khadir[1], and Julie Dugdale[2]

[1] Laboratoire de Gestion Electronique de Documents,
Department of Computer Science,
University Badji Mokhtar, P.O. Box 12, 23000,
Annaba, Algeria
[2] MAGMA – Laboratoire d'Informatique de Grenoble, France
{Ghazi,Khadir}@labged.net, Julie.Dugdale@imag.fr

Abstract. Environmental issues, specifically pollution are considered as major concerns in many cities in the world. They have a direct influence on our health and quality of life. The use of computers models can help to forecast the impact of human activities on ecosystem equilibrium. We are interested in the use of MAS (Multi-Agent System) for modelling and simulating the environmental issues related to pollution. In this paper, we present a review of recent studies using a MAS approach for designing environmental pollution simulation models. Interactions between the three components of the environmental problem (Social, Economic and Ecological) are presented. On the light of these interactions, studies published from 2009 to 2013 are reviewed. Models are presented in terms of: model's purpose, studied variables, used data, representation of space and time, decision-making mechanism and implementation.

Keywords: Multi-Agent System, Multi-Agent Based Simulation, Agent-Based Modelling, Environmental Modelling, Pollution.

1 Introduction

Environmental issues and specifically pollution are considered as major concerns in many cities in the world. They have a direct influence on our health and quality of life. The degradation in air, soil, and water quality has to be estimated before the establishment or the expansion of urban or industrial activities. Environment pollution simulation and decision support tools can help decision-makers to set up environmental management policies in order to preserve the ecosystem and ensure public health. Computer models allow environmental managers to predict the impact of theirs decisions on the environment. Pollution is mainly caused by anthropogenic activities, thus, modelling these activities and including them in the simulation process is a key element. Using these models the world was able to predict the global warming and climatic changes [19]. During the last decades many approaches have been used to model environmental problems. [1] Presents a comparative study of five modelling approaches for environmental problem: System Dynamics, MAS, Bayesian Networks,

J.M. Corchado et al. (Eds.): PAAMS 2014 Workshops, CCIS 430, pp. 13–21, 2014.

Knowledge Base and Coupled Component. To select the suitable model, the authors suggest three considerations: The purpose of the model, which can be: prediction, forecasting, management and decision-making, learning; used data; the representation of time, space and entities included in the simulation. In this paper, the aim is to present a review of recent studies (2009 to 2013) using Multi-Agents Systems or MAS, (also called agent-based or multi-actor modelling) to model environmental issues related to pollution, with a specific consideration to air pollution. The selection of studies was done using these criteria: Agent based modelling of pollution; Agent based Simulation of Pollution; Multi-Agent System modelling of Environmental pollution. This review, forms the first step for designing a MAS based simulation system of air pollution for the region of Annaba (North-East of Algeria).

The paper is organised as follows: Section (2) presents the typical environment problem components and theirs interactions. Section (3) presents a review of recent studies using MAS to model environmental related issues. We end the paper by a conclusion with the possible perspectives of our work.

2   Environmental Problem Components

Many conceptualizations have been proposed to represent the socio-natural system [20]. Figure 1, shows that an environmental simulation system can be represented as an interconnection of three components (or subsystems); each one is represented by a set of variables (attributes) forming its state at time t. The ecological component models the biotic and abiotic[1] parts. The economic component represents the economic point view and regroups the economic variables. The social component represents the human social networks implicated in the simulation; among them are decision-makers, firms and government agencies and etc. The change in the state variable of each component affects other systems' state variables. A typical example of this is the increase in demand of certain kind of fish, which motivates fishermen to intensify their exploitation; this in turn results in changes to the biodiversity. Six interactions may exist between the system components: (A) represents the interaction of the social subsystem with itself, altering some attributes affect other social attributes, for example: when political constraints are used to control the demography of the population; (B) Occurs when natural events alter the ecosystem equilibrium, an example of this is volcanic activities which affects the air quality; (C) happens between economic component and itself. Thus, economic variables are systemically interconnected, (e.g. prices-inflation); (D) Occurs between social and ecological components, which is the key element for the simulation, understanding this interaction helps preserve environmental resource and sustainability; (E) represents the interaction between social and economic components, for example: the demography-consumption relation.

---

[1] The non-living chemical and physical components of the environment (e.g. soil, water and air).

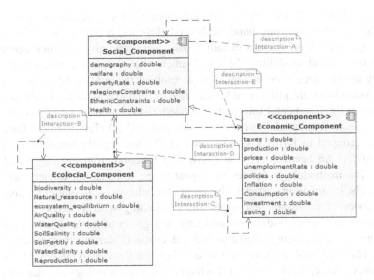

Fig. 1. UML Component Diagram, representing the interaction between ecological, social and economic components

The analysis of the studies focuses on six elements: (1) the purpose of the system, which represents the objectives of the simulation (decision support tools, learning, experimentation, prediction etc); (2) studied variables, according to the simulation objectives, the studied or target variables have to be defined (e.g. air pollution concentration, water pollution, biodiversity of a species, land use, etc) along with economic or social parameters (e.g. poverty rate, house income, demography, etc); (3) space and time representation, environmental problem are always spatially distributed and may include the use of real geographic data. Hence, the simulation system may use a GIS (Geographic Information System). The representation of time is very important because all environment phenomena are time related. In most cases a discrete representation is used; (4) data: some systems use real data collected from: monitoring networks, surveys, or a legacy database. Other systems use randomized data; (5) implementation: here, the technology used to develop the simulation system and the stage of implementation are presented; (6) decision-making model used by the agents (here, the agents generally represent human-beings) to choose an action to perform among all possible actions. For example: CBR (Case Based Reasoning), ANN (Artificial Neural Network), Fuzzy-Logic and coupled or hybrid models.

3   Multi-Agent Based Modelling of Environmental Problems: The State of the Art

MAS has emerged as a promising approach for modelling environmental issues. [2] Argues that the detection of macro-behaviours helps understanding the complex physical and ecological phenomena. MAS model is based on the fundamental principle of representing the interactions; in our case, between social-economic and ecological dynamics. It starts, on one hand, with modelling the actors at the individual level and/or aggregate level (groups of individuals, managers, governmental agencies) and on the other hand modelling the environment that contains a renewable resource. Usually the resource state is altered as a result of the actions performed by agents, whose behaviours are influenced by the state of resource as well. A methodology for building an Environmental Information System (EIS) based on a MAS is presented in [3]. Information about the environment are called EDO (Environment Data Object) that are grouped to forms ES (Environment States). Agents perceive and act upon these EDOs. An agent is seen as a mapping function from environmental state to action. The methodology defines two agent types: information carrier and decision-maker. The information carrier is the agent that behaves as a computing unit perceiving a series of environmental states and responding with a series of actions. The decision-maker agent models human-being or a group of humans-being; these kinds of agents use a reasoning engine to make decision D starting from a set of internal states. The methodology was used to develop two systems: O3RAA for air quality assessment and reporting; ABACUS which deals with metrological radar data surveillance. In [4] the aim is to help decision-makers in order to manage Insular Tropical Environments. An information system for environmental protection is designed using an: agent modelling approach, a database, a GIS and web services. The model is used to simulate and forecast the evolution of species (corals, marine turtles, forest, reef fish, etc). A MAS framework called GEAMAS-NG was used to help modelling the behaviours of agglomerations and urban extensions. The authors presented an approach called dynamic-oriented modelling which takes the dynamics as centre of the modelling process. The agent's behaviours and attributes are formed into two sets, and between them modify/influence relationships are defined. Two MAS were built using this approach: BIOMAS, which deals with the influence of agriculture on an ecosystem. The second is called SMAT which includes models of urban, agriculture and natural dynamics. The ocean ecosystem is subject to pollution especially when extracting and transporting oil. In [5] a simulation system combines MAS and CBR (Case Based Reasoning) to detect oil slicks and give predictions about their evolution and trajectory. The model uses meteorological parameters and satellite images. The coastal ecosystem is subject to disturbances by shellfish farming and aquaculture. To find the best way to exploit coasts without altering the balance of the ecosystem, a decision-maker may benefit from simulation tools. In [6] EcoSimNet is used to simulate the farmers' behaviours in order to forecast the impact of their decisions. The model used to optimize the farmer's actions based on economic parameters. Randomized data was used to feed the simulation model. Because people are spending increasingly more time indoor. Road traffic is the principal cause of air quality degradation in urban area. [7] presents ECROUB, a management system of urban quality based on a MAS. Using physical models, the system was able to generate information on the micro-climate (information about the climate in a very small geographic zone) of the Bari area in Italy. The system shows that a hybrid approach (MAS and physical models) can assist in the understanding and study of urban areas and ecosystems. [8] presents a MAS designed for monitoring air quality in Athena (Greece). It is composed of a set of software agents, controlling a network of sensors installed in different positions of an urban region. Agents verify and stock the data measured by sensors. In case of a sensor being damaged and data about the concentration of pollutant is therefore not available, the system uses a prediction given by an Artificial Neural Network. This prediction is used to estimate air quality. Real data about ozone concentration and meteorological data was used to feed the simulation system. In [9], a MAS is used to model air pollution in an urban area. The environment is represented by a two-dimensional grid $G(N, M)$. The purpose of the simulation is to find the dispersion of air pollution on the grid. Each cell $C(X, Y)$ of the grid has a value of pollutant concentration. Neighbours with a close pollution rate (according to an initially set threshold) form a cluster. The pollution sources are represented by homogeneous agents that emit pollution in their areas (polluters). Each agent pollutes with an emission rate of ED. The pollution decay is modelled according to a destruction rate (evaporation) ER. As the simulation runs, clusters are formed with different values of pollution concentration. At the end, a single cluster is formed, thus, the dispersion of pollution is estimated. The results are used to give the dispersion of pollution specifying the number of polluters and the time required for the overall cluster shape. This model does not include meteorological parameters, does not address a specific pollutant types and does not use real data. The prototype was implemented using Repast Symphony framework. To understand pollution and health related problems. [10], presents DeciMas, a hybrid agent based decision support system. It includes data mining technique to extract dependent variables. The authors use MAS to evaluate environmental impact upon human health. The aim is to help experts to identify the relationship between some pollutants and diseases. The data used includes datasets from different sources: health care system and environmental monitoring agencies. All these data were used to feed the simulation with real data. A list of 30 variables is used, with different forecasting models: Artificial Neural Network and linear regression. In order to reduce air pollution emitted from transport traffic, [11] presents a MAS for optimizing the fuel consumption in road intersection. The system models intersection as an agent and every vehicle is equipped with driver-assistant agent. Interactions between agents help to adapt the waiting time. It shows a reduction of 28% of fuel consumption. The model calculates the fuel consumption based on energy, air drag force, engine capacity, acceleration and speed. In [12] a MAS model is deployed on a grid-computing environment in order to gives visual simulation of the water pollution in the river. The Globus platform is used to build the computing grid. The water basin was modelled as a 3D mass, composed of numbers of agents called *WaterAgent*, cooperating with their neighbours in order to compute the influence of river flow on pollution propagation. [13] Presents an improvement of Agripolis(a MAS simulation system of land-use) to take into account the effects of agricultural policy on land use as well as biodiversity. The environment is represented by a matrix of $N \times M$ cells. Each cell represents a portion of the cultivable land with three fertility levels. The land may be owned, rented or abandoned. Each farmer (agent) may own or rent cells. As the simulation runs, the farmer-agent must make decisions about: the product to cultivate, the land to sell, or rent or buy, the abandon or not of the farming activity. The goal is to see how the farmers' behaviours can emerge and affect the structure of the ecosystem in the studied area. A MAS-Genetic algorithm model is presented in [14]. The model is used to optimize the management of waste to prevent the water pollution on the Urumqi river in Xinjiang (China). Each agent has attributes (energy, position in the grid of $N \times N$ cells). The competition between agents and theirs neighbours identify how the system will optimize the process of waste treatment and help escaping from the local minimum. One of the principal advantages of MAS is the ability to model the human decision-making process. The poorly parameterized decision-making models lead to less realistic results and this can be a key weakness. [15] presents a framework for the parameterization of human behaviours in a MAS based environmental model. There are a several empirical methods used for the parameterization of agent behaviours modelling human decision-makers, the authors list: expert knowledge, participant observation, social survey, interviews, census data, field experiments, role-playing game, cluster analysis, asymmetric mapping and the Monte-Carlo method. The presented framework helps modellers to choose the appropriate methods for the parameterization of the behaviours of the decision-maker agent. The framework is used for the design of two MAS models: SimPaSI for simulating the socio-ecological system of the island of Java (Indonesia). The system includes agents that represent farmer, householders, and as outcomes the system gives information about the effect of fuel pricing policy on the socio-ecological system. The second system is used to simulate the response of farmers to changes in agricultural policy in a rural Dutch region. To understand human-environment interaction in agriculture system, [16] present a software package called MP-MAS (Mathematical Programming Multi-Agent System). MP-MAS helps to simulate a population of farmers subject to: Market dynamics; Environmental change; Policy intervention; Change in agriculture technologies. The objective of the simulation is to forecast the impact of these changes on agro-ecological resource such as water, or soil fertility. In MP-MAS the agent's decision-making about which activity to do is based on MP and constraint optimization problem. The agent before taking a decision

$$\max(z) = \sum_{j=1}^{N} C_j \times X_j \qquad (1)$$

has to find the max value for Z (the farmer income). Where X is an activity among N possible farm activities and C is the expected return of the activity. In [17] the aim is to use a MAS based model to help investigate and understand environmental sustainability. The agents represent citizens and decision-makers, each of them have a set of behaviours designed to preserve energy and water resources. The approach selects be the most suitable behaviours for optimizing the use of energy and water. Citizens' behaviours are influenced by policy-makers agents (media agency, environmental protection etc.). Agents representing citizens are free to choose the appropriate behaviour according to their context. The process of restoration of a damaged ecosystem needs the interventions of experts from different domains (scientists, environmental management agencies, land owners, farmers etc).

Table 1. Summary table

Ref#	Name	Users	Purpose	Studied variables	Space / Time scale	Validation Data	Technologies	Decision-making model
[3]	O₃RAA	Gov. Agencies	Air pollution	Ozone concentration	N/A	Monitoring network data	JADE, WEKA, Protégé2000,	ANN, Expert System,CBR, decision tree
	ABACUS	Gov. Agencies	Meteorological parameters	Meteorological	N/A	Meteorological data	PMML2,JESS	
[4]	BIOMAS	Agriculture policy planners	Agricultural dynamics on ecosystems	Collective organic matter fluxes	GIS,	N/A	GEAMAS-NG, ArcGIS	Mathematical model
[5]	OSM	Not mentioned	Oil slicks	Oil slicks expansion	2D space, Time representation not mentioned	Satellite images meteorological data	Web services,	Case based reasoning, ANN, BDI.
[6]	EcoSimNet	Not mentioned	Costal ecosystem and aquaculture	Biodiversity	1120 cells (32 x 35), spatial resolution of 500m. Time-step of 30 seconds; Horizon 1.5 year.	Economic parameters		Simulated Annealing algorithm
[7]	ECROUB	Not mentioned	Air pollution	Air quality	GIS	Meteorological ,measure data	GIS	Mathematical model
[8]		Not mentioned	Air pollution	Ozone concentration	6 hour ahead prediction	Metrological data	Jade, MySQL	ANN, Fuzzy logic
[9]		Not mentioned	Air pollution	Air pollution concentration	2D Grid ,	Randomised	Repast Symphony	
[10]	DeciMas	Health and ecologist	Health-pollution	Correlation between pollutant/health problems	N/A	30 parameters :Health care system,	Ontology, JACK, Prometheus	Regression, ANN
[11]		Not mentioned	Air pollution and road traffic	Fuel consumption	Space-continuous, discrete time with 23 minutes step.	Vehicle characteristics and road traffic		Mathematical model
[12]		Not mentioned	Water pollution	Pollution	3D GIS. Discrete time, Time step one second.	Data about Weihe river pollution incident.	Gird computing.	
[13]	Agripolis	agricultural policy makers	Land-use and biodiversity in agriculture	Biodiversity indicator	Grid of N X M cells, Discrete time, 1 year step, horizon 25 years.	Economic and agriculture parameters		
[14]		Not mentioned	Waste and water pollution	waste treatment	Grid of N x M cells			Genetic algorithms
[15]	SimPaSI	Not mentioned	Fuel pricing,/ecology	Forest and Fuel pricing	N/A			
[16]	MP-MAS	Not mentioned	Agriculture/ environment		N/A	Empirical data		Mathematical model
[17]		Not mentioned	Water management	Water-use	N/A			
[18]		Not mentioned	Ecosystem restoration	Forest restoration	N/A	Survey		Mathematical model

The decision-making in this case is a very complex task. In [18] a MAS is designed in order to understand the process of decision-making in ecological restoration. The model is a set of agents in form of hierarchies and groups. The inter-agent and inter-group interaction is used to update agent's choices. If the agents' choice is different than the other agents, the cost of dissent mechanism is used to reduce the respect of the agent on his own choice and increase his respect for other agents with which they interact. Empirical data were used to feed the simulation. Table 1 above presents a summary of the works discussed.

4   Conclusion

Anthropogenic activities are the main causes of pollution and environmental problems. These activities have to be included within the simulation models. Modelling the interaction between social and ecological component is a very important aspect of MAS approaches. MAS allow us to model the social network of human-beings sharing the exploitation of common environmental resource. By manipulating the behaviour at individual and groups levels this helps to gain more knowledge and makes the simulation more realistic. Studies treating air pollution, model well the physical aspect (concentration and dispersion of pollutant), but don't include human-decision about emission source within the simulation, consequently, the human activities causing pollution are not modelled. We hope exploiting this point in the next stage of our work, which aims to build a MAS based simulator of air pollution for the region of Annaba (North-East of Algeria), and taking the emission sources controllers as key element of our approach.

References

1. Kelly Letcher, R.A., Jakeman, A.J., Barreteau, O., Borsuk, M.E., ElSawah, S., Hamilton, S.H., Henriksen, H.J., Kuikka, S., Maier, H.R., Rizzoli, A.E., van Delden, H., Voinov, A.A.: Selecting among five common modelling approaches for integrated environmental assessment and management. Environmental Modelling & Software 47, 159–181 (2013)
2. Aulinas, M., Turon, C., Sànchez-Marrè, M.: Agents as a Decision Support Tool in Environmental Processes: The State of the Art. Whitestein Series in Software Agent Technologies and Autonomic Computing, pp. 5–35 (2009)
3. Athanasiadis, I.N., Mitkas, P.A.: A Methodology for Developing Environmental Information Systems with Software Agents. Advanced Agent-Based Environmental Management Systems. Whitestein Series in Software Agent Technologies and Autonomic Computing, pp. 119–137 (2009)
4. Conruyt, N., Sébastien, D., Courdier, R., David, D., Sébastien, N., Ralambondrainy, T.: Designing an Information System for the Preservation of the Insular Tropical Environment of Reunion Island Integration of Databases, Knowledge Bases and Multi-Agent Systems by using Web Services. In: Advanced Agent-Based Environmental Management Systems, pp. 61–90. Birkhäuser, Basel (2009)

5. Corchado, J.M., Mata, A., Rodriguez, S.: OSM: A Multi-Agent System for Modeling and Monitoring the Evolution of Oil Slicks in Open Oceans. In: Advanced Agent-Based Environmental Management Systems, pp. 91–117. Birkhäuser, Basel (2009)

6. Pereira, A., Reis, L.P., Duarte, P.: EcoSimNet: A Multi-Agent System for Ecological Simulation and Optimization. In: Lopes, L.S., Lau, N., Mariano, P., Rocha, L.M. (eds.) EPIA 2009. LNCS, vol. 5816, pp. 473–484. Springer, Heidelberg (2009)

7. Borri, D., Camarda, D.: Planning for the Environmental Quality of Urban Microclimate: A Multiagent-Based Approach. In: Luo, Y. (ed.) CDVE 2011. LNCS, vol. 6874, pp. 129–136. Springer, Heidelberg (2011)

8. Papaleonidas, A., Iliadis, L.: Hybrid and Reinforcement Multi Agent Technology for Real Time Air Pollution Monitoring. In: Iliadis, L., Maglogiannis, I., Papadopoulos, H. (eds.) AIAI 2012. IFIP AICT, vol. 381, pp. 274–284. Springer, Heidelberg (2012)

9. Ahat, M., Amor, S.B., Bui, M., Lamure, M., Courel, M.-F.: Pollution Modeling and Simulation with Multi-Agent and Pretopology. In: Zhou, J. (ed.) Complex 2009. LNICST, vol. 4, pp. 225–231. Springer, Heidelberg (2009)

10. Sokolova, M.V., Fernández-Caballero, A.: Evaluation of environmental impact upon human health with DeciMaS framework. Expert Systems with Applications 39, 3469–3483 (2012)

11. Pulter, N., Schepperle, H., Böhm, K.: How agents can help curbing fuel combustion: a performance study of intersection control for fuel-operated vehicles. In: The 10th International Conference on Autonomous Agents and Multiagent Systems. International Foundation for Autonomous Agents and Multiagent Systems, vol. 2 (2011)

12. Xie, L.W., Xie, J., Li, J., et al.: Three Dimensional Simulation of Basin Water Pollution Incidents Based on Multi-agent and Grid Technology. In: 2012 Fifth International Symposium on Computational Intelligence and Design (ISCID), pp. 470–473. IEEE (2012)

13. Brady, M., Sahrbacher, C., Kellermann, K., Happe, K.: An agent-based approach to modeling impacts of agricultural policy on land use. biodiversity and ecosystem services. Landscape Ecology 27(9), 1363–1381 (2012)

14. Dong, Q.-J., Lu, F., Yan, D.-H.: Application of Improved MAGA to Water Pollution Control System Planning. In: 2010 Asia-Pacific Conference on Power Electronics and Design (APED), May 30-31, pp. 80–84 (2010)

15. Smajgl, A., Brown, D.G., Valbuena, D., Huigen, M.G.A.: Empirical characterisation of agent behaviours in socio-ecological systems. Environmental Modelling & Software 26(7), 837–844 (2011)

16. Schreinemachers, P., Berger, T.: An agent-based simulation model of human–environment interactions in agricultural systems. Environmental Modelling & Software 26(7), 845–859 (2011)

17. Pedell, S., Sterling, L.: Agent-Based Modelling for Understanding Sustainability. In: Kinny, D., Hsu, J.Y.-j., Governatori, G., Ghose, A.K. (eds.) PRIMA 2011. LNCS, vol. 7047, pp. 398–409. Springer, Heidelberg (2011)

18. Watkins, C., Massey, D., Brooks, J., et al.: Understanding the Mechanisms of Collective Decision Making in Ecological Restoration: An Agent-Based Model of Actors and Organizations. Ecology & Society 18(2) (2013)

19. Murakami, K., Sasai, T., Yamaguchi, Y.: A new one-dimensional simple energy balance and carbon cycle coupled model for global warming simulation. Theoretical and Applied Climatology 101(3-4), 459–473 (2010)

20. De Vries, H.J.M.(B.): Environmental Modelling. In: Principles of Environmental Sciences, pp. 345–373. Springer Netherlands (2009)

Agent-Based Modeling and Simulation for the Design of the Future European Air Traffic Management System: The Experience of CASSIOPEIA

Martin Molina, Sergio Carrasco, and Jorge Martin

Department of Artificial Intelligence
Technical University of Madrid
Campus de Montegancedo S/N 28660 Madrid, Spain
martin.molina@upm.es, {scarrasco,jmartin}@fi.upm.es

Abstract. The SESAR (Single European Sky ATM Research) program is an ambitious research and development initiative to design the future European air traffic management (ATM) system. The study of the behavior of ATM systems using agent-based modeling and simulation tools can help the development of new methods to improve their performance. This paper presents an overview of existing agent-based approaches in air transportation (paying special attention to the challenges that exist for the design of future ATM systems) and, subsequently, describes a new agent-based approach that we proposed in the CASSIOPEIA project, which was developed according to the goals of the SESAR program. In our approach, we use agent models for different ATM stakeholders, and, in contrast to previous work, our solution models new collaborative decision processes for flow traffic management, it uses an intermediate level of abstraction (useful for simulations at larger scales), and was designed to be a practical tool (open and reusable) for the development of different ATM studies. It was successfully applied in three studies related to the design of future ATM systems in Europe.

Keywords: Agent-based modeling, agent-based simulation, air traffic management system, complex adaptive system.

1 Introduction

Air traffic management (ATM) is an example of a complex system with a large number of interacting, heterogeneous individuals (e.g., airlines, air traffic controllers, regulatory entities, passengers, etc.) operating in an intricate and constrained environment (air routes, time schedules, international regulations, etc.). The study of the behavior of ATM systems is important for the development of new methods of improving air transportation performance aspects such as safety, transport capacity, cost efficiency and environmental concerns.

Agent-based modeling and simulation was successfully applied in a number of studies of ATM systems. In recent years, important initiatives have been developed to

J.M. Corchado et al. (Eds.): PAAMS 2014 Workshops, CCIS 430, pp. 22–33, 2014.

modernize ATM systems. For example, the SESAR (Single European Sky ATM Research) program is an ambitious research and development initiative funded by the European Union, Eurocontrol and industry. The ultimate goal of SESAR is to develop a future ATM system for Europe, ensuring the safety and fluidity of air transport over the next thirty years, making flying more environmentally friendly and reducing the costs of air traffic management [14].

The purpose of this paper is to present the results of our research work under the CASSIOPEIA project (Complex Adaptive Systems for Optimization of Performance in ATM) that we developed in the context of the SESAR program. First, we identify new agent-based modeling challenges for the design of future ATM systems and subsequently present an agent-based approach that we designed for these challenges. Using this approach, we developed a solution to simulate new collaboration strategies of ATM stakeholders in large geographic areas at an intermediate level of abstraction that is between the microscopic and macroscopic level. Our approach was developed as a practical tool that is open and reusable for different ATM problems, and it was applied successfully in three different ATM studies.

2   Modeling Challenges for the Design of Future ATM Systems

According to Eurocontrol (European Organization for the Safety of Air Navigation), air traffic management (ATM) concerns the processes, procedures and resources that are involved in ensuring that aircraft are safely guided from their origin to their destination [9]. An ATM system is composed of three main, complementary sub-systems: (1) airspace management (AM), which establishes the best aerial routes for an increasing number of flights; (2) air traffic flow management (ATFM), which matches the flights with the available capacity and (3) air traffic control (ATC), which manages aircraft as they fly and move in the airports.

In general, ATM is a complex, socio-technical system [3], where different stakeholders such as traffic controllers, airport authorities, slot coordinators and air navigation service providers interact with technical systems (navigation aids, runways, taxiways, etc.) that create a social context in which the system operates. Modern ATM is more complex because new organization rules and communication mechanisms create new, geographically dispersed, collaborative decision making processes and involve several stakeholders with their own set of business behaviors (driven by self-interests and partial responsibilities). Distributed decisions exist at multiple levels (strategic, tactical and operational) that follow different temporal and spatial scales. In addition, ATMs operate as adaptive systems, able to self-organize when external conditions change (e.g., airports and airlines can modify transport routes during traffic disruptions). The European ATM system currently manages approximately 26,000 flights daily in a complex network. Since 1989, air traffic flows have increased by 33%, and they are expected to nearly double over the next 20 years [9].

The study of the behavior of ATM systems using modeling and simulation tools can help in the development of new methods of improving air transportation performance. Because of their significant complexity, it is difficult to understand and predict the behavior of ATM systems at a macroscopic scale. The agent-based approach was successfully applied as a solution for developing models that capture air traffic decisions and interactions with an adequate level of detail. After initial studies were performed on cooperation strategies for collision avoidance [4] and real-time traffic control [13], agent-based models gained popularity as an effective approach to modeling and simulating specific dynamics of ATM systems.

Different agent-based approaches were applied in ATM studies concerning air traffic control (ATC). These agent-based models represent air traffic processes such as vehicle trajectories, collision avoidance, airport operation, etc. In this category of models, we can mention Air MIDAS [11][12], ACES [10][18], AgentFly [15] and tools such as AirTop [2] and CAST [6]. These approaches are capable of simulating how air traffic controllers manage aircraft as they fly and move in the airports with a high level of detail. For example, Air MIDAS simulates the behavior of the final approach of aircraft in the terminal airspace and their interaction between the pilots and the flight controllers for risk evaluation.

ATM studies related to air traffic flow management (ATFM) have recently been performed using also agent-based approaches. In general, they simulate ATFM on the day of the flight [1][5][17]. For example, IMPACT [5] simulates the airlines' decisions when meteorological conditions affect flight scheduling, and those conditions result in a constraint on the capacity of some airports. However, studies for future ATM systems must also consider new ATFM processes (e.g., far in advance of the day of the flight). These studies normally require the implementation of new algorithms for collaborative human decision making related to planning and scheduling (see our approach in CASSIOPEA below).

The agent-based models of ATM studies cover different temporal and geographical extensions. In general, the existing models cover a small number of hours or one day of flight in a limited number of airports (five or ten airports, a few dozen at the most). The models are defined at a microscopic level and consider details such as aircraft approach, runways, taxiways, aircraft movements and, occasionally, bus movements, passenger behavior during check-in, etc. Therefore, developing models for large areas with this level of detail requires significant effort and significant amounts of data that are sometimes not available. For the design of a new ATM system in Europe, it is important to understand cause-effect relations between policy decisions and their impact on a large scale. Therefore, it is necessary to use new representations with less detail to model and efficiently simulate areas with larger extensions, taking into account the partial availability of data.

The design of a future ATM system requires the active participation of the research community to conduct several different ATM studies. To promote this, it is important to provide practical tools (e.g., software tools and methodologies) that are easy to use and are open to the community. A number of existing approaches were designed and used as general, reusable tools for different studies (ACES, AirTop and CAST). They provide reusability using libraries of agent classes (ACES) or user interfaces for model configuration using parameter values (AirTop and CAST). In addition to this type of tool, it is also important to develop more practical (open and reusable) solutions that decrease the effort and cost requirements of the studies.

In summary, based on the general goals of the SESAR program in Europe, we identified the following new challenges in agent-based modeling and simulation for the design of future ATM systems: (1) modeling new decision levels in ATM systems (such as strategic decisions related to flow and capacity management with longer temporal horizons), (2) designing new representation methods to simulate at a larger scale (e.g., multinational geographic areas in Europe) taking into account limitations concerning existing data, and (3) creating new practical tools (more easily available to the research community) to support the development of new ATM studies. In the following sections, we describe our agent-based approach in CASSIOPEIA that we designed that addresses these challenges.

3   The Agent-Based Approach in CASSIOPEIA

CASSIOPEIA (Complex Adaptive Systems for Optimization of Performance in ATM) is a project of the SESAR (Single European Sky ATM Research) program of Eurocontrol. The general goal of the CASSIOPEIA project was to propose a modeling approach, using techniques of complex systems and paradigms of computer science, that could provide policy-makers with the means to understand and explore initiatives that affect complex ATM networks, allowing them to test potential concepts, regulations and mechanisms to manage delay propagation, capacity limits, network congestion, and other ATM phenomena.

This project was envisioned as a solution to facilitate an understanding of the cause-effect relation between policy decisions in different sectors of aviation and air traffic performance for different scopes and scales of application of regulations. As a result of the project, an agent-based modeling approach was designed, and it was successfully applied in several studies regarding various regulations in the context of European ATM. In the following, we describe the characteristics of our agent-based model and discuss the results obtained in different studies.

3.1   The Agent-Based Model

The model of CASSIOPEIA includes agents corresponding to different ATM stakeholders. For example, there are agents such as network managers, airlines (with agent subclasses: network airline, cargo airline, low-cost airline, etc.), airports (with information such as geographic location, category, etc.), and aircrafts (with information such as model, capacity, CO emissions, weight, etc.). The model also includes objects related to the environment and general decision-making processes such as flight plans, time slots, and geographical sectors. The agent models follow a BDI approach, with beliefs, goals and plans. Figure 1 shows a partial example of a model for an airline agent, showing the components related to the rescheduling of the network operation plan.

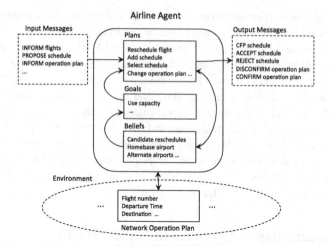

Fig. 1. Summary of the model of the airline agent (related to flight reschedule)

In this model, we implemented algorithms for collaborative decision-making processes corresponding to future ATM systems. For example, we simulate how airports interact with airlines and other airports to propose new schedules for flights (e.g., a new arrival time or new destination). The airline agent can receive input messages from other agents (for example, an airport that proposes a new flight schedule) and the airline uses local decision rules to select the best proposals. Figure 2 summarizes an example of an interaction to establish a new departure time for a flight (numbers in parentheses describe the temporal order of messages). First, the airport *EGLL* interacts with the airport *WSSS* to determine a new departure time for a flight that must be rescheduled. Then, the airline *BAW* receives the new arrival times proposed by two airports (*EGLL* and *EGSS*). Finally the airline accepts one of the proposals and rejects the other one.

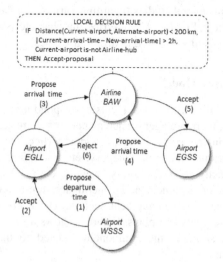

Fig. 2. Partial example of agent interaction during collaborative decision making

In the CASSIOPEIA model, we also implemented algorithms that simulate how airlines interact to bid and sell air traffic slots to reschedule flight plans with lower costs. We implemented various bidding-selling strategies based on new studies of coordination [7]. Airlines use local sets of decision rules to accept or reject bidding proposals. An example of a rule is *if* $[Cost(s_p) - q \cdot k] < Cost(s_r)$ *then Accept(b)*, where s_p is the provided slot by the bidder; s_r is the requested slot by the seller; q is the amount of money provided by the bidder; $Cost(x)$ is the estimated cost; k is a constant between 0 and 1, whose value depends on the selected strategy; and b is the bid proposal.

We implemented algorithms to simulate certain air traffic processes following an intermediate level of abstraction using a stochastic approach. Instead of modeling all the precise details, which is not possible for practical reasons, a number of components are not explicitly modeled, and only the outcomes are estimated using probability distributions. For example, we follow this approach to simulate how airlines coordinate aircrafts in the presence of delays. The model of the airline agent includes plans (using decision rules) to determine how to change the behavior of aircrafts to recover delays. For example, the airline decides that an aircraft, with a delay of 23 minutes, must reduce its delay to 10 minutes. To do this, the airline calculates a new *cost index* for the aircraft (a number used by the aircraft to adjust its speed during the flight) and sends a message to the aircraft with the new cost index. We simulate the movement of aircraft between airports using a stochastic approach (Figure 3).

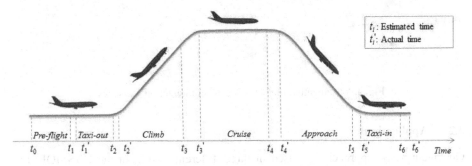

Fig. 3. Simulated events corresponding to the different phases of a flight

The model of the aircraft agent includes a plan that simulates the different phases of flights. The phases are represented as a set of events $E = \{$pre-flight, taxi-out, climb, cruise, approach, taxi-in$\}$. According to this plan, the actual time for an event is generated as $t_i = t_i + \Delta t_i^d + \Delta t_i^n$, where t_i is the estimated planned time of event e_i, Δt_i^d is the accumulative delay for the event e_i, and Δt_i^n is a noise value. The value for Δt_i^n is generated automatically as a random number following the probability distribution $N[0, [\alpha(t_i - t_{i-1})]^2]$, where α is a constant value (for example, $\alpha = 0.015$). We also apply a stochastic approach to simulate other air traffic processes (e.g., the duration of certain phases of flight using a log-normal LnN probability distribution).

Our software architecture in CASSIOPEIA was designed to be a general (open and reusable) tool for use in various ATM studies. The architecture integrates open-source components to facilitate reusability at reduced costs. We used the general, agent-based modeling tool Jadex for agent formalization and simulation control together with a relational database (MySQL) to store agent instances and simulation results. Agent models are specified using the XML declarative language, together with algorithms implemented in the Java language for agent plans, with reusable libraries of classes. The architecture includes a visualization tool, developed in this project, to visualize complex agent interactions with large numbers of messages. This tool aggregates information using different dimensions (spatial, temporal, types of messages, types of agents, etc.) and presents the information using animations on geographic maps (using OpenStreetMaps) and specific types of hierarchies and tables. For example, figure 4 shows on the left a tree of messages between airlines and airports aggregated by consecutive time points. On the right, a geographic map shows the messages corresponding to a specific simulation time.

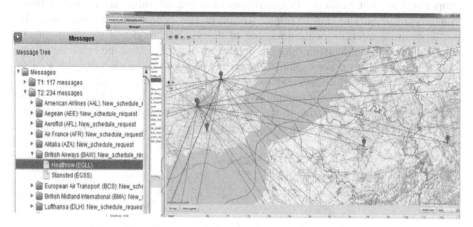

Fig. 4. Visualization tool showing agent interaction messages

3.2   Applications

Our agent-based approach was used in three different studies in the CASSIOPEIA project: (1) *study* 1: analyze the effects of new environmental regulations (e.g., restrictions of night traffic at certain airports to reduce noise pollution), (2) *study* 2: analyze the effect of capacity constraints considering as a new strategy that airlines can exchange traffic slots (i.e., an air traffic slot as a tradable commodity), and (3) *study* 3: analyze the effect of new methods of speed adjustment for aircraft based on environmental conditions.

For these studies, we used data on air transportation in Europe from several sources. The majority of the data was acquired from ALL-FT+, a dataset collected by the PRISME group from Eurocontrol that includes information on trajectories for all flights crossing the European airspace from the 1st of March to the 31st of December 2011 and includes a total of 10.3 million flights. The data was provided in a large text file (more than 350 Gbytes), and it was necessary to appropriately clean, filter, validate and store in a database. We also used data from other sources (Demand Data Repository DDR, OpenFlights, OurAirports and Geonames) to complement these datasets with additional information (geographic names, time zones, etc.).

This data was used as input data for these studies. Each study included several simulations with different input data corresponding to various scenarios. For example, for study 1, we used data from 79,852 flights, 838 airports and 84 airlines and generated approximately 4,500 interaction messages (during one of the simulations). For study 2, we used data from 20,529 flights and 272 airlines and generated 4,938 interaction messages; and for study 3, we used data from 114 airports and 676 flights and generated approximately 2,000 messages. The CASSIOPEIA software architecture was reused to develop the agent models for the three studies. We reused 78% of the agent specifications in the XML language, 72% of the Java code and 91% of the database design.

The data was also used to estimate certain common quantitative parameters for the different scenarios. This was done manually and with simple statistical procedures. We did not use this data to validate the simulation results (these results correspond to new traffic policies for future ATM systems). Instead, we simulated certain ATM scenarios that were similar to the scenarios used in other ATM studies, and the domain experts verified that they generated similar simulation results.

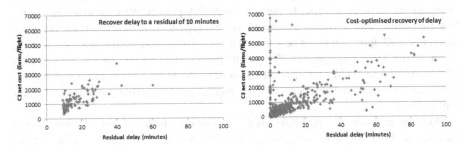

Fig. 5. Simulation results comparing two different strategies for delay recovering: (1) recover delay to a residual 10 minutes, and (2) optimum cost strategy.

The analysis of the results generated conclusions concerning the cause-effect relations in the ATM systems. Examples of the conclusions established by domain experts are as follows: traffic restrictions in the morning have worse economic effects than at night (study 1), direct slot trading between airlines can decrease costs by approximately 30% (study 2), and a reduction in delays is obtained when a new flight strategy for speed adjustment is applied by airlines and aircraft (the dynamic cost index strategy) (study 3).

In general, the results showed simulated effects related to complex adaptive system behavior such as system adaptation, emergent behavior and ripple effects. These cases simulated how the ATM system was able to adapt to environmental constraints using self-organization. For example, we imposed traffic restrictions at certain airports in study 1 (e.g., to reduce noise pollution at night). The simulation showed how airlines and airports could collaborate to adapt to these restrictions by finding alternative paths and new timetables and by rescheduling flight plans.

Certain behaviors of the system at a macroscopic level, which were difficult to anticipate by domain experts at this level of abstraction, emerged as a result of the interaction among agents and their environment. In study 1, for example, an effect emerged concerning traffic accumulation near the borders of restricted time intervals, which was stronger in the morning hours. Another example of emergent behavior is the global effect of local decision strategies concerning delay recovery. Figure 5 shows that the global delay of flights is significantly lower when the strategy of recovery delay to a residual of 10 minutes is applied instead of an optimum cost strategy. The simulations also showed ripple effects for events. In study 1, for example, we observed how the traffic constraints at certain airports were propagated to other airports and airline schedules. Using large scale areas for the simulation (e.g., 79,852 flights corresponding to seven days and 838 airports) was important for the analysis of this type of effect.

4   Discussion

In the context of the SESAR European program, it is important to provide policy makers with the means to analyze initiatives that affect future ATM networks on a multinational scale in Europe. In the CASSIOPEIA project, we explored how agent-based modeling and simulation can help in this regard. In this project, we designed an agent-based approach using new methods for collaborative human decision making in air traffic flow management. We implemented methods based on new models of coordination in ATM that were based on new and more agile communication mechanisms between stakeholders (for example, bidding-selling strategies for air traffic slots).

Our representation in CASSIOPEIA follows an intermediate level of abstraction (a mesoscopic level, between microscopic and macroscopic). A number of air traffic processes were abstracted using a stochastic approach. This level of representation was useful to simulate larger geographic areas (containing hundreds of airports) and larger temporal intervals, using available partial data. The simulations using this approach generated emergent behaviors that were difficult to anticipate by domain experts on a macroscopic scale. Future research concerning models with intermediate levels of abstraction can explore the use of methods for automatic calibration. For example, uncertainty representations (e.g., bayesian networks) can capture, in aggregated models, sets of behaviors with explicit measures of uncertainty. This type of representation could be automatically calibrated using machine learning methods for certain types of agents and subsequently reused for other agents to build complex models.

In air transport, it is difficult to obtain real-world data for ATM studies for various reasons (large amounts of data for large-scale studies, private information, high cost of data acquisition, etc.). In CASSIOPEIA, we had access to the ALL-FT+ dataset on European air traffic from the PRISME group. However, we had delays in obtaining the data (e.g., receiving the appropriate permissions), and a significant amount of effort was required to clean and filter the data. In CASSIOPEIA, it was useful to obtain additional data from open sources such as OpenFlights, OurAirports and Geonames. We expect that in the future, ATM data will become more accessible with the help of initiatives such as Open Data (e.g., data.gov) and Linked Data with explicit standard metadata.

It is important to have practical tools (more open and reusable) and methodologies that facilitate model development for various ATM studies. In CASSIOPEIA, we implemented a software architecture following an open concept with declarative representations for ATM agents and open-source tools. We used the XML language to formulate explicit declarative definitions for agents (e.g., airlines, airports, etc.) that were reused in various ATM studies. The software architecture was developed by integrating open software tools (Jadex, MySQL, OpenStreetMaps, etc.) to facilitate reusability at reduced costs. Jadex was useful for agent model specification and simulation control, although we found certain problems (partial documentation and a number of execution errors) that should be solved in a more mature version of this tool. Future research on the reusability of agent models for ATM systems can explore the use of declarative languages for agent model specification (such as XML) in combination with standard ontologies concerning ATM systems [16]. This combination can be used to provide more usable general models with representations that are closer to the ATM domain.

In our project, we designed and implemented a visualization tool to help analyze complex agent interactions containing thousands of messages. This was useful to configure simulations and to analyze certain global behaviors (e.g., ripple effects in ATM networks). In general, it is important to have advanced visualization tools for ATM studies with large amounts of data. Future research can explore the use of data analysis methods in combination with new graphical views, which are useful for ATM studies, to generate aggregated presentations that anticipate useful displays for the user, following a mixed-initiative, user-system interaction. For example, we are currently experimenting with new graphical displays that combine new versions of AUML diagrams with agent ontologies in the ATM domain to visualize summaries of agent interactions.

5   Conclusions

Agent-based modeling and simulation was successfully used for ATM studies (e.g., for air traffic control problems). However, the design of future ATM systems, as it is defined by the SESAR program in Europe, presents new challenges such as modeling new strategic decision levels, developing new representation methods for large-scale simulation using partial data, and creating more practical tools to facilitate the development of studies for the research community.

In the CASSIOPEIA project, we developed an agent-based approach for these challenges and obtained several results. We formulated new algorithms for distributed-collaboration decision making for strategic decision levels and used intermediate abstraction levels for simulations using stochastic approaches. Our software architecture in CASSIOPEIA was designed as a general tool, open and reusable, for the development of different ATM studies.

We proved the generality and applicability of our approach using three different ATM studies in the European airspace, which included strategic decisions concerning air traffic flow management and air traffic control. In comparison to previous related studies, we simulated new ATM decision processes, and they were applied to larger areas (with hundreds of airports and longer temporal scales). Our software architecture was used for the three ATM studies with high percentages of reuse (more than 70%) of the different components.

The majority of the implemented agent models and algorithms in CASSIOPEIA are specific to the ATM domain. However, part of our design for the architecture (e.g., integration of software tools and visualization methods) could be reused to simulate complex systems with distributed decisions and geographically dispersed stakeholders in other transportation problems (road traffic, rail transport, ship management, etc.) and other domains (water management, electrical distribution management, etc.).

In the future, we plan to continue our research to provide additional solutions for the ATM challenges using new agent-based approaches (e.g., with uncertainty models with machine learning methods for large-scale, agent-based simulations) together with practical software tools and methodologies.

Acknowledgements. The research presented in this paper was carried out under the CASSIOPEIA project. This project received financial support from Eurocontrol under the SESAR program (Single European Sky ATM Research). The consortium members of the CASSIOPEIA project were the Innaxis Research Institute, the Technical University of Madrid (Department Artificial Intelligence and Department of Air Transport) and the University of Westminster (Department of Transport Studies). The authors would like to thank a member of our research group, Nataliia Stulova, for the implementation of the visualization tool.

References

1. Agogino, A.K., Tumer, K.: A multiagent approach to managing air traffic flow. Autonomous Agents and Multi-Agent Systems 24(1), 1–25 (2012)
2. Airtop: Air Traffic Optimization, http://www.airtopsoft.com
3. Bouarfa, S., Blom, H.A., Curran, R., Everdij, M.H.: Agent-based modeling and simulation of emergent behavior in air transportation. Complex Adaptive Systems Modeling 1(1), 1–26 (2013)
4. Cammarata, S., McArthur, D., Steeb, R.: Strategies of Cooperation in Distributed Problem Solving. In: Proc. 8th International Joint Conference on Artificial Intelligence, Karlsruhe, Germany (1983)
5. Campbell, K., Cooper, W., Greenbaum, D., Wojcik, L.: Modeling Distributed Human Decision-Making in Traffic Flow Management Operations. In: Third USA/Europe Air Traffic Management Research and Development Seminar, The MITRE Corporation, McLean, VA (2000)
6. CAST, Airport Research Center, http://www.airport-consultants.com

7. Castelli, L., Pesenti, R., Ranieri, A.: The design of a market mechanism to allocate air traffic flow management slots. Transportation Research Part C: Emerging Technologies 19(5), 931–943 (2011)
8. De Jonge, H., Seljée, R.: Optimisation and Prioritisation of Flows of Air Traffic through an ATM Network. NLR-TP-2011-567, NLR, Amsterdam (2011)
9. Eurocontrol: The European Organisation for the Safety of Air Navigation, http://www.eurocontrol.int
10. George, S., Satapathy, G., Manikonda, V., Wieland, F., Refai, M.S., Dupee, R.: Build 8 of the Airspace Concept Evaluation System. In: AIAA Modeling and Simulation Technologies Conference (2011)
11. Gore, B.F., Corker, K.M.: Increasing aviation safety using human performance modeling tools: an Air Man-machine Integration Design and Analysis System application. Simulation Series 34(3), 183–188 (2002)
12. Gore, B.F.: Man-machine integration design and analysis system (MIDAS) v5: Augmentations, motivations, and directions for aeronautics applications. In: Human Modelling in Assisted Transportation, pp. 43–54. Springer (2010)
13. Ljunngberg, M., Lucas, A.: The OASIS Air Traffic Management System. In: Proc. 2nd Pacific Rim Conference on AI, Seoul, South Korea (1992)
14. Sesar: Single European Sky ATM Research, http://www.sesarju.eu
15. Sislak, D., Pechoucek, M., Volf, P., Pavlicek, D., Samek, J., Mařík, V., Losiewicz, P.: AGENTFLY: Towards Multi-Agent Technology in Free Flight Air Traffic Control. In: Defense Industry Applications of Autonomous Agents and Multi-Agent Systems, ch. 7, pp. 73–97. Birkhauser Verlag (2008)
16. Van Putten, B., Wolfe, S., Dignum, V.: An Ontology for Traffic Flow Management. In: ATIO 2008, Anchorage, Alaska (2008)
17. Wolfe, S., Jarvis, P., Enomoto, F., Sierhuis, M., Putten, B., Sheth, K.: A Multi-Agent Simulation of Collaborative Air Traffic Flow Management. In: Bazzan, A., Klugl, F. (eds.) Multi-agent Systems for Traffic and Transportation. IGI Global Publishing (2009)
18. Zelinski, S.: Validating the Airspace Concept Evaluation System Using Real World Data. In: AIAA Modeling and Simulation Technologies Conference and Exhibit, AIAA-2005-6491, San Francisco, California (2005)

Risk Management in Construction Project Using Agent-Based Simulation

Franck Taillandier[1] and Patrick Taillandier[2]

[1] UMR 5395 I2M -Univ. Bordeaux- 351 cours de la Libération, 33400, Talence
[2] UMR IDEES - Université de Rouen - 7 rue Thomas Becket, 76821 Mont Saint-Aignan
`franck.taillandier@u-bordeaux1.fr`, `patrick.taillandier@gmail.com`

Abstract. In recent years, intensive research and development have been done in the area of construction project risk management. Indeed, an efficient risk management is mandatory to project success. However, implementing such a management is complex because of the diversity and the dynamic nature of the risk. Moreover, each of the project stakeholders has his/her own risks, his/her own vision and his/her own action on the project and on risks. In this paper, we propose an agent-based model called SMACC to assess the impact of risks on the project. This model allows to test different risk mitigation strategies to measure their impact on the project. An application on a real project is also proposed to demonstrate the operability and the value of the proposed approach.

Keywords: Construction project, Risk management, Agent-based modeling.

1 Introduction

Construction projects are subject to many risks (organizational, human or economic). These risks can have a deep impact on the success of the project. Being able to manage them is one the major aims of project management. To answer this aim, many methods and tools have been developed to identify and evaluate the risks [1]. However, the complexity inherent to construction projects makes very difficult their global management. An important margin exists to improve project risk management but this improvement is constrained by current practice and the lack of global knowledge. Strong gaps have been identified in terms of organization and general management throughout the project, particularly with regard to the interfaces between the actors, whose objectives may be different, even sometimes contradictory. The pressure on project delay and cost, the need for improved performance in the construction industry and increasing contractual obligations, lead to the necessity of a more effective risk management approach [2].

In this article, to address risk analysis issues in construction projects, an agent-based model called SMACC (Stochastic Multi-Agent simulation for Construction projeCt) is proposed. SMACC can be used to simulate the progress of a project while integrating possible risks causes and to evaluate their impact on the project. By running the simulation a large number of times, a statistical view on project results under

J.M. Corchado et al. (Eds.): PAAMS 2014 Workshops, CCIS 430, pp. 34–43, 2014.

risk can then be built. It is also possible to simulate the impact of different possible strategies in order to analyze their performance. After presenting some related works (Section 2), we will introduce the SMACC model (Section 3). Finally, we will present the application of the SMACC model to a real project to illustrate its performance (Section 4).

2   Related Works

Some researchers have already tried to develop MASs to solve problems in the area of construction industry. Their application is often limited to a small part of the global process:

- Project design (ADLIB - Multi-agent system for design collaboration [3]) ,

- Procurement and specification of construction products (APRON - Agent-based Specification and Procurement of Construction Product [4], EPA: Electronic Purchasing Agent [5] and MASSS: a multi-agent system for suppliers sourcing [6]),

- Supply chain coordination (ABS3C: Agent-based framework for supply chain coordination in construction [7]) and schedule coordination (DSAS: Distributed Subcontractor Agent System [8]).

These different MASs are interesting, but consider only a specific domain of the construction project and they do not consider uncertainties. Few MASs developed for construction project take into consideration risk or uncertainties. It is the case of MASCOT -A multi-agent system for Construction Claims Negotiation [9] is based on Bayesian learning approach to simulate negotiation between contractor and designer (on project design) or contractor and client (for risk allocation). Nevertheless, this model still considers only a limited part of the global project process.

Rojas and Mukherjee [10] proposed a MAS to simulate the whole construction phase of a project. The model aims at assisting students and young engineers in understanding the construction process and decision-making process by simulating the construction project. Users can interact with the system by changing project parameters such as the resources requirements. The simulation is based on user interactions, and stochastic events that may arise during the course of the project. The developed MAS do not automatically generate decisions; this task being left to the user. Our challenge with SMACC will be, as in Rojas and Mukherjee model, to consider a stochastic environment, but also to integrate a decision model for stakeholders within the simulation.

3   Model Description

The purpose of SMACC is to simulate a construction project throughout its life cycle, from the feasibility phase to the end of the implementation phase, considering potential risks. It proposes a neutral perspective on risks, considering the whole project and all stakeholders. As results, SMACC estimates the project cost and duration, and the quality of the project activities/tasks. The simulation results can aid in the decision making process by testing different risk mitigation strategies and by measuring their impact on the project. SMACC is based on a chronological perspective of the project, highlighting the role of the stakeholders during the progress of the project.

The model is composed of many entities that have to be taken into account to simulate in a realistic way the dynamic reference system. In SMACC, we chose to represent all the entities composing the reference systems as agents, even when they are non-living entities (contract, operator instructions, etc). This choice helps to simplify the interaction process between the entities.

SMACC considers four agent families and nine types of agent:

(1) Project: Project agent (one global agent),

(2) Initial project descriptors: Stakeholder (project manager, contractor, etc.), Task (excavation work, painting, etc.), Resources (monetary resources, human resources, etc.), Contract (engagement of a company to perform a task with defined time, quality, etc.),

(3) Instructions: Instruction Agent (instruction of a manager to an operator to perform a task with expected delay, quality, etc.),

(4) Risks: Risk factor (high rate of work, low security level, etc.), Risk event (working accident, error on design, etc.) and Risk consequence (task delay, additional cost, etc.).

The Project agent is a global agent which is characterized by a set of tasks, the project objectives and constraints (time, expected performances and resource allowed), the price of each unit of resources (reusable or consumable) and the current situation (time spent, resources used...).

The second family of agents groups the various agents describing the project contents. Stakeholders correspond to the various people working on the project (they can be described as organisms, services or individuals). Stakeholder can have two roles: manager and operator. The operator role is the task execution. Each task has one person in charge (manager) who is responsible for its good realization. The responsibility of each task is directly assigned by the contract. Into this agent family, Contract agent has a center place. It includes all documents making a link between stakeholders and the project requirements according to each task. Contract specifies for a task the resources allowed, the expectations (delay, quality), the manager and the operator. To work on a task, operators have to call up resources (reusable and consumable). Tasks are characterized by a quantity of minimal and maximal resources of each type (reusable and consumable). Minimal resources correspond to the minimal quantity of resource necessary to make the task progress. Maximal resources correspond to the maximal quantity of useful resources to work on a task.

The third family contains Instruction agents. These agents correspond to the communication between a manager and an operator. The manager gives instructions to the operator of a task to favor cost, productivity, or quality. The operator must understand and translate these instructions into concrete actions.

Risk agents (risk factor, risk event and risk consequence) are defined in order to model risks, from their cause to their consequences. A risk factor is a project situation that could have an impact on project risks (for example "A low quality of the landscaping" that could increase the risk event "Problem of foundations realization"). A risk factor is described by a threshold on a variable which describes a stakeholder, a resource, a task or a contract. Risk events are events which can affect a parameter of the project, and thus, the project objectives. They are linked to a task or to a stakeholder and are defined by a probability of occurrence and by an impact on a variable. For example, the risk event "Error on the plan" could have a probability of 0.1 and an impact on the construction task progress. Risk consequences are the sum of consequences due to the risk events which occurred for a defined task or stakeholder.

SMACC is based on project planning. Tasks can be performed successively or simultaneously. The planning considers the precedence relationships between tasks. For each task, a contract defines an operator (contractor, designers…) and a manager. The progress rate, the cost and the quality of the work done by the operators depend on the characteristics of operators and on those of the manager. Risk events (natural hazard, worker accident…) could have an impact on cost, delay and quality. Risk events occur randomly following predefined laws.

Each step of the simulation corresponds to a working day. At each working day, the following processes are carried out, as described on Figure 1:

Process 1 - Update task status: each task updates its status. A task is considered as completed if the work progress on this task reaches 1. A task becomes executable is all the previous task are completed.

Process 2 - Check end condition: the project checks the status of all tasks. If all the tasks composing the project have the status "finished", the project is considered as completed and the simulation ends. There are two other conditions which can end the simulation: if the simulated project duration exceeds twice the planned/target duration or if the simulated project cost exceed twice the budget, the project is considered as failed and the simulation ends.

Process 3 - Assess priorities: each task assesses its priority. Tasks belonging to the critical path have the highest priority. Other tasks allow a delay of one or several days without impacting the total duration of the project and have a priority that depends on this margin; the higher the margin, the lower the priority. PERT diagram [11] is used to calculate the margin.

Process 4 – Give instructions: each manager of an executable task establishes a strategy by giving prior direction– i.e. creates an *instruction* agent - to operators. This instruction is built by choosing a Productivity/Quality/Cost vector value. The instructions depend on (a) the current status of the project and (b) the specific interest this stakeholder has regarding these three dimensions. Risk events can modify the instruction (increase or decrease normal values). For example, a bad perception of a delay situation can lower the importance given to the Productivity value.

Process 5 - Understand instructions: when an operator receives instructions, he/she can follow them or not. His/her behavior may depend on a variety of factors, like misunderstanding the manager instructions, or an exterior pressure on the operator to quickly finish his/her task. An operator has to build his/her own PQC vector by considering all orders he/she has received, his/her preferences and potential risk consequences.

Process 6 - Assign resources: for each task, each manager chooses the monetary resources to share between the operators that must take the task in charge. The quantity of monetary resources by day given by the manager to an operator depends on the will of the manager to limit the cost, the duration, on corrective penalty in case of work of low quality or delay and on risk consequences. The money given by the manager for each task can be freely used by the operators. The operator can divide the money as he/she wants to his/her tasks. This repartition is described in process 7. The assigned money is added to the monetary resources of the stakeholder and is withdrawn from the project monetary resource.

Process 7 - Allocate resources (Operator): each operator that has to work on one or several tasks distributes his/her resources on the tasks. For this, she/he assesses the ideal resources (quantity and quality) for the task which correspond to the minimum quantity and quality necessary to reach the task objectives (without considering risks). Then, the operator analyzes his/her available resources and can buy consumable resources or rent reusable resources using his/her own monetary resources. Risk events can also modify the purchasing or rental costs (e.g. "new tax on the temporary workers", "Increase of iron market price"). Finally, the operators distribute their resources between their tasks. The distribution of owned reusable resources is based on the difference between ideal resources and rented resources, weighted by the productivity indicator. More a task requires a high productivity and higher the quantity of resources to reach the ideal resources is, more the operator allocates resources.

Process 8 - Make progress tasks (Task): each task computes its progresses according to the resources used (quantity and quality), its characteristic and the consequences of the occurred risk events (accident, material failure...). The task quality depends on the quality of the resource, the quality instruction (higher the quality instruction higher the quality) and the possible occurrence of risk event impacting quality (e.g. "design options not adapted to working constraints").

Process 9 – Pay the managers: when a task is completed, the manager of the task is paid. The quantity of money paid to the manager depends on the contract (due monetary amount), the task achievement in terms of time/duration (comparison between the time spent and the time allowed) and quality (comparison between required quality and task quality), resources used (comparison between assigned and expected resources) and risk events (e.g. "financing fault"). The quantity of money paid, i.e. quantity of monetary resources, is removed from the project resources and added to the manager resources.

Process 10 – Update stakeholder's characteristics: the evolution of the project or external events can modify the motivation and the expertise of stakeholders. For example, the retirement of a skillful employee can reduce the technical expertise of a stakeholder. A bad communication between the manager and the operator can reduce his motivation. This action is executed once by step and stakeholder characteristics are updated.

Process 100 – Update risk factors: the risk level depends on the entities concerned by the risk factor (stakeholders, task, contract, instruction or other risks) and on the risk factor characteristics (threshold and importance). The more the value exceeds the threshold and the higher is the importance of the risk factor, the more the probability of the risk event will be impacted.

Process 101 – Update risk events: each risk event updates its probability of occurrence according to the risk factors that can induce this risk event.

Process 102 – Simulate risks: The risk event simulation consists in a random draw. If the random number is inferior to the risk event probability, the risk event occurs and then induces consequences; otherwise nothing happens at this time step. SMACC simulates each risk event and sums the consequences that concern the same stakeholder or the same task to evaluate their impact on the project.

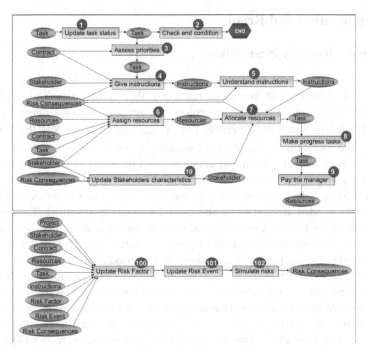

Fig. 1. Processes of the model

The model was implemented with the GAMA open-source agent-based simulation platform [12]. This platform provides a complete modeling and simulation development environment for building multi-agent simulations. Figure 2 illustrates the SMACC interface. The left screen shows the current situation of the model: in green, executable and completed task – the height of the task represents its progress; in red, the non-executable tasks; the spheres represent the stakeholder agents. The right screen monitors the project evolution (cost, time and quality) and compares it to expected values.

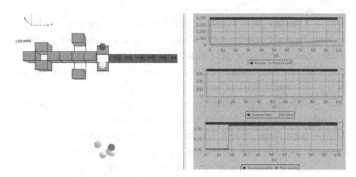

Fig. 2. Snapshot of a simulation (with the GAMA platform)

4   Application and Results

4.1   Application Case Presentation

In this section, we present an application of SMACC concerning the comparison of different risk management strategies regarding their efficiency. The application project is derived from a real public project: the construction of a nursing training institute located in South-West France. The project budget is 3.9 M€; the total time allowed to the project is 18 months (352 working days). Seven stakeholders are considered. For each of them, the initial value of motivation and expertise are set to 0.5 (mean value). Importance values were determined according to stakeholders' preferences. The project is considered at a global level, containing seventeen tasks. For each task, the needed amount of resources of each type is specified. To ensure the achievement of the project's objectives, seventeen contracts were proposed, defining for each task the demanded/requested (quality, duration and cost). 42 risk factors (difficult working conditions, bad crane installation, good communication, high security condition...) and 95 risk events were considered (work accident, difficulty to obtain building permit, underestimation of material need...). Risk events and risk factors can have beneficial (or detrimental) consequences on the project analysis and the construction company feedback. The risk event data (probability and impact) were chosen for simulation after a careful analysis of relevant literature [13-14] and risk manager experience in past similar projects.

Three strategies were simulated. The first strategy (S0) corresponds to that which would be usually chosen for the real project. The second strategy, called "safe strategy" aims at improving the safety during work by safety training and a special monitoring on this point. This strategy implies more time to perform tasks 12, 13, 14 and 15 (four tasks on working site) due to the new working conditions and training (this was simulated by adding 5% to D value for these tasks D). This strategy allows reducing the initial probability of risk events "Accident" by a factor 10. The third strategy called "High quality requirement" was proposed. In this strategy the required quality on every task was increased by 0.1. In the same time, the budget allowed to every task was increased by 10%.

4.2   Results and Discussion

In order to explore the possible solutions in the stochastic universe, Monte-Carlo simulations were performed by repeating 1000 times each strategy. Figure 3 provides the resulting distributions for quality, time and cost of the project for the three strategies.

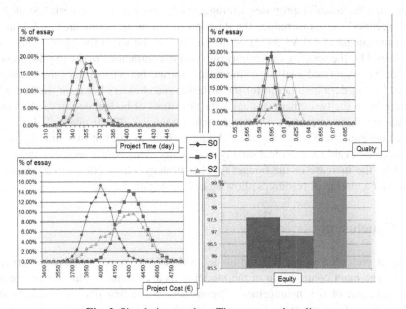

Fig. 3. Simulation results – Time, cost and quality

A fourth index was added regarding the equity between stakeholders. It is estimated by computing the percentage of stakeholders ending the project without a monetary deficit. A situation is considered as better if the equity criterion is higher. This criterion offers an additional view, which can prevent to use a strategy which would induce loser/winner situations.

The total time used by the real project was 331 working days (for 352 granted) and the budget was also respected (3.9 M€). The input data having been fitted with experts involved in the real project or similar ones, a first comparison can be carried out between the performance of the real project and those predicted by simulation using Strategy 0. It appears that the real project delay is in the lower part of the distribution curve. In fact, in the real project no serious hazard occurred, except a bad weather (important rains) during landscaping, causing a delay during this phase, but this delay was caught up during construction phases by increasing the human resources. This result is not surprising: risks are inherently stochastic and it may happen (without necessarily considering that the estimation was wrong) that the project was in an advantageous situation compared with the expected mean value. The theoretical mean value corresponds, in theory, to what could be expected in case of "many similar projects", and it is impossible to derive definitive conclusions from feedback of a single project. The real project cost is close to the mean simulation result. For the same reasons than for delay, the only possible statement is that this is not inconsistent. Quality is more difficult to analyze. An in-depth analysis would require discussion with the client to assess at what level his expectancies were satisfied by the real works.

The result shows that each of the three strategies has its advantages and drawbacks. Strategy 0 ("Standard") proposes average results on the four criteria. Strategy 1 ("High security") leads to reduce the duration of the project compared to S0 but increases the budget (4303 Vs 3972). Strategy 1 is also the worst for equity. This could be explained by the security constraints imposed to contractor (increasing the pressure on the delay). A refined analysis of the results shows that S1 increases the number of cases of budget deficit situation for the different stakeholders but limit the lost when occurred. With the two others strategies the situations of budget deficit are less common but are more important when occurred. Strategy 2 ("high quality") leads to a project cost equal to S1 and a project duration equal to S0, but this strategy allows increasing noticeably the project quality and equity. This equity increase can be explained by the increase of the budget for this strategy which allows to give to each stakeholder a margin of resources allowing to face negative events.

5   Conclusion

This paper presented an agent-based model, SMACC, to manage risk in construction projects. The main contribution of the model is its accounting of the dynamic nature of a project and of risk management. It considers at the first place the stakeholders and their capacity of reaction. This aspect, which is often not considered in classical risk analysis, is crucial. The dynamic nature of the model makes also possible to consider risk interactions, which is a significant innovation. The model was implemented on the GAMA platform and used for simulating the course of real construction projects. It allows to simulate the different possible events that could occur and the response of the stakeholders to these events. It gives a more accurate view about the possible ways the project can take. Simulations can be used to compare various project management strategies and risk mitigation processes.

SMACC has, in its present state of development, several limitations (robustness, etc.), but it already provides a significant basis for an efficient agent-based risk analysis simulation. The model will be enriched in the near future so as to better account the description of the organization of the project. Another perspective is to propose a method to generate the best strategy from user's preferences rather than just comparing different ones.

References

1. Walewski, J., Gibson, E.G.: International Project Risk Assessment: Methods, Procedures, and Critical Factors, Center Construction Industry Studies Report, 31, University of Texas, Austin (2003)

2. Carr, V., Tah, J.H.M.: A fuzzy approach to construction project risk assessment and analysis: construction project risk management system. Advances in Engineering Software 32, 847–857 (2001)
3. Anumba, C.J., Ren, Z., Thorpe, A., Ugwu, O.O., Newnham, L.: Negotiation within a Multiagent System for the Collaborative Design of Light Industrial Buildings. Advances in Engineering Software 34(7), 389–401 (2003)
4. Obonyo, E.A.: APRON: Agent-based Specification and Procurement of Construction Product. PhD Thesis, Loughborough University, UK (2004)
5. Hadikusumo, B.H.W., Petchpong, S., Charoenngam, C.: Construction material procurement using internet-based agent system. Automation in Construction 14, 736–749 (2005)
6. Li, W.: An agent-based negotiation model for the Sourcing of construction suppliers. PhD Thesis, University of Hong Kong (2008)
7. Xue, X.L., Li, X.D., Shen, Q.P., Wang, Y.W.: An agent-based framework for supply chain coordination in construction. Automation in Construction 14(3), 413–430 (2005)
8. Kim, K., Paulson, B.C.: An agent-based compensatory negotiation methodology to facilitate distributed coordination of project schedule changes. Journal of Computing in Civil Engineering 17(1), 10–18 (2003)
9. Ren, Z., Anumba, C.J., Ugwu, O.O.: Multiagent system for construction claims negotiation. Journal of Computing in Civil Engineering 17(3), 180–188 (2003)
10. Rojas, E., Mukherjee, A.: A multi-agent framework for general purpose situational simulations in the construction management domain. Journal of Computing in Civil Engineering 20(6), 1–12 (2006)
11. Kerzner, H.: Project Management: A Systems Approach to Planning, Scheduling, and Controlling, 8th edn. Wiley (2003)
12. Grignard, A., Taillandier, P., Gaudou, B., Vo, D.A., Huynh, N.Q., Drogoul, A.: GAMA 1.6: Advancing the art of complex agent-based modeling and simulation. In: Boella, G., Elkind, E., Savarimuthu, B.T.R., Dignum, F., Purvis, M.K. (eds.) PRIMA 2013. LNCS, vol. 8291, pp. 117–131. Springer, Heidelberg (2013)
13. Mehdizadeh, R.: Dynamic and multi-perspective risk management of construction projects using tailor-made Risk Breakdown Structures. PhD Thesis, Uni Bordeaux 1, France (2012)
14. Taroun, A.: Towards a better modelling and assessment of construction risk: Insights from a literature review. International Journal of Project Management 32(1), 101–115 (2014)

Doubt Removal for Dependant People from Tablet Computer Usage Monitoring

Clément Raïevsky, Annabelle Mercier, Damien Genthial, and Michel Occello

LCIS - COSY, Grenoble University, rue Barthélémy de Laffemas, Valence, France
{clement.raievsky,annabelle.mercier,damien.genthial,
michel.occello}@lcis.grenoble-inp.fr

Abstract. This article describes an agent which detects and handle potentially abnormal situations from the monitoring of applications usage on a tablet computer. The main purpose of this agent is to improve dependent people's safety by signaling potentially risky situations to caregivers. Indeed, such signaling can improve response time, thus reducing the consequences of such situations. The detection of abnormal situations is based on the construction of a user profile from the monitoring of used applications. When a user is inactive during a certain period of time, the recent activity is compared to the learned user's profile to decide if this is normal or not. Once an abnormal situation has been identified, the system will try to confirm that the situation is actually abnormal by prompting the user for input. In order to be as less intrusive as possible, the input request is an application suggestion. The suggested application will be the one that is usually the most used during the time period corresponding to the inactivity. When a situation is confirmed as abnormal, the tablet agent will send an intervention request to the user's caregivers. A simple coordination mechanism aimed at reducing redundant interventions and improving caregivers response time is proposed. The main contribution of this work is to propose a mechanism which monitors elderly people's applications usage on a tablet computer and is therefore able to complement existing monitoring devices in the detection of abnormal situations.

Keywords: Activity Monitoring, Doubt removal, Anomaly Detection.

1 Introduction

The increasing number of elderly and dependent people causes a diminution of the time spent by caregivers with them. Safety is a key concern because it is directly associated with the reduction of caregivers availability. Indeed, the less caregivers spend time with dependent people, the longer it will take to detect and handle a problematic situation. The induced delays have potentially terrible consequences.

The main challenges when giving elderly people's access to information technologies are acceptability, reliability, and cost of the chosen technology on one hand and privacy concerns on the other hand. Acceptability of a technology is

J.M. Corchado et al. (Eds.): PAAMS 2014 Workshops, CCIS 430, pp. 44–53, 2014.

closely related to how much this technology is perceived as obtrusive and/or intrusive. Another aspect related to acceptability is the adaptability of the system to the user.

The research described in this paper is part of the SIET project which aims at evaluating the benefits that adapted tablet computers can bring to dependent people in specialized institutions or at home. The SIET project especially aims at improving elderly people's well being by giving them means to communicate more easily with their caregivers (family and health worker) using information technologies. In order to improve dependent people's safety we added an agent to these tablets. This agent is designed to detect and handle abnormal situations. It is based on the construction of a user profile from the monitoring of used applications. When a user is inactive during a certain period of time, the recent activity is compared to the learned user profile to decide if this is normal or not. Once an abnormal situation has been identified, the system will try to confirm that the situation is actually abnormal by prompting the user for input. If the user does not answer this input request, an intervention request is sent to the user's caregivers. This process can help reduce response time to problematic situations.

Regarding acceptability, this solution is kept as less intrusive as possible since no dedicated device is added to the dependent person's environment or body. Furthermore, specific actions required from the user are kept to a minimum. There is no explicit training phase during which the user is required to perform specific tasks. Another advantage of using tablet computers is the fact that they are not perceived as segregative. Some devices dedicated to abnormal situations detection, such as fall detection devices, are perceived as ageing symbols and are sometimes not well accepted. This is not the case with tablet computers.

Choosing off-the-shelf devices ensures some confidence in their reliability and reduces their cost compared to custom-made, dedicated devices. Furthermore, since the monitoring process does not require continuous communication between several computing units, the chosen solution is less sensitive to communication failures.

Regarding adaptability, our solution involves the construction of a personal user profile which is aimed at making anomaly detection more accurate and less intrusive. This kind of adaptability to the user may reduce the number of useless input requests from the user and intervention requests from caregivers, thus improving perceived utility of the agent.

Another concern of seniors regarding automated monitoring systems is privacy [1,2]. Not only does storing or transmitting sensitive data raise ethical issues, but it also reduces the acceptability and thus the potential benefits of the technology. In our approach, only summarized application usage history is stored and generic requests are transmitted. Furthermore, our solution is not handling any sensitive data such has health records or prescriptions. The potential impact of the proposed solution on elderly people's privacy is thus low.

The proposed solution is composed of three agents: one running on tablet computers given to elderly people and responsible for monitoring application usage; one running on a distant server and responsible for checking if tablets are switched off; and one running on caregivers hand-held devices, responsible for alerting them about intervention requests and coordinating intervention intentions.

The remainder of this article starts by presenting related work, following is a description of the different mechanisms involved in the detection and confirmation of abnormal situations. The way an abnormal situation is handled is described and the mechanism used to coordinate caregivers interventions are presented in Section 4. An illustrative example is depicted in Section 5 along with planned experiments. Some considerations regarding the modeling process plasticity are presented in Section 6. The last section concludes this paper and proposes some extensions to the work presented here.

2   Related Work

Passive monitoring of elderly or dependent people is not a new topic, and some advanced commercial solutions are available[1]. Those systems include continuous or on demand video and audio forwarding, and various forms of remote sensing. However active monitoring, which includes alarm triggering, decision making and/or pro-activity is still an active research area.

Many research and industrial projects have studied the safety improvement given by adding specific sensors to the elderly people's environment or body. These sensors include accelerometers to detect falls [3,4], blood oxygenation sensors [5], or dedicated sensors (bed pressure, bath overflow, etc) [6].

Other teams use generic sensors to assess elderly people's situation for example, [7] use microphones to detect falls, [8,9] use video data to also detect falls. Some other works use a multi-modal approach using a combination of these techniques [10,11].

Until recent time, computers or cell-phones were rarely used by the elderly. Reduction of the costs and improvements in user interfaces usability has made computer more accessible to elder people. Tablet computers, removing the major obstacle that mouse and keyboard are, increased further the accessibility of information technology to the elderly. It is therefore becoming possible to consider monitoring usage of these technology to assess elderly people situation. One of the research topic of the SIET project is precisely to identify which are the most important ergonomic choices to make a tablet computer usable by a senior.

Even before tablet computers have been widely available, computer usage monitoring has been used to assess the cognitive performances evolution of elderly people [12]. Smart-phone, a device similar to the one used in the work presented here, has been identified as a reliable tool to assess the cognitive function in the elderly [13]. To our knowledge, no research project reports the monitoring of tablet computer usage to assess elderly people situation.

The main differences between our project and existing work are the nature of what we monitor, tablet computer usage, and the fact that we integrate the alarm

---

[1] e.g. www.clariscompanion.com

mechanism with a simple caregivers coordination scheme. Our work does not aim at replacing dedicated devices or health-related sensors, but at complementing those systems to widen the range of identified risky situations, thus improving dependent people safety.

3   Doubt Identification

The tablet agent, which is responsible for detecting anomalies and sending intervention requests, is integrated in a dedicated Android application running on the tablet. This application allows elderly people to use some predefined applications and prevents them from accessing the configuration interface of the tablet or using applications which are not adapted to them. These restrictions have the positive consequence to prevent novice users from worrying about breaking things on the tablet.

The abnormal situations identification mechanism is composed of three parts:

- a monitoring process which builds a profile of the way the dependent person uses applications available on the tablet computer;
- a process which checks general user activity to detect periods of inactivity;
- an anomaly detection algorithm which compares built user profile with recent activity to determine if detected inactivities are normal or not.

These three parts are described in the next three sections.

3.1   Usage Profile Modeling

In order to detect potentially abnormal situations, the tablet agent monitors matching between applications usage and a model of the user usage profile. This user profile is represented by histograms and built from application usage sampling. At each sampling step, the current active application is logged with a time stamp and the corresponding histogram bin is incremented. In order to remove "seasonal" effect on the profile modeling, there is a histogram for each day of the week. To be able to suggest the most used application when trying to confirm a situation as abnormal, each application has its own histogram.

The modeling process parameters are the sampling rate and the histograms bin size. The application sampling rate has been set to 5 minutes in order to capture most of tablet use while keeping memory footprint low (1 year of logging amounts to approximately 800Mo of disk space).

Even though elderly people often have quite fixed routines, it is interesting for the modeling process to be able to capture changes in user habits. To do so, the tablet agent always updates the user profile, the training phase does not have a finite duration. One problem of this choice is that the agent will potentially take a long time to capture a new habit: the time during which frequencies of new behaviour observations will stay low is proportional to the training time. To solve this problem, usage frequencies are computed on a finite time period. The duration of this time window determines the reactivity of the

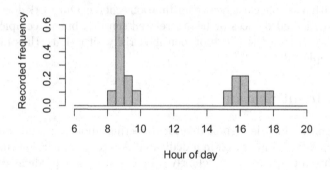

Fig. 1. User profile example for one day and one application

system to new behaviours. It should not be too short however because interesting observations may fall out of the time window and be forgotten, preventing an actually recurrent behaviour to be captured.

3.2   Inactivity Detection

Current user activity is checked against the built model only when an inactivity is detected. The duration of the inactivity period which triggers the model checking determines the reactivity of the detection process. Inactivity detection is carried out by a rule matching engine. According to Equation 3, this engine computes the accumulated time during which no activity has been reported (i.e. no application has been used) on a sliding time window (w in Equation 2). It then checks if this accumulated time is above a threshold. The user is considered inactive when this test fails. The parameters of this detection mechanism are the time window length and inactivity threshold. The user activity is checked every 10 minutes for inactivity to keep the load on the system low. This sampling rate is different from the applications usage sampling rate because it used to detect inactivities, not to build the user profile.

$$active_i(t) = \begin{cases} 1 & \text{if application } i \text{ is active at } t \\ 0 & \text{otherwise} \end{cases} \tag{1}$$

$$a_i = \int_{-w}^{0} active_i(t)\mathrm{d}t \tag{2}$$

$$activity = \sum_i a_i \tag{3}$$

3.3   Anomaly Detection

Once the user is considered inactive, the user profile is used to check if this inactive state is normal. In order to determine if an inactivity state is an anomaly, the agent computes the usual activity frequency during a time period. This usual activity frequency is the sum of the recorded frequencies over the time lapse of interest. It represents the information captured about user application usage over the time lapse corresponding to the recent past. If this usual activity frequency is greater than a threshold, the detected inactivity is considered abnormal. The current situation is therefore identified as an anomaly.

The parameters of the anomaly detection process are the length of the considered time window and the anomaly threshold.

3.4   Switched-off Tablet Detection

All previous mechanisms can be executed only if the dependent person's tablet computer is switched-on. In order to handle situations where the tablet is switched-off, another agent is running on a remote computer. This remote agent monitors the reception of "awake" messages from the tablet agent. When the remote agent detects that the tablet agent has not sent messages since a defined time, the current situation is considered to be an anomaly.

4   Doubt Handling

When the tablet agent detects a potential anomaly, it first tries to confirm that the situation is abnormal. To do so, it tries to interact with the dependent person. In order to be as less intrusive as possible, this interaction is an application suggestion. The suggested application is the one that has usually been the most used over the time period corresponding to the inactivity that triggered the anomaly detection process. The user is first presented with an unobtrusive message (an android notification) that suggests him to use this application. The possible answers are to launch the suggested application or to delete the notification. If the user responds to the suggestion, either by launching the application or deleting the notification, the agent considers that the current situation is not abnormal. The inactivity counter is reset. If the user accepts the suggestion, the application is started and the user profile is updated by the modeling process. If the user declines the suggestion, no application is launched and the frequency of observations related to the anomaly detection is "naturally" decreased by the modeling process.

If the user does not respond to the application suggestion after some time, an audible reminder is emitted. If the user still does not respond to this signal after some time, an intrusive message is displayed and an alarm is triggered. If the user does not stop this alarm, an intervention request is sent to caregivers. This process is described in the next section.

4.1   Caregivers Coordination

When an anomaly has been identified either by the tablet agent or the remote agent, an intervention request is generated. This request is sent by the agent which detected the anomaly to the caregivers in the dependent person's network. A third agent, running on portable devices owned by caregivers, is responsible for informing the caregivers of the request. The caregivers, are able, through this agent, to declare their intention regarding the request or to acknowledge the request. Possible intentions regarding an intervention request are to decline it or to indicate a time at which the caregiver may respond to the request. Intervention intentions are forwarded to the other caregivers' agents in order to avoid redundant intervention. It is possible for a caregiver to indicate an intervention time that is sooner than an existing intention, making it possible to decrease response time.

5   Realization

5.1   Illustration

As an illustration of the whole process, let us consider an elderly woman who is at home and was given, three months ago, a tablet computer with dedicated services such as video chat, e-mail, social games, news, and photo sharing. Each week day morning, around 8 o'clock, she checks if she has received new e-mails. She sometimes plays bridge for some time with friends around half past ten. She rarely uses the tablet between noon and 3 o'clock in the afternoon, except on Sundays, when she makes video calls with her family. She usually checks the news after her nap, around 4 o'clock in the afternoon. She usually meets with friends on Sundays afternoon and therefore does not read the news on this day. She regularly looks at some photos or plays some game on Saturday evenings. The tablet agent has built a model of these habits, depicted by the diagram on the left of Figure 2, and is therefore able to alert her family and/or caregiver if, for example, she cannot stand up from her bed in the morning or if she has fallen in the bathroom and cannot reach the phone. It will also be able to know that it is normal that no interaction occurs during her nap time and will conveniently not trigger alarms during this time.

5.2   Planned Experiments

Currently, 35 elderly people have been given a tablet computer. From these persons 75% are female and are 80 years old in average. They live in retirement homes. The tablets do not yet the agent responsible for usage monitoring. We plan to add our monitoring agent into the next release of the dedicated application which users interact with. In this preliminary version, the agent will only monitor activity and log anomaly detection and identification events. No action will be taken in response to anomaly detection since people in a retirement home do not need an abnormal situation detection system because there is almost always an available caregiver. This will however allow us to collect actual data about the load our system puts on the tablets and analyse the generated profiles and the frequency and relevance of detected anomaly.

The next phase of the SIET project, which this research is part of, includes the deployment of tablets at elderly people's home. This will allow us to actually evaluate our system in terms of intrusiveness, false alarm rates, and accuracy.

6   Tests

6.1   Model Plasticity

One important property of the model is its plasticity, that is to say its ability to capture new behaviour and to modify already learned habits. This property is important because it greatly influences the perceived intrusiveness of the whole mechanism. If the agent is not able to modify its model of the user behaviour while it is changing, many false alarms will be generated, annoying the user. Conversely, if the model varies too easily, some alarms will be missed.

In order to test the plasticity of the modeling process, we measured the time (in days) to forget a usual activity. This experiment simulates the situation where a senior has a new weekly medical appointment and modifies a habit accordingly. In the experiment, we first give the agent application usage logs. These logs are generated by randomly sampling normal distributions which have properties matching those described in the illustration example of Section 5.1. The simulated time of this initial observations spans over 70 days. Diagram on the left of Figure 2 depicts a summarized view of the behaviour model the agent has built from these logs. In this figure, application models are not distinguished. Once this model has been built, we feed the agent with logs generated from normal distributions with different properties. The new properties correspond to the postponing of the e-mails checking from 8 o'clock to 10 o'clock. Diagram

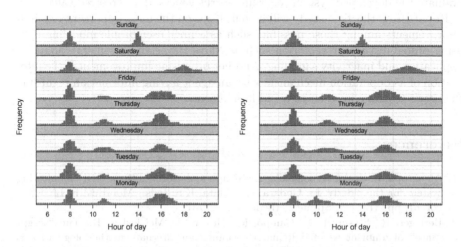

Fig. 2. Summarized user profile examples; original model (left), after adaptation to habit change (right). Frequencies of all applications have been summed.

on the right of Figure 2 depicts the result of the adaptation of the model to this new situation after some time. It can be seen that the built profile captured successfully the activity shift. The time after which the previous habit will be overridden by the new one can be tuned using the length of the time window over which the observations are considered (see Section 3.1).

6.2   Monitoring Load

Regarding the load applied on the tablet computer by the modeling and monitoring processes, log size and application sampling have very low impact on the tablet usability. The inactivity detection process' low sampling rate causes no hard load on the tablet CPU and is therefore not intrusive. All these processes have an overall small footprint in term of power consumption.

7   Conclusion and Future Work

This paper presented a system aimed at improving elderly people safety using an agent running on a tablet computer to detect and identify abnormal situations, an agent on a server to detect switched-off tablets, and an agent on caregivers' hand-held devices to ease their coordination. The described mechanism allows the agent running on the tablet to adapt to its user's profile and make the monitoring process as less intrusive as possible. The usage modeling process can be fine-tuned to obtain a suitable plasticity of the model, improving its adaptability and reducing its intrusiveness. Overall, the described agents offer an interesting ratio between their cost, intrusiveness and senior safety improvement.

The next main step of our research project is to carry out field studies to evaluate the developed system regarding intrusiveness and perceived safety.

Results from this field study will help us focus on the most important required improvements among those possible, such as a finer user profile modeling (e.g. using probabilistic representation such as Naive Bayesian Classifiers), adaptive application and inactivity sampling. Another promising improvement is the integration of a cooperation mechanism with an agent having information regarding the user's schedule in order to avoid false alarms.

References

1. Alakärppä, I., Hosio, S., Jaakkola, E.: SNS as a platform of the activity monitoring system for the elderly. In: Godara, B., Nikita, K.S. (eds.) MobiHealth. LNICST, vol. 61, pp. 413–420. Springer, Heidelberg (2013)
2. Beringer, R., Sixsmith, A., Campo, M., Brown, J., McCloskey, R.: The "acceptance" of ambient assisted living: Developing an alternate methodology to this limited research lens. In: Abdulrazak, B., Giroux, S., Bouchard, B., Pigot, H., Mokhtari, M. (eds.) ICOST 2011. LNCS, vol. 6719, pp. 161–167. Springer, Heidelberg (2011)

3. Bagalà, F., Becker, C., Cappello, A., Chiari, L., Aminian, K., Hausdorff, J.M., Zijlstra, W., Klenk, J.: Evaluation of Accelerometer-Based Fall Detection Algorithms on Real-World Falls. PLoS ONE 7(5) (2012)
4. Bourke, A., O'Brien, J., Lyons, G.: Evaluation of a threshold-based tri-axial accelerometer fall detection algorithm. Gait & Posture 26(2), 194–199 (2007)
5. Ahmed, M.U., Banaee, H., Loutfi, A.: Health Monitoring for Elderly: An Application Using Case-Based Reasoning and Cluster Analysis. ISRN Artificial Intelligence (2013), http://dx.doi.org/10.1155/2013/380239
6. Mahoney, D.F., Mahoney, E.L., Liss, E.: AT EASE: Automated Technology for Elder Assessment, Safety, and Environmental monitoring. Gerontechnology 8(11-25) (2009)
7. Li, Y., Ho, K., Popescu, M.: A microphone array system for automatic fall detection. IEEE Transactions on Biomedical Engineering 59(5), 1291–1301 (2012)
8. Foroughi, H., Aski, B., Pourreza, H.: Intelligent video surveillance for monitoring fall detection of elderly in home environments. In: 11th International Conference on Computer and Information Technology, ICCIT 2008, pp. 219–224 (2008)
9. Rougier, C., Meunier, J., St-Arnaud, A., Rousseau, J.: Fall detection from human shape and motion history using video surveillance. In: 21st International Conference on Advanced Information Networking and Applications Workshops, AINAW 2007, vol. 2, pp. 875–880 (2007)
10. Alemdar, H.Ö., Yavuz, G.R., Özen, M.O., Kara, Y.E., Incel, Ö.D., Akarun, L., Ersoy, C.: Multi-modal fall detection within the wecare framework. In: Abdelzaher, T.F., Voigt, T., Wolisz, A. (eds.) IPSN, pp. 436–437. ACM (2010)
11. Crispim-Junior, C.F., Joumier, V., Hsu, Y.L., Pai, M.C., Chung, P.C., Dechamps, A., Robert, P., Bremond, F.: Alzheimer's patient activity assessment using different sensors. Gerontechnology 11(2) (2012)
12. Jimison, H., Pavel, M., McKanna, J., Pavel, J.: Unobtrusive monitoring of computer interactions to detect cognitive status in elders. IEEE Transactions on Information Technology in Biomedicine 8(3), 248–252 (2004)
13. Brouillette, R.M., Foil, H., Fontenot, S., Correro, A., Allen, R., Martin, C.K., Bruce-Keller, A.J., Keller, J.N.: Feasibility, Reliability, and Validity of a Smartphone Based Application for the Assessment of Cognitive Function in the Elderly. PLoS ONE (June 11, 2013)

Development of Electrolarynx by Multi-agent Technology and Mobile Devices for Prosody Control

Kenji Matsui[1], Kenta Kimura[1], Alberto Pérez[2],
Sara Rodríguez[2], and Juan M. Corchado[2]

[1] Osaka Institute of Technology, Osaka, Japan
[2] Computer and Automation Department. University of Salamanca. Spain
`matsui@elc.oit.ac.jp, e1610024@st.oit.ac.jp,`
`{srg,alberto.pgarcia,corchado}@usal.es`

Abstract. The feasibility of using a motion sensor to replace a conventional electrolarynx (EL) user interface was explored. A mobile phone motion sensor with multi-agent platform was used to investigate on/off and pitch frequency control capability. A very small battery operated ARM-based control unit was also developed to evaluate the motion sensor based user-interface. The control unit was placed on the wrist and the vibration device was placed against the throat using support bandage. Two different conversion methods were used for the forearm tilt angle to pitch frequency conversion: linear mapping method and F0 template-based method. A perceptual evaluation was performed with two well-trained normal speakers and ten subjects. The results of the evaluation study showed that both methods were able to produce better speech quality in terms of naturalness.

Keywords: multi-agent system, agents, prosody, electrolarynx, hands-free.

1   Introduction and Background

As a result of technological advances, intelligent systems have become an important part of our lives. These systems can be found in multiple places and provide a huge range of facilities. Disabled people face increasing difficulties daily. Most buildings and facilities are not adapted to their disabilities, so they find barriers, which they cannot overcome alone. However, with the help of these new intelligent systems disabled people are now able to overcome difficulties they encounter. People who have had laryngectomies have several options for restoration of speech, but no currently available device is satisfactory. An electrolarynx (EL) introduces a source vibration into a vocal tract by producing vibrations in the external wall. It is easy for patients to master, but the intelligibility of consonants they articulate is diminished and the speech is uttered at a monotone frequency since it does not produce airflow. Alternatively, esophageal speech does not require any special equipment, but requires speakers to insufflate, or inject air into the esophagus, and limits the pitch range and intensity. Both esophageal speech and tracheoesophageal speech are characterized by low average pitch frequency, large cycle-to-cycle perturbation in pitch frequencies,

J.M. Corchado et al. (Eds.): PAAMS 2014 Workshops, CCIS 430, pp. 54–65, 2014.
© Springer International Publishing Switzerland 2014

and low average intensity. Age has also been found to be an important factor for utilizing esophageal speech. When patients get older, they face difficulty in mastering the esophageal speech, or continue to use esophageal speech because of their waning strength. For that reason, the EL is an important device even for the people who use esophageal speech.

There are many advantages of the EL. To begin, one can speak in long sentences that are easily understood. Additionally, no special care requirements are needed; the EL need only to be placed up against the neck and turned on. Finally, the EL can be used by almost everybody, regardless of the post-operative changes in the neck. In those few cases where scarring prevents proper placement of the EL, an intraoral version can be used. On the other hand, there are also some disadvantages. Firstly, the EL has a very mechanical tone that does not sound natural. There is usually little change in pitch or modulation. Secondly, its appearance is far from normal. Pitch frequency control is one of the important mechanisms for EL users to be able to generate naturally sounding speech. There are some commercially available EL devices using a single push button with a pressure sensor to produce F0- contours [1], [2]. There are also similar studies of pitch controlling methods [3],[4]. However, none are hands-free. Some approaches for generating F0-contour without manual inter-action have been proposed. Saikachi et al. use the amplitude variation of EL speech [5]. Another approach is to generate an F0-contour using an air-pressure sensor that is put on the stoma [6][7]. Also, recently, a machine learning F0- contour generation from EL speech has been proposed [8]. Although most of those studies are in the early stages of research, the results show substantial improvement of EL speech quality. An EL system that has a hands-free user interface could be useful for enhancing communication by alaryngeal talkers. Also, the appearance can be almost normal because users do not need to hold the transducer by hand against the neck. Almost all people frequently use gestures when they talk. It would be quite convenient if the EL users could utilize gestures to control the device. Furthermore, because hands can generate various types of motion, gesture control has a lot of potential to handle not only the on/off function, but many other functions as well. However, if users are not able to use hand gestures, we need to consider other part of body movement, or a completely different technique, such as EMG based hands-free EL control [9].

As for the total system management issue, multi-agent is one of the key technology trends. There are many multi-agent frameworks, which help and facilitate working with agents [16][17][18][19][20][21][22][23][24][25][26][27]. The main drawback of these systems is that they are for general purposes. General purpose was considered a major issue twenty years ago, but it is much less the case now, at a time where personal computers, devices, mobile phones and alike, have grown exponentially. In addition, the needed architecture must be able to assume tasks for integrating disabled people. Moreover, differences among disabled people are very different. Some of the most known European multi-agent systems projects oriented in the direction of our research direction are [28][29][30][31][32].

The present study was undertaken to explore the feasibility of using multi-agent technology and mobile devices (replacing the conventional EL user interface) to control both on/off function, and pitch frequency. The specific goals were: 1) to make the generated speech natural, and 2) to make the appearance normal.

The paper is structured as follows: Section 2 presents a revision on the system requirements as indicated by the participants involved in the study. Afterwards, the system implementation is approached for the reader to fully understand the system design. Finally the article briefly explains the results and conclusions obtained from the study.

2   System Requirements

A set of techniques - including user observations, interviews, and questionnaires - were used to understand implicit user needs. The total number of laryngectomized participants in the questionnaire survey was 121 (87% male, 13% female), including 65% esophageal talkers, 12% EL users, 7% both, and 21% used writing messages to communicate.

Almost all of the participants claimed that most public areas are difficult for oral communication due to the noisy environment. Typical public areas include train stations, inside of train cars, inside of vehicles, restaurants/pubs, and conventions/gatherings.

The noisy environment issue is a well-known problem and people usually use portable amplifier; however, we have been investigating a smaller, lighter, and low profile speech enhancement system for both esophageal speech [10] and EL. Other needs confirmed from the survey are: (i) Natural sounding voice, without a mechanical tone. (ii) Light weight device. (iii) Smaller device, low profile. (iv) Hands-free, easy to use. (v) Low cost. Based on those survey results, the present study was conducted to meet the essential user needs.

3   System Implementation

The system implementation was carried out by using PANGEA (Platform for Automatic coNstruction of orGanizations of intElligents Agents) [14], [33]. It is modeled as a virtual organization of agents. These agents are connected with the PANGEA platform [22], a multi-agent platform designed on the basis of virtual organizations[34][35][36], aimed at creating intelligent environments which are able to be connected to any kind of device, as explained in [37]. The system uses a smartphone, which has powerful processing capabilities, provides any functionality needed to connect to, and allows the use of its integrated accelerometer to calculate the desired output.

The following subsections explains how the system is integrated, paying special attention to the UI design, the integration of the system with PANGEA platform – multi-agent design, the design of the hardware to include in the system, and the two algorithms used to contrast data.

3.1   Hands Free UI Design: Gesture and Pitch Control

Gesture control UI can be developed through the use of a system based on photo detector, camera, or accelerometer. Based on the survey results, a three-axis MEMS accelerometer was used in this study. MEMS sensors are very small, low cost, and fit the system requirements well [12].

A MEMS accelerometer accurately measures acceleration, tilt, shock and vibration in applications. The challenge in designing the pitch control algorithm that uses a MEMS accelerometer output to control pitch contour is to reconcile the numerical ranges between two types of data. MEMS output bytes are integers within the range -128 to 127 for a range of ±2G. This issue can often be easily reconciled by linear mapping of one range of values (such as MEMS data values - 128 to 127) into another range (such as 67 to 205 expected as the typical male pitch range).

Another possible pitch control method is to utilize a pitch contour generation model, such as Fujisaki's model [11]. The system needs to have a strategy to generate both the phrase component and the accent component from the MEMS output. The F0 template-based method is easier to generate relatively stable pitch contour, however, it may lose some flexibility to generate various pitch patterns.

In this study, both the simple linear mapping method and the F0 template-based method were prototyped and examined to evaluate pitch control performance. Also, the comparison study was performed between conventional EL, the linear map-ping method and the F0 template-based method.

```
<test> help

<sensorAgent> C000
<sensorAgent> C001: getValue <int: number_of_values>: This message
   returns the specified number of last read values, from 1 to 10.
<sensorAgent> C002 End of help
```

Fig. 1. Message format offered by the sensor agent in PANGEA

3.2   Multiagent Design

In order to integrate the system with the PANGEA platform, a virtual organization was developed, named the "alaryngeal talkers organization". This organization includes the following three kinds of agents, all of which improve the complete system because of the advantages inherent to a multi-agent structure:

- *Sensor agent:* this kind of agent is in charge of obtaining measures from the smartphone's accelerometer sensor and providing this data when required by other agent members of the system who are authorized to communicate with it.
- *Config agent*: this kind of agent allows establishing certain configuration data, which are required when establishing a pitch frequency to be the base when readjusting the frequency. This is an important factor to fit the frequency with a person's physical appearance, which will be estimated from the data entered. With this, an even more natural result is achieved.

```
<test> help
<configAgent> C000
<configAgent> C001: setGender <bool: gender>: This message sets the
   gender of the current user. 0=male, 1=female.
<configAgent> C001: setWeight <int: kilograms>: This message sets the
   weight of the current user.
<configAgent> C001: setHeight <int: centimeters>: This message sets
   the height of the current user.
<configAgent> C001: bool getGender: This message returns the gender
   of the current user if it is established.
<configAgent> C001: int getWeight: This message returns the weight of
   the current user in kilograms
<configAgent> C001: int getHight: This message returns the height of
   the current user in centimeters.
<configAgent> C002 End of help
```

Fig. 2. Message format offered by the configuration agent in PANGEA

- *Analogic agent*: this kind of agent is responsible for generating and providing an analogue output from the data obtained from the agents involved (sensor and configuration agents). These agents can now only communicate with each other and with control agents that the PANGEA platform offers, but with the possibility of eliminating this restriction or even expanding the system in future extensions.

3.3   Hardware System Design

We have been using Android-based mobile devices. Android is an open-source operating system (OS) and has a large market share in terms of OS for smartphones and PC tablets. The basic idea is to utilize an accelerometer of an Android mobile device to control on/off function and pitch frequency. Users can control without seeing the display using sensors.

A block diagram of the hardware architecture is shown in Figure 3. An Android mobile device sends PWM signals to a pair of EL transducers through an amplifier. The Amplifier requires a 9V battery so that the EL transducers can generate sufficient speech output. The EL transducer is placed against the neck with the neck-bandage. Figure 4 shows the entire system, including the EL transducer and the amplifier.

3.4   Pitch Control (Linear Mapping Method)

Hand gestures are a very important part of language. A preliminary UI study using forearm movement was conducted in order to evaluate the feasibility of the pitch control mechanism.   Figure 6 shows the forearm tilt and the MEMS output (x-axis) when the controller was placed on the wrist. The normal pitch control zone extends from the horizontal position ($0°$) to the $75°$ upward position. The fading out zone extends from the horizontal position to the $-25°$ downward position, and is where the phrase ending pitch pattern is adjusted based on the forearm moving speed. As for the conversion from the MEMS output to the pitch frequency, there are four pitch ranges. Figure 7 shows the relationship between the MEMS output and the four ranges of pitch frequency, i.e. high, mid-high, mid-low, and low. Users can select one of the four ranges.

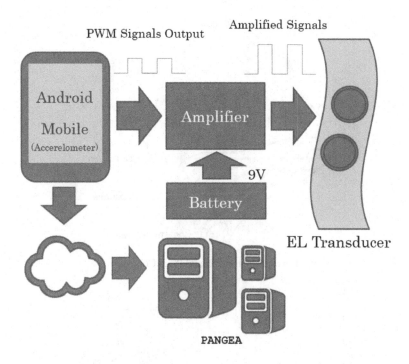

Fig. 3. Block diagram of the Hardware Architecture

Fig. 4. EL transducer, amplifier and entire system (upper left: EL transducer with neck-bandage, upper right: a pair of EL transducer, lower left: amplifier in a box, lower right: entire system)

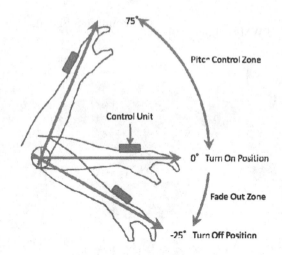

Fig. 5. Forearm Tilt and Pitch Control

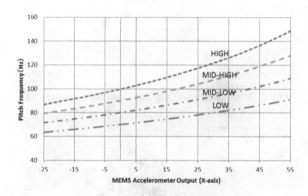

Fig. 6. Relation between MEMS Output and Pitch (linear mapping method)

3.5   Pitch Control (F0 Template-Based Method)

The linear mapping method is straightforward approach; however, it requires precise sensor control to avoid unnatural pitch behavior. The F0 template-based method applies a basic F0 template to the fine F0 contour generation. The phrase component of Fujisaki's model was used to generate the F0 template F0(t). While the system is intended to generate both phrase control and accent control, during the first step of testing the template, we utilized only the phrase component.

$$\text{Ln } F0(t) = \ln F \min + Ap \cdot Gp(t) \tag{1}$$

where

$$Gp(t) = \alpha^2 \, t \exp(-\alpha t) \tag{2}$$

The symbols in equations (1) and (2) indicate:

- Fmin is the minimum value of the speaker's F0.
- Ap is the magnitude of phrase command.
- α is natural angular frequency of the phrase control mechanism.

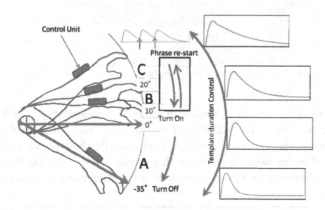

Fig. 7. Relation between Forearm tilt and F0 template generation (F0 model-based Method) A-zone: -35°~0° B-zone 0°20°, and C-zone: 20°~

In this study, those values are: Fmin = 80Hz, α=1.5 and Ap = 0.75. The calculated F0 template data is stored in the controller software. Figure 7 shows the F0 contour generation mechanism using the MEMS sensor output and the F0 template. The oscillation starts at 10° upward from the horizontal position. The template duration is controlled based on the forearm tilt angle as shown in the Figure 7. The figure also how to re-start the F0 template is shown. Basically, the forearm movement (C-zone → B-zone → C-zone) is required. A-zone is -35°~0°, B-zone is 0°~20°, and C-zone is 20°~, respectively.

4   Evaluation and Results

Although we confirmed the two types of pitch control functions using the mobile device based system, this time, we took an ARM-based hardware unit for the pitch control algorithm evaluation. Subjective evaluation tests (by rating scale method) were made with 2 male well-trained normal speakers, and 10 (one female and nine male) subjects. Each speaker read the phonetically balanced test materials as shown in table 1. We used one commercially available EL device (SECOM EL- X0010), proto-type-A (linear mapping method, with 70Hz mode), and prototype-B (F0 template-based method). Those 60 speech stimuli (2 speakers *3 devices *10 sentences) were recorded, and two sets of differently randomized stimuli were prepared. 5 subjects evaluated one set of stimuli, and another 5 subjects rated the other set of stimuli. Each speech stimulus was presented two times.

Table 1. Phonetically balanced Japanese test sentences

1	Papa mo mama mo minna de mamemak· o shita
2	takai takai tokoro e nobotte iku tokoro da.
3	Achirakara mo kochirakara mo dochirakara mo ikukoto ga dekiru.
4	Aoi o ueru.
5	Anohito wa bunkajin to yobareru no ga fusawashi.
6	Shichi gatsu kara hanshin densha de nikir shite ima su
7	Ginkô mo gakkô mo aruite ikeru kyori ni ari masu.
8	Kinkô ga tore te iru no de kukkô ga yoi.
9	shijû gamu o kamuno ga syûkan ni natte iru.
10	Hana o ottari ana o hottari sanzanna meni atta.

The subjects rated the speech stimuli in terms of "intelligibility (Clarity)", "naturalness of the prosody", and "stability of the prosody" using five level scaling. As shown in Figure 8, the subjective evaluation indicated that both prototype-A(LM) and B(FU) obtained higher naturalness scores than the EL device(EL). On the other hand, intelligibility (clarity) and stability shows almost no difference among those devices.

	LM	FU	EL
Intelligibility	2.99	2.98	2.98
Naturalness	3.11	3.03	2.255
Stability	3.3	3.17	3.345

Fig. 8. Average evaluation scores

Without losing intelligibility (clarity) and stability of the prosody, both prototype-A and B showed substantial improvement in terms of the naturalness of the prosody. Results of this study indicate that both, usability and speech quality of EL speakers could be improved by MEMS accelerometer based hands-free UI controller. The ability to control the pitch contour of EL speech with the proposed linear mapping method and F0 template-based method implies that hand gesture control may be adequate for implementation of the hands free user interface for the EL device. Our assumption about the performance difference between the two proposed methods is that the F0 template-based method may be easier to learn and the pitch contour easier to stabilize. However, there was almost no difference between those two methods. We plan to run the same evaluation with actual EL-users, and confirm if the proposed methods perform similarly. Also, a more detailed and precise study across the talkers, sentences, and learning curve has to be performed. As for the gesture control, we tested only the forearm movement; however, it is necessary to test other body locations where users might be able to control the EL device more easily and naturally. According to the user requirements, the evaluation of appearance also needs to be considered. In the study, we set a relatively narrow pitch range in order to avoid wild swings in pitch. A better pitch control range needs to be investigated.

5   Conclusions

An MEMS accelerometer, integrated in a smartphone, hands free UI for EL device was proposed. A hand gesture system was designed and prototyped using a smartphone. Two types of pitch contour generation methods were proposed and tested together with conventional EL device. Results of the evaluation indicated that the proposed methods have a potential to make the EL output prosody more natural, easy to use, and with a less distinct appearance. In addition, the developed multi-agent system provides several advantages. A simple application with multi-profile capacity is achieved, which allows the speaker to obtain an even more natural way of speech. Similarly, the system could be expanded in terms of sensors or even complexity thanks to the characteristics provided by the integration with PANGEA multi-agent platform [13]. It also allows us to keep a record of all messages produced in the system [14], which can lead to future studies to improve the system based on the generated knowledge.

A disadvantage of using the PANGEA platform is that the mobile device must necessarily have a connection with the server, either by local network or the Internet. For a situation where a connection is not possible, there is an alternative design, already developed and presented, which can be seen in [15]

However, a more detailed and precise study across the talkers, sentences, and learning curve has to be performed.

Acknowledgements. This work has been carried out by the project *Sociedades Humano-Agente: Inmersión, Adaptación y Simulación*. TIN2012-36586-C03-03. Ministerio de Economía y Competitividad (Spain). Project co-financed with FEDER funds.

References

[1]   SECOM company Ltd., Electrolarynx "MY VOICE",
      http://www.secom.co.jp/personal/medical/myvoice.html
[2]   Griffin laboratories, Tru Tone users guide
[3]   Kikuchi, Y., Kasuya, H.: Development and evaluation of pitch adjustable electrolarynx. In: SP 2004, pp. 761–764 (2004)
[4]   Takahashi, H., Nakao, M., Ohkusa, T., Hatamura, Y., Kikuchi, Y., Kaga, K.: Pitch control with finger pressure for electrolaryngial or intra-mouth vibrating speech.Jp. J. Logopedics and Phoniatrics 42(1), 1–8 (2001)
[5]   Saikachi, Y.: Development and Perceptual Evaluation of Amplitude-Based F0 Control in Electrolarynx Speech. Journal of Speech, Language, and Hearing Research 52, 1360–1369 (2009)
[6]   Uemi, N., Ifukube, T., Takahashi, M., Matsushima, J.: Design of a new electrolarynx having a pitch control function. In: Proceedings of 3rd IEEE International Workshop on Robot and Human Communication, RO-MAN, Nagoya, Japan, July 18-20, pp. 198–203 (1994)

[7] Nakamura, K., Toda, T., Saruwatari, H., Shikano, K.: The use of air-pressure sensor in electrolaryngeal speech enhancement. In: INTERSPEECH, Makuahari, Japan, September 26-30, pp. 1628–1631 (2010)

[8] Fuchs, A.K., Hagmüller, M.: Learning an Artificial F0- Contour for ALT Speech. In: INTERSPEECH, Portland, Oregon, September 9-13 (2012)

[9] Kubert, H.L.: Electromyographic control of a hands-free electrolarynx using neck strap muscles. J. Commun. Disord. 42(3), 211–225 (2009)

[10] Matsui, K., et al.: Enhancement of Esophageal Speech using Formant Synthesis. Journal of Acoustical Society of Japan (E) 23(2), 66–79 (2002)

[11] Fujisaki, H.: In Vocal Physiology: Voice Production, Mechanisms and Functions. Raven Press (1988)

[12] Matsui, K., et al.: A preliminary user interface study of speech enhancement system. In: Proc. of the 1st International Conference on Industrial Application Engineering, pp. 53–56 (2013)

[13] Sánchez, A., Villarrubia, G., Zato, C., Rodríguez, S., Chamoso, P.: A gateway protocol based on FIPA-ACL for the new agent platform PANGEA. In: Pérez, J.B., et al. (eds.) Trends in Pract. Appl. of Agents & Multiagent Syst. AISC, vol. 221, pp. 41–51. Springer, Heidelberg (2013)

[14] Zato, C., Villarrubia, G., Sánchez, A., Bajo, J., Corchado, J.M.: PANGEA: A New Platform for Developing Virtual Organizations of Agents. International Journal of Artificial Intelligence 11(13), 93–102 (2013)

[15] Matsui, K., et al.: Development of Electrolarynx with Hands-Free Prosody Control. In: The Proc. of the 8th ISCA, August 31, pp. 273–277 (2013)

[16] Poslad, S., Buckle, P., Hadingham, R.: The FIPA-OS agent platform: Open Source for Open Standards. In: Proceedings of Autonomous Agents AGENTS 2000, Barcelona (2000)

[17] Argente, E., Giret, A., Valero, S., Julian, V., Botti, V.: Survey of MAS Methods and Platforms focusing on organizational concepts. In: Vitria, J., Radeva, P., Aguilo, I. (eds.) Recent Advances in Artificial Intelligence Research and Development, Frontiers in Artificial Intelligence and Applications, pp. 309–316 (2004)

[18] McCabe, F.G., Clark, K.L.: APRIL—Agent PRocess Interaction Language. In: Wooldridge, M.J., Jennings, N.R. (eds.) Proceedings of the Workshop on Agent Theories, Architectures, and Languages on Intelligent Agents (ECAI 1994), pp. 324–340. Springer-Verlag New York, Inc., New York (1995)

[19] Bicharra García, A.C., Sanchez-Pi, N., Correia, L., Molina, J.M.: Multi-agent simulations for emergency situations in an airport scenario. Advances in Distributed Computing and Artificial Intelligence Journal (2013) ISSN: 2255-2863

[20] Bordini, R.H., Hübner, J.F., Vieira, R.: Jason and the Golden Fleece of agent-oriented programming. In: Bordini, R.H., Dastani, M., Dix, J., El Fallah Seghrouchni, A. (eds.) Multi-Agent Programming: Languages, Platforms and Applications, ch. 1, pp. 3–37. Springer (2005)

[21] Tapia, D.I., Abraham, A., Corchado, J.M., Alonso, R.S.: Agents and ambient intelligence: case studies. Journal of Ambient Intelligence and Humanized Computing 1(2), 85–93 (2010)

[22] Bajo, J., Corchado, J.M.: Evaluation and monitoring of the air-sea interaction using a CBR-agents approach. In: Muñoz-Ávila, H., Ricci, F. (eds.) ICCBR 2005. LNCS (LNAI), vol. 3620, pp. 50–62. Springer, Heidelberg (2005)

[23] Tapia, D.I., Rodríguez, S., Bajo, J., Corchado, J.M.: FUSION@, a SOA-based multi-agent architecture. In: International Symposium on Distributed Computing and Artificial Intelligence 2008 (DCAI 2008), pp. 99–107 (2008)

[24] Rodríguez, S., Pérez-Lancho, B., De Paz, J.F., Bajo, J., Corchado, J.M.: Ovamah: Multiagent-based adaptive virtual organizations. In: 12th International Conference on Information Fusion, FUSION 2009, pp. 990–997 (2009)

[25] Tapia, D.I., De Paz, J.F., Rodríguez, S., Bajo, J., Corchado, J.M.: Multi-agent system for security control on industrial environments. International Transactions on System Science and Applications Journal 4(3), 222–226 (2008)

[26] Rodríguez, S., de Paz, Y., Bajo, J., Corchado, J.M.: Social-based planning model for multiagent systems. Expert Systems with Applications 38(10), 13005–13023 (2011)

[27] Pinzón, C.I., Bajo, J., De Paz, J.F., Corchado, J.M.: S-MAS: An adaptive hierarchical distributed multi-agent architecture for blocking malicious SOAP messages within Web Services environments. Expert Systems with Applications 38(5), 5486–5499

[28] CommonWell Project (2010), http://commonwell.eu/index.php

[29] Monami project (2010), http://www.monami.info/

[30] DISCATEL (2010), http://www.imsersounifor.org/proyectodiscatel/

[31] INREDIS (2011), http://www.inredis.es/

[32] INCLUTEC (2011), http://www.idi.aetic.es/evia/es/inicio/ contenidos/documentacion/documentacion_grupos_de_trabajo/ contenido.aspx

[33] Zato, C., Villarrubia, G., Sánchez, A., Bajo, J., Corchado, J.M.: PANGEA: A New Platform for Developing Virtual Organizations of Agents. International Journal of Artificial Intelligence 11(A13), 93–102 (2013)

[34] Pavon, J., Sansores, C., Gomez-Sanz, J.J.: Modelling and simulation of social systems with INGENIAS. International Journal of Agent-Oriented Software Engineering 2(2), 196–221 (2008)

[35] Rodríguez, S., de Paz, Y., Bajo, J., Corchado, J.M.: Social-based planning model for multiagent systems. Expert Systems with Applications 38(10), 13005–13023 (2011)

[36] Garijo, F., Gómes-Sanz, J.J., Pavón, J., Massonet, P.: Multi-agent system organization: An engineering perspective. Pre-Proceeding of the 10th European Workshop on Modeling Autonomous Agents in a Multi-Agent World, MAAMAW 2001 (2001)

[37] Zato, C., Sánchez, A., Villarrubia, G., Bajo, J., Rodríguez, S.: Integration of a proximity detection prototype into a VO developed with PANGEA. In: Casillas, J., Martínez-López, F.J., Corchado, J.M. (eds.) Management of Intelligent Systems. AISC, vol. 171, pp. 197–204. Springer, Heidelberg (2012)

A BDI Emotional Reasoning Engine
for an Artificial Companion

Carole Adam[1] and Emiliano Lorini[2]

[1] LIG CNRS UMR 5217, UJF Univ. Grenoble-Alpes, Grenoble, France
carole.adam@imag.fr
[2] IRIT CNRS UMR 5505, Toulouse, France
emiliano.lorini@irit.fr

Abstract. In this paper, we present an agent that is able to reason about the user's emotions and to perform or suggest coping strategies to deal with them in order to improve the user's well-being. Concretely, this agent uses the PLEAID reasoning engine that we extended to implement Dastani and Lorini's BDI logic for graded emotions and coping strategies. We explain the difficulties behind such an implementation, that proves the computational tractability of the underlying logic. We then illustrate the possibilities offered by this agent on a short scenario involving an artificial companion interacting with a human user.

Keywords: Artificial companions, Emotions, Coping Strategies, BDI Logics.

1 Introduction

A companion agent is an intelligent agent able to naturally interact with its user on the long-term and establish a relationship with them [Bickmore and Picard, 2005]. Several projects have investigated such companions and their relationships with humans: for instance Paro, a plush seal robot, was used in a nursing home to improve elderly people's well-being [Taggart et al., 2005]; similarly, virtual characters with relational abilities interacting with older adults helped them develop social connections and subsequently reduce health problems and mortality [Vardoulakis et al., 2012]; companions were also used as weight loss advisors [Kidd and Breazeal, 2007]. When interacting with such companions, human users tend to use and expect the same social norms as when interacting with humans [Reeves and Nass, 1996]. Therefore, the design of such companions should rely on a theoretical model of human-companion interactions based on theories of human-human interaction [Kramer et al., 2011]. In this paper we focus on one particular aspect of social interactions and relationships: emotions. We argue that an artificial companion should be endowed with a model of emotions that allows it to reason about the user's emotions, understand them and react appropriately.

Companion Agents are usually endowed with the ability to recognise the user's emotions from various cues: facial expressions, paralinguistic and semantic analysis of speech, body language and posture, physiological cues...

J.M. Corchado et al. (Eds.): PAAMS 2014 Workshops, CCIS 430, pp. 66–78, 2014.

(*e.g.* [D'Mello and Graesser, 2010], or see [Calvo and D'Mello, 2010] for a review). Another approach consists in endowing the agent with a logical model of emotions allowing it to infer hypotheses on the user's emotions [Adam, 2007]; the advantage of this approach is that the agent can reason about these emotions and their causes, and by extending the logical model with a description of coping strategies, the agent becomes able to offer emotion regulation help to the user.

Models of emotions for artificial agents are usually inspired by the cognitive appraisal theories of human emotions [Ortony et al., 1988], [Lazarus, 1991], [Frijda, 1987]. According to these, an agent continuously **appraises** its situation, *i.e.* evaluates its subjective significance, and a **coping** mechanism selects strategies to deal with this subjective appraisal. As a result of these two processes, the individual **feels** an emotion with a certain intensity [Keltner and Ekman, 1996], which then affects its behaviour. Lots of agents are based on *ad hoc* computational models (*e.g.* EMA [Gratch and Marsella, 2004]) and cannot easily be compared together, while more theoretical models such as logical models enable formal deductions from the underlying theory but often lack an actual implementation. In order to bridge this gap, we propose to use PLEIAD, a BDI agent framework that allows the implementation of logical models of emotions.

In this paper, we first discuss several approaches to artificial emotions for agents, namely computational models such as EMA vs formal logical models such as Dastani and Lorini (Section 2); we argue that formal logical approaches have interesting advantages but they lack a working implementation to prove useful in real agents. We detail D&L's formal model of appraisal and coping (Section 3) which is the one we chose to implement here. We then describe PLEIAD, an implemented BDI architecture allowing the integration of various formal logical models of appraisal and coping, and use it to implement D&L's logic (Section 4). Next, we demonstrate this implementation and illustrate its potential by running a short scenario and detailing the reasoning processes involved (Section 5). We finally conclude about this work and perspectives for future works (Section 6).

2 Emotions for Agents

On the one hand, logical models of emotions allow us to reason, infer properties of the underlying theories, and compare them. But although psychological models of emotion emphasize the role of emotion intensity and its role in the coping mechanism [Ortony et al., 1988], most existing works on logical modeling of emotions have ignored either the intensity of emotions or the coping strategies. [Adam et al., 2009] have proposed a logical formalisation of the OCC theory, while [Lorini and Schwarzentruber, 2011] have formalised counterfactual emotions such as regret and disappointment, but both approaches ignore the quantitative aspect of emotions. [Lorini, 2011] later formalised emotion intensity in a similar logic, but did not consider coping strategies. Finally [Dastani and Lorini., 2012] formalised both appraisal and coping in a quantitative logic. [Steunebrink et al., 2009] also provide a formal model of emotions extended with their intensities (an intensity function is assigned to each appraised emotion to determine its intensity at each state of the model) and a coping mechanism (inspired by [Frijda, 1987]'s theory of action tendencies, according to which specific emotions set the tendencies to change the agent's relation to its subjectively perceived environment) to reduce intensity of negative emotions. However, unlike D&L, [Steunebrink et al., 2009] takes emotion intensity as a primitive without explaining how it depends on more primitive cognitive ingredients such as belief strength and goal strength; the other important difference is that D&L provide a decidable logic of emotion with a complete axiomatisation, whereas [Steunebrink et al., 2009] do not provide any decidability result or complete axiomatisation.

On the other hand, lots of agents are based on *ad hoc* computational models, that do not allow formal comparison of their underlying theories, but have the strong advantage of being already implemented and readily usable in real applications. [Gratch and Marsella, 2004,Marsella and Gratch, 2009] propose such a computational model. It is not based on formal logics, instead the eliciting conditions of emotions are defined in terms of quantitative measures such as desirability and likelihood of events. It considers both emotion intensity and coping strategies: several thresholds determine when emotions are elicited and how emotions are coped with. Its implementation, called EMA, is applied in particular to generate predictions about human emotions and their coping strategies.

The advantage of BDI logic is that it is based in folk psychology, and therefore offers a formalisation in terms of high level concepts, mental attitudes, that are easily understandable by humans, making it possible for an artificial companion to explain its behaviour to its user. But the drawbacks of formal logic is that they are often very complex and not computationally tractable, which is a prohibitive obstacle to their actual use in practical applications. In this paper, we propose to bridge the gap between these two approaches by using the PLEIAD system for implementing D&L Logic of Emotions.

3   A Logic of Emotions: Appraisal and Coping

3.1   Logical Framework

D&L's logic of emotions is a logic of graded mental attitudes designed to represent beliefs (with degree of plausibility), goals (with degree of desirability), and intentions. It is parameterised by a set of propositional variables $Atm = \{p, q, \ldots\}$, a finite set of positive integers $Num = \{0, \ldots, \mathsf{max}\}$ with $\mathsf{max} > 0$ for measuring strengths of beliefs and desirability of the consequences of the agent's actions, and a finite set of physical actions $PAct = \{a, b, \ldots\}$. The set of negative integers $Num^- = \{-x : x \in Num \setminus \{0\}\}$ is used to represent undesirability of the consequences of the agent's actions (*i.e.*, the fact that certain consequences might have a negative utility for the agent). Consequences of the agent's actions are represented by literals in the set $Lit = \{p : p \in Atm\} \cup \{\neg p : p \in Atm\}$. The logic supports reasoning about four different kinds of mental attitudes:

1. *graded belief* represented by formulae $\mathsf{B}^h\varphi$ with ($h \in Num$), meaning that "the agent believes that φ is true with strength h";

2. *certain belief* represented by formulae $CB\varphi$, meaning that "the agent strongly believes/is certain that φ is true";
3. *desire* represented by formulae $Des^k c$ (with $k \in Num \cup Num^-$ and $c \in Lit$), meaning that "the consequence c has a degree of desirability k for the agent";
4. *intention* represented by formulae Int_a (with $a \in PAct$), meaning that "the agent has the intention to perform the physical action a".

Differently from degree of belief that is either equal to or greater than zero, degree of desirability can be positive, negative or equal to zero. Suppose $k > 0$. Then $Des^k c$ can also be read "the agent wishes c to hold with strength k", whereas $Des^{-k} c$ means that "the agent wishes c not to hold with strength k". $Des^k 0$ means that "the agent is indifferent about k" (*i.e.*, the agent does not care whether c is true or false). The following abbreviations are used:

$$AchG^k c \overset{\text{def}}{=} Des^k c \text{ for } k > 0$$

$$AvdG^k c \overset{\text{def}}{=} Des^{-k} c \text{ for } k > 0$$

where $AchG$ and $AvdG$ respectively stand for achievement and avoidance goal.

3.2 Appraisal Patterns

The logic of graded mental attitudes discussed above is used by D&L to formalise appraisal patterns of basic emotions such as hope, fear, joy and sadness with their corresponding intensities.

Following current psychological and computational models of emotion (see, *e.g.* [Reisenzein, 2009, Gratch and Marsella, 2004, Ortony et al., 1988]), D&L assume that intensity of hope is a monotonically increasing function of the degree of belief that a given event will occur and the desirability of the event, while intensity of fear is a monotonically increasing function of the degree of belief that a given event will occur and the undesirability of the event. This function is denoted by the symbol *merge*.[1]

According to the D&L's definition of hope, a given agent hopes with intensity i that its current intention to do a will lead to the desirable consequence c, denoted by $Hope^i(a, c)$, if and only if there exist two values h and k such that: (1) $merge(h,k) = i$, (2) the agent intends to perform action a, (3) the agent believes with strength h that its current intention to do a will lead to the consequence c, and (4) the agent wishes to achieve c with strength k. Formally:

$$Hope^i(a, c) \overset{\text{def}}{=} \bigvee_{\substack{h,k \in Num \setminus \{0\}: h < max \\ \text{and } merge(h,k) = i}} (B^h \langle\langle a \rangle\rangle c \wedge AchG^k c \wedge Int_a)$$

According to the D&L's definition of fear, a given agent fears with intensity i that its current intention to do a will lead to the undesirable consequence c, denoted by $Hope^i(a, c)$, if and only if there exist two values h and k such that: (1) $merge(h,k) = i$, (2) the agent intends to perform action a, (3) the agent believes

---

[1] The simplest merging function one might consider is the *product*.

with strength h that its current intention to do a will lead to the consequence c, and (4) the agent wishes to avoid c with strength k. Formally:

$$\text{Fear}^i(a,c) \stackrel{\text{def}}{=} \bigvee_{\substack{h,k \in Num\setminus\{0\}:h<\max \\ \text{and } merge(h,k)=i}} (B^h\langle\langle a\rangle\rangle c \wedge \text{AvdG}^k c \wedge \text{Int}_a)$$

In the preceding definitions of hope and fear it is assumed that h < max becausehope and fear require some level of uncertainty. This is the main difference between hope and fear and joy and distress that are based on certainty. D&L define joy and distress based on the notion of certain belief as follows:

$$\text{Joy}^i(a,c) \stackrel{\text{def}}{=} \bigvee_{\substack{k \in Num\setminus\{0\}: \\ merge(\max,k)=i}} (CB\langle\langle a\rangle\rangle c \wedge \text{AchG}^k c \wedge \text{Int}_a)$$

$$\text{Distress}^i(a,c) \stackrel{\text{def}}{=} \bigvee_{\substack{k \in Num\setminus\{0\}: \\ merge(\max,k)=i}} (CB\langle\langle a\rangle\rangle c \wedge \text{AvdG}^k c \wedge \text{Int}_a)$$

where $\text{Joy}^i(a,c)$ has to be read "the agent is joyful with intensity i that its current intention to do a will lead to the desirable consequence c", and $\text{Distress}^i(a,c)$ has to be read "the agent is distressed with intensity i that its current intention to do a will lead to the undesirable consequence c".

3.3   Coping Strategies

D&L's logical analysis of coping strategies is largely inspired by Gratch & Marsella's EMA ([Gratch and Marsella, 2004,Marsella and Gratch, 2009]). It mainly concentrates on emotion-focused coping (*i.e.*, coping with the emotion by modifying one or more mental attitudes that triggering it). Three kinds of coping strategies are considered: coping strategies affecting beliefs, coping strategies affecting desires, and coping strategies affecting intentions. Each kind of coping strategy is formally expressed by a corresponding operator in the logic:

- **Operators $\varphi\uparrow^B$ and $\varphi\downarrow^B$ for coping strategies affecting beliefs:** increase ($\varphi\uparrow^B$) or decrease ($\varphi\downarrow^B$) the strength of the belief that φ of a given value ω_1,
- **Operators $c\uparrow^D$ and $c\downarrow^D$ for coping strategies affecting desires:** increase ($c\uparrow^D$) or decrease ($c\downarrow^D$) the desirability of the consequence c of a given value ω_2,
- **Operators $+a$ and $-a$ for coping strategies affecting intentions:** generate ($+a$) or remove ($-a$) the intention Int_a.

Following Lazarus's psychological theory of coping [Lazarus, 1991], in D&L's logic each coping strategy is characterised by a corresponding triggering condition. For instance, it is assumed that an agent that is fearful or distressed because its intention a will lead to the undesirable consequence c will possibly reconsider its intention. Such an intention reconsideration strategy is formulated as follows:

$$Trg(-a) = \bigvee_{\substack{c \in Lit, \\ i \in EmoInt: i \geq \theta}} ((\text{Fear}^i(a,c) \vee \text{Distress}^i(a,c)) \wedge B \text{ Ctrl } c)$$

with:

$$\text{Ctrl } c \stackrel{\text{def}}{=} \bigvee_{b \in PAct} \langle\langle b \rangle\rangle \neg c$$

This means that the coping strategy of reconsidering the intention to perform action a is triggered if and only if (1) the agent is either fearful or distressed with intensity at least θ that its intention to perform the action a will lead to an undesirable consequence c, and (2) the agent believes that he has control over c, in the sense that he can prevent the undesirable result c to be true by performing a different action. θ is a threshold which captures the agent's sensitivity to negative emotions (the lower is θ, and the higher is the agent's disposition to discharge a negative emotion by coping with it). This kind of coping strategy is called *behavioural disengagement* [Carver et al., 1989].

D&L also formalise the triggering condition of *wishful thinking*, the proto-typical coping strategy affecting beliefs, and *positive reinterpretation*, the pro-totypical coping strategy affecting desires. It is assumed that an agent that is fearful or distressed because it believes that its intended action a will realise the undesirable consequence c on which it has no control will either (1) decrease the strength of the belief that action a will lead to the undesirable consequence c (wishful thinking) or, (2) increase the desirability of c (positive reintepretation). Formally:

$$Trg(\langle\langle a \rangle\rangle c \downarrow^B) = \bigvee_{\substack{i \in EmoInt: \\ i \geq \theta}} ((\text{Fear}^i(a,c) \vee \text{Distress}^i(a,c)) \wedge \neg B \text{ Ctrl } c)$$

$$Trg(c \uparrow^D) = \bigvee_{\substack{i \in EmoInt: \\ i \geq \theta}} ((\text{Fear}^i(a,c) \vee \text{Distress}^i(a,c)) \wedge \neg B \text{ Ctrl } c)$$

4 The PLEIAD System

4.1 PLEIAD Architecture

The PLEIAD system (ProLog Emotional Intelligent Agent Designer) [Adam, 2007] is a SWI-Prolog agent with a BDI architecture, endowed with reasoning capabilities (planning, etc) and emotions. Concretely it enables implementation of various log-ical models of emotions, such as the OCC theory [Adam et al., 2009], or a model of complex emotions (*i.e.* emotions based on counterfactual reasoning and reasoning about responsibility) and their expression in language [Riviere et al., 2012]. The advantage of implementing different models in this one system is to allow comparing their influence on the agent's behaviour in similar situations. PLEIAD is composed in particular of:

- Perception module: interprets stimuli in terms of mental attitudes to be added to the agent's knowledge base (KB);
- Reasoning engine: applies a set of deduction rules (*e.g.* modus ponens);
- Knowledge Base manager: handles assertion of new mental attitudes while avoiding conflicts with previous ones;
- Planning module: computes the agent's plan to reach its current intention ;
- Appraisal module: has definitions of emotions in terms of mental attitudes, and applies them on the KB to infer triggered emotions and their intensity ;
- Coping module: contains specification of triggering conditions and effects of the coping strategies presented above.

PLEIAD also allows to specify agents with different personality traits: sensitiveness (intensity threshold for feeling emotions); introversion (intensity threshold for expressing a felt emotion); optimism (decay speeds for intensity of positive and negative emotions); and coping style (order of preferred coping strategies).

4.2   Emotional Appraisal

The agent's KB is first updated after any new perception by inferring all new consequences, and then appraised by using the emotions definitions, which results in triggering one or several emotions (about either the same or different objects). The intensity of each emotion is computed as the merge (*i.e.* here the product) of the strengths of the triggering mental attitudes (plausibility of belief, desirability of goal). The agent's personality defines two intensity thresholds: the intensity of an emotion should exceed the first threshold for the emotion to be felt, and exceed the second threshold for the felt emotion to be expressed. The intensity of emotions then decays over time, until it eventually falls below the *feeling threshold* and the emotion disappears.

4.3   Coping

Once one or several emotions have been triggered by the appraisal module[2], the agent can cope with them, starting with the most intense negative one. Coping strategies relevant to this emotion are listed by the coping module. The controllability of the situation is then assessed to make a choice between two types of coping (problem oriented vs emotion oriented). If several coping strategies are still applicable, the choice is made based on the agent's personality, and in particular its coping style (concretely an ordered list of preferred coping strategies can be specified in each agent's KB as part of its personality).

Once a preferred coping strategy is selected to deal with the agent's highest negative emotion, it is actually applied, causing a revision of the agent's mental

---

[2] Multiple instances of the same emotion type but with different objects are considered as different emotions, and are coped with separately.

attitudes (goals, intentions or beliefs), and the KB is then saturated by applying all deduction rules. The modified agent's KB is then re-appraised by the emotional appraisal module, possibly triggering different emotions. The effect of coping strategies is thus ultimately a shift in emotions. As long as the most intense emotion is still negative, the agent keeps coping, and each coping strategy decreases the intensity of this stressing emotion; after some iterations, the intensity of negative emotions will be lower than that of positive emotions. Said differently, the coping process will eventually succeed in getting the agent back from a state of stress to a state of well-being [Lazarus and Folkman, 1984].

4.4 Relation to the Logic

Let us explain in more detail in which sense the logical model presented in Section 3 provides a formal specification for the computational model implemented in the PLEIAD system. **First** of all, the set of axioms and deduction rules implemented in the PLEIAD's reasoning engine is a subset of the set of axioms and deduction rules of the logic. For instance, both in the logic and in the computational model implemented in PLEIAD, beliefs are supposed to be closed under logical consequence (*i.e.*, if an agent believes φ and believes that φ implies ψ, then he believes that ψ). In this sense, the implemented model is sound with respect to the logical model. **Secondly**, every primitive assertion handled by the PLEIAD's KB manager correspond to a specific formula of the logic (*e.g.* , the fact that the agent believes that φ is true with strength h, described by the logical formula $B^h\varphi$, corresponds to the PLEIAD predicate $b(a, \varphi, h)$). In the implementation the maximal value for degrees is set to 10. **Third**, the definitions of the cognitive structures of hope, fear, joy and distress implemented in the PLEIAD's reasoning module exactly correspond to those given in our logical model. The merge function used to determine the intensity of an emotion from the strength of the triggering mental attitudes is the product. **Fourth**, the triggering conditions for the coping strategies implemented in the PLEIAD's coping module exactly correspond to those specified in our logical model.

Of course the model had to be tweaked to be computationally tractable (in particular the depth of encapsulated mental attitudes was limited in PLEIAD to avoid infinite inference loops, which is why it is sound but not complete) and to match the implemented system (for instance the logic uses qualitative intensity degrees while PLEIAD works with a continuous intensity function).

5 Application Scenario

By providing an implementation of D&L logic in PLEIAD, we proved that it is computationally tractable and can be actually used in agents. In this section we actually run a short scenario where an artificial companion endowed with this model reasons about a human user's emotions in order to comfort them by offering coping advice, but also to enable more natural interactions with them.

In this scenario we consider an artificial companion endowed with our logical model of emotions, and having a model of a human user *killua* wanting to do a hike and dealing with adverse conditions. The companion's initial model of the user's knowledge base (KB) contains the following mental attitudes:

- `int(killua,done(killua,hike,_))` : user's intention to perform the action `hike`
- `b(killua,after(killua,hike,tired),6)` : user's belief that doing a hike might be tiring (with plausibility 6)
- `b(killua,after(killua,hike,happy),7)` : belief that doing a hike will also make him happy (with plausibility 7)
- `b(killua,raining->after(killua,hike,wet),9)` : belief that if it rains, then hiking will make him wet
- `achg(killua,happy,7)`: achievement goal to be happy
- `avdg(killua,tired,10)` : goal to avoid being tired
- `avdg(killua,wet,10)` : goal to avoid getting wet
- `b(killua,after(killua,playgames,not(tired)),10)` : belief that playing games will be restful

With our definitions of emotions (as given above), the **appraisal** of this KB triggers two different emotions:

- `emo(killua,fear,[hike,tired],6)` : emotion of fear that the hike will tire him, with intensity 6. This is the most intense negative emotion;
- `emo(killua,hope,[hike,happy],4)` : hope that the hike will make him happy, with intensity 4.

There is one coping strategy to deal with the stressor (risk that the hike will make the agent tired): behavioural disengagement. Indeed this stressor is *controllable* due to the availability of another action (playing games) that leads to not being tired. The `cope(killua,Strat)` predicate thus applies the behavioural disengagement strategy, consisting in abandoning the intention to go for a hike,

Figure 1 shows a variant of this scenario, where we suppressed the goal to avoid getting tired from the initial KB, but send an undesirable event stimulus. Below we detail how the agent reasons about user *killua*'s state.

- At the start of the simulation, user *killua* observes that there is a storm and it is raining; the reasoning engine deduces that in these conditions, hiking might make him wet.
- The appraisal module triggers fear of getting wet (undesirable consequence of the intended action of hiking), which means that the agent believes that the user probably fears getting wet if hiking under the rain.
- This time, the stressor is *not controllable* (no other available action will prevent *killua* from getting wet), so the coping module suggests two emotion-oriented strategies: wishful thinking (lowering the plausibility of the belief that hiking will make him wet) and positive reinterpretation (lowering the undesirability of the goal to avoid getting wet). Both strategies thus decrease the intensity of fear.
- These are the strategies that the agent can advise the user to use. Here the agent randomly selects one strategy (positive reinterpretation) to apply it. Concretely, this could result in the companion agent saying something like "getting wet is not that bad".

```
?- stimulus(killua,event(storm,raining)),saturer_bc(killua).
true.

?- most_intense_emotion(killua,E).
E = emo(killua, distress, [hike, wet], 6) .

?- list_coping_strategy(killua,S).
S = strategy(wishful_thinking, hike, wet) ;
S = strategy(positive_reinterpretation, hike, wet).

?- cope(killua,S).
S = strategy(positive_reinterpretation, hike, wet).

?- emo(killua,E,P,D).
E = hope,
P = [hike, happy],
D = 6 ;
E = hope,
P = [playgames, happy],
D = 4 ;
E = distress,
P = [hike, wet],
D = 3 .
```

Fig. 1. Second run of the companion scenario

- As a result, the undesirability of getting wet is decreased, and the most
  intense emotion is now the positive emotion of hope that the hike will make
  killua happy. The agent thus now believes that the user is in a positive
  emotional state and does not need to cope anymore.

6 Conclusion

In this paper we have exposed the implementation of an emotional reasoning
engine for companion agents. Concretely, we implemented D&L logical characterisation of graded emotions, considering both appraisal and coping, in the
PLEIAD system. We then illustrated the functioning of this reasoning engine
on a short scenario where a companion agent predicts the user's emotions and
tries to help them regulate negative emotions when facing adverse conditions
hindering their goals.

BDI logics have many advantages, in particular their folk psychology basis that allows agents to explain their behaviours in terms of high level easily
understandable concepts: mental attitudes. The work presented in this paper
shows that such a complex logic can still be computationally tractable. Another advantage of such an implementation is to enable a formal comparison
with other psychological theories and models implemented in the same system. PLEIAD has been previously used to implement the OCC appraisal theory
[Adam, 2007], and some coping strategies from Carver, Scheier and Weintraub's
theory [Adam and Longin, 2007]. The next step is now to run agents endowed

with these two different models of appraisal and coping and compare their emotions and emotional behaviour in similar situations, in order to precisely compare their underlying models. Our first observation is that D&L logic of emotion implemented here only covers a few emotions and coping strategies. Therefore in future work we also intend to extend this logical model in several directions.

First we want to consider more emotions than those defined here; indeed we only considered here prospective emotions about the agent's own intentions and actions. We believe that these definitions can be extended to also account for non-prospective emotions (such as joy that the container is at its target location), for emotions triggered by events that are independent from the agent's intentions or actions (such as joy that the sun is shining), and for social emotions (such as reproach to another agent for doing something wrong). To this aim we can rely on our previous work of formalisation of various emotions [Adam et al., 2009,Lorini and Schwarzentruber, 2011].

Second we want to consider more coping strategies; in this paper we limited our account to three strategies concerning negative emotions. This could be extended to include strategies for positive emotions, such as focusing on an intention that triggers joy or hope at the expense of the other intentions. There are also more strategies to consider for negative emotions, such as shifting blame to another agent in order to deal with guilt or shame, or mentally disengaging from an intention that triggers negative emotions. The concept of focus available in PLEIAD allows us to implement such a strategy in terms of a change in the degree of focus on the object of the emotion [Adam and Longin, 2007].

It is also interesting to investigate the link between coping and language, in order to account for such coping strategies as apologising for a fault to deal with guilt, venting anger, or expressing sadness to get support. Such strategies are key for agents interacting with humans in a social setting (for example to help them interact with an intelligent environment [Adam et al., 2006,Adam et al., 2011]. To this aim we could integrate coping strategies in our multimodal communication language that was designed and integrated in PLEIAD in previous work [Riviere et al., 2012]. Such work will find its main applications in agents that deal with humans, in particular companion agents that have to develop a long-term relationship with their user. To this end it is essential that these agents have a believable behaviour, which includes having emotions, expressing them and coping with them. But it is also essential that these agents understand their human user's emotions, and can offer not only empathy but also coping advice. Such emotionally intelligent companions could significantly improve their user's well-being, which is what they are designed for.

Acknowledgements. The authors acknowledge the support of the French ANR project EmoTES (ANR-11-EMCO-0004). Carole Adam also acknowledges the support of the French ANR project MoCA (ANR-2012-CORD-019-02).

References

Adam, 2007. Adam, C.: The emotions: from psychological theories to logical formalisation and implementation in a BDI agent. PhD thesis, INP Toulouse (2007)

Adam et al., 2006. Adam, C., Gaudou, B., Herzig, A., Longin, D.: A logical framework for an emotionally aware intelligent environment. In: 1st ECAI Workshop on Artificial Intelligence Techniques for Ambient Intelligence (AITAmI). IOS Press (2006)

Adam et al., 2011. Adam, C., Gaudou, B., Login, D., Lorini, E.: Logical modeling of emotions for ambient intelligence. In: Mastrogiovanni, F., Chong, N.-Y. (eds.) Handbook of Research on Ambient Intelligence and Smart Environments: Trends and Perspectives, pp. 108–127 (2011)

Adam et al., 2009. Adam, C., Herzig, A., Longin, D.: A logical formalization of the OCC theory of emotions. Synthese 168(2) (2009)

Adam and Longin, 2007. Adam, C., Longin, D.: Endowing emotional agents with coping strategies: From emotions to emotional behaviour. In: Pelachaud, C., Martin, J.-C., André, E., Chollet, G., Karpouzis, K., Pelé, D. (eds.) IVA 2007. LNCS (LNAI), vol. 4722, pp. 348–349. Springer, Heidelberg (2007)

Bickmore and Picard, 2005. Bickmore, T.W., Picard, R.W.: Establishing and maintaining long-term humancomputer relationships. ACM Transactions on Computer Human Interaction (ToCHI) 12(2), 293–327 (2005)

Calvo and D'Mello, 2010. Calvo, R.A., D'Mello, S.K.: Affect detection: An interdisciplinary review of models, methods, and their applications. IEEE Transactions on Affective Computing 1(1), 18–37 (2010)

Carver et al., 1989. Carver, C.S., Scheier, M.F., Weintraub, J.K.: Assessing coping strategies: A theoretically based approach. Journal of Personality and Social Psychology 56(2), 267–283 (1989)

Dastani and Lorini., 2012. Dastani, M., Lorini, E.: A logic of emotions: from appraisal to coping. In: AAMAS, pp. 1133–1140. ACM Press (2012)

D'Mello and Graesser, 2010. D'Mello, S., Graesser, A.C.: Multimodal semi-automated affect detection from conversational cues, gross body language, and facial features. User Modeling and User-adapted Interaction 20(2), 147–187 (2010)

Frijda, 1987. Frijda, N.: The Emotions. Cambridge University Press (1987)

Gratch and Marsella, 2004. Gratch, J., Marsella, S.: A domain independent framework for modeling emotion. Cog. Syst. Research 5(4) (2004)

Keltner and Ekman, 1996. Keltner, D., Ekman, P.: Affective intensity and emotional responses. Cognition and Emotion 10(3), 323–328 (1996)

Kidd and Breazeal, 2007. Kidd, C.D., Breazeal, C.: A robotic weight loss coach. In: Twenty-Second Conference on Artificial Intelligence, AAAI (2007)

Kramer et al., 2011. Kramer, N.C., Eimler, S., von der Putten, A., Payr, S.: Theory of companions: What can theoretical models contribute to applications and understanding of human-robot interaction? Applied AI 25(6), 474–502 (2011); Special Issue: Social Engagement with Robots and Agents

Lazarus, 1991. Lazarus, R.S.: Emotion and adaptation. Oxford Univ. Press (1991)

Lazarus and Folkman, 1984. Lazarus, R.S., Folkman, S.: Stress, Appraisal and Coping. Springer Publishing Company (1984)

Lorini, 2011. Lorini, E.: A dynamic logic of knowledge, graded beliefs and graded goals and its application to emotion modelling. In: van Ditmarsch, H., Lang, J., Ju, S. (eds.) LORI 2011. LNCS, vol. 6953, pp. 165–178. Springer, Heidelberg (2011)

Lorini and Schwarzentruber, 2011. Lorini, E., Schwarzentruber, F.: A logic for reasoning about counterfactual emotions. Artificial Intelligence 175(3-4), 814–847 (2011)

Marsella and Gratch, 2009. Marsella, S., Gratch, J.: EMA: A process model of appraisal dynamics. Cognitive Systems Research 10 (2009)

Ortony et al., 1988. Ortony, A., Clore, G.L., Collins, A.: The cognitive structure of emotions. Cambridge University Press (1988)

Reeves and Nass, 1996. Reeves, B., Nass, C.: The Media Equation: How People Treat Computers, Television, and New Media Like Real People and Places. Cambridge University Press (1996)

Reisenzein, 2009. Reisenzein, R.: Emotions as metarepresentational states of mind: naturalizing the belief-desire theory of emotion. Journal of Cognitive Systems Research 10, 6–20 (2009)

Riviere et al., 2012. Riviere, J., Adam, C., Pesty, S.: A reasoning module to select eCA's communicative intention. In: Nakano, Y., Neff, M., Paiva, A., Walker, M. (eds.) IVA 2012. LNCS, vol. 7502, pp. 447–454. Springer, Heidelberg (2012)

Steunebrink et al., 2009. Steunebrink, B.R., Dastani, M., Meyer, J.-J.C.: A formal model of emotion-based action tendency for intelligent agents. In: Lopes, L.S., Lau, N., Mariano, P., Rocha, L.M. (eds.) EPIA 2009. LNCS, vol. 5816, pp. 174–186. Springer, Heidelberg (2009)

Taggart et al., 2005. Taggart, W., Turkle, S., Kidd, C.D.: An interactive robot in a nursing home: Preliminary remarks. In: Toward Social Mechanisms of Android Science. Cognitive Science Society (2005)

Vardoulakis et al., 2012. Vardoulakis, L.P., Ring, L., Barry, B., Sidner, C.L., Bickmore, T.: Designing relational agents as long term social companions for older adults. In: Nakano, Y., Neff, M., Paiva, A., Walker, M. (eds.) IVA 2012. LNCS, vol. 7502, pp. 289–302. Springer, Heidelberg (2012)

Assessment of Agent Architectures for Telehealth

Daniel Jørgensen[1], Kasper Hallenborg[1], and Yves Demazeau[2]

[1] University of Southern Denmark
The Maersk McKinney Moller Institute
DK-5230 Odense, Denmark
{dbj,hallenborg}@mmmi.sdu.dk
[2] CNRS – LIG,
F-38000 Grenoble, France
yves.demazeau@imag.fr

Abstract. On government level, Denmark has published both strategies and technical guidelines to strengthen implementation and use of telehealth in the Danish healthcare sector in the future. Consequently telehealth solutions will become an integrated part of the daily life of the patients equipped with these solutions. This paper proposes an architecture for a multi-agent system to be implemented together with the telehealth solution in a patient's home. The purpose of the multi-agent system is to incorporate more intelligence into the gathering of healthcare related data and thereby learn about the behavior and level of physical activity of the patient, and other interesting context information.

Keywords: BDI, infrastructure, healthcare, telehealth, user modeling.

1 Introduction

The societal challenges dictated by the aging population over the next decades needs no further introduction. The general awareness of the consequences has increased over the last years, and politicians have highlighted it in the context of the financial crises.

Healthcare expenses will increase dramatically over the coming years unless solutions are found that empower users to be more self-maintained and take more responsibility for their care and rehabilitation. Chronic disease management is a serious burden to all healthcare systems – 70-80% of healthcare budgets in European countries are spend on chronic patients.

Telehealth is envisioned to be one of the primary cost-savers, and medical devices to monitor vital parameters in the home of the patients are both available and reliable. However, the infrastructure to bridge communication both ways between the home and healthcare professionals (primarily hospitals and practitioners), and within the home setting is not yet mature. Standards are too complex for most developers and with telehealth being part of the daily life activities of the patients, more focus on user preferences and individualization will make the solutions much more flexible, and thereby more focused on the individual user and quality of life.

J.M. Corchado et al. (Eds.): PAAMS 2014 Workshops, CCIS 430, pp. 79–88, 2014.

A multi-agent based architecture provides some of the characteristics requested for systems in this domain; adaptability, customization, and the ability to handle dynamics and complexity. Thus, in this paper we will evaluate different general architectures for multi-agent systems in the perspective of telehealth, and we will introduce our proposal for an agent based architecture for telehealth solutions in the context of the Danish healthcare sector and the standards used within.

2   Architectures for Multi-agent Systems

2.1   BDI

BDI [1], an abbreviation for Belief-Desire-Intention, is an architecture for designing intelligent agents, the main software components of multi-agent systems, henceforth MAS. The BDI theory is based on the three concepts of beliefs, desires, and intentions [1]. By combining and implementing those three concepts into a software agent, it becomes an intelligent agent capable of practical reasoning like the process humans go through multiple times daily in their everyday life [2].

The 'belief' component represents the knowledge base of the agent [3]. The term belief is preferred to that of knowledge because the information may be imperfect, and not true outside the scope of a certain agent. An agent must store information about its beliefs, possibly about both the surroundings and itself, for it to be able to make decisions on an updated foundation.

The second component 'desire' describes the motivational state of an agent, i.e. descriptions of the objectives the agent wishes to accomplish [1]. An agent may have multiple desires. With multiple desires it is the internal reasoning of the agent that has the task of deciding which objective to achieve at a certain point. Information such as payoffs and priorities, associated with the objectives, can be used in the reasoning process.

The third and final component of the BDI architecture is 'intention'. The intention states which desires the agent has committed to achieve [2]. When an agent have decided upon an intention, it will try to achieve the desire through execution of plans containing a set of actions the agent can perform [1, 3]. Agents operate in dynamic environments, where the surroundings can change, hence the belief component. Based on the information about the environment and the desires of the agent, the intention component has the purpose of deciding if and when the agent should commit to achieving another desire, and leave the previous one unachieved.

2.2   ACT-R

ACT-R [4] is an abbreviation for Adaptive Control of Thought-Rational. ACT-R is an architecture that enables modeling of cognitive tasks, such as learning, decision making, and working memory [4, 5]. According to [5] ACT-R can be used in the MAS to play the role of a human because ACT-R is capable of predicting and explaining human behavior. The architecture of ACT-R is found in Fig. 1.

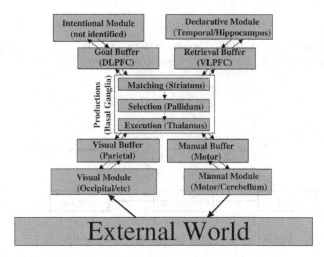

Fig. 1. The ACT-R architecture [4]

As can be seen from Fig. 1 the ACT-R architecture consists of five different components. Based on [4, 5], each of the components are described shortly.

- The Intentional module keeps track of the intentions of the human/agent being modeled, as well as the behavior and sub goals that is expected to lead to the intentions. The intention modules in ACT-R and BDI are alike in that both contain plans/behavior/sub goals leading towards a certain target. However, the purposes of the two modules are quite different. In BDI, when an agent decides upon a certain intention to pursue, it will execute the actions in the plan expected to lead toward the fulfillment of that intention. In ACT-R, on the other hand, the behavior of the intention will not be executed until the Production module has retrieved the intention through the goal buffer.
- The Declarative module is the memory of the architecture. The information found in this module is the facts and experiences of the agent. The declarative information can be retrieved by the Productions module based on the activation level of the information.
- The Productions module is the central component of the architecture. It communicates with the other four components through buffers, each with a capacity of one piece of information at a time. Through production rules, and the information in the buffers, the production system decides upon the operations to be performed by the agent.
- The Visual module is one of two components that communicate with the external world. The purpose of this module is to identify objects in the external world
- The Motor module is the component that is capable of changing the external world.

2.3   AT

AT, an abbreviation for Activity Theory, is a psychological theory, that defines a framework for studying how an activity leads to an outcome [6, 7].

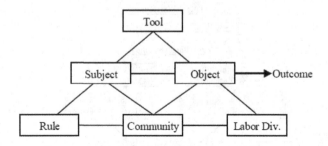

Fig. 2. Components in an Activity Theory system [7]

From Fig. 2 it can be seen that AT defines six different components. Within these components it is possible to describe the elements pertaining to an activity, which lead to an outcome/goal [7-9]. The six components are [7-9]:

- Tool refers to instruments that the subject can utilize to achieve an objective. Tools can be both psychological and physical. In the agent paradigm the tools can be the actions an agent can execute.
- Subject is the individual that works towards achieving the objective. In the agent paradigm the subject is an agent.
- Object is the purpose of the activity.
- Rule mediates between the subject and a community. This mediation includes social relations and norms.
- Community contains all the subjects in the environment, in which the activity happens. According to [9] AT *"rejects the isolated human being as an adequate unit of analysis"*. That means for an agent to be able to achieve an object it has to part of a MAS.
- Division of labor mediates between the community and the object. This component describes how the subjects in the environment are related to object, i.e. who does what in terms of achieving the outcome.

Though AT is a psychological theory it is relevant in the context of this paper, because there are examples of scientific work, where AT is used within the multi-agent paradigm or discussed in relation to it [6-8].

Unlike the BDI and ACT-R; AT has a more holistic view on the whole system, i.e. the elements in the surroundings of the subject (the specific agent), than the subject' cognitive capabilities, to be used to achieve its objects/goals/intentions. An example of this is [7], where AT is used in the context of healthcare, to understand and simplify the complex activities in the domain. Ricci et al. [6] do present some interesting thoughts on the coordination of MAS. At a later point these thoughts may be considered in relation to the MAS that will be implemented in the Patient@Home project (http://www.patientathome.dk/).

2.4   Comparison of BDI and ACT-R

Table 1 shows a concise comparison of BDI and ACT-R in relation to the architecture described in section 3.

Table 1. Comparison of BDI, ACT-R, and AT

	Advantages	Disadvantages
BDI	- Is situated, goal directed, reactive, and social [10]. - Ability to handle and work in a dynamic environment.	- In the original BDI were there no mechanisms of learning from experiences [10].
ACT-R	- Based on cognitive psychology and brain imaging and thereby able to simulate human cognition and behavior.	- Each of the buffers only has a capacity of one element. - Developed to simulate the human brain and behavior [10], however the architecture includes other components that need to be modeled and developed as well.

3   System Architecture

Fig. 3 is a high-level illustration of our thoughts for a system architecture in a Danish telehealth context.

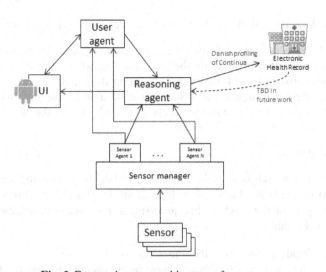

Fig. 3. Expected system architecture of agent system

The data collected and used within the system will come from state-of-the-art healthcare device/sensors for the personal use in the context of telehealth. The devices can, for instance, be wearable, connected to training equipment, and/or location constrained (e.g. home setting). In the future another source of data can be the EHR systems in Denmark. However, at this point, no standard has yet been agreed upon of how to implement bidirectional exchange of healthcare data with the Danish EHR systems. This is a challenge, which is expected to be focused on at a later stage in the Patient@Home project. Therefore at the moment the agent architecture in Fig. 3 will be focused on data collected from the devices for personal use.

The MAS proposed in this paper consists of three types of agents: sensor, reasoning, and user. The remainder of this section is dedicated to describing the purposes and capabilities of each of these agents.

3.1   Sensor Agents

The purpose of the sensor agents will be to handle data concerning new readings from state-of-the-art telehealth devices. A later study will identify the exact devices and standards to build the architecture upon. Stated briefly, obvious candidates are devices based on the ISO/IEEE 11073 standard and/or ANT+ [11]. The ISO/IEEE 11073 is the standard chosen by the Continua Health Alliance [12] for their certified devices. Denmark, as the first country worldwide, has decided that the future national infrastructure for telehealth should be based on the initiatives of CHA [13-15]. The strength of ANT+ is that the number of devices and possible managers implementing the ANT+-stack increases rapidly.

Compared to the other types of agents in the MAS, the sensor agents will have a limited scope. The sensor agent must be able to:

- Observe new readings from its environment.
- Parse a new reading into the language used within the MAS for agent communication.
- Communicate to the rest of the MAS, that a new reading has been observed.

As mentioned above the sensors providing the data for system can be used in many different locations, and depending on the situation a non-fixed-subset of the sensors may be in close proximity with the manager/hosting device collecting the data. Despite the changing environment the system must be able to continue its execution without failure in data collection and unnecessary disturbance for the user.

3.2   User Agent

The focus of this research is to make the future telehealth systems in Denmark even more centered on the individuals, using them as an integrated part of their everyday life. The user agent of the MAS will be an essential component to achieve this. The user agent must be able to:

- Receive new readings data from the sensor agents.
- Store user preferences. The preferences must be changeable through the UI.

- Respond to various requests by the reasoning agent about preferences and Activities of Daily Living (ADL) [16].

Through the data received from the sensor agents, the user agent will be a *Doppelgänger* [17] of the actual user. The user agent is expected to learn the behavior of the user (e.g. eating patterns, patterns in the intake of medication, when telehealth devices are preferably used), the user's level of physical activity, the "normal" level/threshold values of vital signs from medical devices. All this context information, contributes to an understanding of the patient's ADL.

3.3   Reasoning Agent

The reasoning agent is the most central component in the system architecture depicted on Fig. 3. The reasoning agent must be able to:

- Receive new readings data from the sensor agents.
- Receive data about the user. These data will affect the decision making within the reasoning agent.
- Send data to the UI component to be presented to the user.
- If integrated with the rest of the Danish healthcare sector; to send healthcare data based on the HL7 PHMR document format, and to receive relevant patient related data from the Danish healthcare sector to provide the patient with a full picture of his/her condition. The last element (shown on Fig. 3 with a dotted line) is a challenge that will be addressed at a later stage in the Patient@Home project.

In section 3.2 the concept of ADL was mentioned. According to [16] keeping track of the patient' ADL can help the identification of deterioration of well-being. This will be an important task of the reasoning agent. As stated above, the reasoning agent is supposed to send healthcare data to other systems in the Danish healthcare sector. Through the data about ADL and new readings, the reasoning agent can add appropriate context information to the healthcare data, and thereby give the healthcare professionals additional and possibly valuable data to evaluate.

4   Discussion

This section is dedicated to identifying the agent architectures (BDI or ACT-R), which fits the different intelligent agents (sensor, user, and reasoning) in the MAS best.

Considering the capabilities of sensor agents the obvious choice of design architecture is BDI: The belief of the agent will be a new reading; the desire of the agent is to inform the MAS about new readings; and the intention of the agent is to send information about the a new reading as soon as it is received and properly parsed.

The user agent in the MAS will be a doppelgänger for the actual patient through gathering of sensor data, but it will also contain preferences, that the user him/her-self can change. Being a cognitive architecture, ACT-R, was a consideration as agent architecture for modeling the user in this MAS. However, after reading existing litera-ture by Nunes et al. [18, 19] on developing user models and personal preferences in MAS, BDI has been chosen as the architecture to build the user agent upon. In their work on user modeling Nunes et al. have contributed with a domain independent software framework to support the development of Personal Assistance Software (PAS). Telehealth solutions in home settings are PAS applications. The PAS software framework contains a user model, one of the most fundamental components, which is created and evolves upon the preferences of the user. In [18] the BDI architecture is recommended, in relation to user modeling, because it *"facilitates the implementation of user customizations in a modular fashion so that components can be added and removed as the user model changes"*.

Both the sensor agents and user agents will be based on the BDI architecture, and so will the reasoning agent. Besides making sense in terms of the MAS simpler by using only one agent architecture, BDI is the most applied architecture for delibera-tive agents [20], which is the behavior the reasoning agent is expected to expose.

5   Conclusion and Future Work

This paper constitutes the foundation for the development of a software platform for the telehealth domain. The platform will be a multi-agent system based on the BDI architecture with three different types of agents: user, reasoning, and sensor. The pur-pose of the agent architecture is to incorporate more intelligence into the gathering and handling of patients' telehealth data through the ability to understand and use relevant context information.

The work described in this paper is one of the initial steps towards the development of the complete agent architecture. The next step in the development of the architec-ture is to design an ontology, which will define the concepts, properties, and interrela-tionships in the telehealth domain. The purpose of the ontology in the Patient@Home project is to make it easier to integrate new applications in the system described in section 3, through a shared vocabulary which is a foundation for securing semantic interoperability.

The ontology will be designed based on the state-of-the-art in terms of 1) devices and other data sources available for both monitoring and context information, and 2) existing ontologies for the healthcare domain, context aware systems, and user model-ing. The identification of the state-of-the-art in these areas is currently ongoing through the review of relevant literature.

The implementation of this agent based architecture will begin when the ontology has been designed. The agent platform is expected to be implemented in the Java based framework BDI4JADE [21]. This decision is due to previous experiences with the JADE framework, and the identified need for the BDI architecture. The ontology is expected to be built in the Protégé ontology editor [22].

Acknowledgment. This paper has been conducted under the Patient@Home project, which is supported by Danish Strategic Research Council, the Danish Council for Technology and Innovation, and Growth Forum in the Region of Southern Denmark.

References

1. Rao, A.S., Georgeff, M.P.: BDI Agents: From Theory to Practice. In: 1st International Conference on Multi-Agent Systems, ICMAS 1995, pp. 312–319. AAAI, San Francisco (1995)
2. Wooldridge, M.: Reasoning About Rational Agents. The MIT Press (2000)
3. Georgeff, M., Pell, B., Pollack, M., Tambe, M., Wooldridge, M.: The Belief-Desire-Intention Model of Agency. In: Papadimitriou, C., Singh, M.P., Müller, J.P. (eds.) ATAL 1998. LNCS (LNAI), vol. 1555, pp. 1–10. Springer, Heidelberg (1999)
4. Anderson, J.R., Bothell, D., Byrne, M.D., Douglass, S., Lebiere, C., Qin, Y.: An integrated theory of the mind. Psychol. Rev. 111, 1036–1060 (2004)
5. Taatgen, N., Lebiere, C., Anderson, J.R.: Modeling Paradigms in ACT-R. In: Sun, R. (ed.) Cognition and Multi-Agent Interaction: From Cognitive Modeling to Social Simulation, pp. 29–52. Cambridge University Press (2006)
6. Ricci, A., Omicini, A., Denti, E.: Activity Theory as a Framework for MAS Coordination. In: Petta, P., Tolksdorf, R., Zambonelli, F. (eds.) ESAW 2002. LNCS (LNAI), vol. 2577, pp. 96–110. Springer, Heidelberg (2003)
7. Zhang, P., Bai, G.: An Activity Systems Theory Approach to Agent Technology. International Journal of Knowledge and Systems Science 2, 60–65 (2005)
8. Fuentes, R., Gómez-Sanz, J.J., Pavón, J.: Activity Theory for the Analysis and Design of Multi-agent Systems. In: Giorgini, P., Müller, J.P., Odell, J.J. (eds.) AOSE 2003. LNCS, vol. 2935, pp. 110–122. Springer, Heidelberg (2004)
9. Bertelsen, O.W., Bødker, S.: Activity Theory. In: Carroll, J.M. (ed.) HCI Models Theories, and Frameworks: Toward a Multidisciplinary Science, pp. 291–324. Morgan Kaufmann, San Francisco (2003)
10. Chong, H.-Q., Tan, A.-H., Ng, G.-W.: Integrated cognitive architectures: a survey. Artificial Intelligence Review 28(2), 103–130 (2007)
11. ANT+ (THIS IS ANT) (2014), http://www.thisisant.com/
12. Continua Health Alliance (2013), http://www.continuaalliance.org/
13. Referencearkitektur for opsamling af helbredsdata hos borgeren (2013), http://www.ssi.dk/
14. National handlingsplan for udbredelse af telemedicin. Ministeriet for Sundhed og Forebyggelse (2012)
15. Wicklund, E.: Continua Alliance to help Denmark with telemedicine standards (2012), http://www.healthcareitnews.com/news/continua-alliance-help-denmark-telemedicine-standards?single-page=true
16. Kuusik, A., Reilent, E., Lõõbas, I., Parve, M.: Software architecture for modern telehome care systems. In: 6th International Conference on Networked Computing, INC 2010, pp. 1–6. IEEE (2010)
17. Orwant, J.: Heterogeneous learning in the Doppelgänger user modeling system. User Modeling and User-Adapted Interaction 4, 107–130 (1995)
18. Nunes, I., Luck, M., Diniz, S., Barbosa, J., Miles, S., De Lucena, C.J.P.: Dynamically Adapting BDI Agents Based on High-Level User Specifications. In: Workshop on Advanced Agent Technology, AAMAS 2011 Workshops, pp. 139–163 (2012)
19. Nunes, I., Barbosa, S.D.J., de Lucena, C.J.P.: Increasing Users' Trust on Personal Assistance Software Using a Domain-Neutral High-Level User Model. In: Margaria, T., Steffen, B. (eds.) ISoLA 2010, Part I. LNCS, vol. 6415, pp. 473–487. Springer, Heidelberg (2010)

20. Hallenborg, K., Valente, P., Demazeau, Y.: Accessing Cloud Services through BDI Agents Case Study: An Agent-Based Personal Trainer to COPD Patients. In: Rodríguez, J.M.C., Pérez, J.B., Golinska, P., Giroux, S., Corchuelo, R. (eds.) Trends in PAAMS. AISC, vol. 157, pp. 19–28. Springer, Heidelberg (2012)
21. BDI4JADE (2014), http://www.inf.ufrgs.br/prosoft/bdi4jade/
22. Protégé (2014), http://protege.stanford.edu/products.php

Cognitive Architecture
of an Agent for Human-Agent Dialogues

Jayalakshmi Baskar and Helena Lindgren

Department of Computing Science
UmeåUniversity, Sweden
{jaya,helena}@cs.umu.se

Abstract. This paper proposes a cognitive architecture of an intelligent
agent that can have a dialogue with a human agent on health-related
topics. This architecture consists of four main components, namely, the
Belief Base, the *Dialogue Manager*, the *Task Manager* and the *Plan
Generator*. Each component has sub-components that perform a set of
tasks for the purpose to enable the agent to be enrolled in a dialogue.
In this paper the particular sub-component of the Dialogue Manager,
the *Dialogue Strategy* has been discussed in detail. A notion of *scheme*
is introduced, which functions as a template with variables that are instantiated each time a state is entered. The agent's dialogue strategy is
implemented as a combination of the schemes and the state transitions
that the agent makes in response to the human's request. We used a combination of finite-state and agent-based dialogue strategies for dialogue
management. This combined dialogue strategy enables a multi-topic dialogue between a human and an agent.

Keywords: Human-computer interaction, dialogue, agent architecture.

1 Introduction

This paper proposes a cognitive architecture of an intelligent software agent that
can have a dialogue with a human agent on health-related topics. The main challenge for the agents having a dialogue with a human is deciding *what* information
to communicate to the human and *how* and *when* to communicate it. This highly
contextual and situated perspective on human-agent dialogues was exemplified
in [1], where dialogues were aimed at taking place in an ambient assisted living
environment. A persona of an older adult and a case scenario was introduced,
as illustration of the different building blocks of an architecture for an ambient
assisted living environment, integrating support by a multi-agent system. The
cognitive architecture of the agents presented in this work extends the architecture in [1] by concentrating on the components for constructing an intelligent
agent that interacts with a human in a more autonomous, and purposeful way.

The architecture presented in [1] integrates knowledge repositories, developed
using ACKTUS (Activity Centered modelling of Knowledge and interaction Tai-
lored to USers). ACKTUS is a platform for engineering knowledge-based systems
in the medical and health domain. These repositories are built on semantic models, which were in [2] extended to integrate components vital for enabling agent

J.M. Corchado et al. (Eds.): PAAMS 2014 Workshops, CCIS 430, pp. 89–100, 2014.
© Springer International Publishing Switzerland 2014

dialogues, based on the canonical model for agent architectures presented by Fox and coworkers [3].

An initial design and implementation of an agent-based dialogue system where agents communicate with the end user in a home environment for establishing a baseline user model was presented in [4]. The base for interaction was implemented as information-seeking dialogues through which the user can inform the system about preferences, priorities and interests. Based on this information, the system provides feedback to the user in the form of: 1) suggestions of decisions, 2) advices and 3) suggestions of actions to make for obtaining more knowledge about a situation.

The agent's knowledge was obtained from the ACKTUS repository, which had been created by domain experts in the rehabilitation domain [5]. The knowledge consisted of both factual and procedural knowledge, as well as interactive templates, or protocols for assessment of different aspects. The knowledge had been structured and implemented by the domain experts to be used as assessment protocols by therapists in clinical interviews, or in human-agent dialogues. However, in order to accomplish other types of dialogues, which are less structured than the *information-seeking* dialogues, an agent architecture is needed, which allows the agent to plan the moves based on e.g., the purpose of the dialogue, the situation, the knowledge available, etc.

Therefore, this paper extends earlier work, by concentrating on the components for constructing an intelligent agent that interacts with a human in a more autonomous, and purposeful way.

We deal with a complex environment where there are multiple sources of information to consider for an agent: 1) the information about the human agent's daily activities observed by an activity recognition system at home, 2) the information about the human agent's medical health condition obtained from domain professionals and relatives, and 3) the human's preferences, obtained initially as a part of the baseline assessment, which, however may change.

Our aim is to enable dialogues between a human agent and an intelligent agent. For this purpose, the agent needs the following capabilities, which has to different extent also been described in literature (e.g., [6, 7, 8, 9]):

- Autonomous (e.g., decides upon actions to make, takes initiatives in order to reach a goal),
- Handle knowledge obtained from different heterogenous sources, e.g., in a home environment,
- Reason and make decisions in the presence of uncertain and incomplete information,
- Generate new knowledge (e.g., by learning methods such as machine learning, case-based reasoning, etc.),
- Utilize a shared semantic model between human and agent for communication and knowledge exchange purposes,
- Being cooperative,
- Being able to deal with affective components and topics in a dialogue.

In our proposed cognitive architecture, we aim to combine the above mentioned capabilities to build an intelligent agent that interacts with the human as their personalised assistant, i.e., as a *Coach Agent* as described in [1].

The contribution of this paper is the cognitive agent architecture, that directs and organizes the agent's own internal behavior and the behavior performed by the agent in the interaction with the human agent.

2 Related Work

Research literature shows an increasing number of applications of software agents that interact with human actors for health-related purposes (e.g., [10, 11, 9, 12, 13, 14]). One example is the automated system, which has been developed for older adults with cognitive impairment described in [10]. However, it focuses mainly on generating reminders about the activities of their daily living and takes no part in a complex dialogue with the user. Agent-based systems which interact with human actors through dialogues are less common. They are most commonly developed for a specific task or for a limited domain, and the dialogues are tested in specialized environments [14, 12]. In the healthcare domain, the agents have the potential to support the medical professionals in better diagnosis of their patients (e.g., [15]). An agent provides an effective interface modality especially for the applications that require repeated interactions over longer period of time, such as applications developed for supporting behavior change [16, 17].

Bickmore et. al [14] developed an animated conversational agent that provides information about a patient's hospital discharge plan in an empathic fashion. The patients rated the agent very high on measures of satisfaction and ease of use, and also as being the most preferred over their doctors or nurses in the hospital when receiving their discharge information. This was related to the agent capability to adapt to the user's pace of learning and giving information in a nonjudgmental manner. Another reason for the positive results was the amount of time that the agent spent with users helped them to establish a stronger emotional bond.

An automated counseling dialogue system is discussed in [17], which uses an ontology to represent the knowledge and the user model. In their approach, the agent performs motivational interviewing with its knowledge about behavioral medicine and uses empathy in dialogues. It provides the human agent with some advice about exercise and healthy actions and follows up by asking the human followup questions. However it limits its services to counseling only and does not reason with evidence about the human's change of behavior based on information about their activities.

The canonical model of an agent described by Fox and coworkers [7] is an extension of the Belief-Desire-Intention (BDI) model of an autonomous agent (e.g., [6]) and provides formal semantics for the concepts argumentation, decision-making, action, belief, goal (desire) planning (intention) and learning for agents. Literature describes implementation in systems, however, mainly for multi-agent reasoning and decision making without active participation of a human agent in the process [7]. To our knowledge, this model has not served as a base for dialogues between software agents and human agents beyond simple alerts or providing decisions. These generic concepts are incorporated in our proposed architecture, and the implementation and execution of these are organized by the modules in the architecture.

For an agent to be able to reason about what actions to make in the process of a dialogue, it needs to follow a dialogue strategy. Dialogue systems presented in research literature typically use one of the three following existing dialogue strategies [18]. In *finite-state* strategies, the dialogue path is represented as a finite state machine, in which transitions to new dialogue states are determined by the user's selections from fixed sets of responses to system questions. In *frame-based* strategies, the system constructs the dialogue in order to fill in the slots of a predetermined frame. Finally, in an *agent-based* dialogue path, the system constructs the dialogue as it recognizes and attempts to satisfy the user's objectives.

Recent extensions are concerned with multi-strategy dialogue management, where two or more strategies are combined for question answering applications [19, 20]. However, these approaches mainly focus on combining finite-state and frame-based dialogue strategies. In this work, we developed a strategy similar to a human agent's strategy that has more than one information elicitation strategy and is able to change strategy according to circumstances. This was done by combining finite-state and agent-based dialogue strategies.

3   Human-Agent Dialogue Scenario and Design

The system developed in this paper is designed based on the persona and scenario of a female older adult, and the dialogues aimed for self-care assistance described in [1, 5]. Our persona called Rut [1] shares similarity with some of the participants in a study conducted by Lindgren and Nilsson [21], and is therefore considered representative. Rut is 84 years old, who suffers from pain in her back and legs and suffered from few falls before a hip fracture.

We envision that Rut begins to walk around nighttime, and that she may discuss the situation and her sleep with a nurse. The nurse asks a few specific questions about Rut's activities and health, and the dialogue will wander from one aspect to another, sometimes coming back to a topic already mentioned.

This example of a natural dialogue is rather different from dialogues described in literature, which aims at reaching one particular goal of a dialogue (e.g., [22]. Following the categorization of dialogue types, described by Walton and Krabbe [23], the dialogue with the nurse is a simplified example of a combination of different goals: finding information (*information-seeking* type), generate new knowledge, i.e., conclusions (*inquiry dialogue* type) and deciding upon actions to make (*deliberation* type). In case one of the agents has reasons for arguing for one particular action to be made with the purpose to convince the other, e.g. for safety reasons, the dialogue may include a *persuasive* part, e.g., to convince Rut that she needs to go to the hospital for investigation. Based on this, we can define a set of *generic goals* for the agent to use in its organization of dialogues.

More concretely, the generic outcome of each type of dialogue is the following: *information, new derived knowledge, plan of actions* and a *change of priority*. It may be that all of these types of dialogues need to be conducted in order to fully explore a particular *topic*. These generic goals will correspond to *schemes* described in Section 5.

Consequently, the agent needs to be able to handle nested multi-purposed dialogues with different topics. In order to accomplish this, the agent needs to be able to distinguish between *topic, generic goal* and have a semantic model of how these inter-relate in a particular situation. For instance, if the agent would have the dialogue with Rut instead of the nurse, the agent needs a semantic model for how walking around nighttime relates to sleep patterns, pain, cognitive ability, medication, worries, etc. Moreover, it needs strategies to plan next moves, based on a knowledge model, which may not provide with a pre-defined hierarchically organized plan of actions based on goals and sub-goals to be followed, but rather a collection of prioritized actions, among which the order may become determined and changed by the dialogue evolvement and Rut's line of thinking.

The *topics* relate to the human agent's goals and priorities. Consequently, from the human agent's perspective, goals relate to finding answers to questions, finding and deciding about actions to make in order to increase levels of satisfaction, evaluate actions made, etc. Consequently, for the human agent, goals are purposeful, topic-driven and context dependent.

Therefore, the agent in our approach combines a generic goal with a specific topic, in order to identify the *specific goal* with an action. In the following we give the example of a dialogue, where the topic selected by the human agent is the following: "Sleep pattern may be disturbed", which is a claim representing a belief, which has not been verified. The agent can chose to conduct a dialogue with the purpose to find information about sleep (specific goal) and initiates an information-seeking dialogue. Topics related to sleep are e.g., pain and medication, and consequently, in this situation, the sub-goals are to *find information about pain* and *medication*, respectively.

The following is an example of a part of a dialogue, generated by the system in collaboration with Rut, where CA represents the Coach Agent:

- Rut: Hi Coach, I wonder if not my "Sleep pattern may be disturbed".
- CA: Hi, Rut. Okay, then I would like to ask about *sleep*. Did the sleeping pills work for you tonight?
- Rut: No.
- CA: Why did you not sleep well last night?
- Rut: Needed to pee and pain.
- CA: Now I would like to ask about *pain*. Where do you have pain?
- Rut: In my back.
- CA: How severe is your pain?
- Rut: Severe.
- CA: Let us go back to *sleep*. How often do you need to get up each night?

4　Cognitive Architecture for the Agent

This section introduces the cognitive agent architecture based on the scenario and requirements introduced in the introduction of this paper. It consists of the following four main components (Figure 1); 1) the *Belief Base*, 2) the *Dialogue Manager*, 3) the *Task Manager*, and 4) the *Plan Generator*. Each component is assigned a set of responsibilities that enable the agent to act purposefully. The components are explained in detail in the following sections.

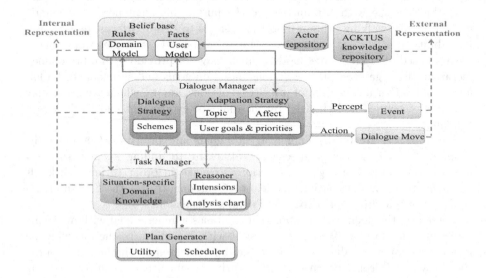

Fig. 1. Cognitive agent architecture

4.1　Belief Base

A belief base consists of a set of beliefs, which can be both facts and rules. The beliefs are extracted from the common semantic model used in ACKTUS for sharing arguments and information. Each agent participating in a dialogue has its own belief base. When a dialogue is initiated, and a topic is selected by human, a *user model* and a *domain model* are created from information relevant to the topic. The domain model may reveal missing information in the user model, and the agent can identify a set of questions, which can constitute templates for the agent to use for the purpose to obtain new facts in dialogues with the human agent or other software agents. When the Coach Agent has answers to these questions, they come in the form of information nodes, which can be interpreted using the semantic model and knowledge context provided by ACKTUS in dialogues and be reasoned about, e.g., a health condition.

Each belief is given a priority value. This value is assigned based on the following: (1) preferences given by the domain experts such as the doctors or the occupational therapist (2) priorities and goals set by the human and (3) follow up by the agent itself in a case where a rule remains to be used from previous dialogue. For example, if the human selects the same topic for a dialogue after a few days, then the agent retrieves any unanswered question from that dialogue and then the agent prioritises that rule in its belief base.

The Coach Agent performs two types of reasoning. Firstly it uses its belief base to reason about the message content of each of its moves during the dialogue. Secondly it uses a component of the task manager to reason about intension behind each move discussed in Section 4.3. The Coach Agent uses its knowledge from its belief base to find opportunities for contributing with help, advices and suggestions of actions to take.

4.2 Dialogue Manager

The agent uses a dialogue manager to decide which of the potential moves will be optimal in each state, to meet the goals of the user. The dialogue manager consists of two sub-components: the *dialogue strategy* and the *adaptation strategy*. The dialogue manager is based on a state machine. Each state specifies a transition state from the current state and the condition to validate that transition, as well as a syntax for what the human can use as response in that state (for example, single-choice option or multi-choice option in the case when a question is posed to the user). State definitions also include the specification of agent *schemes* as templates with variables that are instantiated each time the state is entered. Schemes are a type of protocols, which directs a specific type of dialogue and its completion. The dialogue manager is further described in section 5.

4.3 Task Manager

The task manager contains the situation-specific domain knowledge and the reasoner. The situation-specific knowledge is about the possibilities that exist to make next move in the dialogue. For an information-seeking dialogue for example, the task manager organizes the various questions related to the topic that need to be asked the human if the information is missing. The reasoner is the agent's deliberation module and therefore it organizes the intensions and consists of an analysis chart based on the previous dialogues. The agent uses the reasoner to reason about its intension behind making each move.

4.4 Plan Generator

The plan generator is the final component of the architecture. After making a list of tasks to be performed for a particular dialogue, the plan generator is responsible for deciding about the execution of tasks. In the information-seeking dialogue example, after generating a list of questions to be asked from the human, the plan generator determines the order in which questions need to be asked. It measures the utility of the outcome of each task and prioritizes them. As a result, this module generates a plan for the agent to act upon, which typically needs revision, depending on the human's actions. The agent uses the scheduler to regulate the conditions for when and how the agent will initiate a dialogue with the human.

5   Implementation of the Dialogue Manager

A prototype system for human-agent dialogues has been developed in Java and the Java Agent DEvelopment Framework (JADE) has been used to build the Coach Agent. The knowledge repository used in this system is developed using ACKTUS, and designed for rehabilitation purposes by domain experts [5]. This knowledge is modeled as an ontology, represented in RDF/OWL, and stored in a RDF (Resource Description Framework) repository (Figure 1).

The Dialogue manager utilizes two components in the creation of a dialogue: a *dialogue strategy* and an *adaptation strategy*. The base for adaptation is the priorities and goals defined by the human actor, which the agent obtains from the *Actor repository*, the *topic* for the dialogue, and potential *affective* information.

As previously described, the therapist conducts an interview with the older adult. This baseline assessment results in information about the user regarding their health conditions, medications, preferences, goals and priorities, which is stored in the Actor repository, also based on a semantic model containing assessment events (Figure 1). The information can be interpreted using the ACKTUS semantic model, e.g., when the Coach Agent needs to build a *user model* for a situation. The information about the user, represented as information nodes in the Coach Agent's belief base, is supplemented with a *domain model* relevant to the selected dialogue *topic*.

The dialogue moves are currently visualized to the user as texts, and the user contributes to the dialogue by selecting among a limited set of answer alternatives determined by the domain experts' implementation in the case of a question, and among a list of topics obtained from the repository in case the user is initiating the dialogue. In the following section the dialogue strategy will be further described.

5.1   Dialogue Strategy

Apart from the understanding of human's message and having reliable reasoning techniques, there is a challenge for the agent to know *what it should send as next move* in response to the human's previous move. A message is the request or response that is selected and sent by the human to the agent. Dialogue management is a challenge, as described in [13]. In our case, it is important to prioritize the order in which, e.g., the questions need to be addressed the user by the agent in the case of an information-seeking dialogue, or when an advice should be given. Therefore, an agent in a healthcare system, having a dialogue with human, needs to follow a strategy to decide which of the potential moves will be optimal in each state.

Our method for dialogue strategy selection combines the application of multi-strategy dialogue management [19] with adaptation strategies, and a method for calculating agent's performance based on a utility function. Since the dialogue manager is based on a state machine, each state specifies a transition state from the current state and the condition to validate that transition, as well as a syntax for what the human can use as response in that state State definitions also include the specification of agent *schemes* as templates (e.g., Figure 2), with variables that are instantiated each time the state is entered.

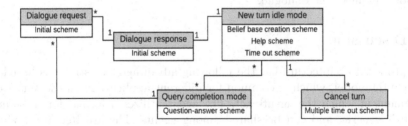

Fig. 2. Entity relationship diagram of a dialogue. Each entity represents a state and its scheme.

An agent's dialogue strategy is implemented as a combination of the schemes and the state transitions that the agent makes in response to the human's request. The schemes are protocols for regulating some generic goal-oriented tasks to be conducted by the agent as sub-tasks to the dialogue, and as such they are different from the *argumentation schemes* defined in [24]. The following schemes are defined:

1. An *initiation scheme*, which regulates how the agent behaves in the initiation of a dialogue.
2. A *belief-base creation scheme*, which regulates how the agent populates its belief base containing relevant information for the current situation and dialogue, based on the knowledge and Actor repository, and previous states.
3. A *dialogue body execution scheme*, which directs how both participants send and receive requests and responses on time. In our example of an information-seeking dialogue we utilize a *question-answer scheme*
4. A *help scheme*, which regulates how the agent may take action for referring responsibility to an external actor such as a nurse or therapist.
5. *Multiple time-out schemes*, which regulate the handling of interruptions, pauses or cancellation of dialogues, e.g., in the case when the human agent does not respond.

The transitions between states are driven by the user's conversational behavior, such as whether he/she makes a move, the content of a move, or the interpretation of the human's request. We introduce the following states and corresponding behaviors for an agent participating in a human-agent dialogue:

1. The *dialogue request state*, in which the request from human to have a dialogue is received.
2. In *dialogue response state*, the agent follows an initial scheme to acknowledge the human agent regarding its availability to have a dialogue.
3. On successful initiation of dialogue, the agent enters the *new turn idle mode* where it creates a belief base.

4. In the *query completion mode*, after the creation of the belief base and within the question-answer scheme, the agent asks questions to the human agent.
5. The *cancel turn state* is entered in the case when no response is received at some point of the dialogue.

6   Discussion

The proposed architecture has the following advantages. Firstly, it is based on a semantic model, which is common for different applications in the smart environment in which the agents act. The agent utilizes a format for reasoning, which is generic, and can be shared among agents. The architecture modules add cognitive models for the agent's internal behavior, which corresponds to goal-directed behavior, with the possibility to adapt its behavior depending on a situation. These characteristics make it reusable, scalable and applicable to any health-related domain, which shares the common semantic model.

The schemes can be used regardless if the other agent is a human or another software agent. In order to meet the agent's goal to conduct the dialogue body, a number of different schemes need to be defined, partly corresponding to the different types of dialogues, which the agent should be able to participate in. Apart from the question-answer scheme, which meets the goal to find new information (i.e., conduct an information-seeking dialogue), we envision schemes for the purpose to conduct deliberation (reason about actions, what to do) or persuasive (reason about why conduct an activity) dialogues. If the question-answer scheme is extended with some possibilities to also create new knowledge (for instance, assert conclusions based on argumentation), then the scheme may regulate inquiry dialogues. Moreover, a particular scheme can be designed for conducting dialogues with affective topics or content.

While argumentation schemes represent patterns of reasoning in argumentative dialogues [24] the dialogue strategy schemes can be seen as templates for dialogues at a higher level, where argumentation schemes can be utilized in the execution of a particular part of a dialogue body.

The current implementation partly implements the cognitive architecture and dialogues, and ongoing work includes the implementation of the dialogue manager's protocols for the dialogue initiation and termination that regulate the conditions for when and how the agent will initiate and terminate a particular type of dialogue with the human. We are exploring this issue in ongoing work, as well as extending the dialogues with additional schemes, for the agent to be more flexible in how the agent approaches the generic purposes of a dialogue (e.g., create new knowledge, learn, make decisions, seek information, deliberation, persuasion, etc.).

7   Conclusions and Future Work

The capabilities required for an intelligent software agent to be interacting with a human agent in dialogues about health-related topics has been outlined and discussed. A cognitive architecture was proposed for an agent consisting of the four main components belief base, dialogue manager, task manager and plan generator.

An initial prototype of the dialogue manager with a set of schemes added to an agent's dialogue strategy was presented and discussed. During the conduction of a human-agent dialogue, an agent transits from one state to another and the scheme of dialogue strategy also changes. The advantage of this approach is that the agent can decide which state to navigate to from the current state, based on the scheme. This is different compared to the multi-agent dialogues in which an agent follows linearly ordered dialogue protocols. Consequently, the schemes enable an agent to be more flexible in making a decision about its next dialogue move based on the human agent's response. The task manager and the plan generator will be implemented in future work.

References

[1] Lindgren, H., Surie, D., Nilsson, I.: Agent-supported assessment for adaptive and personalized ambient assisted living. In: Corchado, J.M., Pérez, J.B., Hallenborg, K., Golinska, P., Corchuelo, R. (eds.) Trends in PAAMS. AISC, vol. 90, pp. 25–32. Springer, Heidelberg (2011)

[2] Lindgren, H.: Towards context-based inquiry dialogues for personalized interaction. In: Demazeau, Y., Pěchouček, M., Corchado, J.M., Pérez, J.B. (eds.) Adv. on Prac. Appl. of Agents and Mult. Sys. AISC, vol. 88, pp. 151–161. Springer, Heidelberg (2011)

[3] Fox, J.: Towards a canonical framework for designing agents to support health-care organisations. In: Proc. of the European Conference of AI (ECAI) Workshop Agents Applied in Healthcare (2006)

[4] Baskar, J., Lindgren, H.: Towards personalised support for monitoring and improving health in risky environments. In: VIII Workshop on Agents Applied in Health Care (A2HC 2013), Murcia, Spain, pp. 93–104 (2013)

[5] Lindgren, H., Nilsson, I.: Towards user-authored agent dialogues for assessment in personalised ambient assisted living. International Journal of Web Engineering and Technology 8(2), 154–176 (2013)

[6] Castelfranchi, C., Falcone, R.: Founding autonomy: The dialectics between (Social) environment and agent's architecture and powers. In: Nickles, M., Rovatsos, M., Weiss, G. (eds.) AUTONOMY 2003. LNCS (LNAI), vol. 2969, pp. 40–54. Springer, Heidelberg (2004),
http://dx.doi.org/10.1007/978-3-540-25928-2_4

[7] Fox, J., Glasspool, D., Modgil, S.: A canonical agent model for healthcare applications. IEEE Intelligent Systems 21(6), 21–28 (2006)

[8] Isern, D., David Sánchez, A.M.: Agents applied in health care: A review. International Journal of Medical Informatics, 145–166 (2010)

[9] Bickmore, T., Caruso, L., Clough-Gorr, K., Heeren, T.: 'it's just like you talk to a friend' relational agents for older adults. Interacting with Computers, 711–735 (2005)

[10] Pollack, M., Brown, L., Colbry, D., McCarthy, C.E., Orosz, C., Peintner, B., Ramakrishnan, S., Tsamardinos, I.: An intelligent cognitive orthotic system for people with memory impairment. Robotics and Autonomous Systems, 273–282 (2003)

[11] Bickmore, T., Cassell, J.: Social dialogue with embodied conversational agents. In: Advances in Natural, Multimodal Dialogue Systems, pp. 4–8 (2005)

[12] Susan, R., Traum, D.R., Ittycheriah, M., Henderer, J.: What would you ask a conversational agent? observations of human-agent dialogues in a museum setting. In: International Conference on Language Resources and Evaluation, pp. 69–102 (2008)

[13] Alistair, K., Vlugter, P.: Multi-agent human–machine dialogue: issues in dialogue management and referring expression semantics. Artificial Intelligence 172(2-3), 69–102 (2008)

[14] Bickmore, T., Mitchell, S., Jack, B., Paasche-Orlow, M.: Response to a relational agent by hospital patients with depressive symptoms. Interacting with Computers, 289–298 (2010)

[15] Yan, C., Lindgren, H.: Hypothesis-driven agent dialogues for dementia assessment. In: VIII Workshop on Agents Applied in Health Care (A2HC 2013), Murcia, Spain, pp. 93–104 (2013)

[16] Kennedy, C.M., Powell, J., Payne, T.H., Ainsworth, J., Boyd, A., Buchan, I.: Active assistance technology for health-related behavior change: An interdisciplinary review. Journal of Medical Internet Research (2012)

[17] Bickmore, T.W., Schulman, D., Sidner, C.L.: A reusable framework for health counseling dialogue systems based on a behavioral medicine ontology. Journal of Biomedical Informatics, 183–197 (2011)

[18] McTear, M.F.: Spoken dialogue technology: Enabling the conversational user interface. ACM Computing Surveys 34(1), 90–169 (2002)

[19] Chu, S.W., ONeill, I., Hanna, P., McTear, M.: An approach to multi-strategy dialogue management. In: Proceedings of INTERSPEECH, Lisbon, Portugal, pp. 865–868 (2005)

[20] Sonntag, D.: Towards combining finite-state, ontologies, and data driven approaches to dialogue management for multimodal question answering. In: Proceedings of the 5th Slovenian First International Language Technology Conference (2006)

[21] Lindgren, H., Nilsson, I.: Designing systems for health promotion and autonomy in older adults. In: Gross, T., Gulliksen, J., Kotzé, P., Oestreicher, L., Palanque, P., Prates, R.O., Winckler, M. (eds.) INTERACT 2009. LNCS, vol. 5727, pp. 700–703. Springer, Heidelberg (2009)

[22] Black, E., Hunter, A.: An inquiry dialogue system. Autonomous Agents and Multi-Agent Systems 19(2), 173–209 (2009)

[23] Walton, D., Krabbe, E.: Commitment in dialogue: Basic concepts of interpersonal reasoning. SUNY Press (1995)

[24] Walton, D., Reed, C.: Diagramming, argumentation schemes and critical questions. In: Proceedings of the Fifth International Conference on Argumentation (ISSA), Amsterdam, pp. 881–885 (2002)

A Different Approach in an AAL Ecosystem:
A Mobile Assistant for the Caregiver

Angelo Costa[1,*], Oscar Gama[2], Paulo Novais[1], and Ricardo Simoes[2,3,4]

[1] CCTC-Computer Science and Technology Center, University of Minho, Braga, Portugal
{acosta,pjon}@di.uminho.pt
[2] Institute for Polymers and Composites - IPC/I3N, University of Minho,
Campus de Azurém, 4800-058 Guimarães, Portugal
osg@di.uminho.pt, rsimoes@dep.uminho.pt
[3] Life and Health Sciences Research Institute (ICVS), School of Health Sciences,
University of Minho, Campus de Gualtar, 4710-057 Braga, Portugal
[4] Polytechnic Institute of Cavado and Ave, Campus do IPCA, 4750-810 Barcelos, Portugal
rsimoes@ipca.pt

Abstract. Currently the Ambient Assisted Living and the Ambient Intelligence areas are very prolific. There is a demand of security and comfort that should be ensured at people's homes. The AAL4ALL (ambient assisted living for all) project aims to develop a unified ecosystem and a certification process, allowing the development of fully compatible devices and services. The UserAccess emerges from the AAL4ALL project, being a demonstration of its validity. The UserAccess architecture, implementation, interfaces and test scenario are presented, along with the sensor platform specially developed for the AAL4ALL project.

Keywords: Ambient Assisted Living, Ambient Intelligence, Intelligent Environments, AAL4ALL, e-Health, Active Ageing, Artificial Intelligence, Sensor Platform.

1   Introduction

In the last 20 years modern society has witnessed several technological evolutions, as the birth of high speed internet, smartphones, GPS systems, smart TV's, among others devices [1]. Furthermore, we can state that the proliferation of these devices on a home environment induced behavioural changes in the youngest generations. Even older people have progressively accepted and adopted these devices on their work or at home, thus, we can say that society considers these devices as a common good and being always present [2]. Moreover, with the current advances, some devices have transcended from being tools to perform a task to being the motive of the human interaction with them. As an example, the smartphone has started as work facilitator tool, providing everywhere internet access and office tools, to become an entertainment

---

* Corresponding author.

J.M. Corchado et al. (Eds.): PAAMS 2014 Workshops, CCIS 430, pp. 101–110, 2014.

centre, with music, videos and games. Even the way people communicate has changed due to these devices, shaping the language and the social interaction between humans [3, 4].

Historically, the main driving forces behind the evolution of these technologies were the medical, military and engineering fields. To solve complex problems they require pioneering technology, which is obtained through massive investments [5]. Even spinoff products are of use and important, if not to the area they were produced, to other areas, branching into other lines of investigation. Also, the people who adopted emerging technology contributed greatly to the investment in home version of industrial devices.

Home automation is one field that displayed abundant progression due to the adoption of technology developed to other fields. The crescent use of automated devices on common homes have forced a cost reduction of them, thus allowing a greater panoply of choices in terms of features and complexity. The merge of home automation devices with computational systems resulted in the Ambient Intelligence concept (AmI).

AmI aim is integrating all devices in an ecosystem and the obtaining the environment's context [6, 7]. These two goals can be described in the following way:

- Integration: allows different devices, such as sensors and actuators, to communicate with the rest of them, being communication protocol agnostic. The homogenization of the communication protocol leads to the possibility of using devices from different makers, or easily changing the device's topology and placement. The ecosystem created is permeable to changes and allows new additions to the network;
- Context: enables the capture of information relative to the environment's state. Simple sensor information only provide a limited spectrum of the environment. Context is usually the outcome of information fusion, which provides a broader perspective of the environment. Therefore, complex information can be obtained from simple sensor data, in some cases outlining unexpected states that each sensor by itself was unable to do. Context also places itself on high-level communicating process, transmitting clear information that encapsulates simple actions.

The evolution of the AmI was allowed due to the four main aspects:

- Device miniaturization: allowing complex systems be encapsulated in a small form factor;
- Information availability: datasets from heterogeneous sources and classification of said data allowed the generation of knowledge that can be implemented directly on the developing systems.
- Computing power: allowing the ability to consume information and processing it faster than ever before, obtaining results instantaneously;
- Ubiquity: allowing integration of computerized system in common appliances, providing them with the capability of communication and integration with the ecosystem, transforming them in a sensor/actuator terminal.

AmI's are structured to be constructed over very different scenarios, such as home environments, offices, industrial factories, hospitals, day-care centres, among others. Although this architectural feature is important, allowing everyone access to this technology, it presents an implementation problem. It is easy to grasp that a hospital environment is very different of a factory environment, and so are the requirements of each of them. Thus, the adaptation to each environment that is going to be implemented is essential, and the areas that care for the home and medical environments is named Ambient Assisted Living (AAL).

1.1   AAL

The AAL concept is fundamentally the one of the AmI, but with the directed towards a specific population and environments, being mainly the elderly and the people with disabilities [8–12]. They require special attention due to their limitations leading the systems to be sensible enough to accommodate them properly. Adaptation is key in these cases and the AAL provide it. As the name shows, the AAL can be defined by a sentient environment that helps sensibly the people in it, on their daily living [13, 14].

To be sentient, a system has to be intelligent. Alike humans, which are able to perceive a scenario and sort the elements and events happening, these systems must also have to be able to capture and contextualize the information obtained by the sensors.

Sensor systems are very useful as they provide an array of sensors, able to capture different environment aspects, but they also present a flaw, they are only able to capture the information according to their specification, and unable to distinguish the "bigger picture". Here, the sum of all parts are usually greater than the parts themselves, where the perspective is fundamental, so having only streams of data it is very difficult, if not impossible, to describe what is really happening in the environment. For instance, if a flood sensor is not paired with a fire alarm, in an event of a small fire that could be easily contained, a flood could occur, damaging valuable propriety.

What currently happens is that most of the home systems rely only on simple logic systems, implemented directly on the system middleware. This approach a proven solution directed for simple smart homes' implementations, with only a few features. A problem emerges when the users and the environments are more exigent. Thus, a simple system is just not enough to respond to the demands.

The AAL aims to provide personalised systems that adapt to the user, not only on implementation but along the user's life. Furthermore, the intended users of the AAL have very specific and complex disabilities so they must have environments that are designed to them, helping them on their daily tasks.

In this paper we present the AAL4ALL project and an AAL system that was developed to validate the project concept.

2   UserAccess: An AAL4ALL Project

The AAL4ALL project [15] is a Portuguese effort on the AAL area, being consortium of private companies and public institutions. The aim is to deliver solutions, in the form of devices or services, and a certification process so that other developers (outside the consortium) can obtain a national *approved for sale* seal. Being an AAL project, the AAL4ALL goal is to ease the life of the elderly and disabled by offering an ecosystem adjusted to them, having into account the social and monetary conditions.

The distinctive feature from other projects is the ecosystem's integration. The integration procedures were assured since the project conception, thus, a large effort was done by all project partners to construct products and services that were compliant with the rest. Additionally, the project relied on a social sphere created to support the user constituted by formal and informal caregivers, and family and friends. It is clear that some procedures must be accompanied by humans, justifying the need to resort to caregivers, so allowing the inclusion of caregiving companies.

The core architecture of the project is open, allowing access to anyone that desires developing a solution to it. The components heterogeneity enforces the integration of them, and the homogeneity of the final product requires that every device must be able to trade information as effectively and as perceivable as possible.

One of the AAL4ALL solutions is the UserAccess, consisting in a devices and service structure, aimed mainly to the caregivers, creating a digital bridge between the user and the caregiver.

2.1   UserAccess

The UserAccess project is an AAL implementation based on but presenting a different approach of the project shown in [14, 16]. The project's goal is to deliver user information to the caregiver, thus assisting the caregiver on him/her daily task, by retrieving information from sensor platforms and formulating knowledge about the environment's context.

Most of the AAL projects rely on a human assistance network, which provide help on critical situations or by user demand. They act as a medical proxy, providing assistance and social support remotely so the user can stay at home and trial the simpler cases without needing to go to a hospital constantly. The main issue with these services is that they require on the user interaction, meaning that the usually is the user who must phone them if there is any case wrong. They act very passively and in the critical cases are little to no user of the user. In the last years there was a proliferation of "panic buttons" consisting of a hardware device that had a unique button and with a press it calls the caregiving services or the emergency medical services. Additionally to passing the user information to the services, the panic button could establish a phone call or text messaging, resulting on a few different services that can be offered, depending on the device capabilities. The point is that none of them (caretaking services and panic buttons) are truly a good solution to the user. One is unable to act in critical situations, and other acts only when a critical situation is ongoing.

In this project the importance of the caretaking services is acknowledged, as we consider that the human supervision it is still the best approach when medical related events happen. With this in mind, the UserAccess is built to help caregivers, and may be modestly explained as: receiving the information from the house's sensors system, process it and deliver it to the caregiver in human-readable form. The system is constituted by a server and a mobile platform, preferably a smartphone or tablet and can monitor several users at the same time.

The information that is presented to the caregiver is related to the context rather than to each sensor, although some sensors (e.g. sos button) are directly reported in form of a notification, with the maximum priority possible.

Architecture. As stated before, the UserAccess is constituted by a software service and hardware devices, thus the architecture of the project also reflects those features. The UserAccess follows the integration standards that were defined on the AAL4ALL, and because it is an AAL4ALL project it uses its structure to communicate.

The communication is assured be the AAL4ALL Node which serves as a communication bridge, providing channels form publishing and consuming information. Due to the heterogeneity of the sensor systems the sustaining platform requires that they communicate at higher level information, thus, the sensor platform has to provide a middleware component to process the raw data.

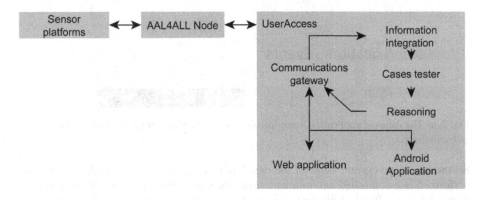

Fig. 1. UserAccess architectural components

As depicted in the Figure 1, the UserAccess receives high-level information, such as "user exited home" or "lights are on" trough the *Communications gateway*, which performs a verification of the incoming data checking the validity and restructures it according the internal communication method. Thereon, the information sent to the *Information integration* and is merged with the previous user state, updating the environment's context, forming new knowledge about the user's actions.

The context aspect is essential, thus a vector is formed containing the previous knowledge, the new knowledge and the base rules. In the *Cases tester* the vector is tested to verify if it is already in the knowledge base, and if any response was previously defined. If a case is present (according to the similarity) then same approach is used, but if it is not present the event is saved for further analysis.

The next step is the *Reasoning*, and it contains the previous actions and a similarity analysis process that compares the cases and retrieves them along with the rules, obtaining the action to be performed. Finally, the set of actions are transformed into information or notifications to send to the caregiver mobile platform.

The *Cases tester* and *Reasoning* are based over Case Based Reasoning and Bayesian Networks concepts, as in this project were considered as the best approach due to the information type and the relational knowledge. Also, what is called *action* on the UserAccess process is a bundle of events that must be performed by the interfaces, such as displaying certain messages or notifications, as shown in Figure 2. A bilateral communication process was implemented to validate the test scenario consisting in an electrical switch actuator that was responsible of turning on or off a light.

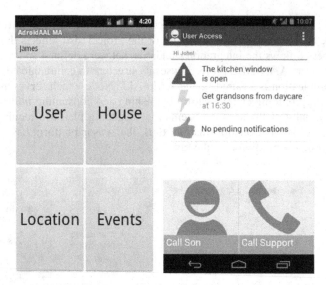

Fig. 2. a) The Android application home interface. **b)** Alpha stage caregiver interface (warnings and activities).

Scenario. At the current stage of the development the system must undergo on tests performed in a controlled environment, using the sensor platform and a local server. It is critical that a finished product is presented to the user, thus it is critical having a testing process recurring to predefined scenarios.

The sensors used are shown in the Figure 3. They use the ZigBee protocol to communicate, and possess a base station connected to a Raspberry Pi computer, acting as middleware. The sensors displayed on the Figure 3 are: (on the front) two motion sensors, a light and environment temperature and relative humidity sensor, two door/window open/close sensor, a SOS button, and on the back the electrical switch actuator.

The base station received the information from these devices and communicated with the middleware, being the speed of the communication negligible as it was immediate. The middleware also has enough power to process raw data and transform it into information accepted by the server. The middleware saves the direct previous states (5 to 10) to deliver stable information and to filter errors. Furthermore, it also detects the sensor's battery level and connection quality.

The server is constructed following a multi-agent system concept, being constituted by several modules that are responsible for the knowledge process. Currently the system is unable to form new knowledge, being the information saved in a knowledge base and after each test the WEKA tool is used to find correlations.

Five tests were performed in the proposed scenario, each with 10 attempts, being the following list:

- Test 1: the user gets up from a seated position and exits the door;
- Test 2: the user gets up from a seated position and open and closes the door;
- Test 3: the user enters the house;
- Test 4: the user gets close to the door but does not open it;
- Test 5: Press the SOS button.

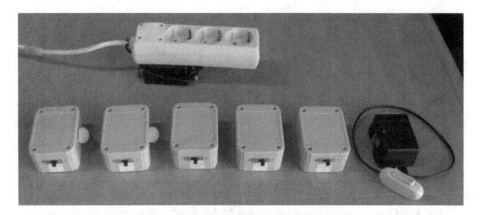

Fig. 3. Sensors used in the scenario setup

Of those tests, the system was able to correctly detect the procedures (7 of 10) having difficulty when noise was introduced in some of the events. In all cases the caregiver received a notification and a threat assessment. In the failed tests, the main issues were caused by the sensor's latency, causing a deviation to the expected event. To perform these tests a logic construction was devised and implemented in each agent. For instance, to detect the user going outside the agent monitored the sensors that retrieved that information, usually being more than one, and in this particular case, three (the two motion sensors and the door sensor).

As stated before, the stabilization time is an issue that directly impacts the states detection and even the actions to be performed. For instance, the motion detection sensors take 5 to 10 seconds to stabilize, which means that for that period of time the system has no idea of what is happening. For instance, if the user has full mobility he/she could open the door, exited, go back inside and stand still until the sensors stabilize and in the best case scenario the system would detect that the user is still inside. This perilous example shows the dependency of the software has over the information of the hardware. In our perspective, a compromise can be reached to overcome the stabilization problem, having two solutions: a redundant system, or other sensor formats.

Other sensor formats means that, for instance, for the motion detection, the current sensors should be replaced by other sensors, such as floor sensors, cameras or even laser sensors. The major issue with this solution is that we aim to have a sensor platform that is monetarily accessible thus, the use of high-end sensors rapidly inflates the expected budget and compromises the acceptance by the users.

The redundant set of sensors consists in equipping the environment with more sensors, being the same type or other cheap ones. This way in addition to have motion detection inside a house, a few more can be place outside the house or even placed in other angles. This solution is the most inexpensive and, with a fine tuned logic associative procedure, can in fact outperform the system with more advanced but with less number of sensors. With different stabilization times is expected that the software will be receiving information at all times thus covering the shortcomings of each sensor. In the case of the motion detection sensors, in the Figure 4 is showed the current setup (in the left) and the right side the possible setup of an entry hall.

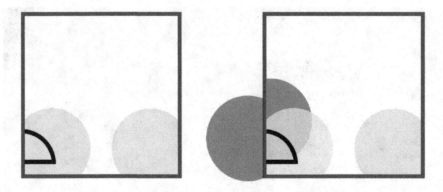

Fig. 4. a) Current motion sensor positioning. b) Advanced motion sensor positioning.

In Figure 4, on the b) image, it is clear that the additional information about the motion can easily provide full information about the user location. As the motion detection sensors only act when the user is moving they do not know where they are within the scope of the sensor. Thus with several sensors it is possible to verify the several activation sequence and stabilization procedure thus, we can obtain the exact user action.

A similar conclusion can be obtained to all other sensors, for instance, in terms of temperature, light and electrical switches. They are inexpensive and easy to implement, thus the number of available devices can be greatly increased, increasing also the quality of the obtained information.

The UserAccess agent-based architecture is able to easily support sensor additions to the platform, being the requirement only to comply with the API and the communication ontologies. The agents can be updated to find other sensors of the same type and the logical procedures adapted to receive blocks of information with the only requirement of setup the sensor sequences to each action.

3   Conclusions and Future Work

In this paper was presented the AAL4ALL project and the UserAccess project. The AAL4ALL project is already an important landmark, presenting novelty features such as the integration methods and the certification procedures. The UserAccess is an effort towards the validation of the AAL4ALL concept, among the other partners' projects.

The AAL4ALL project is now shifting towards an integrated solution, being the aim to implement all the sensor communications and early processing to a set-top box, which presents the information locally in a television. The heavy data processing will be done on the cloud, where the UserAccess is expected to be placed. The aim of the UserAccess remains the same, being to display the information to the user and the caregiver, in a functional webpage. Moreover, the agent-base system is also maintained, being currently adapted to receive high-level information, as the initial processing system is placed on the home set-top box. This releases the UserAccess of the sensor data processing tasks to being more focused in providing real actions relations, being able to provide personal information and a profile. We are aiming to detect potentially hazardous actions and provide information to the caregiver about them, allowing to act preventively.

In terms of future architecture and technical work, we expect to implement a load balancing feature on the server, and an optimized interface structure. Establishing a better communication protocol between the server and the mobile platform, optimizing the message weight and establishing ontologies to structure all content.

In terms of the sensor platform, the current challenges are the miniaturization and the battery life. To proceed to a field test, we need to use devices that are nearly at the end-product phase so the invisibility and duration are key factors to a successful experiment, allowing a smooth and functional operation.

Currently, we can state that the UserAccess is at an advanced stage, being the architecture and most of the modules developed. The reasoning of the system is undergoing on several developments and is expected to be operational in the near future.

Acknowledgements. Project "AAL4ALL", co-financed by the European Community Fund FEDER, through COMPETE - Programa Operacional Factores de Competitividade (POFC). Foundation for Science and Technology (FCT), Lisbon, Portugal, through Project PEst-C/CTM/LA0025/2013 and the project PEst-OE/EEI/UI0752/2014.

Project CAMCoF - Context-aware Multimodal Communication Framework funded by ERDF -European Regional Development Fund through the COMPETE Programme (operational programme for competitiveness) and by National Funds through the FCT - Fundação para a Ciência e a Tecnologia (Portuguese Foundation for Science and Technology) within project FCOMP-01-0124-FEDER-028980.

References

1. Cozza, R., Milanesi, C., Zimmermann, A., Glenn, D., Gupta, A., Shen, H.J.D.L.V., Lu, C., Sato, A., Huy, T., Sandy, N.: Market Share: Mobile Communication Devices by Region and Country, 3Q11 (2011)
2. Markopoulos, P., Mavrommati, I., Kameas, A.: End-User Configuration of Ambient Intelligence Environments: Feasibility from a User Perspective. In: Markopoulos, P., Eggen, B., Aarts, E., Crowley, J.L. (eds.) EUSAI 2004. LNCS, vol. 3295, pp. 243–254. Springer, Heidelberg (2004)
3. Shuler, C.: Industry Brief: Pockets of Potential: Using Mobile Technologies to Promote Children's Learning (2009)
4. Common Sense Media: Zero to Eight: Children's Media Use in America 2013 (2013)
5. Jorge, J.A.: Adaptive tools for the elderly. In: Proceedings of the 2001 EC/NSF Workshop on Universal Accessibility of Ubiquitous Computing Providing for the Elderly, WUAUC 2001, p. 66. ACM Press, New York (2001)
6. Russell, S., Norvig, P.: Artificial Intelligence: A Modern Approach. Prentice Hall (1995)
7. Augusto, J.C., Callaghan, V., Cook, D., Kameas, A., Satoh, I.: Intelligent Environments: a manifesto. Human-Centric Computing and Information Sciences 3, 12 (2013)
8. Kurschl, W., Mitsch, S., Schönböck, J.: Modeling Situation-Aware Ambient Assisted Living Systems for Eldercare. In: 2009 Sixth International Conference on Information Technology: New Generations, pp. 1214–1219. IEEE (2009)

9. O'Grady, M.J., Muldoon, C., Dragone, M., Tynan, R., O'Hare, G.M.P.: Towards evolutionary ambient assisted living systems. Journal of Ambient Intelligence and Humanized Computing 1, 15–29 (2009)
10. Botia, J.A., Villa, A., Palma, J.: Ambient Assisted Living system for in-home monitoring of healthy independent elders. Expert Systems with Applications 39, 8136–8148 (2012)
11. Nehmer, J., Becker, M., Karshmer, A., Lamm, R.: Living assistance systems: an ambient intelligence approach. In: Proceedings of the 28th International Conference on Software Engineering, pp. 43–50 (2006)
12. Novais, P., Costa, R., Carneiro, D., Neves, J.: Inter-organization cooperation for ambient assisted living. Journal of Ambient Intelligence and Smart Environments 2, 179–195 (2010)
13. Lima, L., Novais, P., Costa, R., Bulas Cruz, J., Neves, J.: Group decision making and Quality-of-Information in e-Health systems. Logic Journal of IGPL 19, 315–332 (2010)
14. Costa, Â., Castillo, J.C., Novais, P., Fernández-Caballero, A., Simoes, R.: Sensor-driven agenda for intelligent home care of the elderly. Expert Systems with Applications 39, 12192–12204 (2012)
15. AAL4ALL - Ambient Assisted Living For All, http://www.aal4all.org
16. Vardasca, R., Costa, A., Mendes, P.M., Novais, P., Simoes, R.: Information and Technology Implementation Issues in AAL Solutions. International Journal of E-Health and Medical Communications 4, 1–17 (2013)

RETRACTED CHAPTER: HomeCare, Elder People Monitoring System and TV Communication

Victor Parra[1], Vivian López[1], and Mohd Saberi Mohamad[2]

[1] Department of Computer Science and Automation, University of Salamanca
Plaza de la Merced, s/n, 37008, Salamanca, Spain
{parra,vivian}@usal.es
[2] Center for Information and Communication Technology (CICT),
Universiti Teknologi Malaysia, 81310 UTM Skudai, Johor, Malaysia
saberi@utm.my

Abstract. For seniors who require continuous care and do not have the resources to have an assistant continuously, have a low cost system that monitors their environment allows them to have independence, while moving in a secure environment. In addition, accessing to basic services through a platform accessible to all people, including TV, facilitates their integration into the online society.

Keywords: Context aware system, multi-agent system, Wireless sensor networks.

1   Introduction

Today, access to information and numerous services is clearly geared to the network. Thanks to cheaper mobile devices as well as connections to the Internet and social networks we live interconnected almost 24 hours. However, despite the popularity of touchscreens, smartphones, tablets, etc., communication interfaces with electronic devices remain relatively traditional, as they are geared mostly to young or adult audience accustomed to working with them, leaving outside this range a large sector, such as the elderly. In a society that lives permanently connected, older people who cannot fully care for themselves need personal assistance or admission to a residence, situations that cannot always afford. The availability of a system that would allow them to get in touch with the outside world in a simple way from home [4] facilitate the independence of this sector of society, he could feel more useful, while they would be remotely monitored by experts and can be addressed quickly if necessary.

In this paper a system that is able to monitor a house and manage communication through television, as input interface using the four colors that the remote control is presented. By installing non-intrusive sensors and a low cost unit, a control of the areas in which the person is moving is maintained as well as possible changes in their routine. Moreover, through the television, they can offer personal services to facilitate tasks such as booking appointment at the physician or transport to a day center.

The original version of this chapter was retracted: The retraction note to this chapter is available at https://doi.org/10.1007/978-3-319-07767-3_35

J.M. Corchado et al. (Eds.): PAAMS 2014 Workshops, CCIS 430, pp. 111–120, 2014.
© Springer International Publishing Switzerland 2014, corrected publication 2024
https://doi.org/10.1007/978-3-319-07767-3_11

This article is divided into the following sections: Section 2 describes a state of the art; Section 3 presents the model and the proposed architecture; Section 4 presents the results and conclusions, respectively.

2   Background

Today's automation systems are geared mostly to home security, so are oriented mostly to access through doors and windows, as well as the use of cameras and microphones, which can sometimes seem intrusive for tenants. However, a proper arrangement of the sensors in the home can provide much more information. With the present sensors including low cost can be extracted activity patterns [1] that allow additional routines in order to increase safety and energy savings. Not only restricted to housing this possibility, but also the information is accessible remote [2 3, 17] enabling act if abnormalities in routine. It is especially useful for a routine of an elderly person in your home [4] without a 24/7 assistant. Including fall sensors can even detect emergencies immediately [5, 29, 30, 31, 32, 33] without intrusive sensors such as cameras.

However, these systems either behave reactively or just extract information to define the behavior. The interaction with a human being usually takes place via computer or Smartphone, which usually requires some knowledge of handling such devices. Smart TV systems menus provide access to services that require sailings not always intuitive menus. This makes people not related to new technologies, such as the sector of the elderly, and not able to enjoy access to online services. Projects like [7] propose the use of television as a tool to integrate people with reduced abilities, being the sole mechanism for the provision of services and obtaining information, without access to the monitoring of the person. On the other hand, the European project Monami proposes a comprehensive framework to provide services to elderly and disabled people, focusing on providing services to foster a more independent life style. However, it provides no information to Physicians or alarm systems.

3   Proposed Reasoning System

The system proposed in this paper combines the collection of data from distributed sensors in a home for a routine of a person and to detect any abnormalities caused by a problem. The system would permanently be connected to a medical center, which would receive an alert with the conditions given. Thus, a person would not require admission to a residence or the need for a 24/7 wizard. The doctor may communicate directly with the person to carry a medical control of it in real time. Furthermore, we propose the use of television as a method of two-way interaction, so that the person could receive information through it, as well as reminders on taking pills, and also may request certain services, such as an appointment with Physician, transport to the reserve day or a food menu. Communication with television posed by the remote control of television, taking advantage that it is a physical interface friendly and known for virtually all of the current population to full.

Agents and multi-agent systems have been successfully implemented in areas such as e-commerce, medicine, oceanography, robotics, etc. [15. 16, 18, 19, 20, 21, 22, 23, 24, 25, 26, 27, 28]. To perform the operation of the entire system, use of multi-agent architecture is PANGEA [10, 34], on which different organizations have been included in order to delegate responsibilities and facilitate the distribution and decentralization. This allows us to divide the system into a smaller, easier to maintain and to update sections. Fig. 1 shows the organization created, only the roles associated to the system not including PANGEA own account. As one can see it is the control that handles sensors monitor the sensor value changes and react to these organization. The agent communication is responsible for managing notifications, communication and user interaction with the system.

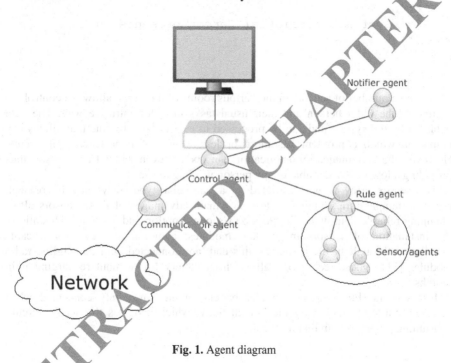

Fig. 1. Agent diagram

3.1   Sensor Control

On the one hand, the sensors are read by agents dedicated to them, making the readings periodically and storing the information. Each of these agents would monitor a sensor such that it can detect a failure in the reading or a change in value in the same. If this anomaly or change detected, you will notify the agent that plays the role of management rules, which apply an order based on the rules. These rules are grouped into a "library" that defines a typical daily activity plan. An example would be "If the bed sensor is active for more than eight hours, an alert is generated." To configure the Drools rules engine is used [8], which is a system for managing business rules (known in English as BRMS Business Rule Management System) with a rules engine based on forward chaining inference, using an object-oriented implementation of the Rete algorithm [9]. Thus, the semantics is exposed using the domain specific language (DSL). The re-icing are expressed by the Drools rule language, called DRL that allows you to embed Java code or MVEL for the implementation of the rules. It also supports the ability to write in EXCEL files. An example of a simple rule, with integrated Java code could be next:

```
rule "Presence"
    salience 100 // Importance of the rule on other
    when
        s : Presence()
    then
        System.out.println("Detect presence in the
room.");
end
```

Having a number of sensors in the various rooms of the house allows to control the routine of the older person and their usual tasks in a non-intrusive way. The data obtained by the system and can be processed to extract a set routine that allows key points on which a problem has more or less weight of importance if it occurs. However, the communication application can operate even without any sensor, thus providing a low-cost accessible to any person wishing to use.

The sensor array is not restricted to a particular type, they may be present, pressure, temperature, humidity, etc... The main advantages of these sensors allow obtaining reliable data with minimum power consumption and low cost. This allows the installation of sensors in wireless modules, avoiding the need for a cable installation throughout the home. To this end, are connected with the ZigBee radio modules [11], whose technology allows high battery life without recharging it in months.

PIR sensors (Fig. 2) allow greater battery saving since only consumed when detected emitted radiation by the human body, which activates the sensor circuit, consuming power only in that moment.

Fig. 2. Presence sensor PIR

Moreover, pressure sensors allow to obtain a reading of places where the person usually is, as for example in the bed, so that an activation of the sensor for more than X times could be a problem. A more detailed description about the sensor features can be seen in this previous work 12.

3.2   User Control Events

Moreover, the control agent role is in the computer connected to the TV and is in charge of collecting the throwing events the user through the remote control, in addition to displaying menus and alerts issued by the agents and notification rules (which manages periodic alerts or reminders). The Notification Agent is responsible for managing the user-programmed or assistant alerts, such as taking pills, when the doctor's appointment, etc.

The local exchange is a low cost computer and very low power consumption, so it just means a significant investment and saving the high costs of ongoing care of an elderly person. This unit only requires a power internet access and an HDMI connection to the TV (Fig. 3).

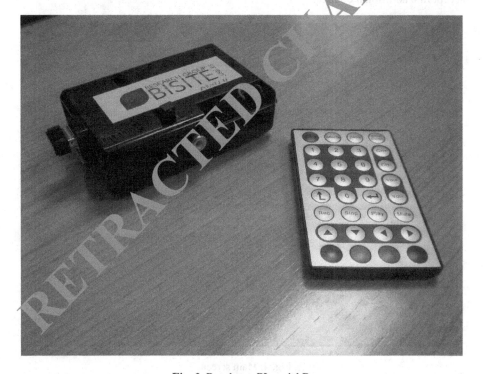

Fig. 3. Raspberry PI model B

The HDMI connection allows two-way communication device to the TV, making it unnecessary to use an additional command to access the available services. Also, the system is able to control the channel tuning, allowing the display off warnings even when the person is watching TV. These notifications would be monitor and reminded, making the automatic agenda. If you do not have a TV with HDMI connection, the system carries an infrared receiver that allows the mapping of the TV's remote, which recognizes recorded codes and would be associated with key management options. This protocol uses CEC (Consumer Electronics Control) which is supported by a variety of manufacturers. It allows the user to control and monitor up to ten CEC devices connected via HDMI using a single remote. The CEC protocol uses a single bidirectional wire serial bus for communication. As an example of important commands we have: to activate a device which is in standby status, playback control, tuning menus and other devices. Since the target audience to whom the purpose of this article is geared is mainly old people, it is intended the control system to be as simple and intuitive as possible. Thus, it is proposed to use only the colored buttons of the remotes, which allow the creation of graphical interfaces that can be associated immediately with the option to select. The entire system is designed with the aim that no more buttons are needed and they should be as simple as possible and also they should get rid off of unnecessary navigation between levels in menus.

If the TV does not have HDMI connection, the system carries an infrared receiver that will map the remote control codes, so it can also be used without the need to incorporate additional control.

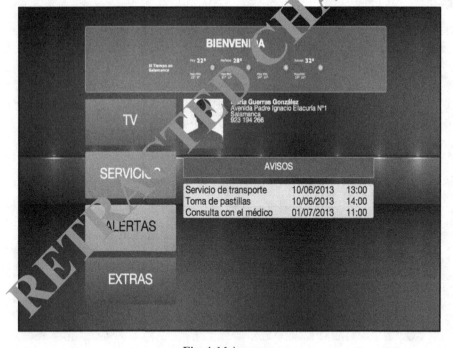

Fig. 4. Main screen

The communication interface consists only of the four colored buttons (red, green, yellow and blue) that provide specific functionality for each screen. The red button is associated in all cases with the "back" so that it becomes associated immediately. On the home screen, as it can be seen in Fig. 4, the main menu provides access to the offered services as well as viewing alerts or add-ons, which are rated with lower priority. Among the available services, one of the most important can automatically make an appointment with the doctor. The user simply selects the option, the system takes care of the hospital contact and booking appointment, getting the user both a visual confirmation by the monitor and a call phone. Similarly, according to the appointment date approaches, the user receives reminder alerts on your television character. This feature is especially geared to seniors who are in early stages of Alzheimer's disease.

Regardless of reminder alerts, you can schedule automatic alerts or even perform them manually, with the goal of achieving an active monitoring. Thus, you can control whether you have taken medication rightful, and get the answer that the user transmits through the remote control. This system is also used for the detection of alarms in the house itself, if the person has a sensor on the door to notify you when you leave it open, or fail sensor, which would first alert asking the user if you are alright. All management of alarm based on the value of the sensors is performed as indicated in Section 3.2. Failure to receive a response within a specified time, the system considers that the person is not able to reach the control, so it would launch a medical alert service.

4   Results and Conclusions

The obtained results with the system have shown that integration with older people has been completely successful. The use of colors when associating with the actions of the menus has allowed a very steep learning curve, and the combination of red button with the option to back the more easily accepted. On the other hand, access of older people to the possibility of requesting services instantly without the need of relying on a phone has enabled them to increase their sense of individualism and independence. The system of reminders for taking medication or transportation schedules doctor's appointment and avoid the need to constantly check the schedules, managing largely dispel the feeling of anxiety.

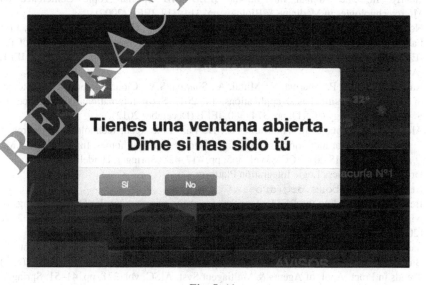

Fig. 5. Alert

Moreover, the use of low-cost devices allows installation in homes at an affordable price, being more relevant the cost of internet connection as the system itself. This allows the installation of a monitoring system for the elderly without the high cost of entry into a residence or a 24/7 assistant.

The rules engine allows to modify the behavior of agents at runtime without requiring the platform stopping for behavior modification. In future work, agents for the automatic learning will be added, allowing the detection of anomalous situations by implementing the function regarding the sensor values. Formerly already been done some research in this area [13].

Acknowledgments. Work partially supported by the Spanish Government through the project iHAS (grant TIN2012-36586-C03).

References

1. Tapia, E.M., Intille, S.S., Larson, K.: Activity recognition in the home using simple and ubiquitous sensors. In: Ferscha, A., Mattern, F. (eds.) PERVASIVE 2004. LNCS, vol. 3001, pp. 158–175. Springer, Heidelberg (2004)
2. Noury, N., Hervé, T., Rialle, V., Virone, G., Mercier, E., Morey, G., Porcheron, T.: Monitoring behavior in home using a smart fall sensor and position sensors. In: 1st Annual International Conference on Microtechnologies in Medicine and Biology, pp. 607–610. IEEE (2000)
3. Lymberopoulos, D., Bamis, A., Savvides, A.: Extracting spatiotemporal human activity patterns in assisted living using a home sensor network. Universal Access in the Information Society 10(2), 125–138 (2011)
4. Noury, N.: A smart sensor for the remote follow up of activity and fall detection of the elderly. In: 2nd Annual International IEEE-EMB Special Topic Conference on Microtechnologies in Medicine & Biology, pp. 314–317. IEEE (2002)
5. Noury, N., Fleury, A., Rumeau, P., Bourke, A.K., Laighin, G.O., Rialle, V., Lundy, J.E.: Fall detection-principles and methods. In: 29th Annual International Conference of the IEEE Engineering in Medicine and Biology Society, EMBS 2007, pp. 1663–1666. IEEE (August 2007)
6. Rao, B., Saluia, P., Sharma, N., Mittal, A., Sharma, S.V.: Cloud computing for Internet of Things & sensing based applications. In: 2012 Sixth International Conference on Sensing Technology (ICST), pp. 374–380. IEEE (December 2012)
7. Alonso, R.S., Tapia, D.I., Villarrubia, G., De Paz, J.F.: Agent technology and wireless sensor networks for monitoring patients in residences and their homes. In: Corchado, J.M., et al. (eds.) PAAMS 2013. CCIS, vol. 365, pp. 417–428. Springer, Heidelberg (2013)
8. Drools. The Business Logic Integration Platform, http://www.jboss.org/drools/
9. Berstel, B.: Extending the RETE algorithm for event management. In: On Proceedings of Ninth International Symposium on Temporal Representation and Reasoning, TIME 2002 (2002)
10. Sánchez, A., Villarrubia, G., Zato, C., Rodríguez, S., Chamoso, P.: A Gateway Protocol Based on FIPA-ACL for the New Agent Platform PANGEA. In: Pérez, J.B., et al. (eds.) Trends in Pract. Appl. of Agents & Multiagent Syst. AISC, vol. 221, pp. 41–51. Springer, Heidelberg (2013)

11. ZigBee Standards Organization: ZigBee Specification Document 053474r13. ZigBee Alliance (2006)
12. Alonso, R.S., Tapia, D.I., Bajo, J., García, Ó., de Paz, J.F., Corchado, J.M.: Implementing a hardware-embedded reactive agents platform based on a service-oriented architecture over heterogeneous wireless sensor networks 11(1), 151–166 (January 2013)
13. de Paz, J.F., Alonso, R.S., Tapia, D.I.: A Case-Based Planning Mechanism for a Hardware-Embedded Reactive Agents Platform. In: Casillas, J., Martínez-López, F.J., Corchado, J.M. (eds.) Management of Intelligent Systems. AISC, vol. 171, pp. 121–130. Springer, Heidelberg (2012)
14. Bajo, J., Corchado, J.M.: Evaluation and monitoring of the air-sea interaction using a CBR-agents approach. In: Muñoz-Ávila, H., Ricci, F. (eds.) ICCBR 2005. LNCS (LNAI), vol. 3620, pp. 50–62. Springer, Heidelberg (2005)
15. Bajo, J., De Paz, J.F., Rodríguez, S., González, A.: Multi-agent system to monitor oceanic environments. Integrated Computer-Aided Engineering 17(2), 131–144 (2010)
16. Borrajo, M.L., Baruque, B., Corchado, E., Bajo, J., Corchado, J.M.: Hybrid neural intelligent system to predict business failure in small-to-medium-size enterprises. International Journal of Neural Systems 21(04), 277–296 (2011)
17. Carneiro, D., Castillo, J., Novais, P., Fernández-Caballero, A., Neves, J.: Multimodal Behavioural Analysis for Non-invasive Stress Detection. Expert Systems With Applications 39(18), 13376–13389 (2012) ISSN: 0957-4174
18. Corchado, J.M., Aiken, J.: Hybrid artificial intelligence methods in oceanographic forecast models. IEEE Transactions on Systems, Man, and Cybernetics, Part C: Applications and Reviews 32(4), 307–313 (2002)
19. Corchado, J.M., De Paz, J.F., Rodríguez, S., Bajo, J.: Model of experts for decision support in the diagnosis of leukemia patients. Artificial Intelligence in Medicine 46(3), 179–200 (2009)
20. Corchado, J.M., Bajo, J., De Paz, J.F., Rodríguez, S.: An execution time neural-CBR guidance assistant. Neurocomputing 72(13), 2743–2753 (2009); De Paz, J.F., Rodríguez, S., Bajo, J., Corchado, J.: Case-based reasoning as a decision support system for cancer diagnosis: A case study. International Journal of Hybrid Intelligent Systems 6(2), 97–110 (2009)
21. Fdez-Riverola, F., Corchado, J.M.: CBR based system for forecasting red tides. Knowledge-Based Systems 16(5), 321–328 (2003)
22. Fraile, J.A., Bajo, J., Corchado, J.M., Abraham, A.: Applying wearable solutions in dependent environments. IEEE Transactions on Information Technology in Biomedicine 14(6), 1459–1467 (2011)
23. Garijo, F., Gomez-Sanz, J.J., Pavón, J., Massonet, P.: Multi-agent system organization: An engineering perspective. Pre-Proceeding of the 10th European Workshop on Modeling Autonomous Agents in a Multi-Agent World (MAAMAW 2001) (2001)
24. Griol, D., García-Herrero, J., Molina, J.M.: Combining heterogeneous inputs for the development of adaptive and multimodal interaction systems. Advances in Distributed Computing and Artificial Intelligence Journal
25. Pavon, J., Sansores, C., Gomez-Sanz, J.J.: Modelling and simulation of social systems with INGENIAS. International Journal of Agent-Oriented Software Engineering 2(2), 196–221 (2008)
26. Pinzón, C.I., Bajo, J., De Paz, J.F., Corchado, J.M.: S-MAS: An adaptive hierarchical distributed multi-agent architecture for blocking malicious SOAP messages within Web Services environments. Expert Systems with Applications 38(5), 5486–5499

27. Rodríguez, S., Pérez-Lancho, B., De Paz, J.F., Bajo, J., Corchado, J.M.: Ovamah: Multiagent-based adaptive virtual organizations. In: 12th International Conference on Information Fusion, FUSION 2009, pp. 990–997 (2009)
28. Rodríguez, S., de Paz, Y., Bajo, J., Corchado, J.M.: Social-based planning model for multiagent systems. Expert Systems with Applications 38(10), 13005–13023 (2011)
29. Sánchez-Pi, N., Carbó, J., Molina, J.M.: A Knowledge-Based System Approach for a Context-Aware System. Knowledge-Based Systems 27, 1–17 (2012)
30. Tapia, D.I., Alonso, R.S., De Paz, J.F., Corchado, J.M.: Introducing a distributed architecture for heterogeneous wireless sensor networks. In: Omatu, S., Rocha, M.P., Bravo, J., Fernández, F., Corchado, E., Bustillo, A., Corchado, J.M. (eds.) IWANN 2009, Part II. LNCS, vol. 5518, pp. 116–123. Springer, Heidelberg (2009)
31. Tapia, D.I., Abraham, A., Corchado, J.M., Alonso, R.S.: Agents and ambient intelligen case studies. Journal of Ambient Intelligence and Humanized Computing 1(2), 85–93 (2010)
32. Tapia, D.I., Rodríguez, S., Bajo, J., Corchado, J.M.: FUSION@, a SOA-based multi-agent architecture. In: International Symposium on Distributed Computing and Artificial Intelligence 2008 (DCAI 2008), pp. 99–107 (2008)
33. Tapia, D.I., Alonso, R.S., García, Ó., de la Prieta, F., Pérez-Lancho, B.: Cloud-IO: Cloud Computing Platform for the Fast Deployment of Services over Wireless Sensor Networks. In: Uden, L., Herrera, F., Bajo, J., Corchado, J.M. (eds.) 7th International Conference on KMO. AISC, vol. 172, pp. 493–504. Springer, Heidelberg (2013)
34. Zato, C., et al.: PANGEA – platform for automatic coNstruction of orGanizations of intElligent agents. In: Omatu, S., Paz Santana, J.F., González, S.R., Molina, J.M., Bernardos, A.M., Rodríguez, J.M.C. (eds.) Distributed Computing and Artificial Intelligence. AISC, vol. 151, pp. 229–240. Springer, Heidelberg (2012)

A Multi-Agent Approach to the Multi-Echelon Capacitated Vehicle Routing Problem

Paweł Sitek[1], Jarosław Wikarek[1], and Katarzyna Grzybowska[2]

[1] Kielce University of Technology, Institute of Management and Control Systems
{sitek,j.wikarek}@tu.kielce.pl
[2] Poznan University of Technology, Faculty of Engineering Management
katarzyna.grzybowska@put.poznan.pl

Abstract. The paper presents a concept and application of a multi-agent approach to modeling and optimization the Multi-Echelon Capacitated Vehicle Routing Problem. Two environments (mathematical programming (MP) and constraint logic programming (CLP)) and two types of agents were integrated. The strengths of MP and CLP, in which constraints are treated in a different way and different methods are implemented, were combined to use the strengths of both. The proposed approach is particularly important for the decision models with an objective function and many discrete decision variables added up in multiple constraints. The Two-Echelon Capacitated Vehicle Routing Problem (2E-CVRP) is an extension of the classical Capacitated Vehicle Routing Problem (CVRP) where the delivery depot-customers pass through intermediate depots (called satellites). Multi-echelon distribution systems are quite common in supply-chain and logistic systems. The presented multi-agent approach will be compared with classical mathematical programming on the same data sets.

Keywords: vehicle routing, multi-echelon systems, multi-agent, constraint logic programming, mathematical programming, optimization.

1 Introduction

The freight transportation and logistics industry are one of the sources of employment and supports the country's economic growth. In freight transportation there are two main distribution strategies: direct shipping and multi-echelon distribution. In the direct shipping, vehicles, starting from a depot, bring their freight directly to the destination, while in the multi-echelon systems, freight is delivered from the depot to the customers through intermediate.

In two-echelon distribution systems, freight is delivered to an intermediate depot and, from this depot, to the customers.

The majority of multi-echelon systems presented in the literature usually explicitly consider the routing problem at the last level of the transportation system, while a simplified routing problem is considered at higher levels [1].

In recent years multi-echelon systems have been introduced in different areas:

J.M. Corchado et al. (Eds.): PAAMS 2014 Workshops, CCIS 430, pp. 121–132, 2014.

- Logistics enterprises and express delivery service companies.
- Hypermarkets and supermarkets products distribution.
- Multimodal freight transportation and supply chains.
- E-commerce and home delivery services.
- City and public logistics.

The vast majority of models of decision support and/or optimization in freight transportation and logistics industry have been formulated as the mixed integer programming (MIP) or mixed integer linear programming (MILP) problems and solved using the operations research (OR) methods [2]. Their structures are similar and proceed from the principles and requirements of mathematical programming [2], [9].

Unfortunately, high complexity of decision-making models and their integer nature contribute to the poor efficiency of OR methods. Therefore a new approach to solving these problems was proposed. This approach relies on the logical and functional division into smaller areas and the application of different modeling and programming paradigms. As the best structure for the implementation of this approach, multi-agent systems were chosen [7], [18,19].

It seems that better results will be obtained by the use of the constraint programming paradigms (CP/CLP) especially in modeling. The CP-based environments have the advantage over traditional methods of mathematical modeling in that they work with a much broader variety of interrelated constraints and allow producing "natural" solutions for highly combinatorial problems. The CP/CLP environments have declarative nature [8], [11].

The main contribution of this paper is multi-agent approach (mixed CP with MP paradigms) to modeling and optimization Two-Echelon Capacitated Vehicle Routing Problem (2E-CVRP) or the similar problems. In addition, some extensions and modifications to the standard 2E-CVRP are presented.

The paper is organized as follows. In Section 2 the literature related to Multi-Echelon Vehicle Routing Problems has been reviewed. Next section is about our motivation and contribution. In Section 4 the concept of multi-agent approach to modeling and solving, and the multi-agent solution framework have been presented. Then, the general description of Multi-Echelon Vehicle Routing Problems and mathematical model of 2E-CVRP has been discussed. Finally test instances for 2E-CVRP and some computational results were discussed in Section 6.

2   Literature Review

The Vehicle Routing Problem (VRP) is used to design an optimal route for a fleet of vehicles to service a set of customers' orders (known in advance), given a set of constraints. The VRP is used in supply chain management in the physical delivery of goods and services. The VRP is of the NP-hard type.

Nowadays, the VRP literature offers a wealth of heuristic and metaheuristic approaches, which are surveyed in the papers of [3,4] because exact VRP methods have a size limit of 50 – 100 orders depending on the VRP variant and the time-response requirements.

There are several variants and classes of VRP like the capacitated VRP (CVRP), VRP with Time Windows (VRPTW) and Dynamic Vehicle Routing Problems (DVRP), sometimes referred to as On-line Vehicle Routing Problems etc. [3].

Different distribution strategies are used in freight transportation. The most developed strategy is based on the direct shipping: freight starts from a depot and arrives directly to customers. In many applications and real situations, this strategy is not the best one and the usage of a multi-echelon and particular two-echelon distribution system can optimize several features as the number of the vehicles, the transportation costs, loading factor and timing.

In the literature the multi-echelon system, and the two-echelon system in particular, refer mainly to supply chain and inventory problems [1]. These problems do not use an explicit routing approach for the different levels, focusing more on the production and supply chain management issues. The first real application of a two-tier distribution network optimizing the global transportation costs is due to [12] and is related to the city logistics area. They developed a two-tier freight distribution system for congested urban areas, using small intermediate platforms, called satellites (intermediate points for the freight distribution). This system is developed for a specific situation and a generalization of such a system has not already been formulated. The complete mathematic model of 2E-CVRP with the solution for sample test data in the classical approach has been proposed by [4], complemented with the method for boosting the computing efficiency (see Section 5).

3   Motivation and Contribution

Based on [2,3,4,5,6], [11] and our previous work [8,9,10] we observed some advantages and disadvantages of both (CP/MP) paradigms.

An integrated approach of constraint programming/constraint logic programming (CP/CLP) and mixed integer programming/mixed integer linear programming (MIP/MILP) can help to solve optimization problems that are intractable with either of the two methods alone [13,14,15]. Although Operations Research (OR) and Constraint Programming (CP) have different roots, the links between the two environments have grown stronger in recent years.

Both MIP/MILP and finite domain CP/CLP involve variables and constraints. However, the types of the variables and constraints that are used, and the way the constraints are solved, are different in the two approaches [13,15].

MIP/MILP relies completely on linear equations and inequalities in integer variables, i.e., there are only two types of constraints: linear arithmetic (linear equations or inequalities) and integrity (stating that the variables have to take their values in the integer numbers). In finite domain CP/CLP, the constraint language is richer. In addition to linear equations and inequalities, there are various other constraints: disequalities, nonlinear, symbolic (*alldifferent, disjunctive, cumulative* etc). In both MIP/MILP and CP/CLP, there is a group of constraints that can be solved with ease and a group of constraints that are difficult to solve. The easily solved constraints in MIP/MILP are linear equations and inequalities over rational numbers.

Integrity constraints are difficult to solve using mathematical programming methods and often the real problems of MIP/MILP make them NP-hard.

In CP/CLP, domain constraints with integers and equations between two variables are easy to solve. The system of such constraints can be solved over integer variables in polynomial time. The inequalities between two variables, general linear constraints (more than two variables), and symbolic constraints are difficult to solve, which makes real problems in CP/CLP NP-hard. This type of constraints reduces the strength of constraint propagation. As a result, CP/CLP is incapable of finding even the first feasible solution.

Both environments use various layers of the problem (methods, the structure of the problem, data) in different ways. The approach based on mathematical programming (MIP/MILP) focuses mainly on the methods of optimization and, to a lesser degree, on the structure of the problem. However, the data is completely outside the model. The same model without any changes can be solved for multiple instances of data. In the approach based on constraint programming (CP/CLP), due to its declarative nature, the methods are already built-in. The data and structure of the problem are used for its modelling in a significantly greater extent.

To use so much different environments and a variety of functionalities such as modeling, optimization, transformation, etc., the multi-agent approach was adopted.

The motivation and contribution behind this work was to create a multi-agent method for constrained decision problems modelling and optimization instead of using mathematical programming or constraint programming separately.

It follows from the above that what is difficult to solve in one environment can be easy to solve in the other.

Moreover, such a multi-agent approach allows the use of all layers of the problem to solve it.

In our approach to modelling and optimization these problems we proposed the environment, where:

- Knowledge related to the problem can be expressed as linear, logical and symbolic constraints;
- The decision models solved using the proposed approach can be formulated as a pure model of MIP/MILP or of CP/CLP, or it can also be a hybrid model;
- The problem is modelled in the constraint programming environment by CLP-based agents, which is far more flexible than the mathematical programming environment;
- Transforming the decision model to explore its structure has been introduced by CLP-agents;
- Constrained domains of decision variables, new constraints and values for some variables are transferred from CP/CLP into MILP/MIP/IP by CLP-agents;
- Merging and final generation of the model is performed by MILP-based agents;
- Optimization is performed by MILP-based agents.

As a result, a more effective multi-agent solution environment for a certain class of decision and optimization problems (2E-CVRP or similar) was obtained.

4   Multi-Agent Solution Framework (MASF)

Both environments have advantages and disadvantages. Environments based on the constraints such as CLPs are declarative and ensure a very simple modeling of decision problems, even those with poor structures if any. In the CLP a problem is described by a set of logical predicates. The constraints can be of different types (linear, non-linear, logical, binary, etc.). The CLP does not require any search algorithms. This feature is characteristic of all declarative backgrounds, in which modeling of the problem is also a solution, just as it is in Prolog, SQL, etc. The CLP seems perfect for modeling any decision problem.

Numerous MP models of decision-making have been developed and tested, particularly in the area of decision optimization. Constantly improved methods and mathematical programming algorithms, such as the simplex algorithm, branch and bound, branch-and-cost etc., have become classics now [2].

The proposed method's strength lies in high efficiency of optimization algorithms and a substantial number of tested models. Traditional methods when used alone to solve complex problems provide unsatisfactory results. This is related directly to different treatment of variables and constraints in those approaches (Section 3).

This schema of the Multi-Agent Solution Framework (MASF) and the concept of this framework with its agents (A1..A5, AG) is presented in Fig. 1. The names and descriptions of the agents and the implementation environment are shown in Table 1.

Table 1. Description of agents

Agent	Description
A1 CLP environment	The implementation of the model in CLP, the term representation of the problem in the form of predicates.
A2 CLP environment	The transformation of the original problem aimed at extending the scope of constraint propagation. The transformation uses the structure of the problem. The most common effect is a change in the representation of the problem by reducing the number of decision variables, and the introduction of additional constraints and variables, changing the nature of the variables, etc.
A3 CLP environment	Constraint propagation for the model. Constraint propagation is one of the basic methods of CLP. As a result, the variable domains are narrowed, and in some cases, the values of variables are set, or even the solution can be found.
AG CLP environment	Generation by the AG: • The model for mathematical programming. Generation performed automatically using CLP predicate; • Additional constraints on the basis of the results obtained by agent A3; • Domains for different decision variables and other parameters based on the propagation of constraints. Transmission of this information in the form of fixed value of certain variables and/or additional constraints to the MP.
A4 MILP environment	Merging files generated by agent AG into one file. It is a model file format in MILP system.
A5 MILP environment	The solution of the model from the previous stage by MILP solver. Generation of the report with the results and parameters of the solution.

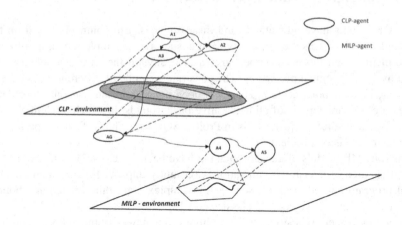

Fig. 1. The scheme of the Multi-Agent Solution Framework (MASF)

5   Two-Echelon Capacitated Vehicle Routing Problem

The Two-Echelon Capacitated Vehicle Routing Problem (2E-CVRP) is an extension of the classical Capacitated Vehicle Routing Problem (CVRP) where the delivery depot-customers pass through intermediate depots (called satellites). As in CVRP, the goal is to deliver goods to customers with known demands, minimizing the total delivery cost in the respect of vehicle capacity constraints. Multi-echelon systems presented in the literature usually explicitly consider the routing problem at the last level of the transportation system, while a simplified routing problem is considered at higher levels [4], [12].

In 2E-CVRP, the freight delivery from the depot to the customers is managed by shipping the freight through intermediate depots. Thus, the transportation network is decomposed into two levels (Fig. 2): the 1st level connecting the depot (d) to intermediate depots (s) and the 2nd one connecting the intermediate depots (s) to the customers (c). The objective is to minimize the total transportation cost of the vehicles involved in both levels. Constraints on the maximum capacity of the vehicles and the intermediate depots are considered, while the timing of the deliveries is ignored.

From a practical point of view, a 2E-CVRP system operates as follows (Fig. 2):

- Freight arrives at an external/first/base zone, the depot, where it is consolidated into the 1st-level vehicles, unless it is already carried into a fully-loaded 1st-level vehicles;
- Each 1st-level vehicle travels to a subset of satellites that will be determined by the model and then it will return to the depot;
- At a satellite, freight is transferred from 1st-level vehicles to 2nd-level vehicles.

The formal mathematical model (MILP) was taken from [4]. Table 2 shows the parameters and decision variables of 2E-CVRP. Figure 2 shows an example of the 2E-CVRP - transportation network for this model.

Table 2. Summary indices, parameters and decision variables

Symbol	Description
	Indices
n_s	Number of satellites
n_c	Number of customers
$V_0 = \{v_o\}$	Deport
$V_s = \{v_{s1}, v_{s2}, v_{s3}, \ldots v_{sn_s}\}$	Set of satellites
$V_c = \{v_{c1}, v_{c2}, v_{c3}, \ldots v_{cn_c}\}$	Set of customers
	Parameters
M_1	Number of the 1st-level satellites
M_2	Number of the 2nd-level satellites
K_1	Capacity of the vehicles for the 1st level
K_2	Capacity of the vehicles for the 2nd level
d_i	Demand required by customer i
$c_{i,j}$	Cost of the *arc (i,j)*
s_k	Cost of loading/unloading operations of a unit of freight in satellite k
	Decision variables
$X_{i,j}$	An integer variable of the 1st-level routing is equal to the number of 1st-level vehicles using *arc (i,j)*
$Y_{k,i,j}$	A binary variable of the 2nd-level routing is equal to 1 if a 2nd-level vehicle makes a route starting from satellite k and goes from node i to node j and 0 otherwise
$Q_{i,j}^1$	The freight flow *arc (i,j)* for the 1st-level
$Q_{k,i,j}^2$	The freight *arc (i,j)* where k represents the satellite where the freight is passing through.
$z_{k,j}$	A binary variable that is equal to 1 if the freight to be delivered to customer j is consolidated in satellite k and 0 otherwise

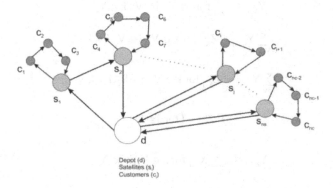

Fig. 2. Example of 2E-CVRP transportation network

$$\min \sum_{i,j \in V_0 \cup V_s} (c_{i,j} \cdot X_{i,j}) + \sum_{k \in V_s} \sum_{i,j \in V_s \cup V_c} (c_{i,j} \cdot Y_{k,i,j}) + \sum_{k \in V_s} (s_k \cdot Ds_k) \tag{1}$$

$$\sum_{i \in V_s} X_{0,i} \le M_1 \tag{2}$$

$$\sum_{j \in V_s \cup V_0, j \ne k} X_{j,k} = \sum_{i \in V_s \cup V_0, i \ne k} X_{k,i} \text{ for } k \in V_s \cup V_0 \tag{3}$$

$$\sum_{k \in V_s} \sum_{j \in V_c} Y_{k,k,j} \le M_2 \tag{4}$$

$$\sum_{i \in V_c, j \in V_c} Y_{k,i,j} = \sum_{i \in V_c, j \in V_c} Y_{k,j,i} \text{ for } k \in V_s \tag{5}$$

$$\sum_{i \in V_0 \cup V_s, i \ne j} Q^1_{i,j} - \sum_{i \in V_s, i \ne j} Q^1_{j,i} = \begin{cases} Ds_j & j \text{ is not the deport} \\ \sum_{i \in V_c} -d_i & \text{otherwise} \end{cases} \text{ for } j \in V_s \cup V_0 \tag{6}$$

$$Q^1_{i,j} \le k_1 \cdot X_{i,j} \text{ for } i,j \in V_s \cup V_0, i \ne j \tag{7}$$

$$\sum_{i \in V_s \cup V_c, i \ne j} Q^2_{k,i,j} - \sum_{i \in V_c, i \ne j} Q^2_{k,j,i} = \begin{cases} Z_{k,j} d_j & j \text{ is not a satelite} \\ -D_j & \text{otherwise} \end{cases} \text{ for } j \in V_c \cup V_s, k \in V_s \tag{8}$$

$$Q^2_{k,i,j} \le k_2 \cdot Y_{k,i,j} \text{ for } i,j \in V_s \cup V_c, i \ne j, k \in V_s \tag{9}$$

$$\sum_{i \in V_s} Q^1_{i,V_0} = 0 \tag{10}$$

$$\sum_{j \in V_c} Q^2_{k,j,k} = 0 \text{ for } k \in V_s \tag{11}$$

$$Y_{k,i,j} \le Z_{k,j} \text{ for } i \in V_s \cup V_c, j \in V_c, k \in V_s \tag{12}$$

$$Y_{k,j,i} \le Z_{k,j} \text{ for } i \in V_s, j \in V_c, k \in V_s \tag{13}$$

$$\sum_{i \in V_s \cup V_c} Y_{k,i,j} = Z_{k,j} \text{ for } k \in V_s, j \in V_c, i \ne k \tag{14}$$

$$\sum_{i \in V_s} Y_{k,j,k} = Z_{k,j} \text{ for } k \in V_s, j \in V_c, i \ne k \tag{15}$$

$$\sum_{i \in V_s} Z_{i,j} = 1 \text{ for } j \in V_c \tag{16}$$

$$Y_{k,i,j} \le \sum_{l \in V_s \cup V_0} X_{k,l} \text{ for } k \in V_s, i,j \in V_c \tag{17}$$

$$Y_{k,i,j} \in \{0,1\}, Z_{k,l} \in \{0,1\} \text{ for } k \in V_s, i,j \in V_s \cup V_c, l \in V_c \tag{18}$$

$$X_{k,j} \in Z^+ \text{ for } k, j \in V_s \cup V_0 \tag{19}$$

$$Q^1_{i,j} \geq 0 \text{ for } i, j \in V_s \cup V_0; Q^2_{k,i,j} \geq 0 \text{ for } i, j \in V_s \cup V_c, k \in V_s \tag{20}$$

$$\sum_{i,j \in S_c} Y_{k,i,j} \leq |S_c| - 1 \text{ for } S_c \subset V_c, 2 \leq |S_c| \leq |V_c| - 2 \tag{21}$$

$$Q^2_{k,i,j} \leq (k_2 - d_j) \cdot Y_{k,i,j} \text{ for } i, j \in V_c, k \in V_s \tag{22}$$

$$Q^2_{k,i,j} - \sum_{l \in V_s} Q^2_{k,j,l} \leq (k_2 - d_j) \cdot Y_{k,i,j} \text{ for } i, j \in V_c, k \in V_s \tag{23}$$

$$Ds_k = \sum_{l \in V_c} (d_j \cdot Z_{k,j}) \text{ for } k \in V_s \tag{24}$$

The objective function minimizes the sum of the routing and handling operations costs. Constraints (3) ensure, for $k = V_0$, that each 1st-level route begins and ends at the depot, while when k is a satellite, impose the balance of vehicles entering and leaving that satellite. Constraints (5) force each 2nd-level route to begin and end to one satellite and the balance of vehicles entering and leaving each customer. The number of the routes in each level must not exceed the number of vehicles for that level, as imposed by constraints (2) and (4). The flows balance on each network node is equal to the demand of this node, except for the depot, where the exit flow is equal to the total demand of the customers, and for the satellites at the 2nd-level, where the flow is equal to the demand (unknown) assigned to the satellites which provide constraints (6) and (8). Moreover, constraints (6) and (8) forbid the presence of sub-tours not containing the depot or a satellite, respectively. In fact, each node receives an amount of flow equal to its demand, preventing the presence of sub-tours. Consider, for example, that a sub-tour is present between the nodes i, j and k at the 1st level. It is easy to check that, in such a case, does not exist any value for the variables $Q^1_{i,j}, Q^1_{j,k}$, and $Q^1_{k,i}$, satisfying the constraints (6) and (8). The capacity constraints are formulated in (7) and (9), for the 1st-level and the 2nd-level, respectively. Constraints (10) and (11) do not allow residual flows in the routes, making the returning flow of each route to the depot (1st-level) and to each satellite (2nd-level) equal to 0. Constraints (12) and (13) indicate that a customer j is served by a satellite k ($Z_{k,j} = 1$) only if it receives freight from that satellite ($Y_{k,i,j} = 1$). Constraint (16) assigns each customer to one and only one satellite, while constraints (14) and (15) indicate that there is only one 2nd-level route passing through each customer and connect the two levels. Constraints (17) allow to start a 2nd-level route from a satellite k only if a 1st-level route has served it. Constraints from 17 to 20 result from the character of the MILP-formulated problem. Additional constraints were introduced by [4] to increase the solution search efficiency. They strengthen the continuous relaxation of the flow model. In particular, authors in [4] used two families of cuts, one applied to the assignment variables derived from the sub-tour elimination constraints (edge cuts) and the other based on the flows. The edge-cuts explicitly introduce the well-known sub-tours elimination constraints derived from the TSP (Traveling Sales Problem). They can be expressed as constraints (21). The inequalities explicitly forbid the presence in the solution of sub-tours not containing the depot, already forbidden by the constraints (8). The number of potential valid inequalities are exponential, so that each customer reduces the flow of an amount equal to its demand d_i –constraints (22) and (23).

A possibility to transform the model by the CLP-based agent (A2) is an important aspect of that approach. The our transformation of this model in this approach focused on the resizing of $Y_{k,i,j}$ decision variable by introducing additional imaginary volume of freight shipped from the satellite and re-delivered to it. Such transformation resulted in two facts. First of all, it forced the vehicle to return to the satellite from which it started its trip. Secondly, it reduced decision variable $Y_{k,i,j}$ to variable $Y_{i,j}$ which decreased the size of the combinatorial problem.

6   Computational Tests – Two-Echelon Capacitated Vehicle Routing Problem

For the final validation of the proposed multi-agent approach, the benchmark data for 2E-CVRP was selected. 2E-CVRP, a well described and widely discussed problem, corresponded to the issues to which our approach was applied.

The instances for computational examples were built from the existing instances for CVRP [16] denoted as E-n13-k4. All the instance sets can be downloaded from the website [17]. The instance set was composed of 5 small-sized instances with 1 depot, 12 customers and 2 satellites. The full instance consisted of 66 small-sized instances because the two satellites were placed over twelve customers in all 66 possible ways (number of combinations: 2 out of 12). All the instances had the same position for depot and customers, whose coordinates were the same as those of instance E-n13-k4. Small-sized instances differed in the choice of two customers who were also satellites (En13-k4-4, En13-k4-5, En13-k4-6, En13-k4-12, etc.).

Numerical experiments were conducted for the same data in three runs. The first run was a classical implementation of model (1)..(20) and its solution in the MILP environment (E1). The second run used the same environment for model (1)..(24) with additional edge-cuts (E2). In the final run the model (1)..(20) and its solution were implemented in the proposed multi-agent solution framework (E3). The calculations were performed using a computer with the following specifications: Intel(R) Core(TM) 2, 2x 2,40GHZ RAM 1,98 GB. The analysis of the results for the benchmark instances demonstrates that the multi-agent approach may be a superior approach to the classical mathematical programming. For all examples, the solutions were found 4–16 times faster than they are in the classical approach (Table 3). In many cases the calculations ended after 600 s as they failed to indicate that the solution was optimal. Number of constraints (C) and decision variables/integer (V /int V) was for examples E1, E2, E3, respectively C=1262, V=744/368 for E1, C=1982 , V=744 /368 for E2 and C=21, V=1082/1079 for E3.

Table 3. The results of numerical examples for 2E-CVRP

E-n13-k4	MASF (E3)		MILP+Edge-Cuts (E2)		MILP (E1)	
	T	Fc	T	Fc	T	Fc
E-n13-k4-04	10,09	218	44	218	65	218
E-n13-k4-05	9,58	218	48	218	108	218
E-n13-k4-06	11,05	230	78	230	154	230
E-n13-k4-11	19,91	276	159	276	600*	276
E-n13-k4-12	24,38	290	600*	290	600*	290
E-n13-k4-13	18,14	288	600*	288	600*	288
E-n13-k4-22	9,97	312	600*	312	600*	312
E-n13-k4-61	12,20	338	600*	338	600*	338
E-n13-k4-66	11,91	400	600*	400	600*	400

*calculations stopped after 600 s, the feasible value of the objective function
Fc   the optimal value of the objective function
T   time of finding solution

As the presented example was formulated as a MILP problem, the MASF was tested for the solution efficiency. Owing to the multi-agent approach the 2E-CVRP models can be extended over logical, nonlinear, and other constraints. At the next stage logical constraints were introduced into the model. The logical relationship between mutually exclusive variables was taken into account, which in real-world distribution systems means that the same vehicle cannot transport two types of selected goods or two points cannot be handled at the same time. Those constraints result from technological, marketing, sales or safety reasons. Only declarative application environments based on constraint satisfaction problem (CSP) make it possible to implement constraints such as. Table 4 presents the results of the numerical experiments conducted for 2E-CVRPs with logical constraints relating to the situation where two delivery points (customers) can be handled separately but not together in one route.

Table 4. The results of numerical examples for 2E-CVRP with logical constraints

E-n13-k4	Fc	T	C	V	exCustomer*
E-n13-k4-04	248	12,09	21	774(771)	1,2; 1,3; 1,6; 2,7; 2,8; 2,9
E-n13-k4-12	294	25,34	21	774(771)	1,2; 1,3; 1,6; 2,7; 2,8; 2,9
E-n13-k4-32	276	12,23	21	774(771)	1,2; 1,3; 1,6; 2,7; 2,8; 2,9
E-n13-k4-66	426	43,43	21	774(771)	1,2; 1,3; 1,6; 2,7; 2,8; 2,9

* pairs of customers that cannot be served on one route

7   Conclusion and Discussion on Possible Extension

The efficiency of the proposed approach is based on the reduction of the combinatorial problem and using the best properties of both environments. The multi-agent approach (Table 3, Table 4) makes it possible to find solutions in the shorter time.

In addition to solving larger problems faster, the proposed approach provides virtually unlimited modeling options with many types of constraints. Therefore, the proposed solution is recommended for decision-making problems that have a structure similar to the presented models (Section 5). This structure is characterized by the constraints and objective function in which the decision variables are added together. Further work will focus on running the optimization models with non-linear and other logical constraints, multi-objective, uncertainty etc. in the multi-agent optimization framework. The planed experiments will employ MASF for Two-Echelon Capacitated VRP with Time Windows, Two-Echelon Capacitated VRP with Satellites Synchronization and 2E-CVRP with Pickup and Deliveries.

References

1. Verrijdt, J., de Kok, A.: Distribution planning for a divergent n-echelon network without intermediate stocks under service restrictions. International Journal of Production Economics 38, 225–243 (1995)
2. Schrijver, A.: Theory of Linear and Integer Programming. John Wiley & Sons (1998)
3. Kumar, S., Panneerselvam, R.: Survey on the Vehicle Routing Problem and Its Variants. Intelligent Information Management 4, 66–74 (2012)
4. Perboli, G., Tadei, R., Vigo, D.: The Two-Echelon Capacitated Vehicle Routing Problem: Models and Math-Based Heuristics. Transportation Science 45, 364–380 (2012)
5. Bocewicz, G., Banaszak, Z.: Declarative approach to cyclic steady states space refinement: periodic processes scheduling. International Journal of Advanced Manufacturing Technology 67(1-4), 137–155 (2013)
6. Relich, M.: Project prototyping with application of CP-based approach. Management 15(2), 364–377 (2011)
7. Barbati, M., Bruno, G., Genovese, A.: Applications of agent-based models for optimization problems: A literature review. Expert Systems with Applications 39, 6020–6028 (2012)
8. Sitek, P., Wikarek, J.: A Declarative Framework for Constrained Search Problems. In: Nguyen, N.T., Borzemski, L., Grzech, A., Ali, M. (eds.) IEA/AIE 2008. LNCS (LNAI), vol. 5027, pp. 728–737. Springer, Heidelberg (2008)
9. Sitek, P., Wikarek, J.: Cost optimization of supply chain with multimodal transport. In: Federated Conference on Computer Science and Information Systems (FedCSIS), pp. 1111–1118 (2012)
10. Sitek, P., Wikarek, J.: A hybrid approach to supply chain modeling and optimization. In: Federated Conference on Computer Science and Information Systems, pp. 1223–1230 (2013)
11. Apt, K., Wallace, M.: Constraint Logic Programming using Eclipse. Cambridge University Press (2006)
12. Crainic, T., Ricciardi, N., Storchi, G.: Advanced freight transportation systems for congested urban areas. Transportation Research Part C 12, 119–137 (2004)
13. Jain, V., Grossmann, I.E.: Algorithms for hybrid MILP/CP models for a class of optimization problems. INFORMS Journal on Computing 13(4), 258–276 (2001)
14. Milano, M., Wallace, M.: Integrating Operations Research in Constraint Programming. Annals of Operations Research 175(1), 37–76 (2010)
15. Achterberg, T., Berthold, T., Koch, T., Wolter, K.: Constraint Integer Programming: A New Approach to Integrate CP and MIP. In: Trick, M.A. (ed.) CPAIOR 2008. LNCS, vol. 5015, pp. 6–20. Springer, Heidelberg (2008)
16. Christofides, N., Elion, S.: An algorithm for the vehicle dispatching problem. Operational Research Quarterly 20, 309–318 (1996)
17. ORO Group Web-page, http://www.orgroup.polito.it/
18. Grzybowska, K., Kovács, G.: Developing Agile Supply Chains - system model, algorithms, applications. In: Jezic, G., Kusek, M., Nguyen, N.-T., Howlett, R.J., Jain, L.C. (eds.) KES-AMSTA 2012. LNCS, vol. 7327, pp. 576–585. Springer, Heidelberg (2012)
19. Pawlewski, P.: Situated MAS Approach for Freight Trains Assembly. In: Corchado, J.M., et al. (eds.) PAAMS 2013. CCIS, vol. 365, pp. 106–117. Springer, Heidelberg (2013)

Mixing ABS and DES Approach to Modeling of a Delivery Process in the Automotive Industry

Jakub Borucki, Pawel Pawlewski, and Wojciech Chowanski

Poznan University of Technology
jakub.borucki@doctorate.put.poznan.pl,
pawel.pawlewski@put.poznan.pl,
wojciech.chowanski@student.put.poznan.pl

Abstract. Today in the automotive industry, reconfigurability, flexibility and high availability are as important as the level of automation, cost effectiveness, and maximum throughput. In this paper two main delivery strategies (JIT – Just in Time, JIS – Just in Sequence) in the automotive industry are presented and two approaches to modeling and to simulate that strategies are described (DES - Discrete-Event and ABS - Agent-Based Simulation). Authors discuss that DES approach to JIS strategy is insufficient and propose to mixing DES and ABS in simulation of delivery processes in the automotive. The case study of proposed solutonion is described.

Keywords: agent based modeling, simulation, manufacturing.

1   Introduction

Car manufacturers are constantly competing for customers, offering vehicles in an increasing number of variants. This applies to personal cars as well as delivery trucks. Therefore, a concept of "built-to-order" has been developed, with the effect that practically every vehicle on the assembly line is different. It is assumed that the average car consists of 35,000 parts. Delivery trucks are usually offered in tens variants of bodybuilding, whereas personal cars, occur in up to four different bodies. Quoted market conditions are forcing manufacturers to use effective tools for organization and supervision of processes in the supply chain. One such tool is the JIT (Just In Time) strategy and its sequential option JIS (Just In Sequence) [3].

Main delivery strategies in automotive industry are:

- Classic model of inventories based on information level of stock.
- Supermarket with baskets filled with parts from warehouse.
- JIT – where production system call demand (based on Kanban method) for delivery and this is realized in precisely time and quantity. This is used to a recurrent parts.
- JIS – where means of transport are controlled by computer system and parts are delivered with the same order as cars are assembled on the line. Deliveries is also realized in precisely time [10].

With such an sophisticated process with a high variability, tools such as a spreadsheet are insufficient, therefore decided to use the simulation.

J.M. Corchado et al. (Eds.): PAAMS 2014 Workshops, CCIS 430, pp. 133–143, 2014.
© Springer International Publishing Switzerland 2014

The main objective of this paper is present to combine two approaches to simulation of different delivery processes – JIT and JIS. All of an assembly activities on the assembly line are realized with using a process approach and reflected in the simulation using DES. Highlights are:

- Present the differences between JIT and JIS.
- Demonstrate that the DES (discrete-event simulation) method is insufficient to modeling all parts of delivery process.
- Identify areas where ABS is more appropriate, mixing that methods and identify points of interaction with DES.

This paper is organized as follow: in section 2 the main features and differences between JIT and JIS are described. Section 3 presents modeling techniques (DES and ABS) of delivery strategies (JIT and JIS). Case study with application of mixing simulation techniques are included in section 4. Finally, conclusions are stated in section 5.

2   Discussion of JIT and JIS Features

In the automotive industry distinguishes a few kind of deliveries. In the last years two main were elaborated: JIT and JIS. JIT strategy was developed by Toyota within TPS – Toyota Production System [5]. It is used with a moving assembly line (invented by Ford) and mainly relates to the repetitive parts. Deliveries are realized with use the Kanban technique, which consists in the fact that in the assembly point there is a buffer which contains the same repetitive parts. The installer collects parts and when a level of them falls below a predetermined level, demand on delivery to the same buffer is generated, using Kanban card. This method is consistent with the process approach. The process to realize, demands resource (specified parts to assembly). This resource is in the buffer and if this is available, process is realized without disruptions. Otherwise the process is stopped. Availability of the resource (part for assembly) provides delivery process which is called when level of buffer is low. Delivery must be realized at such time that the buffer is not empty.

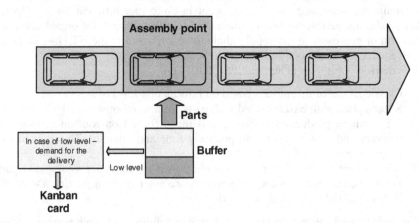

Fig. 1. Assembly and delivery of repetitive parts with JIS using Kanban card

Practically every vehicle on the assembly line is different. For example there are 20 types of the wing mirrors. In a sequence of cars on the assembly line, mirrors ate not repeated. If we would like to apply JIT, we would have 20 buffers. In practice, there is not enough place nearby assembly line and that solution is impossible to realize. To solve this problem, Just in Sequence was developed [3].

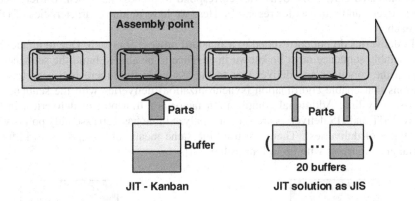

Fig. 2. JIT solution as JIS with a huge number of buffers

Parts in the transport container are placed with the same order as cars are assembled on the line. This order must be known much earlier to prepare the sequence of parts in the container and deliver to the assembly line. Containers are built in the building sequences container area which is usually away from the assembly plant about a few hundred meters to a few/over a dozen kilometers.

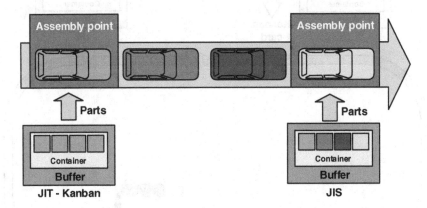

Fig. 3. JIS solution with sequence container

3   Simulation Modeling of JIT and JIS

DES (Discrete-Event Simulation) has been the main way for the process simulation of manufacturing and logistics for about four decades. This is adequate for problems that consist of queuing simulations and a variability is represented through stochastic distributions [9]. This approach is applicable in simulate of manufacturing and supply chain processes. DES models are characterized by [9] a process oriented approach. They are based on a top-down modeling approach and have one centralized control point.

As indicated earlier JIT deliveries correspond to process approach. Buffers occur here as queue and requests for resources. Here we have unique characteristics of DES approach.

JIS deliveries do not correspond to a standard process approach. Due to a fact, that the assembly sequence must be known in advance to be able to build the sequence of parts in the container and deliver that to the assembly line, there is a need to seek solutions that enable coordination (synchronization) deliveries with the sequence in the assembly line. Additional complication factor is a transport of deliveries. In the Figure 3 JIT and JIS deliveries are shown (analyzed line has 126 assembly points with both types of deliveries). There are used the same means of transport – forklifts or special electric trains with up to four trolleys [4].

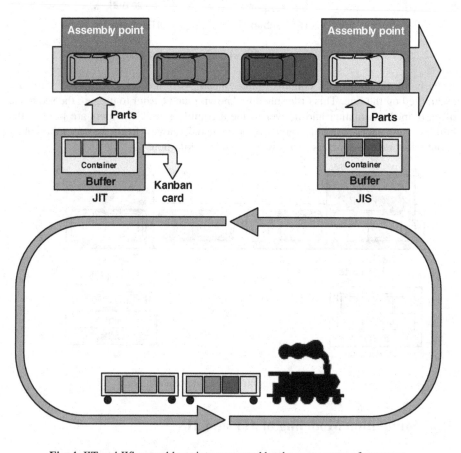

Fig. 4. JIT and JIS assembly points supported by the same mean of transport

The system defined in that way, require decision-making center which decides when and what is to be transported. The means of transport should have the ability to realization a task list, because it can be used to carry different amounts of deliveries in the different placements. To model such a complex system, the traditional process approach is insufficient. In the literature can be found proposals modeling decision-making approach using ABS. ABS modeling seems to be also useful for modeling of vehicles, which have their own "intelligence", where the intelligence means the ability to complete changeable task lists. In this case means of transport must have the ability to receive and send messages to the adoption of a task list, send a message about the execution or termination of realization the task list. In the literature this approach is also referred to Task Driven [1].

ABS is a simulation technique that models the overall behavior of a system through use of autonomous system components (also referred to as agents) that communicate with each other by using [8]. The behavior incorporated into an agent determines its role in the environment, its interaction with other agents, its response to messages from other agents, and indeed whether its own behavior is adaptable [6]. These dependencies are reflected in Figure 5 [7].

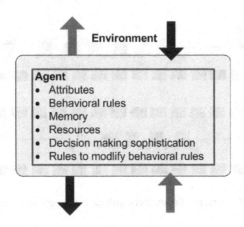

Fig. 5. General view of simulation

4   Mixing ABS and DES Approach – Case Study

This case is based on research in a factory belonging to one of the biggest global automotive company. This is divided to three production department: car body building, paint shop and final assembly. Research focuses on assembly area.

In analyzed factory there are 126 positions on an assembly line. Parts are delivered with JIS system to 26 of them. Each of positions are accompanied by two buffers for containers with parts. Containers are delivered from logistics center by trucks and loaded on electric trains with a capacity of four containers. This loading point is marked in the upper right corner of Figure 6.

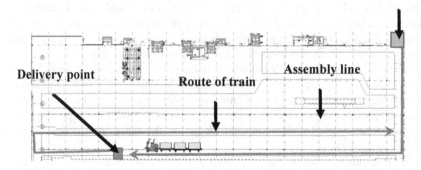

Fig. 6. Route of electric train from loading point to positions on assembly line

Near the target delivery position, an empty container is replaced by a full one. These steps are repeated in the next three (or less) positions. This part of process is shown in Figure 7.

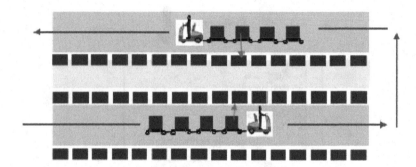

Fig. 7. Delivery of containers with parts to specific positions

The control system is based on production plan. The order of cars on assembly line is known more than two hours before enter cars to assembly area. This information is stored in the computer system and on this basis containers are filled in the logistics center. Control of trains is described in the next section.

The paramount objective of this system is to prevent the line from stopping due to lack of parts to assembly. The constraints of this system include:

-    All transport roads are one-way.
-    Trains cannot reverse.

Actually all of activities in assembly area are based on process approach. Main process (production line) call demand for parts. Trains move with constant time intervals. Trains' assignment to lines is also constant – there are four lines and four trains. A general view of simulation, with assembly lines and transport routes, is shown in Figure 8. It was created with the use of Flexsim Simulation Software.

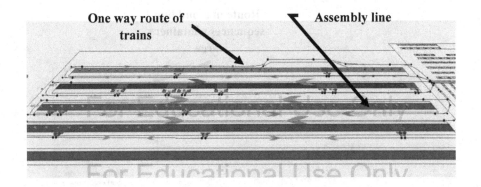

Fig. 8. General view of simulation

In the simulation model trains are contractors of transport tasks. They are driven by opening and closing input ports. Transport resources are constantly assigned to process. This solution is identical to the one implemented in the public transport system [2].

In practice there are situations where the assigned transport resources significantly exceed the demand. For example a train transport a only one container as shown in Figure 9. Of course this generates considerable costs and deteriorates the competitiveness of the company. In this case trains must perform more courses and their utilization is low.

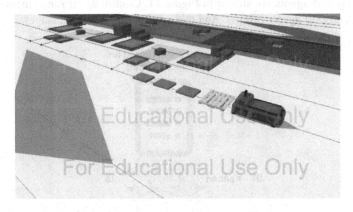

Fig. 9. One train only partially loaded

In JIS deliveries a process approach is insufficient. Near assembly points there is a place for a maximum of two containers with parts. The proposed solution of a control system of delivery trains is changing approach in JIS field to task driven and giving "intelligence" to means of transport. In the analyzed company building sequences containers area is the immediate neighborhood of the assembly plant. This is shown in Figure 10. Therefore, the authors expand the simulation model to combination DES and ABS, which will be described in the next section.

**Route in a building
sequences containers
area**

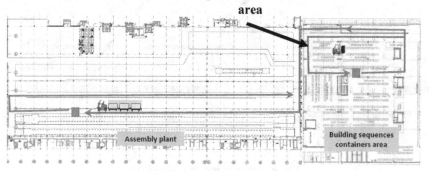

Fig. 10. General view of simulation

The main assumptions of a new idea of design model based on ABS are:

- Constant assignment to routes and replaced by a dynamic way.
- Flexible intervals of trains rides.
- Control of two groups of agents by a paramount agent.

Specificity of JIS solution require using ABS with features presented above. Authors propose design of control system and simulation as follow:

Two types of agents are shown in Figure 11. Control agent sends messages to the group of transport agents (trains). And this groups send return messages.

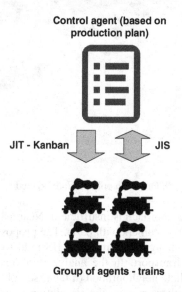

Fig. 11. Relations between agents

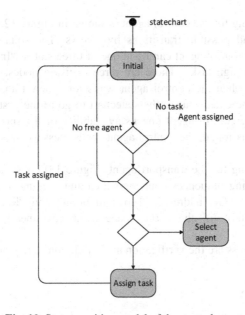

Fig. 12. State transition model of the control agent

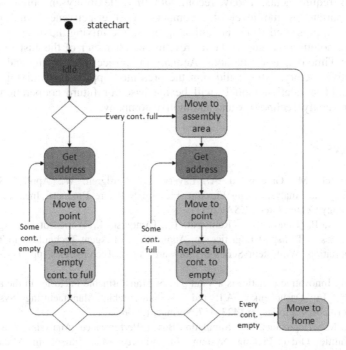

Fig. 13. State transition model of transport agent

Statechart modeling for the control agent is shown in Figure 12. Possible states are shown by boxes and possible transitions by arrows. The square shapes illustrate decision nodes. The control agent can be in one of three states: "Initial" state, "Select agent" state and "Assign task". There are three decision nodes. The "Initial" state represents the state when the control agent waits for a new transport task from the production plan. A new task causes the statechart to go to the first decision node. At the second node, the control agent checks availability of transport agent. When the free transport agent is found, the control agent sends message and assigns task to the transport agent.

Statechart modeling for the transport agent (Figure 13) consists two main blocs – moving in the building sequences containers area and moving in the assembly area. Sequence of tasks – "Get address", "Move to point" and "Replace container" is repeated to completely fill the cargo space (four containers) by full or empty containers.

Currently in progress are the verification and validation of the current state model.

5   Conclusion

The evolution of supply chain in the automotive industry puts forward new challenging requirements. Today, reconfigurability, flexibility and high availability are as important as the level of automation, cost effectiveness, and maximum throughput. In presented work the authors propose the mixing the discrete-event and agent-based solution, because it better reveals the character of the Just In Sequence and Just In Time deliveries methods. Actually the project is verifying and validating in automotive factory. After validation the presented approach of mixing DES and ABS to build simulation model will be the base for future cooperation between Poznan University Technology and automotive company.

References

1. Beaverstock, M., Greenwood, A., Lavery, E., Nordgren, W.: Applied Simulation. Modeling and Analysis using Flexsim. Flexsim Software Products, Inc., Canyon Park Technology Center, Orem, USA (2011)
2. Davidsson, P., Henesey, L., Ramstedt, L., Törnquist, J., Wernstedt, F.: Agent-Based Approaches to Transport Logistics. In: Applications of Agent Technology in Traffic and Transportation. Whitestein Series in Software Agent Technologies, pp. 1–15. Springer (2005)
3. Graf, H.: Innovative logistics is a Vital part of Transformable Factories in the automotive industry. In: Dashchenko, A.I. (ed.) Reconfigurable Manufacturing Systems and Transformable Factories, pp. 423–457. Springer (2006)
4. Güller, M., Hegmanns, T.: Simulation-Based Performance Analysis of a Miniload Multishuttle Order Picking System. In: Variety Management in Manufacturing. Proceedings of the 47th CIRP Conference on Manufacturing Systems (2014)
5. Liker, J.K.: The Toyota way: 14 management principles from the world's greatest manufacturer. McGraw-Hill Professional (2004)

6. Mustafee, N., Bischoff, E.E.: A Multi-Methodology Agent-Based Approach For Container Loading. In: Jain, S., Creasey, R.R., Himmelspach, J., White, K.P., Fu, M. (eds.) Proceedings of the 2011 Winter Simulation Conference (2011)
7. Macal, C.M., North, M.J.: Agent-Based Modeling And Simulation. In: Rossetti, M.D., Hill, R.R., Johansson, B., Dunkin, A., Ingalls, R.G. (eds.) Proceedings of the 2009 Winter Simulation Conference (2009)
8. North, M.J., Macal, C.M.: Managing business complexity: Discovering strategic solutions with agent-based modeling and simulation. Oxford University Press, New York (2007)
9. Siebers, P.O., Macal, C.M., Garnett, J., Buxton, D., Pidd, M.: Discrete-Event Simulation is Dead, Long Live Agent-Based Simulation! Journal of Simulation 4(3), 204–210 (2010)
10. Wagner, M.S., Silveira-Camargos, V.: Decision model for the application of just-in-sequence. In: Decision Sciences Institute Proceedings of the 40th Annual Conference, New Orleans, USA (2009)

Agent Based Approach
for Modeling Disturbances in Supply Chain

Patycja Hoffa and Pawel Pawlewski

Poznan University of Technology, ul.Strzelecka 11, 60-965 Poznań
patrycja.hoffa@doctorate.put.poznan.pl,
pawel.pawlewski@put.poznan.pl

Abstract. The aim of the paper is to present the agent based approach for modeling disturbances in supply chain. An introduction to the issue of Agent-Based Modeling is provided. The paper describes in detail the modeled area of a supply chain, taking into account different modeling techniques. Disturbances (selected and highlighted by the authors) are identified and modeling methods are discussed. Two selected disturbances are modeled using of agent-based approach. The research highlights of the performed works are as follows: identifying disturbances in a supply chain, which can be modeled with use of the ABS approach and demonstrating how to model the chosen disturbances by using the above method of modeling.

Keywords: supply chain, agent based systems, transport, modeling, simulation.

1   Introduction

Currently, there are two trends concerning the methods of simulating processes in a supply chain. The first is Discrete-Event Simulations (DES). DES is used in queuing simulations and complex networks of queues. DES is a good option when we deal with well-known processes, for which the situations of uncertainty are defined using statistical distributions [3, 6, 12]. DES models are characterized by the process approach – they focus on the modeling of the system in detail, not on the independent units. The other method of simulating a the supply chain is Agent-Based Simulation (ABS). In contrast to DES, ABS focuses on individual elements (resource, participants in the process), which are characterized by their own distinct behaviors [11]. When discussing ABS, we should consider the following elements of this model: attributes and behaviors of individual agents, relations and interactions between agents and the environment that we model [11]. When applying ABS to modeling supply chains, it is good to know that the individual chain participants (companies, manufacturers, wholesalers and retailers) can be treated as agents who have their own goals and skills and their common goal is to produce and deliver a product to a specific customer [15]. Agent-Based Simulation is discussed in more detail in [1, 7, 9, 11]. There are also numerous articles dedicated to agent modeling and multi-agent modeling in the transport and supply chains [2, 4, 5, 10, 14].

J.M. Corchado et al. (Eds.): PAAMS 2014 Workshops, CCIS 430, pp. 144–155, 2014.

The aim of the present article is to present the agent-based approach for modeling supply chain disturbances. The article consists of five parts. Section 1 provides an introduction to the issue of Agent-Based Modeling. Part 2 describes in detail the modeled area of a supply chain, taking into account different modeling techniques. Section 3 discusses disturbances (selected and highlighted by the authors) in the analyzed section of a supply chain and determines the method of modeling these disturbances. Part 4 discusses the use of agent-based approach for the two selected disturbances. Section 5 summarizes the possibility of using agent-based approach for modeling disturbances in a supply chain and provides prospects for further investigations.

The research highlights of the performed works are as follows: identifying disturbances in a supply chain, which can be modeled with use of the ABS approach and demonstrating how to model the chosen disturbances by using the above method of modeling.

2   Supply Chain in Terms DES/ABS

Each supply chain consists of at least two participants (sender and receiver). It often includes a series of intermediary entities, such as wholesalers, storage or transport service providers. On the one hand, each company creates a separate entity and operates independently (e.g. manufacturing a given product); on the other hand, it works with other participants of the chain in order to achieve the intended purpose (e.g., product distribution to selected customers). From the standpoint of agent-based modeling, each user of a supply chain (each entity) is a separate agent that makes his/her own decisions. Each agent represents the internal and external functions of companies, reflecting the mechanisms of cooperation within the chain [14].

The growing globalization and increasing cost pressure force the companies (both manufacturing and servicing ones) to search for new solutions for their businesses [8]. When discussing the issue of a supply chain, companies focus on increasing the efficiency of operation, by reducing the delivery time, increasing the filling of the transport or just-in-time delivery [13]. After the analysis of a supply chain, the authors decided to focus primarily of the aspect of time in implementing a particular transport order. Having considered the timescale, the authors decided to take into account not only the transport time from the point of origin to the point of acceptance but also the time of loading and unloading at various points. According to the authors, activities in these two points have a large impact on the turnaround time of transport. However, in order to limit the analyzed area, aspects related to the production and inventory are not taken into account.

The entity that connects all the elements of the analyzed chain is the means of transport, which carries the load. Therefore, it is the subject of analysis in the following part of the work.

The implementation of a transport order from point A (starting point) to point B (destination point) can be modeled in several ways, depending on the rigorousness of the model and the entered data. The applied ways of modeling are as follows:

1) A vehicle covers the distance from point A to point B without regard to any changes in the course of order execution (the vehicle is not assigned to any intelligence, at the time of loading the maximum amount of the product it begins to realize transport order from point A to point B) – figure 1.

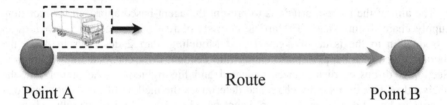

Fig. 1. First way of route modelling

Activities at point A and B (i.e. loading and unloading) can be described by discrete events (modeling DES) – the time needed to complete each operation is described by statistical distributions. In contrast, the means of transport is treated as an agent of the specified attributes and behaviors (in this case strongly limited).

2) A vehicle covers the distance from point A to point B according to the specified timetable (the vehicle operates according to a timetable set by the modeler; the schedule includes the amount of cargo, the starting time of the order; in case of a larger number of unloading points, it determines the order of unloading points and the number of unloaded goods) – figure 2.

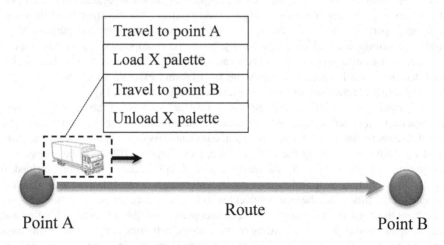

Fig. 2. Second way of route modelling

As above, the steps in section A and B can be described by statistical distributions (modeling DES). The means of transport is the agent of the specified attributes and behaviors (in this case it has a list of tasks, according to which all operations are implemented).

3) A vehicle covers the distance from point A to point B according to the schedule, taking into account changes during the order execution (as in point 2, in addition it is possible to change the route, for example: in case of road blocks) – figure 3.

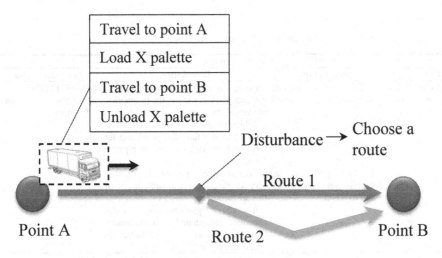

Fig. 3. Third way of route modelling

Again, the activities carried out at point A and B are defined by statistical distributions. The means of transport is an agent that has some kind of intelligence – it realizes the steps according to the list of tasks, but in case of unforeseen situations (disturbances), it makes the decisions concerning further implementation of the order. This option also takes into account the relationship between the agent and the environment in which it operates.

3   Disturbances

Analyzing the supply chain and, to be more exact, the transport turnaround time, it is necessary to take into account a number of variables. The time of finishing the race depends on many factors, such as the type of road on which the means of transport is traveling, the weather conditions, driving skills, capabilities of means of transport and other factors.

Some of these factors are constant: they are known in advance, while others are characterized by variability (e.g. weather conditions). In the present study, authors characterize a series of disturbances that affect the implementation of the transport order. The emphasis is put mainly on the aspect of time, however, the loading and unloading operations at various points are also taken into consideration. The present article does not deal with the aspect of ensuring the availability of the goods to be transported and, therefore, disturbances related with this issue are not analyzed.

The disturbances are divided into 6 groups, as we can see at table 1 on the left side.

Table 1. Disturbances in supply chain

Disturbances			
General type	Special type	Description	The modeling way
Related with means of transport	1. Failures of the means of transport	- a failure is random; based on historical data you can predict the probability of such a situation; - failure of the means of transport is associated with the time of waiting for help, and the time required to repair a fault;	MTBF/MTTR characteristics for DES/ABS
	2. Not providing a vehicle on time (e.g. due to theft)	- a disturbance is random; it is necessary to determine the probability of this situation; - it results in significant delay in order execution (associated with the search for a replacement car), or failure in order execution;	DES
Related with the route	1. Traffic congestion	- random factor; based on historical data it is possible to determine the volume of traffic in a changeable geographical /spatial area; - it shortens or extends the duration of the transport order;	ABS
	2. Road traffic accidents (so-called "black spots")	- random aspect; based on historical data it is possible to determine the probability of an accident in so-called "Black spots"; - vehicle accident without participation of the vehicle executing the transport order: it is associated with a stoppage at the accident site; - an accident involving a vehicle performing a transport order: it is associated with longer duration of order execution due to the need to provide roadside assistance, as a result of damages it may impossible to execute the order;	ABS
	3. Weather conditions (sudden bad weather)	- this disturbance is random in nature; based on historical data and weather maps it is possible to determine the points with frequent breaks in the weather; the disturbance is defined for the changeable geographical / spatial areas; - it results in a significant lengthening of order execution (associated with a lower traveling speed);	ABS
	4. If a vehicle travels on toll roads, the toll-collection points must be taken into account	- the time of paying the fee should be determined as a variable (depending on the number of cars waiting to pay the toll and the individual characteristics of particular drivers);	DES

Table 1. *(continued)*

Resulting from the fault of the sender	1. The time needed for loading (lengthening related with a limited number of employees)	- depends on the number of employees participating in the loading; - the time of loading may possibly be shortened or lengthened;	DES
	2. incorrect date or amount of loading	- it has a random character; based on historical data it is possible to determine the probability of the disturbance; - it results in lengthening the time of loading;	DES
	3. No enough ramps for loading	- the disturbance is of random character, based on historical data it is possible to determine the probability of this disturbance; - it results in lengthening the time of loading;	DES
Resulting from the fault of the receiver	1. The time needed for unloading (lengthening associated with a limited number of employees)	- it depends on the number of employees participating in the unloading; - the time of loading may possibly be shortened or lengthened;	DES
	2. incorrect date of unloading	- the disturbance is of random character, based on historical data it is possible to determine the probability of this disturbance; - it results in lengthening the time of loading;	DES
	3. No enough ramps for unloading	- the disturbance is of random character, based on historical data it is possible to determine the probability of this disturbance; - it results in lengthening the time of loading;	DES
Related with the driver	1. Driver skills	- it affects the traveling speed and the time needed to reach the loading / unloading point	Scale of skill level (1,3,5); the conversion factors for particular activities of a driver : (1 - lowest rating - 1,2xTime, 3 – average rating - 1,1xTime, 5-highest rating - 1xTime)
	2. Driver working time	- breaks in the driver work should be taken into account, as they affect the time of order execution;	Message informing of a break at work, in accordance with current regulations
Others	1. Natural disasters (hurricanes, floods, etc.) and other situations that slow down traffic on the road (e.g. strikes)	- the disturbance is completely random in nature, it involves a changeable geographical/spatial area affected by the disturbance; - it results in significant lengthening of order execution (associated with a slower traveling speed), or failure in order execution;	ABS
	2. Failure of IT system used by companies to communicate	-the disturbance has a random character, based on historical data it is possible to determine its probability; - it results in significant lengthening of order execution or failure in order execution;	MTBF/MTTR – characteristic of DES/ABS

4   Detailed Presentation of the Method of Modeling Selected Disturbances with Use of ABS

4.1   Modeling Traffic Congestion with Use of Agents

Traffic congestion at a given point is modeled with use of agents. Depending on the volume of traffic at a given point (representing the statistical distribution of traffic at particular times) the radius of congestion is defined This disturbance can be modeled in several ways with use of agents:

Method 1 (figure 4) - traffic congestion at a given point is represented by an agent with a specific range. The agent, like a radar, checks at a specified time interval (e.g. 1 unit of simulation) whether in his/her coverage area there is an unfamiliar object (in this case, means of transport). In case a means of transport appears within the agent's functioning area, the agent sends a message to the vehicle informing about the distur-bance, i.e. traffic congestion. This message contains information about the volume of traffic and the traveling speed of the vehicle in a certain distance. The truck, after re-ceiving the message, changes the traveling speed according to the given information.

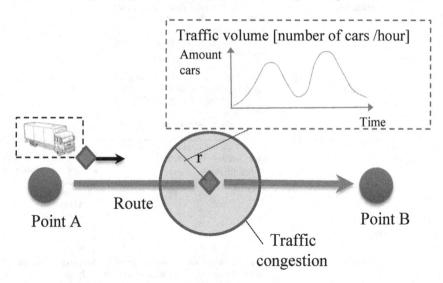

Fig. 4. A traffic congestion represented by an agent – way 1

Method 2 (figure 5) - Traffic congestion at a given point is represented by an agent with a specific range of operation. In addition, the means of transport has its own range of operation – an area in which it checks if there are other agents (including their range of action), representing certain disturbances. The transport area is represented by a half of the circle, as in this case we are interested in only the area in front of the vehicle (the area behind is no longer taken into account). In this case, it is agent representing the truck who checks, according to a defined unit of time, whether any disturbance occurs in the area. If so, he/she sends a message (kind of a request) to the disturbance asking about constraints. After receiving the message, he/she changes the travelling speed according to the given information.

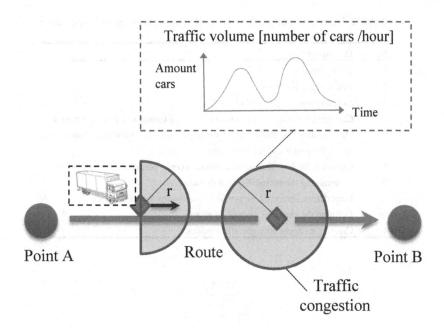

Fig. 5. A traffic congestion represented by an agent – way 2

Both presented methods make it possible to correctly and accurately map the specified disturbance and its effect on the executed operation (transport order).

4.2 Modeling Sudden Weather Changes (Breaks in the Weather) Using Agent-Based Methods

Historical data and information obtained from the weather maps are commonly used when modeling sudden changes of the weather (such as blizzards, downpour, sleet, black ice). After determining the routes for a transport order, the model checks the current weather conditions at certain strategic points (the distance between various points on the route is about 50 km). When we have information about the possible occurrence of significant deterioration of weather conditions, it is necessary to create an agent, who represents this disturbance. The attributes of this agent are the duration of this weather event, the area of operation, which depends on the expected duration of difficulties, and information on traveling speed in the area of operation. When discussing a break in the weather, two areas of this event should be taken into account – the center of the weather change, where the culmination of the phenomenon is observed, and its periphery, where the weather conditions are difficult, but to a smaller extent than in the center. As in case of downpours accompanying the storm – first we find ourselves in the rain, then heavy rain, and again in the rain. According to this approach, an agent has two ranges of action, with specific restraints for each of them. The block diagram (Figure 6) shows how to create an agent representing a given disturbance. The description of each item of the block diagram is presented in Table 2.

Table 2. Description of block diagram of creation of agent for disturbances

No.	Description
1	Transport orders
2	Determination of route
3	Defining points on the route
4	Checking the current weather conditions (disturbances) at certain points
5	Determining the disturbance, duration, intensity (determination of two areas: the center and the periphery)
6	Checking the historical weather data at certain points
7	Determining the probability of a disturbance
8	Final determination of the possible disturbance at a given point
9	Defining the characteristics of an agent
10	Creating an agent with specific qualities

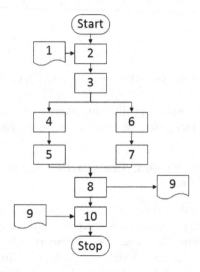

Fig. 6. Block diagram of creation of agent for disturbances

This disturbance can be modeled in several ways with use of agents:

Method 1 - difficult weather conditions at a given point are represented by an agent with the two specified ranges of action (figure 7). These areas are as follows: a circle with a specified radius, representing the center of change in the weather and a ring (the operating range is defined by two rays), which forms the area surrounding the center. The agent checks, in specified units of time, whether in his area there is another agent representing a means of transport. If there is one, it sends information to the vehicle about the occurring disturbance (message about the type of disturbance, the area of operation, reduced speed). Due to the rapidly changing weather conditions, it is impossible to assume that a vehicle covers a particular distance in the surrounding area, next it enters the center of changes, and then goes back to the surrounding area following the same information (invariable in all the covered areas). Assuming sudden changes in the weather, it is necessary to take into consideration their dynamic nature, and therefore in accordance with the user-defined unit of time (e.g. at one simulation unit), the agent sends information to the vehicle about the current conditions and related restraints. The vehicle, after receiving the message, changes the traveling speed according to the given information.

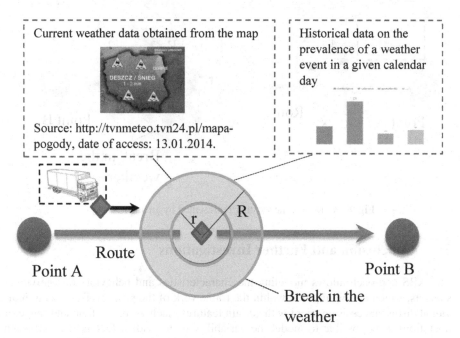

Fig. 7. A break in the weather represented by an agent – way 1

Method 2 – as in case 1, the agent representing the difficult weather conditions at a given point has two areas (center and surrounding area) – figure 8. In addition, the means of transport has its range of operation – a fixed area, in which it checks whether there are other agents (including their range of action) representing disturbances. The transport area is represented by a half of the circle, as in this case we are interested in only the area in front of the vehicle (the area behind is no longer taken into account). In this case, the agent that represents the vehicle, checks whether there are disturbances in this area. If there is one, he/she sends a message to the disturbance to get information about limiting conditions (changes). After receiving the message, he/she changes the traveling speed according to the given information.

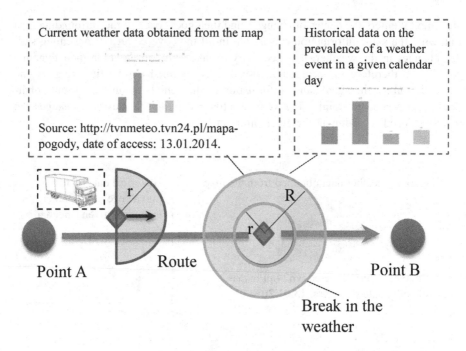

Fig. 8. A break in the weather represented by an agent – way 2

5   Conclusion and Further Investigations

The ABS approach allows modeling the characteristics and behaviors for individual subjects, which are highlighted within the framework of the process. By treating individual disturbances as an agent with certain features (such as, place, time and range of operation), it is possible to model the variability of individual factors that influence the process (and time) of the transport order. Through the representation of the different subjects and disturbances as agents (having their own goals and being characterized by specific features) it was possible to show their impact on the environment, and thus on the analyzed process, which is the implementation of the transport task. Some agents affect others (a disturbance has an impact on a vehicle) and, as a result we deal with a specific reaction and effect. Depending on the assumed rigorousness level of the entered data, we encounter various levels of disturbances. Yet, it must be noted that too much information introduces chaos in the model.

Obviously, there is an opportunity for further development of the proposed agent-based approach to disturbance modeling in a supply chain. The paper presents three methods of modeling the implementation of a transport order (part 2). Another, a more advanced model, is the one with a manager and several vehicles. The manager distributes orders to individual vehicles, based on the received information (orders) and the analysis of them. The analysis aims at searching for optimal routes for individual orders; it is also possible to combine the orders so that the means of transport is fully loaded. Therefore, in this model an extra agent, representing the manager (dispatcher), is created: he/she is above all the other highlighted agents (vehicles and disturbances).

Acknowledgements. Presented research are carried out under the LOGOS project (Model of coordination of virtual supply chains meeting the requirements of corporate social responsibility) under grant agreement number PBS1/B9/17/2013.

References

1. Bae, J.W., Lee, G., Moon, I.: Introductory tutorial: Agent-Based Modeling and Simulation. In: Winter Simulation Conference, pp. 3809–3820 (2012)
2. Balbo, F., Pinson, S.: Dynamic modeling of a disturbance in a multi-agent system for traffic regulation. Decision Support System 41, 131–146 (2005)
3. Banks, J., Carson II, J.S., Nelson, B.L., Nicol, D.M.: Discrete-event system simulation, 4th edn., pp. 68–86. Prentice Hall (2004) ISBN 0-13-144679-7
4. Baykasoglu, A., Kaplanoglu, V.: A multi-agent approach to load consolidation in transportation. Advances in Engineering Software 42, 477–490 (2011)
5. Bocewicz, G., Nielsen, P., Banaszak, Z., Dang, Q.V.: Multimodal Processes Cyclic Steady States Scheduling. In: Corchado, J.M., et al. (eds.) PAAMS 2013. CCIS, vol. 365, pp. 73–85. Springer, Heidelberg (2013)
6. Cassandras, C.G., Lafortune, S.: Introduction to Discrete Event Systems, 2nd edn., pp. 557–615. Springer (2008) ISBN-13: 978-0-387-33332-8
7. Chan, W.K.V., Son, Y., Macal, C.M.: Agent-Based Simulation tutorial – simulation of emergent behavior and differences between Agent-Based Simulation and Discrete-Event Simulation. In: Winter Simulation Conference, pp. 135–150 (2010)
8. Jasiulewicz-Kaczmarek, M.: Sustainability: Orientation in Maintenance Management—Theoretical Background. In: Golinska, P., et al. (eds.) Eco-Production and Logistics. Emerging Trends and Business Practices, pp. 117–134. Springer, Heidelberg (2013)
9. Kim, S.-H., Robertazzi, T.G.: Modeling Mobile Agent Behavior. Computers and Mathematics with Applications 51, 951–966 (2006)
10. Krejci, C.C., Beamon, B.M.: Modeling food supply using Multi-Agent Simulation. In: Winter Simulation Conference, pp. 1167–1178 (2012)
11. Macal, C.M., North, M.J.: Introductory tutorial: Agent-Based Modeling and Simulation. In: Winter Simulation Conference, pp. 362–376 (2013)
12. Siebers, P.O., Macal, C.M., Garnett, J., Buxton, D., Pidd, M.: Discrete-Event Simulation is Dead, Long Live Agent-Based Simulation! Journal of Simulation 4(3), 204–210 (2010)
13. Sitek, P., Wikarek, J.: A hybrid approach to supply chain modeling and optimization. In: Federated Conference on Computer Science and Information Systems (FedCSIS), pp. 1223–1230 (2013)
14. Zhan, H.-P., Huang, D.-C.: Plan and Coordination of Agile Supply Chain Based on Multi-Agent. Energy Procedia 13, 10134–10142 (2011)
15. anylogic.com (2014), http://www.anylogic.com/agent-based-modeling
16. tvnmeteo (2014), http://tvnmeteo.tvn24.pl/mapa-pogody

Combining Simulation and Multi-agent Systems for Solving Enterprise Process Flows Constraints in an Enterprise Modeling Aided Tool

Paul-Eric Dossou[1], Pawel Pawlewski[2], and Philip Mitchell[1]

[1] ICAM, Site de Vendée, 28 Boulevard d'Angleterre,
85000 La Roche-Sur-Yon, France
[2] Poznan University of Technology, ul.Strzelecka 11
60-965 Poznań
`paul-eric.dossou@icam.fr`, `pawel.pawlewski@put.poznan.pl`,
`philip.mitchell704@orange.fr`

Abstract. European economies have been deeply affected by different crises. The impact of the economic crisis on enterprises is now recognized by everybody. Enterprises need to reorganize in order to be better adapted to this situation. GRAI Methodology is one of the three main methodologies for enterprise modeling. GRAIMOD is a software tool being developed for supporting this methodology and facilitating enterprise improvement. The concepts elaborated for this tool combine reasoning like Case Based Reasoning (CBR), Decomposition or transformation reasoning and multi-agent systems like training agent. This paper introduces these concepts and presents how to complete them with simulation concepts for improving enterprise performance. An example will be used for illustrating the concepts presented through a detailed case study.

Keywords: Multi-agent systems, Expert system, Simulation, Reference models, Rules, Knowledge.

1 Introduction

Since 2008 and the beginning of the crisis, the deficiencies of a system based on capitalism have been becoming more apparent with many European countries submitted to unbelievable constraints. European enterprises are searching for the best way to be efficient faced with ever-increasing globalization. Nobody has yet fully understood exactly how to address the situation not only in terms of the global economy but also in terms of performance for individual enterprises.

Many of these enterprises have understood that for being efficient, they need to satisfy not only customers and shareholders, but also suppliers and employees. This implies a complete reorganization based on performance criteria.

GRAI Methodology [4] is one of the three main methodologies (with PERA, CIMOSA) of enterprise modeling. To support this methodology different tools are being developed. GRAIMOD is the latest one being developed by using JAVA technology, JADE and JESS platforms, and an open architecture and structure.

J.M. Corchado et al. (Eds.): PAAMS 2014 Workshops, CCIS 430, pp. 156–166, 2014.

This paper summarizes the research done at Icam Vendee in this area. The basic concepts of GRAIMOD are presented. GRAIMOD is used for improving enterprise performance. The main criteria used for this improvement were quality, cost and lead time (QCD). Nowadays, these criteria are no longer sufficient for making the most adapted improvements. The improvements envisaged have an impact not only on the enterprise environment but also on society and the general public. For instance, Danone has chosen to locate its manufacturing plant near suppliers in order to reduce its carbon footprint and to implement policies with a positive impact for the local population. So, a further criterion called CSSE for carbon management together with social, societal and environmental dimensions has been added to the already existing QCD. The changes due to integration of a special module GRAI_SSE for social, societal and environmental dimensions will be presented in this paper. The advantage is clearly the possibility of using ISO 26000, environmental norms, energy reduction parameters, carbon reduction norms, waste reduction processes for complementing improvements in QCD. GRAI_SSE is composed of two sub-modules GRAICARB destined for carbon footprint management and GRAISO being developed for social and environmental responsibility management. Then, the combination of Case Based Reasoning (CBR) and multi-agent systems is presented. The use of JESS, JADE and JAVA for developing GRAIMOD is studied. Finally the combination of these concepts with simulation is shown through an example.

2   GRAIMOD: Existing Concepts and Architecture

GRAI Methodology is one of the three main methodologies used for analyzing and designing enterprises. The GRAI approach is composed of four phases: An initialization phase to start the study, a modeling phase where the existing system is described, an analysis phase to detect the inconsistencies of the studied system and a design phase during which the inconsistencies detected are corrected and a new system proposed. These concepts could be used to ensure the transformation of enterprises to meet real market needs (globalization, relocation, capacity to be proactive, cost optimization, lead time, quality, flexibility, etc....) and have to be adapted.

An enterprise is completely described according to GRAI Methodology by finding five models: functional (functions of the enterprise and their links), physical (the production system), informational (the net, tools and informational flows), process (series of sequences or tasks), and decisional (structure of orders, hierarchic organisation). Then these models could be improved for increasing enterprise performance.

GRAIMOD is a new tool being developed by ICAM Engineer School for proposing concrete solutions to improve enterprises according to new market evolutions. Nowadays, it contains five modules working around three sub modules (figure 1).

GRAIKERN is a graphic editor, an interface used for representing the different models associated to GRAI methodology. GRAIWORKER is the work base elaborated for managing, modifying and capitalising knowledge about the case studied. GRAITRANS is a Transfer Interface used for putting the new case in GRAIXPERT in order to improve its Cases Base [1], [2], [3]. The reference model elaborated for each enterprise domain will be improved by the acquisition of this new model in GRAIXPERT between the different modules.

GRAIXPERT is a hybrid expert system for managing the analysis of the existing system and proposing a new system [12], [16]. It is composed of two sub-modules in interaction with GRAIKERN: the Knowledge Capitalization (KCM) and the Knowledge Based System (XPERTKBM). GRAIMANAGER is a management module used for organising the different interactions between the modules of GRAIMOD. It controls and manages the system's interactions with the users [5], [6].

GRAISUC is a module used for managing the choice of an ERP or SCM tool for an enterprise. It is composed of two sub-modules SpeMM and SpeCM. The Specification Management Module (SpeMM) is used for choosing the appropriate ERP or SCM Tool of an enterprise. The specifications obtained are capitalised in the Specification Capitalisation Module (SpeCM).

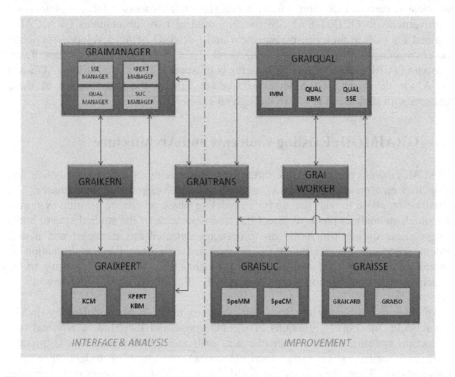

Fig. 1. New Architecture of GRAIMOD (five modules for analysis and improvements and 3 sub-module operative tasks)

GRAIQUAL is a module used for managing quality approach implementation or quality improvement in an enterprise [7]. It contains two sub-modules IMM and QUALKBM. The Improvements Management Module (IMM) is used for managing the different quality action plans of the enterprise. The Quality Knowledge Base Module (QUALKBM) is being elaborated for containing the rules related to quality certifications in order to use them for improving or elaborating quality in an enterprise. The module GRAIQUAL of GRAIMOD is both able and efficient for defining how to improve enterprises based on criteria such as quality, lead time and cost. Indeed, a fourth criterion allowing carbon management has been put forward. Then this criterion has to be combined to the others to really improve enterprises according to the actual context of enterprises today.

GRAI_SSE is the new module being developed specifically for integrating social, societal and environmental dimensions in the improvement of enterprises. It is composed of a sub-module GRAICARB destined to manage carbon footprint and GRAI_SO being elaborated for improving the other aspects of environmental, social and societal dimensions.

It appears that a focus needs to be made on the use of this criterion. A new module GRAI_SSE is being added to GRAIMOD in order to pinpoint the environmental, societal and social dimensions in enterprises. This module would integrate, for example, changes associated to carbon management, ISO 26000, ISO 14000 implementations, social and societal evolutions impacts on enterprises but also impact on local authorities (states, associations, districts, etc.) [9]. The objective is not to dissociate this criterion but to obtain the best combination by really studying this aspect of the enterprise in order to propose appropriate solutions. The difficult enterprise context due to the crisis and the search for alternative solutions to the basic QCD optimization are the cause of this new focus on how important social, societal and environmental dimensions have indeed become and how beneficial it is for enterprises to find a new optimized solution by focusing on these aspects.

The architecture of this system contains three different bases for managing the study of a new case. A model base is used for managing elaborated reference models. A rule base is used for analyzing the models of the system in question. And a case base is defined for capitalizing different studies for future use. This tool proposes the combination of CBR (Case Based Reasoning) and Multi-agent systems for solving enterprise modeling problem and improving enterprise performance.

3 Use of Multi-agent Systems

GRAIMOD is being developing by using Java. The platform used for multi-agent systems is JADE. This method combines different reasoning such as Case Based Reasoning, decomposition reasoning, generalization and particularization reasoning and transformation reasoning.

For designing a new enterprise organization, a problem solving method is defined. This process starts with the new functional model realization, followed by the new physical model (figure 2). Then global and local decision models are elaborated. Finally the informational model is specified. For instance, for designing the new functional model, generalization reasoning is used for obtaining a functional reference model which would be extracted during a new modeling phase.

Each reference model is considered as an object with a structure. The CBR mechanism uses an algorithm «extract - select - transform» to choose the reference model that is suitable for the system studied. In fact, there are in the case base different types of objects. The first step consists in choosing the object class C_i on which the mechanism will be applied (associated activity domain). Each class has different objects: $C_i = \{O_{i1}, O_{i2}, ...O_{in}\}$. The extractor allows the choice of the reference class. The selector chooses the reference model suitable to the study.

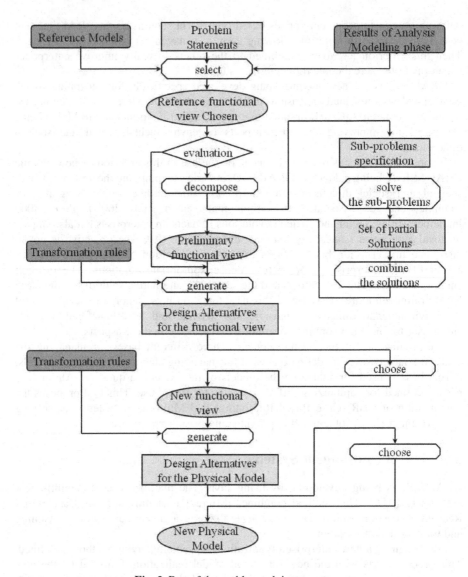

Fig. 2. Part of the problem solving process

An object Oij of the class Ci is chosen by comparing the parameters of the object Om to design, from the result of the modelling/analysis phase and the design objectives, with the objects Oij of the class Ci. Then the object Oij is used for realizing the design of O_m. The transformer manages the process of reference model specification.

The previous problem solving process and different reasoning associated are combined with multi-agent systems for developing GRAIMOD. The use of case based reasoning implies the acquisition of different cases, the defining of reference models from the obtained cases and adaptation of these reference models to the studied case.

It is clear that the agents defined for the phases related to enterprise performance improvement have to learn quickly in accordance with the possible changes (previous cases, reference models associated to typology, etc.). Indeed, the choice was difficult because of the advantages of BDI architecture, but we chose the training agents because of their particularity to learn [13]. This system is used for defining how to improve the enterprise performance and for capitalizing the process followed. The language associated to Jade platform is FIPA ACL (Agent Communication Language) [10, [11], [14]. The training agent structure is adapted to the requirements of GRAIMOD. This choice is in coherence with the problem solving method used for defining concepts of GRAIMOD.

For instance, the agents are used for production system diagnosis and improvement. The objective is to use these agents for elaborating models of an enterprise, making diagnosis of these models and designing new models and appropriate improvements.

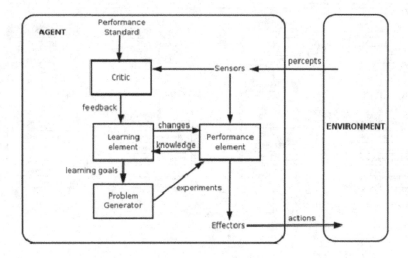

Fig. 3. Training agents

The development of GRAIMOD by using these concepts allows to obtain the architecture in figure 4. This architecture is adapted to the concepts of GRAIMOD.

The first difficulty is to translate these concepts into terms appropriate for IT developers. The choice of the use of Java technology and Jade Platform integrates some constraints. GRAIXPERT contains cases, rules and reference models [8]. The use of Multi-agents makes the tool more efficient by giving the opportunity to choose which kind of improvement is desired. The rule engine JESS is used for implementing rules. The rules (through the training multi-agents) could be used on the existing enterprise model for finding inconsistencies, but the different studied cases could also be used and the reference models could be exploited too. Then the management of these possibilities needs the use of training agents.

GRAIMOD is used for modeling and improving enterprise performance. This improvement includes the supply chain. The idea is to propose the definition of agents for managing relations with an existing tool FLEXIM used for realizing simulation of processes. Indeed, the propositions of improvement by GRAIMOD need sometimes to be tested. For instance, a new implementation, or a new production process could be tested by using simulation and finding the best solution according to simulation before really implementing it. The objective here is to use advantages of simulation for improving the response given to users. It seems that the training agent would be adapted in the development of this interface. The interface managed by the defined training agent would also allow to integrate in GRAIXPERT the best results obtained by using FLEXSIM and to capitalize them. The structure of this interface is being developed and will be presented during the conference.

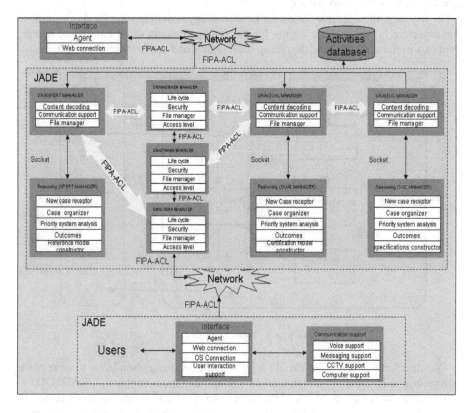

Fig. 4. Architecture of GRAIMOD in a Java environment

The following example is used for validating hypotheses made for this tool and the exploitation of the results will come soon.

4   Example

The enterprise SOLISO is specialized in sun protection. The products are numerous and divided into types: blinds, sun blinds, roller blinds, textile frontages, awnings and pergolas. This enterprise is a SME founded in 1947 and located in the west of France near Nantes. There are generally about 100 employees reinforced with seasonal workers. The number of customers is very high: more than 3000. The surface area is 9000 m2 divided into two manufacturing workshops. The enterprise has no sales shop but the strategy is to sell the different products to tradesmen, retailers, carpenters, blind manufacturers and specialized hypermarkets. The context of the enterprise is simple: due to the economic crisis and the weather, the turnover decreased in 2013. It means that SOLISO has had to think about how to reduce cost on the supply chain, to improve quality and to respect delivery dates in order to win the loyalty of customers, and anticipate future improvements by integrating for instance the social, societal and environmental dimensions. The study is for reorganizing the enterprise, by using concepts developed in GRAIMOD. The enterprise accepted to be used as a case in the database of GRAIMOD. The deal is:

- For SOLISO the improvement of its global performance,
- And for ICAM Industrial Organization Research Team the definition of a reference model for multi-product enterprises.

The study started with context acquisition, and then the modeling of the existing system was done. Different formalisms were used for achieving this modeling. The formalism actigramme was used for modeling the physical and the functional systems. A zoom was made on each workshop (decomposition reasoning) in order to study in detail the supply chain. During this phase the kernel of GRAIMOD was used for elaborating models. Based on Object Oriented Design, the concepts used in this module allow to show links between the different parts of the physical and the functional systems in order to detect inconsistencies.

Other models have also been elaborated by using this kernel. For instance, the entire decisional structure of the enterprise was studied by establishing the GRAIgrid and the GRAInets of the enterprise. The processes of this enterprise were also elaborated and the structure of informational data shown. Interviews were held with staff to elaborate these models. It was also opportunity to know exactly the desire of operators in terms of ergonomics, their suggestions for improvement, their problems, their expectations. The module GRAISSE was used for the existing environmental, social and societal dimensions of SOLISO. A zoom was made on energy, carbon and waste management.

The analysis of these models allows to detect inconsistencies in the enterprise. The module GRAIXPERT (containing rules) was used for this task. In addition to the previous models, a Value Stream Mapping (VSM) formalism was used for calculating flow times and showing inconsistencies. A simulation tool (Flexsim) was also used for modeling the manufacturing implantation and showing bottlenecks and finding inconsistencies on the enterprise manufacturing processes. This tool will also be used for the design phase for proposing adapted and optimized process organization. It appears that the interface being developed would be interesting:

- For modeling the existing processes
- For putting out data from GRAIMOD (GRAIXPERT) in order to analyse processes obtained
- And for using reference models for proposing new adapted solutions to the enterprise concerned.

From these inconsistencies, strengths and weaknesses of the enterprise were deduced. We noted the desire of management team at SOLISO to both progress as quickly as possible and to carry out the necessary improvements noted in this process. The following points were immediately taken into account for being addressed:

- Storage according to raw materials, semi-products and products
- Process organization
- Quality of products and system
- Non-respect of delivery dates
- Quantity of energy used
- Waste management
- High production costs

Fig. 5. Simulation of the enterprise processes

In order to improve these points, approaches, tools and methods contained in the module GRAIQUAL were used for finding the best way for solving the problem detected and proposing the appropriate solution. The module GRAISSE was used for proposing improvements according to ISO26000 principles, energy, carbon and waste reduction.

5   Conclusion

Enterprise modelling is one of the main tools available for enterprises to help them successfully come through the present crisis. In this paper, GRAIMOD a new tool for supporting GRAI methodology is presented. For the development of this tool, a combination of different concepts was elaborated. Case based reasoning and generalisation reasoning were combined with multi-agent theory and simulation concepts in order to achieve improvement in enterprise efficiency. The particularity of Icam Vendee (Icam Group), where students spend 50% of their Engineering degree course in industrial apprenticeship, is the great opportunity for the research team to obtain applications for concepts developed on Case Based Reasoning and on Multi Agent Systems Theories. GRAIMOD is being developed in a Java environment, particularly with Jade platform and FIPA-ACL Language.

Furthermore, a crucial new criterion including social societal and environmental dimensions has been elaborated in addition to QCD criteria to take into account changes in our society.

GRAIMOD serves for managing the different phases of GRAI Methodology and is used for improving enterprise performance. The example given shows that this tool is efficient and will certainly be transformed into a reference model for multi-product companies.

Future prospects point to further development of this tool. Other reference models will be elaborated upon in the future and the opportunity to combine the tool with simulation tools will be demonstrated. The concepts associated with the new criterion will be set out in detail in order to demonstrate their capability to reduce costs and increase profits which constitutes the main argument for convincing enterprises and particularly SMEs.

References

1. Aamodt, A.: Case-Based Reasoning: foundational issues, methodological variations, and system approaches. Artificial Intelligence Communications 7(1), 39–59 (1994)
2. Burke, E.K., et al.: Structured cases in case-based reasoning – reusing and adapting cases for time-tabling problems. The Journal of KBS 13(2-3), 159–165 (2000)
3. Brown, D.C., Chandrasekaran, B.: Expert system for a class of mechanical design activities. Knowledge Engineering in CAD. Elsevier, Amsterdam (1985)
4. Chen, D., Doumeingts, G., Vernadat, F.B.: Architectures for enterprise integration and interoperability. Past, present and future. Computers in Industry 59, 647–659 (2008)
5. Dossou, P.E., Mitchell, P.: Using case based reasoning in GRAIXPERT. In: FAIM 2006, Limerick, Ireland (2006)
6. Dossou, P.E., Mitchell, P.: Implication of Reasoning in GRAIXPERT for modeling Enterprises. In: DCAI 2009, Salamanca, Spain (2009)
7. Dossou, P.E., Mitchell, P.: How Quality Management could improve the Supply Chain performance of SMES. In: FAIM 2009, Middlesbrough, United Kingdom (2009)
8. Dossou, P.-E., Pawlewski, P.: Using multi-agent system for improving and implementing a new enterprise modeling tool. In: Demazeau, Y., et al. (eds.) Trends in PAAMS. AISC, vol. 71, pp. 225–232. Springer, Heidelberg (2010)

9. European commission: Responsabilité sociale des entreprises: une nouvelle stratégie de l'UE pour la période 2011-2014, Brussels, Belgium (2011)
10. Ferber, J.: Multi-agent system: An Introduction to distributed Artificial Intelligence. Addison Wesley Longman, Harlow, ISBN 0-201-36048-9
11. Friedman-Hill, E.: JESS, the rule engine for the JAVA platform, version 7.1p2. Sandia National Laboratories (2008)
12. Russell, S.J., Norvig, P.: Artificial Intelligence. A Modern Approach. Prentice-Hall, Englewood Cliffs (1995)
13. Sen, S., Weiss, G.: Learning in Multiagent Systems. In: Weiss, G. (ed.) MultiagentSystems: A Modern Approach to Distributed Artificial Intelligence, ch. 6, pp. 259–298. The MIT Press, Cambridge (1999)
14. Sycara, K.P.: Multi-agent systems. AI Magasine, American Association for Artificial Intelligence (1998) 0738-4602-1998
15. Wooldridge, M.: Intelligent Agents. In: Weiss, G. (ed.) Multiagent Systems: A Modern Approach to Distributed Artificial Intelligence, ch. 1, pp. 27–77. The MIT Press, Cambridge (1999)
16. Xia, Q., et al.: Knowledge architecture and system design for intelligent operation support systems. The Journal Expert Systems with Applications 17(2), 115–127 (1999)

A Proposal for Processing
and Fusioning Multiple Information Sources
in Multimodal Dialog Systems

David Griol, José Manuel Molina, and Jesús García-Herrero

Computer Science Department
Carlos III University of Madrid
Avda. de la Universidad, 30, 28911 - Leganés, Spain
{david.griol,josemanuel.molina,jesus.garciaherrero}@uc3m.es

Abstract. Multimodal dialog systems can be defined as computer systems that process two or more user input modes and combine them with multimedia system output. This paper is focused on the multimodal input, providing a proposal to process and fusion the multiple input modalities in the dialog manager of the system, so that a single combined input is used to select the next system action. We describe an application of our technique to build multimodal systems that process user's spoken utterances, tactile and keyboard inputs, and information related to the context of the interaction. This information is divided in our proposal into external and internal context, user's internal, represented in our contribution by the detection of their intention during the dialog and their emotional state.

Keywords: Multimodal Systems, Conversational Agents, Fusion Techniques, Dialog management, User Modeling.

1   Introduction

Research on multimodal interaction has grown considerably during the last decade, as a consequence of the development of innovative input interfaces, as well as the advances in research fields such as speech interaction and natural language processing [1, 2]. However, multimodal fusion has not evolved at the same rate, which has lead to minor advances at the different possibilities of combining input modalities [3, 4].

Multimodal dialog systems [5–7] are dialog systems that process two or more combined user input modes. According to [8], fusion of input sources in these systems must be approached in a global way: from the point of view of the architecture of a multimodal system as a whole, then, from the point of view of multimodal dialog modeling, and finally from an algorithmic point of view.

The architectural perspective focuses on necessary features of an architecture to allow usability in the integration of a fusion engine. Most of the current systems have been developed following the basis for multimodal interaction defined by important projects like Smartkom [7]. Smartkom's interaction metaphor was

J.M. Corchado et al. (Eds.): PAAMS 2014 Workshops, CCIS 430, pp. 167–178, 2014.

based on the idea that the user delegates a task to the virtual communication assistant which is visualized as a life-like character. Among the input modalities considered there were spoken dialog, graphical user interfaces, gestural inter-action, facial expressions, physical actions, and biometrics. In the output, it provided an anthropomorphic user interface that combined speech, gesture, and facial expressions.

Multimodal dialog modeling refers to the module of the multimodal system that controls the interaction: the dialog manager. This module decides the next action of the multimodal system [9–11], interpreting the incoming semantic rep-resentation of each input modality in the context of the dialog. In addition, it resolves ellipsis and anaphora, evaluates the relevance and completeness of user requests, identifies and recovers from recognition and understanding errors, re-trieves information from data repositories, and decides about the next system's response. Fusion techniques in multimodal dialog systems are usually integrated in the dialog manager [12].

Finally, the algorithmic perspective studies logic and algorithms used to in-tegrate data coming from different input recognizers into an application-usable result. Fusion of input modalities can be achieved at a number of different levels of abstraction, as well as considering increasing levels of complexity. Multi-sensor data fusion can be performed at four different processing levels, according to the stage at which the fusion takes place: signal level, pixel level, feature level, and decision level [13].

In this paper we propose a general-purpose approach to cost-efficiently de-velop an adapt a multimodal dialog system. The main objective is to reduce the effort required for both the implementation of a new system and the adaptation of systems to deal with user's specific features, a new task or modality. Our proposal follows an architecture that integrates several modules dealing with in-put modalities, as speech or visual and tactile interaction, and also the context of the interaction. We differentiate between two types of context: *internal* and *external*. The former describes the user state, modeled in our proposal by the user's intention during the dialog and the user's emotional state, whereas the latter refers to the environment state (e.g. location and temporal context).

We also propose a multimodal fusion methodology that is integrated in the dialog manager of the system. This module takes the input information sources into account to generate and encode a single input used for the selection of the next system action.

2   Proposal for Developing Multimodal Dialog Systems

The general architecture used for the development of multimodal applications can be separated in four different components: input modalities and their rec-ognizers, output modalities and their respective synthesizers, the integration committee, and the application logic [8]. Indeed, using multimodality efficiently implies a clear abstraction between the results of the user's input analysis, the processing of this input, answer generation and output modalities selection.

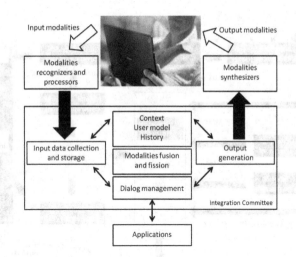

Fig. 1. General architecture for the generation of multimodal dialog systems

As Figure 1 shows, this clear separation is achieved with help of the integration committee, responsible for management of all input and output modalities.

The integration committee can itself be separated in five different subcomponents. First, input modalities are collected into the input data collection and storage module, which is in charge of identifying and storing input data. The Modalities fusion and fission module manages input data prepares it for processing by the application logic. When the fusion and fission engines reach an interpretation, it is passed to the dialog management module.

Figure 2 describes the process for adapting the general architecture presented in Figure 1 by introducing the key points of our proposal. A spoken dialog system integrates five main tasks to deal with user's spoken utterances in natural language: automatic speech recognition (ASR), natural language understanding (NLU), dialog management (DM), natural language generation (NLG), and text-to-speech synthesis (TTS).

Speech recognition is the process of obtaining the text string corresponding to an acoustic input [14]. It is a very complex task as there is much variability in the input characteristics, which can differ depending on the linguistics of the utterance, the speaker, the interaction context and the transmission channel. Linguistic variability involves differences in phonetic, syntactic and semantic components that affect the voice signal. Inter-speaker variability refers to the big difference between speakers regarding their speaking style, voice, age, sex or nationality.

Once the conversational agent has recognized what the user uttered, it is necessary to understand what he said. Natural language processing is the process of obtaining the semantic of a text string [15, 16]. It generally involves morphological, lexical, syntactical, semantic, discourse and pragmatical knowledge. Lexical and morphological knowledge allow dividing the words in their

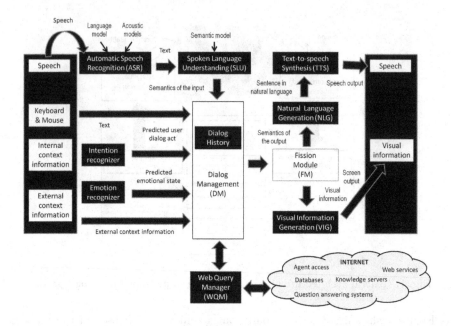

Fig. 2. Proposed framework for the generation of multimodal dialog systems

constituents distinguishing lexemes and morphemes. Syntactic analysis yields a hierarchical structure of the sentences, while semantic analysis extracts the meaning of a complex syntactic structure from the meaning of its constituents. In the pragmatic and discourse processing stage, the sentences are interpreted in the context of the whole dialog.

There is not a universally agreed upon definition of the tasks that a dialog manager has to carry. Traum and Larsson [17] state that dialog managing involves four main tasks: i) updating the dialog context, ii) providing a context for interpretations, iii) coordinating other modules and iv) deciding the information to convey and when to do it. Thus, the dialog manager has to deal with different sources of information such as the NLU results, database queries results, application domain knowledge, and knowledge about the users and the previous dialog history [11].

Natural language generation is the process of obtaining texts in natural language from a non-linguistic representation. The simplest approach consists in using predefined text messages (e.g. error messages and warnings). Finally, a text-to-speech synthesizer is used to generate the voice signal that will be transmitted to the user.

As explained in the introduction section, a multimodal dialog system involves user inputs through two or more combined modes, which usually complement spoken interaction by also adding the possibility of textual and tactile inputs provided using physical or virtual keyboards and the screen. In our contribution, we want also to model the context of the interaction as an additional valuable information source to be considered in the fusion process.

With regard to external context, our proposal is based on additional agents used to capture and provide this information to the spoken conversational agent. Regarding internal context, our proposal merges the traditional view of the dialog act theory, in which communicative acts are defined as intentions or goals, with the recent trends that consider emotion as a vital part for social communication. To do so, we contribute a user state prediction module based on an intention recognizer and an emotion recognizer.

Finally, we also propose a statistical methodology that combines multimodal fusion and dialog management functionalities. To do this, a data structure is introduced to store the information provided by the user's inputs and the context of the interaction. This information is coded taking into account the confidence measures provided by the modules that capture and process the different information sources. This data structure is taking into account in a classification process whose result allows the selection of the next system response. The following subsections describe the different methodologies proposed to develop the main modules of the multimodal dialog system.

2.1 Modeling User's Intention

Research in techniques for user modeling has a long history within the fields of language processing and dialog systems. The main purpose of a simulated user in this field is to improve the usability of a dialog system through the generation of corpora of interactions between the system and simulated users [18]. Two main approaches can be distinguished to the creation of simulated users: rule based and data or corpus based. In a rule-based simulated user the researcher can create different rules that determine the behavior of the system [19]. The main objective of data-based techniques is to automatically explore the space of possible dialog situations and learn new potentially better dialog strategies [20].

The statistical technique that we propose to model user's intention is described in [21]. The proposed technique carries out the functions of the ASR and SLU modules, i.e., it estimates user's intention providing the semantic interpretation of the user utterance in the same format defined for the output of the SLU module. A data structure, that we call *User Register* (UR), contains the information provided by the user throughout the previous history of the dialog. For each time i, the proposed model estimates user's intention taking into account the sequence of dialog states that precede time i, the system answer at time i, and the objective of the dialog $\mathcal{O}$. The selection of the most probable user answer U_i is given by:

$$\hat{U}_i = \arg \max_{U_i \in \mathcal{U}} P(U_i | UR_{i-1}, A_i, \mathcal{O})$$

The information contained in UR_i is a summary of the information provided by the user up to time i. That is, the semantic interpretation of the user utterances during the dialog and the information that is contained in a user profile (e.g., user's name, gender, experience, skill level, most frequent objectives, additional information from previous interactions, user's neutral voice, and additional parameters that could be important for the specific domain of the system). We propose to solve the previous equation by means of a classification process, which takes the current state of the dialog (represented by means of the set $UR_{i-1}, A_i, \mathcal{O}$) as input and provides the probabilities of selecting the different user dialog acts. Figure 3 shows the described process followed by the proposed intention recognizer and its interaction with the rest of modules of the multimodal dialog system.

2.2 Modeling User's Emotional State

Although emotion is receiving increasing attention from the dialog systems community, most research described in the literature is devoted exclusively to emotion recognition [22] and not to the use of this valuable information in the fusion and dialog management processes. Emotions change people voices, facial expressions, gestures, and speech speed. They can also affect the actions that the user chooses to communicate with the multimodal system.

Our emotion recognition method, based on the previous work described in [23], firstly takes acoustic information into account to distinguish between the emotions which are acoustically more different, and secondly dialog information to disambiguate between those that are more similar. We were interested in recognizing negative emotions that might discourage users from employing the system again or even lead them to abort an ongoing dialog. Concretely, we considered three negative emotions: anger, boredom, and doubtfulness, where the latter refers to a situation in which the user uncertain about what to do next).

The proposed emotion recognizer employs acoustic information to distinguish anger from doubtfulness or boredom and dialog information to discriminate between doubtfulness and boredom, which are more difficult to discriminate only by using phonetic cues. This process is shown in Figure 3. The first step for emotion recognition is feature extraction. The aim is to compute a list of 60 features from a speech input which can be relevant for the detection of emotion in the users' voice [23]. The second step of the emotion recognition process is feature normalization, with which the features extracted in the previous phase are normalized around the user neutral speaking style. Once we have obtained the normalized features, we classify the corresponding utterance with a multilayer perceptron (MLP) into two categories: *angry* and *doubtful_or_bored*. If the utterance is classified as *doubtful_or_bored*, it is passed through an additional step in which it is classified according to two dialog parameters: depth and width.

2.3 Acquiring and Processing External Context

External contextual information is usually measured by hardware or software-based sensors (such as GPS and monitoring programs), or provided by the users. Typically, sensors rely on low level communication protocols to send the collected context information or they are tightly coupled within their context-aware systems. Since sensing techniques are well developed, existing sensors utilize these techniques through instrumentation or polling mechanisms, and extend their capability by acquiring context information from existing systems.

As described in [24], we propose the use of a Facilitator and Positioning Systems to acquire and process external contextual information. The Positioning System communicates with the ARUBA positioning system to extract and transmit positioning information to other agents in the system

The Facilitator System is implemented using the Appear IQ commercial platform (AIQ, www.appearnetworks.com). The platform consists of two main modules: the Appear Context Engine (ACE) and the Appear Client (AC). The ACE is installed in a server, while the ACs are included in the users' devices.

The ACE implements a rules engine, where the domain-specific rules that are defined determine what should be available to whom, and where and when it should be available. These rules are fired by a context-awareness runtime environment, which gathers all known context information about a device and produces a context profile for that device (e.g., physical location, date/time, device type, network IP address, and user language).

The ACE is divided into three modules that collaborate to implement a dynamic management system that allows the administrator to control the capability of each device once they are connected to the wireless network. The Device Management Module provides management tools to deploy control and maintain the set of mobile devices. The Synchronization Module manages the exchange of files between corporate systems and mobile hand-held devices. Finally, the Device Management is continuously provided with updated versions of the configuration files. Figure 3 shows the integration of the Positioning and Facilitator systems in the proposed framework for developing multimodal dialog systems.

2.4   Fusion of Input Modalities and Dialog Management

As previously described, the objective of fusion in multimodal dialog systems is to process the input information and assign a semantic representation which is eventually sent to the dialog manager. Two main levels of fusion are often used: feature-level fusion, semantic-level fusion. The first one is a method for fusing low-level feature information from parallel input signals within a multimodal architecture. The second one is a method for integrating semantic information derived from parallel input modes in a multimodal architecture.

Semantic-level fusion is usually involved in the dialog manager and needs to consult the knowledge source from the dialog history and data repositories. Three popular semantic fusion techniques are used. Frame-based fusion is a method for integrating semantic information derived from parallel input modes [25].

Unification-based fusion is a logic-based method for integrating partial meaning fragments derived from two input modes into a common meaning representation during multimodal language processing. Compared with frame-based fusion, unification-based fusion derives from logic programming, and has been more precisely analyzed and widely adopted within computational linguistics (e.g. [26]).

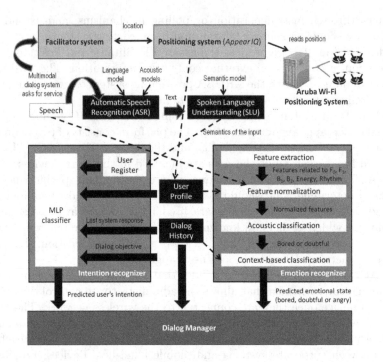

Fig. 3. Schema for the acquisition and processing of external and internal contextual information

Hybrid symbolic/statistical fusion is an approach to combine statistical processing techniques with a symbolic unification-based approach (e.g. Members-Teams-Committee (MTC) hierarchical recognition fusion [27]). Another related work on low-level fusion is sensor fusion, which is the combining of sensory data from disparate sources such that the resulting information is in some sense better than would be possible when these sources were used individually

To deal with the input information sources and transmit this information to the dialog manager, we propose the use of EMMA (Extensible MultiModal Annotation markup language, www.w3.org/TR/emma/), developed by the W3C Multimodal Interaction Framework (www.w3.org/TR/mmi-framework/) and intended for use by systems that provide semantic interpretations for a variety of inputs, including speech recognition, handwriting recognizers, natural language understanding engines, and other input media interpreters (e.g. DTMF, pointing, keyboard), as well that multimodal integration component and the interaction manager.

EMMA is focused on annotating single inputs from users, which may be either from a single mode or a composite input combining information from multiple modes, as opposed to information that might have been collected over multiple turns of a dialog. The language provides a set of elements and attributes that are focused on enabling annotations on user inputs and interpretations of those inputs. The attribute *emma : hook* can be used to mark the elements in the application semantics within an *emma : interpretation*, which are expected to be integrated with content from input in another mode to yield a complete interpretation. Figure 4 shows an example EMMA code in which this attribute is used to integrate a spoken and a visual input.

```
<emma:emma version="1.0"                                          <action>send</action>
    xmlns:emma="http://www.w3.org/2003/04/emma"                      <arg1>
    xmlns:xsi="http://www.w3.org/2001/XMLSchema-instance"               <object emma:hook="ink">
    xsi:schemaLocation="http://www.w3.org/2003/04/emma                     <type>file</type>
      http://www.w3.org/TR/2009/REC-emma-20090210/emma.xsd"               <number>1</number>
    xmlns="http://www.example.com/example">                             </object>
<emma:interpretation id="voice2"                                     </arg1>
    emma:medium="acoustic"                                           <arg2>
    emma:mode="voice"                                                   <object emma:hook="ink">
    emma:function="dialog"                                                 <number>1</number>
    emma:confidence="0.4"                                               </object>
    emma:tokens="I want to go there"                                 </arg2>
    emma:start="1087995961500"                                     </command>
    emma:end="1087995963542">                                    </emma:interpretation>
  <command>                                                      </emma:emma>
```

Fig. 4. Example of EMMA document dealing with several input modalities

The methodology that we propose for the multimodal data fusion and dialog management processes considers the set of input information sources (spoken interaction, visual interaction, user intention modeling, and user emotional state) by means of a machine-learning technique. The dialog manager receives EMMA files containing the results processed by the modules that deal with each input modality. As in our previous work on user modeling and dialog management [21, 11], we propose the definition of a data structure to store the values for the different concepts and attributes provided by means of the different input modalities along the dialog history.

The information stored in this data structure, that we called Interaction Register (IR), is coded in terms of three values, $\{0, 1, 2\}$, for each field according to the following criteria:

- **0**: The value of the specific position of the IR has not been provided by means of any of the input modalities or sources defined as interaction context.
- **1**: The value of the specific position of the IR has been provided with a confidence score that is higher than a given threshold. Confidence scores are provided by different modules that process the information acquired for each input modality (e.g., the ASR and SLU modules for the spoken utterances).
- **2**: The value of the specific position of the IR has been provided with a confidence score that is lower than the given threshold.

The information contained in the IR at each time i has been generated considering the values extracted from the EMMA files along the dialog history. Each slot in the IR can be usually completed by means of more tan one input modality. If just one value has been received for a specific dialog act, then it is stored at the corresponding slot in the IR using the described codification. Confidences scores provided by the modules processing each input modality are used in case of conflict among the values provided by several modalities for the same slot. Thus, a single input is generated for the dialog manager to consider the next system response.

As in our previous work on dialog management [11], we propose the use of a classification process to determine the next system response given the single input that is provided by the interaction register after the fusion of the input modalities and also considering the previous system response. This way, the current state of the dialog is represented by the term (IR_i, A_{i-1}), where A_{i-1} represents the last system response. The values of the output of the classifier can be viewed as the a posteriori probability of selecting the different system responses given the current situation of the dialog.

3   Conclusions and Future Work

In this paper we have described a framework to develop multimodal systems that considers information provided by means of spoken, visual and tactile input modalities. We carry out an additional step towards the adaptation of these systems by also modeling the context of the interaction in terms of external and internal context, which in our case is related to the detection of the user's intention and emotional state.

Several modules have been incorporated in the classical architecture of a spoken dialog system to achieve the integration of the additional input modalities and contextual information sources. These modules respectively allow to predict the next user response for the conversational agent and carry out the fusion of visual and spoken information. The proposed multimodal fusion and dialog management technique allows considering these heterogeneous information sources to select the next system action by means of a classification process.

Although the different methodologies proposed to develop the described modules integrated in the multimodal dialog system have been evaluated in previous works [21, 23, 24, 11], as a future work we propose the application of the described framework to develop and evaluate a practical system in a real environment.

Acknowledgements. This work was supported in part by Projects MINECO TEC2012-37832-C02-01, CICYT TEC2011-28626-C02-02, CAM CONTEXTS (S2009/TIC-1485).

References

1. Filipe, P., Mamede, N.: Ambient Intelligence Interaction via Dialogue Systems, pp. 109–124. Intech (2010)
2. López-Cózar, R., Callejas, Z.: Multimodal Dialogue for Ambient Intelligence and Smart Environments, pp. 559–579. Springer (2010)
3. Jaimes, A., Sebe, N.: Multimodal human-computer interaction: A survey. Computer Vision and Image Understanding 108, 116–134 (2007)

4. Turk, M.: Multimodal interaction: A review. Pattern Recognition Letters 36, 189–195 (2014)
5. López-Cózar, R., Araki, M.: Spoken, Multilingual and Multimodal Dialogue Systems. John Wiley & Sons Publishers (2005)
6. Pieraccini, R.: The Voice in the Machine: Building Computers that Understand Speech. The MIT Press (2012)
7. Wahlster, W.: SmartKom: Foundations of Multimodal Dialog Systems. Springer (2006)
8. Dumas, B.: Frameworks, description languages and fusion engines for multimodal interactive systems. Master's thesis, University of Fribourg, Fribourg, Switzerland (2010)
9. Traum, D., Larsson, S.: The Information State Approach to Dialogue Management, pp. 325–353. Kluwer (2003)
10. Williams, J., Young, S.: Partially Observable Markov Decision Processes for Spoken Dialog Systems. Computer Speech and Language 21(2), 393–422 (2007)
11. Griol, D., Hurtado, L., Segarra, E., Sanchis, E.: A Statistical Approach to Spoken Dialog Systems Design and Evaluation. Speech Communication 50(8-9), 666–682 (2008)
12. Ruiz, N., Chen, F., Oviatt, S.: Multimodal input, pp. 211–277. Elsevier (2010)
13. Dai, X., Khorram, S.: Data fusion using artificial neural networks: a case study on multitemporal change analysis. Computers, Environment and Urban Systems 23(1), 19–31 (1999)
14. Tsilfidis, A., Mporas, I., Mourjopoulos, J., Fakotakis, N.: Automatic speech recognition performance in different room acoustic environments with and without dereverberation preprocessing. Computer Speech & Language 27(1), 380–395 (2013)
15. Wu, W.L., Lu, R.Z., Duan, J.Y., Liu, H., Gao, F., Chen, Y.Q.: Spoken language understanding using weakly supervised learning. Computer Speech & Language 24(2), 358–382 (2010)
16. Minker, W.: Design considerations for knowledge source representations of a stochastically-based natural language understanding component. Speech Communication 28(2), 141–154 (1999)
17. Traum, D., Larsson, S.: The Information State Approach to Dialogue Management. In: Current and New Directions in Discourse and Dialogue. Kluwer Academic Publishers (2003)
18. Möller, S., Englert, R., Engelbrecht, K., Hafner, V., Jameson, A., Oulasvirta, A., Raake, A., Reithinger, N.: MeMo: towards automatic usability evaluation of spoken dialogue services by user error simulations. In: Proc. Interspeech 2006, pp. 1786–1789 (2006)
19. Chung, G.: Developing a flexible spoken dialog system using simulation. In: Proc. ACL 2004, pp. 63–70 (2004)
20. Schatzmann, J., Weilhammer, K., Stuttle, M., Young, S.: A Survey of Statistical User Simulation Techniques for Reinforcement-Learning of Dialogue Management Strategies. Knowledge Engineering Review 21(2), 97–126 (2006)
21. Griol, D., Carbó, J., Molina, J.: A statistical simulation technique to develop and evaluate conversational agents. AI Communication 26(4), 355–371 (2013)
22. Schuller, B., Batliner, A., Steidl, S., Seppi, D.: Recognising realistic emotions and affect in speech: state of the art and lessons learnt from the first challenge. Speech Communication 53(9-10), 1062–1087 (2011)

23. Callejas, Z., López-Cózar, R.: Influence of contextual information in emotion annotation for spoken dialogue systems. Speech Communication 50(5), 416–433 (2008)
24. Griol, D., Carbó, J., Molina, J.: Bringing context-aware access to the web through spoken interaction. Applied Intelligence 38(4), 620–640 (2013)
25. Vo, M., Wood, C.: Building an application framework for speech and pen input integration in multimodal learning interfaces. In: Proc. of ICASSP 1996, pp. 3545–3548 (1996)
26. Johnston, M.: Unification-based multimodal parsing. In: Proc. of ACL 1996, pp. 624–630 (1996)
27. Wu, L., Oviatt, S., Cohen, P.: From members to teams to committee - a robust approach to gestural and multimodal recognition. IEEE Transactions on Neural Networks 13(4), 972–982 (2002)

PHuNAC Model: Creating Crowd Variation with the MBTI Personality Mode

Olfa Beltaief[1], Sameh El Hadouaj[2], and Khaled Ghedira[1]

[1] Laboratory *SOIE*, ISG of Tunis, Tunisia
beltaief.olfa@gmail.com,
khaled.ghedira@isg.rnu.tn
[2] Laboratory *SOIE*, FSEG Nabeul, Tunisia
hadouaj@yahoo.fr

Abstract. Several crowd simulators simulate only homogenous pedestrians. In the reality, there are different personalities. This personality variation affects the pedestrian behavior and the fate of the crowd. In this paper, we extend the HuNAC (Human Nature of Autonomous Crowd) model by providing each pedestrian agent with a personality in order to examine how the emergent behavior of the crowd is affected. We use the MBTI personality theory as a basis for agent psychology. The aim of this work is to improve HuNAC model and consequently to improve results. In this context, we have a new version of our model which we called PHuNAC model (Personalities' Human Nature of Autonomous Crowd). Our PHuNAC model is a multi-agent simulation of pedestrian crowd model .The conducted experiments show that PHuNAC model is able to produce more realistic pedestrian behaviors than the HuNAC model.

Keywords: Agent based simulation, Autonomous crowd model, Complex systems, MBTI theory.

1   Introduction

Pedestrian crowd is a set of people with different personalities who are gathered in the same location. These different personalities shape the crowd's fate and its movements. Indeed, personality is a pattern of behavioral and mental traits for each pedestrian [17]. The simulation of these complex phenomena has attracted considerable attention. However, a great number of these models do not cover all the psychological factors necessary for a pedestrian located in a crowd (see [10] and [18]). Moreover, many of these models simulate only homogenous personalities of pedestrians. In the reality, there are different personalities. Experimentations' results of these models show that they lack realism. For this purpose, the goal of our work is to reproduce realistic pedestrian crowd simulated situations by simulating a realistic pedestrian behavior and personality. In this context, we opted for, firstly, the HuNAC (Human's Nature of Autonomous Crowds) model which includes the necessary psychological factors for a pedestrian located in a crowd [2]. Secondly, we opted for the PHuNAC

J.M. Corchado et al. (Eds.): PAAMS 2014 Workshops, CCIS 430, pp. 179–190, 2014.

(Personnalities' Human's Nature of Autonomous Crowds) version which integrates heterogeneous crowd.

The plan of our paper is as follows: section 2 describes related works. Section 3 presents the research problem. Section 4 introduces psychological studies. Section 5 describes our model. Section 6 presents our experimentations and a discussion of this work. Finally, in section 7 we conclude and we give perspectives for this work.

2   Related Works

Several pedestrians' crowd simulation models were proposed. These models could be classified into two families: macroscopic models and microscopic models. Macroscopic approaches include regression (e.g., [4]) and fluid dynamic models (e.g., [5], [6], etc.). Microscopic approaches include rule-based models (e.g., [14], [15], etc.), social force models (e.g., [9], etc.), cellular automata models (e.g., [12], [13], etc.) and agent-based (e.g., [16], [17], [18], [19], etc.). The macroscopic approaches simulate the behavior of the crowd as a whole. In fact, macroscopic models don't consider individual features such as physical abilities, direction of movement, and individual positioning [7]. This causes a lack of realism [8]. On the other hand, the microscopic approaches are interested in the behavior, actions and decisions of each pedestrian and his interaction with others [8]. Therefore, the microscopic models allow us to obtain more realistic simulations. For this reason, in our work, we adopt a microscopic approach and more specifically on agent-based models. In fact, the agent-based models are able, over others approaches, to be flexible, to provide a natural description of the system and to capture emergent phenomena and complex human behaviors [2], [20]. In other words, they may reflect more the reality. Several models based on multi-agents and psychological theories have been proposed. We cite namely [16], [18], [19], etc. However, a great number of these models do not cover all the psychological factors necessary for a pedestrian located in a crowd (see [10] and [18]). Therefore the produced pedestrian crowd situations lack realism. Indeed, many of these models simulate only homogenous pedestrians. In the reality, there are different personalities. The goal of our work is to reproduce realistic pedestrian crowd simulated situations by simulating a realistic pedestrian behavior. In this context, we proposed, firstly, our HuNAC model [2]. In order to have a realistic simulation, the design of the pedestrian behavior is based on psychosocial and psychophysical studies of normative personalities. Secondly, we opted for the PHuNAC (Personnalities' Human's Nature of Autonomous Crowds) version which integrates heterogeneous crowd.

3   Research Problem

Several studies [21], [31], [32], [33], [3] have shown that the crowd average speed and flow is mainly influenced by two factors: the environment and the different personalities of pedestrian. Hence we can conclude that the pedestrian behavior shape the pedestrian speed [21] (see figure 1). It is important to note that we have considered in our HuNAC model only environmental factor and we have neglected the "behavior of different personalities" factor. In fact, we took into account, in the HuNAC model, only normative personality, but in reality, there are several personalities. Hence we can conclude that there is a lack of balance. This lack of balance can be recovered by adding the missing factor. For this purpose, we performed studies on the different personalities of pedestrians to integrate it in our model with the aim to have best results. In this context, we proposed the PHuNAC model. In what follows we explain the existing different personalities.

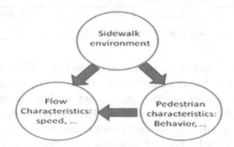

Fig. 1. Relationship between the sidewalk, pedestrian behavior and flow [21]

4   Psychological Studies

There are several theories that classify personality types such as: MBTI, Big Five, NPA, etc. It must be noted that MBTI and Big Five theory are the widely accepted theories by psychologists [22], [23], [25], [27]. However, the Big Five theory is not used in the organizational behavior area in contrast to the MBTI theory [26]. Since the pedestrian crowd behavior is an organizational behavior [24], the MBTI theory is more linked to the crowd pedestrian simulation field. This is the reason for which we choose the MBTI theory.

4.1   The MBTI Theory

The indicator of psychological types Myers-Briggs (MBTI) is based on the theoretical concepts of Carl Jung. The MBTI theory is a way to describe and explain the fundamental differences between people. This theory is the most widely studied and best validated. It describes three fundamental dichotomies of human behavior (such as seeking information, decision making, planning), and adds a fourth dichotomy (such as focusing attention and energy). The following table (see table 1 [34]) explains these four dichotomies:

Table 1. MBTI dichotomies [34]

Where Do You Focus Your Attention And Energy?	EXTRAVERSION: person enjoys interacting with others	INTROVERSION: likes, always, to be alone
How Do You Prefer To seek Information?	SENSING: likes standard methods of seeking details of its path.	INTUITION: prefers to see the overall path's pattern.

Table 1. (*continued*)

How Do You Prefer To Make Decisions?	THINKING: uses logical analysis to satisfy his own interests and also satisfy the around people.	FEELING: considers only what is important for other crowd members.
How to plan?	JUDGING Come to closure; make decisions; organize	PERCEIVING: spontaneous

The MBTI theory contains four dichotomies, and each dichotomy has two preferences. The MBTI theory has three postulates. The first one is the attitudes Extraversion and introversion. An extraverted person enjoys interacting with others while someone introverted likes, always, to be alone. The second postulate is the psychological functions: seeking information and making decisions. The first psychological function is sensing versus Intuition. Pedestrian with sensing's preference likes standard methods of seeking details of its path. Indeed, an intuitive person still prefers to see the overall path's pattern. The second psychological function is thinking versus feeling. A pedestrian who makes feeling decisions considers only what is important for other crowd members. A person who makes thinking decisions, always, uses logical analysis to satisfy his own interests and also satisfy the around people. Finally, the third postulate is the auxiliary function judging versus perceiving. In order to integrate the preferences of the MBTI theory: Judging and Perception, we must look at the dominant psychological function: If the function of "sensing-intuition" is dominant, we should choose the Perceiving preference. If the "Thinking-feeling" function is dominant in this case it is necessary to choose the judgment preference. For this reason, we will focus only on the three first dichotomies: "Where Do You Focus Your Attention And Energy?", "How Do You Prefer To seek Information?", "How Do You Prefer To Make Decisions?"

In fact, there are 16 personality types (according to MBTI theory). It is the combination of the eight preferences and each combination presents a personality. For example, an ESFJ pedestrian is an extraversion, sensing, feeling and judging person:

- Extraversion (E) or Introversion (I)
- Sensing (S) or iNtuition (N)
- Thinking (T) or Feeling (F)
- Judging (J) or Perceiving (P)

4.2   Quantifying the MBTI Method

The dichotomies of the MBTI theory are still qualifying values that we cannot implement and integrate into our HuNAC model. For this reason, we should find a method that quantifies the MBTI theory. In this context, several studies are proposed in the psychological field. As example, we cite namely the 2-qubits method [28], [29], « Jung's Personality Theory Quantified » method [11], etc. it is very important to note that the 2-qubit method is the simplest one because it contains less variables and equations. For this reason, we used the method of 2-qubits. The 2-qubit model can generate artificial personalities, which can be compared to the real world. In this method, we need only three parameters which describe the complete distribution without the need for additional parameters. The three variables are namely τ, θ and α with τ is the entanglement factor and θ and α are the parameters of superposition (for more details see [28], [29]).We can produce various artificial personalities through the following equations [28], [29]:

$$\overline{E} = (2\,\tau^2 - 1)\cos\alpha - 2\tau\sqrt{1 - \tau^2}\sin\alpha \tag{1}$$

$$\overline{T} = (2\,\tau^2 - 1)\cos\theta - 2\tau\sqrt{1 - \tau^2}\sin\theta \tag{2}$$

$$\overline{S} = (2\,\tau^2 - 1)\sin\theta - 2\tau\sqrt{1 - \tau^2}\cos\theta \tag{3}$$

In order to describe any personality, we must just give random values for the three parameters τ, α and θ without any need for other variables. All results of the functions $\overline{E}, \overline{T}$ and $\overline{S}$ (respectively the "extraversion introversion" function, "thinking-feeling" function and "Sensing intuition" function) must be in the interval [-1, 1]. For example, in the "thinking-feeling" case: If the value is greater than 0, the function takes the "thinking" value. Obviously, if the value is less than zero, the function takes the "feeling" value. In order to integrate Judging (J) and Perception (P) preferences, we must look at the dominant function personality: If the function of "sensing-intuition" is dominant, we must choose the preference Perceiving (P) and if the "Thinking-feeling" function is the dominant feature in this case it is necessary to choose the preference judgment (J).

5   Our Model

This section describes briefly the HuNAC model and explains the PHuNAC model in details.

5.1   The HuNAC Model

In our HuNAC model [2], each pedestrian is represented by an agent. Each agent has its own autonomous behavior. Indeed, the behavior of a pedestrian agent is divided into three phases: strategic phase, tactical Phase and operational phase. The strategic phase defines the global plan of a pedestrian agent. The tactical phase represents seeking information and taking decisions. These decisions allow the pedestrian agent to avoid people and obstacles. Each pedestrian agent has its own perception of the environment. Researchers [1], [21] found that pedestrians predict the "cost" of each sidewalk facility in   terms of the convenience and speed to reach a destination and that the cost is based on their personal expectations. For this purpose, the pedestrian agent in our model divides the corridor in which it is situated in a set of lanes (see fig.2). The width of each lane is equal to 60 cm (60 cm is the width of the body ellipse of a normal person [30]).

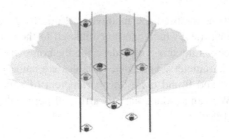

Fig. 2. Lanes' construction

Being situated in a corridor (namely C_i), each time t, the pedestrian agent has to choose the adequate lane (the lane which allows it to minimize the interactions with its environment).   Indeed, the agent has to choose the closest, the fastest, the least dense lane, having its same direction, and allowing it to avoid the collisions. In other words, the pedestrian agent chooses the easiest lane for its movement. To achieve this goal, the pedestrian agent P determines for each lane a score (namely S_L) based on the following attributes (namely A_j):

- Speed: the speed of a lane is the speed of the slower pedestrian in this lane.
- Density: the density of a lane is equal among the number of pedestrians situated in the lane divided by its surface.
- Direction: the direction of a lane is the direction of the majority of pedestrians present on this lane.
- Proportion of pedestrians with the same direction: it is a measure that allows determining the direction of the lane compared of the pedestrian direction.
- Distance of a lane from a pedestrian: it is the Euclidian distance which separates the actual lane of a pedestrian from the lane to be reached.
- Distance of an obstacle, situated in the lane to reach, from the pedestrian: it is the Euclidian distance which separates the pedestrian from the first obstacle which can cross it, placed in the lane to be reached.

Each attribute A_j is balanced by a weight W_j which gives us the following evaluation function:

$$S_L = \sum_j (f(A_j)) * W_j * F_j \tag{4}$$

Note that $f(A_j)$ is the function of the attribute A_j. F_j is the favoring lane variable. F_j is equal to -1 in the case of a penalty and equal to +1 in the case of recompense. For example, if the attribute favors the choice of the lane, this attracts pedestrian to choose the lane in consideration. So the lane score must increase. Therefore F_i must be equal to +1. After determining for each lane L the score S_L the pedestrian agent chooses the lane with the highest score.

Finally, in the operational phase, the pedestrian agent determines the direction and the speed suited to reach the chosen lane in the previous phase.

5.2   The PHuNAC Model

The pedestrian crowd is composed of different personalities. The variation in these personalities influences the crowd movement and more precisely the speed and the traffic flow. To achieve this goal, we conducted a psychological study to incorporate a plausible variation in personality in our PHuNAC model. Several studies [21], [31], [32], [33], [3] have shown that the choice of the lane influences the speed of the pedestrian. It is important to note that our HuNAC model takes into account only the normative personality. A normal person always chooses the optimal path. So the function of the score of HuNAC model was still based on the optimal choice of the way. This explains the imbalance in our model. For this reason, we need to change the score function of our model by integrating the "personality" factor. The choice of path should be sometimes optimal and sometimes not optimal this will depend on the agent pedestrian satisfaction and specifically on its personality. In what follows, we first explain the integration of the MBTI method in the PHuNAC model. Then we present the new score function.

Integration of the MBTI Method in the PHuNAC Model

The choice of personality is through formulas which allow us to correctly determine a personality with consistent manner (see equations 1, 2 and 3). Each personality characteristic is represented by the letter $\bar{C}$ with $\bar{C} \in \{value(\bar{E}), value(\bar{T}), value(\bar{S})\}$. It is important to note that the characteristic value in psychology varies over time with a constant probability. Therefore, we must determine this probability. The likelihood of a feature of personality pedestrian i is represented by $\Psi_i(\bar{C})$ (see equation 5).

$$\Psi_i(\bar{C}) = \frac{\bar{C} * 100}{\max \bar{C}} \tag{5}$$

For reasons of simplification, we have decoupled the characteristics $\bar{T}$ and $\bar{S}$. In order to decouple these characteristics, we use the platonic concept which is called" ideal" [11].   In the present application, Plato's concept of ''ideal'' rigorously suggests matching any maximum possible 100% decoupled attitude score with equivalent 100% scores of the associated original MBTI attitudes. Geometrically speaking, this generates a new coordinate system with axes rotated 45° from the original ones. The combination of two approaches gives the following equation (see equation 9).

$$\Psi_i(\overline{TS}) = \frac{\Psi_i(\bar{T}) + \Psi_i(\bar{S})}{2} \tag{6}$$

The New Lane Score Function

The new score function must consider probability functions $\Psi_i(\overline{TS})$ and $\Psi_i(\overline{E})$. In this context, we consider the extraversion attitude as a new attribute of the score function. Indeed, an extraverted person enjoys interacting with others while someone introverted always likes to be alone (see table 1). So the probability to have an extraverted person in groups is more to see him alone. Besides, the likelihood to have an introverted person alone is more to see him in a group. In the case where the extraversion probability is high, the new extraversion function $f(\Psi(\overline{E}))$ (which we must integrate in the new lane score function) must favor the choice of the path which contains pedestrian's friends or family. Besides, where the value of extraversion probability is low, the extraversion function must neglect the E attribute. The extraversion attribute has also a weight $W_{\bar{E}}$ that determines how a pedestrian is attached to the group. The following equation shows the new extraversion function which will be integrated in the new lane score function.

$$S(\bar{E}) = f(\Psi(\bar{E})) * W_{\bar{E}} \tag{7}$$

In this way, a very extraversion person (i.e. the extraversion probability is very high) who is much attached to his group (i.e. has a very high attachment weight) still favors lanes containing his group. Where the probability or attachment weight decreases, this person is more introverted and he is less attached to his group.

It is important to note that the lane score differs depending on TS function. The TS function is the combination of "seeking information" and "decision making". First, we will explain the "seeking information" that includes intuition and sensation preferences. Indeed, the pedestrian with sensing's preference likes standard methods of seeking the details of the path he undergoes (see table 1). In our PHuNAC model, the agent pedestrian seeks information in lanes of the corridor (lane by lane) as all normative personality of the agent pedestrian. So it calculates the score for each lane (namely S_L, see equation 8) to finally determine the lane with the highest score.

$$S_L = (\Sigma_i f(A_i) * W_i * F_i) * \Psi_i(\overline{TS}) + S(\bar{E}) \tag{8}$$

Regarding the intuitive person, he always prefers to see the overall path (see table 1), that is to say, see all the information in a global manner. In the PHuNAC model, an intuitive pedestrian agent seeks information in the entire corridor. For this reason, it observes overall the corridor C_i to determine the optimal lane score of the corridor designated by $L_{optimal}$ (C_i). The optimal lane of the corridor is a virtual lane that must reflect the whole of the corridor (See equation 12). We note that A_{ci} represents attributes of the corridor C_i.

$$S\left(L_{optimal}(C_i)\right) = \Sigma_i f(A_{C_i}) * W_i * F_i \tag{9}$$

Then the pedestrian seeks the nearest lane to the optimal lane with the least error. See equations 10, 11 and 12. In fact, the score of the nearest lane S (lane $_{nearest}$) represents the minimum score error S_ε of lanes.

$$S(lane_{nearest}) = Min\ (S_\varepsilon) \tag{10}$$

$$S_\varepsilon = (\Sigma_i f_\varepsilon(A_i) * W_i * F_i) * \Psi_i(\overline{TS}) + S(\bar{E}) \tag{11}$$

$$f_\varepsilon(A_i) = f_{optimal\ lane}(A_{C\_i}) - f_{lane_i}(A_i) \tag{12}$$

Regarding the making decision, there are two preferences: thinking and feeling. A pedestrian who makes decisions with feelings, only consider what is important to other members of the crowd (see table 1). This kind of pedestrian is really satisfied only if he ensures that other crowd members around him are satisfied with neglecting his own interests. In the PHuNAC model, the pedestrian agent, in this case, considers only the attributes that ensure respect for the other pedestrians and ignores attributes that ensure its own interests. To do this, we assign the variable F_i of the score function the value 0 when the attribute ensures the interests of the pedestrian. The following equation shows the possible values of F_i:

$$\begin{cases} F_i = 0 \text{ when the attribute } A_i \text{ ensures the interests of the pedestrian} \\ F_i = +1 \text{ if } A_i \text{ favorises the lane} \\ F_i = -1 \text{ if } A_i \text{ defavorises the lane} \end{cases} \tag{13}$$

Concerning a pedestrian who makes thinking decisions, he always uses logical analysis in order to satisfy his own interests and also satisfy the people who surround him (see table 1). In the PHuNAC model, the pedestrian agent, in this case, considers all the attributes. To do this, the variable F_i can have only the values +1 or -1.

6   Experiments and Discussions

We present in this section quantitative experiments. We follow the literature in the measurement of two main features of pedestrian's movements: the average velocity and traffic flow. For this purpose, we have been based on the works achieved by Fruin (see [30]). On the basis of real data, the latter has pointed out laws that describe the walking Level of service. These laws represent the distribution of the average velocity as a function of the crowd density. He has also pointed out laws describing the relation between crowd flow and crowd density.

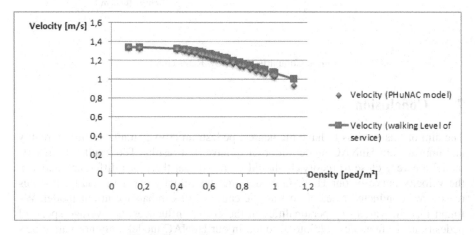

Fig. 3. Comparison of average velocity curves

In order to obtain a curve of average velocity as a function of density, at time t, we created an initial population density of 0.01 pedestrians/ m². Subsequently, we measured the average velocity of the crowd. At time t +1, we added another population of the same density which gives us a density of 0.02 pedestrians /m². Similarly, we measured the average velocity of the crowd. We repeated this experiment several times. At the end of the experiment, we obtained a curve of average velocity as a function of density. Fig.3 compares the curves of the average velocity of the PHuNAC model with curve representing the real data (Fruin [30]). We observe that the velocity curve of our model is very close to the velocity curve representing real data. This is thanks to the integration of different personalities.

It is very important to note that the personality's variation affects the flow characteristics (see fig.1). In fact, the flow characteristics include pedestrian's velocity and pedestrian's flow rates. For this purpose, we must take into consideration not only the velocity but also the flow rates. We repeated the same previous experiment, but this time we measured the flow of pedestrian traffic rather than the average velocity. Fig.4 shows the comparison of the flow rates between PHUNAC model and real data. We observe that the flow rate curve of our model is very close to the flow rates curve representing real data.

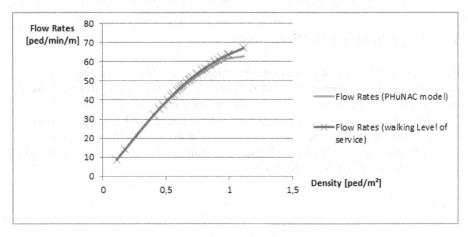

Fig. 4. Comparison of Flow Rates curves

7   Conclusion

The aim of this work is to have the nearest pedestrian crowd simulation to the reality and improve our HuNAC model, in order to have best results. The results of HuNAC model are very close to reality. It should be noted that there is a difference between the velocity curve of our HuNAC model and the velocity curve of reality. For this reason, we conducted research to find the cause of this imbalance in our model. We found that the variety of personalities in the crowd influences the average speed of pedestrians. In fact, we took into account, in our HuNAC model, only normative personality, but in reality, there are several personalities. For this reason, we integrate the different personalities. The conducted experiments show that PHuNAC model is able to produce more realistic pedestrian behaviors more than HuNAC model. It is very important to note that our PHuNAC model doesn't consider emergency situations. We can improve PHUNAC model by considering the evacuation movements.

References

1. Hoogendoorn, S.P.: Pedestrian Flow Modeling by Adaptive Control. Transportation Research Board Annual Meeting (2004a)
2. Beltaief, O., Hadouaj, S., Ghedira, K.: Multi-agent simulation model of pedestrians crowd based on psychological theories. In: 2011 4th International Conference on Logistics (LOGISTIQUA) (2011)
3. Zanlungo, F.: Microscopic dynamics of articial life systems. Springer (2007)
4. Helbing, D.: A fluid-dynamic model for the movement of pedestrians. Complex Systems 6, 391–415 (1992)
5. Smith, R.A.: Density, velocity and flow relationships for closely packed crowds. Safety Science 18, 321–327 (1995)
6. Cusack, M.A.: Modelling aggregate-level entities as a continuum. Mathematical and Computer Modelling of Dynamical Systems 8, 33–48 (2002)
7. Still, G.: Crowd Dynamics, 640–655 (2000)
8. Clegg, C.W., Robinson, M.A., Challenger, R.: Understanding Crowd Behaviours. Cabinet Office Emergency Planning College (2009)
9. Helbing, D., Farkas, I., Moln'ar, P., Vicsek, T.: Simulation of pedestrian crowds in normal and evacuation situations. In: Schreckenberg, M., Sharma, S.D. (eds.) Pedestrian and Evacuation Dynamics, pp. 21–58. Springer, Berlin (2002)
10. Moussaïd, M., Perozo, N., Garnier, S., Helbing, D., Theraulaz, G.: The Walking Behaviour of Pedestrian Social Groups and Its Impact on Crowd Dynamics. PLoS ONE 5(4), e10047+ (2010)
11. Wilde, D.J.: Jung's Personality Theory Quantified (2011) ISBN: 978-0-85729-099-1 (Print) 978-0-85729-100-4
12. Klupfel, H.: The simulation of crowds at very large events. In: Schadschneider, A., Khne, R., Pschel, T., Schreckenberg, M., Wolf, D.E. (eds.) Trafic and Granular Flow 2005. Springer, Berlin (2006) (accepted for publication)
13. Yuan, W., Tan, K.H.: A novel algorithm of simulating multi-velocity evacuation based on cellular automata modeling and tenability condition. Physica A: Statistical Mechanics and its Applications 379(1), 250–262 (2007)
14. Reynolds, C.W.: Flocks, herds, and schools: A distributed behavioral model. In: SIGGRAPH 1987: Proceedings of the 14th Annual Conference on Computer Graphics and Interactive Techniques, pp. 25–34. ACM, New York (1987)
15. Xiong, M., Lees, M., Cai, W., Zhou, S., Low, M.Y.-H.: A Rule-Based Motion Planning for Crowd Simulation. In: Ugail, H., Qahwaji, R., Earnshaw, R.A., Willis, P.J. (eds.) 2009 International Conference on CyberWorlds, Bradford, West Yorkshire, UK, September 7-11, pp. 88–95. IEEE Computer Society (2009)
16. Cherif, F., Chighoub, R.: Crowd simulation influenced by agent's socio-psychological state (2010)
17. Durupinar, F., Allbeck, J.M., Pelechano, N., Badler, N.I.: Creating crowd variation with the ocean personality model. In: Padgham, L., Parkes, D.C., Mller, J., Parsons, S. (eds.) AAMAS (3), pp. 1217–1220. IFAAMAS (2008)
18. Fridman, N., Kaminka, G.A.: Towards a cognitive model of crowd behavior based on social comparison theory. In: AAAI, pp. 731–737 (2007)
19. Musse, S.R., Thalmann, D.: A model of human crowd behavior: Group interrelationship and collision detection analysis. In: Workshop Computer Animation and Simulation of Eurographics, pp. 39–52 (1997)

20. Bonabeau, E.: Agent-based modeling: methods and techniques for simulating human systems. Proceedings of the National Academy of Sciences of the United States of America 99(suppl. 3), 7280–7287 (2002)
21. Burden, A.M.: New york city pedestrian level of service study phase i. Technical report, City of New York (2006)
22. Furnham, A.: The big five versus the big four: the relationship between the Myers-Briggs Type Indicator (MBTI) and NEO-PI five factor model of personality. Personality and Individual Differences (1996)
23. Johnsson, F.: Personality measures under focus: The NEO-PI-R and the MBTI. Griffith University Undergraduate Student Journal 1, 32–42 (2009)
24. Helbing, D., Molnar, P., Farkas, I.J., Bolay, K.: Self-organizing pedestrian movement. Environment and Planning B: Planning and Design 28(3), 361–383 (2001)
25. Wurster, C.D.: Myers-Briggs Type Indicator: A cultural and ethical evaluation. Executive Research Project, National Defense University, Washington D.C. (1993) (retrieved May 5, 2008)
26. Howard, P.J.: The MBTI and the Five Factor Mode. Center for Applied Cognitive Studies (CentACS) Charlotte, North Carolina (2006)
27. McCrae, R.R., Costa Jr., P.T.: Reinterpreting the Myers-Briggs Type Indicator From the Perspective of the Five-Factor Model of Personality. American Psychologist 44(2), 451–452 (1989)
28. Oosterhout, D.: Automatic Modeling of Personality Types, at the Universiteit van Amsterdam (2009)
29. Zevenbergen, R.: Automatic modeling of personality types: the 2-qubit model, Universiteit van Amsterdam (2010)
30. Fruin, J.J.: Pedestrian Planning and Design. Metropolitan Association of Urban Designers and Environmental, New York (1971)
31. Miler, J.S., Begelow, J.D., Garber, N.J.: Calibrating Pedestrian Level-of-Service Metrics with 3-D visualisation. Transportation Research Record 1705, 9–15 (2000)
32. Sharkar, S.: Determination of Service Levels for Pedestrians, with European Examples. Transportation Research Record 1405, 35–42 (1993)
33. Khisty, C.J.: Evaluation of pedestrian Facilities: Beyond the Level of Service Concept. Transportation Research Record 1438, 45–50 (1994)
34. JMH Consultancy, Introducing the Myers Briggs Type Indicator (MBTI) (2006)

Ambient Intelligence: Applications and Privacy Policies

Mar Lopez[1], Juanita Pedraza[2], Javier Carbo[1], and Jose M. Molina[1]

[1] Carlos III University of Madrid, Computer Science Department
[2] Carlos III University of Madrid, Public State Law Department
Avda. Gregorio Peces-Barba Martínez, 28270.Colmenarejo, Madrid, Spain
{mariamar.lopez,javier.carbo,jose.molina}@uc3m.es,
jpedraza@der-pu.uc3m.es

Abstract. In this paper, we present a complete overview of Ambient Intelligence (AmI) focused in its applications, considering the involved domain and technologies. The applications include AmI at home, care of elderly and people with disabilities, healthcare, education, business, public services, leisure and entertainment. The aim of this survey of AmI's applications is to show its socials and ethical implications and specially privacy issues. Intelligent Environments (IE) collect and process a massive amount of person-related and sensitive data. These data must ensure privacy of the users. An important concern in AmI´s applications is privacy. Addressing design by privacy, an important challenge to consider is the development of an architecture that includes the different privacy policies and how can we fusion them in a specific application domain. Ensuring privacy in Intelligent Environments is a difficult problem to solve, as there are different perceptions of privacy and its role in computing for each user. In the so called 'design by privacy' we have to identify the relevant design issues that should be addressed for its developing. Here we present an approach to the dimensions to consider, in order to provide privacy in the design of Ambient Intelligence's applications.

Keywords: Ambient Intelligence, Design Dimensions, Privacy-Policies, User's profile, Intelligent Environments.

1 Introduction

Ambient Intelligence (AmI) involves extensive and invisible integration of computer technologies in people´s everyday lives. Ambient Intelligence [1, 2] consists in the creation of living environments (called Intelligent Environments, IE) [3] where users interact in a natural and intuitive way with computational services which ease the completion of the user´s everyday tasks, being this for leisure, help or work assistance [4, 5]. Ambient Intelligence has potential applications in many areas of life, including home, office, transport, industry, entertainment, tourism, recommender systems, safety systems, healthcare and supported living. Ambient Intelligence will undoubtedly bring substantial economic and social benefits to citizens and industry, but they will come alloyed with many risks.

J.M. Corchado et al. (Eds.): PAAMS 2014 Workshops, CCIS 430, pp. 191–201, 2014.

Ambient Intelligence can be identified as an intelligent, embedded, digital environment that is sensitive and responsive to the presence of people [6], with five related key technology features: embedded, context aware, personalized, adaptive, and anticipatory [7]. The integration of computer technologies in AmI will inevitably open up issues of privacy, risks, acceptance and security. It has been widely acknowledged that is a need for acceptable standards and for laws regulating access, to avoid social and ethical problems [8].

This paper presents a survey of Ambient Intelligence applications focused in the involved domains and technologies. In order to provide a conceptual framework that includes the different privacy policies, privacy issues must be considered in the design in AmI´s applications. The design by privacy in AmI has to include several levels of privacy about how a specific Ambient Intelligence's application, acquires, stores, manages, shares and sends different types of personal dates. The different privacy policies depend on the next elements: ambient ubiquitous, devices, user, services, and legal requirements. Computer scientists who research in AmI must design Ambient Intelligence applications that achieve privacy by design jointly with legal experts.

The related work is organized as follows: Section 2 reviews some of the Ambient Intelligence applications considering the involved domain and technologies. In section 3 we show a study of privacy in AmI. In section 4 we show the design dimensions in the development of these applications in order to provide privacy with the aim to approach a framework for privacy enforcement, based in the domain of Ambient Intelligence and centered in the user. Section 5 presents our conclusions and proposes future work.

2   Ambient Intelligence Applications: A Survey

This section reviews some researches on Ambient Intelligence applications in several domains that include: home, care of elderly and people with disabilities, healthcare, education, business, public services, leisure and entertainment. The employed technologies include several devices as sensor, smart phones, tablet, NFC, RFID, etc.

- **Leisure and Entertainment / Commerce and Business**

The mobile interactions with the physical world are becoming available on the market, using mobile phones equipped with Near-Field Communication (NFC) [9]. The possibilities that NFC brings to users of mobile devices show a large variety in applications domains like shop, tourism and leisure. An important issue that must be considered is the user's interactions with NFC services. The authors of [10] showed potential of improvement and development for future NFC services that make it clear where interaction occurs, where feedback is given, and how the flow of interaction takes place. User problems in the interactions with this technology are strongly related to recognizing the availability of services, as interaction capabilities are often hidden.

A framework for a location based mobile Information and Communications Technology (ICT) system for the tourist industry is presented in [11]. This project is focused on content, information, products and services than can be offered tourists on a mobile platform, typically tablets or smartphones giving the users extra utility value. The solutions are interactive and based on the needs of the customers and the tourist operators. Qualitative feedback is required to improve and develop customized content for mobile tourism services. The lack of this qualitative information about tourist experiences is a path to follow in combination with existing quantitative information. Ethical aspects about collecting customer data through mobile devices in this framework should been clarified.

The automation of baggage management in an airport is presented in [12].The main goal of baggage in an airport is to manage the transport of the luggage via conveyors, carts and planes to right destination. The baggage is tagged at the Check-In, traditionally with barcodes, nowadays more and more with RFID tags. Visibility, security and privacy of baggage events are challenging issues to address.

In [13] an application to tourism in the city of Córdoba is presented. The solution is based in the use of mobile phones provided with Near Field Communications Technology (NFC) and Smart posters spread up along the smart environments offering the users/visitors, in a way easy, intuitive and context-awareness, support for the navigation and localization in urban smart scenarios. The idea proposed in this work is that the user could design its own routes making use of a set of intelligent objects (Smart Posters) augmented by RFID Tags with information about localizations where the tourist could visit.

• **Education**

Mobile learning (m-learning) [14] provides great opportunities to interact with learning materials in different ways while exploring a physical environment both outdoor and indoor. The use of mobile devices like smartphones may expand learning, freeing the user from ties to a particular location. For instance Explore! [15] is an m-learning system implementing a game to help middle school students to acquire historical notions while visiting archaeological parks.

• **Healthcare and Assisted Living**

The qualitative study presented by [16] contributes to the design of Information Technologies supporting diabetics in their daily live. Most IT designed for diabetics have an exclusive medical focus. Aspects of co-operation (in particular the data transfer between people) is possible with the availability of medical devices and self-management tools with communication possibilities. There exists an endless offer of networking possibilities for diabetics (forums, chats, weblog, video or picture sharing sides). Through these networks people strengthen and encourage each other, sharing their thoughts, problems and fears and also their experiences. Thus, co-operation is the central activity, accompanied by informing, finding and planning. In the design of the MaXi-project an important implication to consider is a sustainable privacy and security that give the user full benefit and control of the data-flow.

A personalized system that allows a person and their care givers to monitor the person's health status is described in [17]. Health monitors may be particularly useful for chronically ill people as well as for elderly citizens [18]. Sensors automatically capture health-related data such as heart rate and blood pressure, the location of the person in reference to a room, or the intake of medication. The data needs to be protected from tampering, from external unqualified access, as well as being kept safe for long term storage.

UbiMeds is a mobile application that would allow patients to have easy access to prescription information in a mobile phone platform [19]. This mobile application integrates with current Personal Health Record systems to provide automated scheduling, reminders and tracking of prescription drugs intake, including proactive alerts sent to physicians and relatives then the patient fails to adhere to the prescription regime. Privacy issues are important to consider. This is particularly critical on applications where health related information is involved and when they use third party service such a Google Health or Microsoft Vault to store the health records.

GerAmI (Geriatric Ambient Intelligence) is a system based on agents to facility the care of Alzheimer patients [20]. The system contains ID door readers, ID bracelets for the patients and the nurses, with each bracelet containing an RFID chip, PDAs for nurses, controllable alarms and locks, and wireless access points. The architecture uses a multi-agent structure. The manager and the patient agents run on a central computer and the nurses agents run on mobile devices. The patient agent records the location of the patient hourly and sends the record to a central database.

An application to promote physical exercise for elderly people using the digital televisions is described in a research study about its usability and acceptability [21]. The aim of this study was to obtain feedback from representative elderly people to inform further development of this application. The devices and technologies used were: HD cameras, wide-screen LCD TV connected to a mini-PC unit, video capturing devices like de USB web-camera, wireless connectivity by Bluetooth, Nintendo Wii Fit (NWF).

Building Bridges is a project for social connection to elderly people, their family and friends. It intends to reduce the risk of loneliness and social isolation of them [22]. The communication device used to connect elderly people with their peers, family and friends is based in a touch screen. Further functionality includes individual or group calls, a (textual) messaging service, and a "tea room" which represents a chat forum. The aim of this study was to examine usage and usability of the device communication device for these purposes.

3   Privacy in AmI

The massive collection of data by the Ambient Intelligence technologies that populate Intelligent Environments enables extensive profiling, which in turn is necessary to deliver the benefits promised by Ambient Intelligence. AmI weaves together heterogeneous systems and devices into a seamless architecture able to accommodate the wishes of commercial agents who want access to as much data from as many sources as possible, not only for a higher level of service personalization, but also of security. Data collection and data availability in the AmI world are not the only important issues to be examined, as we also need to consider what "knowledge" is generated from the data. Clearly, the more data, more precise are the profiles [23]. The knowledge about citizen- consumers is often produced to achieve a certain purpose, e.g. to encourage them to buy something or to judge their eligibility for certain services or to assess them as a security risk. Hence, the knowledge does not match the intentions or expectations or interests of the concerned citizen-consumers. The knowledge derived from the use of AmI can create information asymmetries between those who are under surveillance and those who are doing surveillance.

SWAMI (Safeguards in a World of Ambient Intelligence) [24], was a policy-oriented research project focused on social, economic, legal, technological and ethical issues of AmI with particular regard to privacy, trust, security and identity through four dark scenarios that encompass individual-societal and private-public concerns. The results of analysis of each of the scenarios revealed various risks, threats and vulnerabilities posed by AmI in relation to privacy, trust, security, identity and inclusion, among which were greatly increased surveillance and monitoring, a deepening of the digital divide, identity theft, malicious attacks' and so on.

The study presents in [25], involves more than 70 Research and Development projects, from the point of view of what types of scenario they focus on, what assumptions they do about the users, and the control of AmI systems they envisage. The projects cover five application domains: home, health, shopping, work and mobility, leisure and entertainment. In the envisaged and developing applications, where the AmI system was aimed at providing safety or security it had a high level of control. In particular, AmI control is assumed to be very high in envisaged emergency situations, requiring little numbers of communication with humans. On the other hand, where the system had a more advice-giving role it had lower levels of control, possibly subordinate to the user.

In [26] the authors identifies the two central features of AmI that pose the main challenge to privacy: the ability of AmI systems to collect large and detailed amounts of data about individuals' everyday activities over long periods of time, and the enhanced ability for integrating, searching, and retrieving these large amounts of data. These features are central for one of the key objectives of AmI, which is to provide personalized services. AmI can provide sophisticated support for everyday living, but the information capabilities it may use for this purpose can also potentially provide an invisible and comprehensive surveillance network – walls literally can have ears. The authors identify three additional issues to consider in AmI environment: reliability, delegation of control and social compatibility and acceptance.

In [27] the author consider the current European privacy and data protection frameworks and questions if they are applicable and adequate for dealing with the kind of data collection and processing that is at the heart of AmI scenarios and technologies. The European human rights framework incorporates "autonomy in the construction of one's identity", explicitly in the right to privacy. One consequence of this statement, interpreted in courts, is the individual's right to control personal information. The pervasiveness of AmI and the invisibility of data collection and information systems may make it highly unlikely that the individual (the person being observed) will retain control over the data. Furthermore, one objective of AmI systems is to learn user profiles in order to respond to human needs, but these needs are being defined increasingly by the systems themselves, and thus by the designers of the systems, and not by the users. The author [27] shares with [26] the concern about delegation of control in AmI systems that are likely to be distributed systems in which multiple artificial and human agents collaborate and interact. So the notion of human agency, traditional in law for assigning individual responsibility and liability, becomes blurred.

Other features of AmI studied concern information flow, its advantages and dangers. AmI massively increases the amounts of detailed personalized data that is collected and stored, and has the potential to make, and indeed in some applications must make, such data easily available. Furthermore, as [26] has also observed, personalization of data and provision of services, can ultimately lead to the control and filtering of what news or information the users see. Some authors [25] look at data privacy in Ambient Intelligence settings. Their implemented case study concerns to an organization (a university) collecting information about its members accessing Web sites. The purpose of these data is to enable ranking of Web sites and making recommendations to those with similar interests. However, the malicious use of the data can disclose information about what times, and for how long, someone accessed some given Web sites. To counter this, the proposed solution is that users can specify life-cycle policies on data collected on them.

Most of the studies about Ambient Intelligence applications are focused in the technologies, in some cases in the users and in a few cases in the issues of social and privacy impact of AmI technology in order to provide personalized services. In spite of there is much agreement about concerns over security and the social and ethical implications of Ambient Intelligence. It are also crystal clear the reasons why Ambient Intelligences gives rise to security concerns: the collection of large amounts of personal data, the long-term persistence and integration of such data and the possibility of, and in fact often the need for, providing easy access to the data in a technological world increasingly complex.

4   Design Dimensions in Ambient Ingelligence: Design by Privacy

Although most of AmI applications are focused in the technology involved (sensor devices, device´s communication) and in some cases are focused in the user, we consider that the most important element in AmI applications is the user, and so it must be the application the one that adapts itself to the user´s profiles, being the privacy one of the most important issues to be considered. Different levels of privacy should be identified and appropriate mechanisms shall be developed to distinguish life-threatening requests from other applications with various security priorities and appropriate privacy-protections measures.

Hong et al., [28] suggest designers of ubicomp systems need to deploy a privacy risk analysis considering social and organizational content. This type of analysis considers: Who are the users? What kind of personal information is being shared? How is personal information collected? The authors suggest after the initial privacy risk analysis designers need to prioritize the findings and develop a privacy risk management record. Privacy risk model helps designers consider the specific group of users, potential risks and benefits, and the type of feedback users will be giving the system. Privacy risk models will help with designing and understanding social issues as trends move towards ubiquitous computing environments.

The mains dimensions of design by privacy in the AmI's domain and centered in users are:

- Privacy of personal data (data or information privacy). Individuals claim that data about themselves should not be automatically available to other individuals and organizations, and that, even where data is possessed by another party, the individual must be able to exercise a substantial degree of control over their data and its use.
- Privacy of personal behavior (media privacy). This relates to all aspects of behavior, but especially to sensitive matters, such as sexual preferences and habits, political activities and religious practices, both in private and in public places.

- Privacy of personal experience. Individuals gather experience through buying books and newspapers and reading the text and images in them, buying or renting recorder video, conducting conversations with other individuals both in person and on the mobile phone, meeting people in small groups, and attending live and cinema events with larger numbers of people. Until very recently, all of these were ephemeral, none of them generated records, and hence each individual's small-scale experiences, and their consolidated large-scale experience, were not visible to others. During the first decade of the 21st century, reading and viewing activities have migrated to screens, are performed under the control of corporations, and are recorded; most conversations have become 'stored electronic communications', each event is recorded and both 'call records' and content may be retained; many individuals' locations are tracked, and correlations are performed to find out who is co-located with whom and how often; and events tickets are paid for using identified payment instruments. This massive consolidation of individuals' personal experience is available for exploitation, and therefore it is exploited.

In the development on AmI´s Applications an important issue to add from the beginning of the development process is privacy. In order to enforce privacy according to the different privacy policies and how can we fusion them, we propose a conceptual framework (Figure 1) that contain a Privacy Management System and a Privacy Enforcement Controller that takes care of interaction between technologies and devices, users and application's domain.

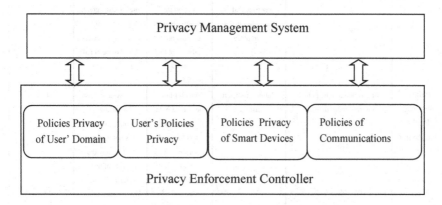

Fig. 1. Proposed conceptual Framework Design by Privacy in Ambient Intelligence

The Privacy Enforcement Controller consists of four different modules:

1. Specific privacy policies of the ubiquitous environment (Policies of User's Domain)
2. Specific privacy policies of the user (User´s Policies Privacy)
3. Specific privacy policies of the devices (Policies Smart Applications Devices and Intelligent Sensors)
4. Specific privacy policies of the communications (Public key certificates)

This conceptual framework can help to determinate the privacy policies in a specific domain in AmI, that should include several levels of data protection of the rights by the privacy about how a specific Ambient Intelligence's application, acquires, stores, manages, shares and sends different types of personal dates (Table 1).

Table 1. Privacy Policies in Application Domain in AmI

	General considerations	User's conditions	Device's characteristics	Communication's characteristics	Levels of data protection
Healthcare	Healthcare determines the life and death of people. The access to a person's health information can be very important in case of emergency.	Patients with autonomous or semi-autonomous life. Patients with limited mental capacity: permanent or transitory (e.g., heart problems and epilepsy).	The character visible or invisible of devices is not so important because there is a Patient Agreement that allows the use of device.	The system must be capable of identify to user. Transmission means must grant: Confidentiality, Integrity, Availability of personal data.	High
Education	In this domain the public interest consists in the protection of personal data.	People interested in enjoy of life-long learning aim, from any place, at any time and at the individual's own place.	The character visible or invisible of the devices is not important because there is an Education Agreement that allows the use of device.	The system must be capable of identify to user. Transmissions means must grant: Confidentiality, Integrity, Availability of personal data.	Medium
Public Services (Public Transport)	In this domain the public interest consists in the protection of personal data.	Public Transport user's.	The user must be agreed with the use of geo-localization services includes in devices.	The system must be capable of identify to device (it is not mandatory to know the identity of user). Transmissions means must grant: Integrity and Availability of data.	Low
Commerce (Tourist /Leisure)	The public interest consists in the protection of personal data (e.g. Prohibits capturing, storing, or reading information from a person's RFID document for particular purpose without that person's prior knowledge and consent).	Consumers	In this domain could be present invisible devices (e.g. RFID chip).	The system must be capable of identify to person. Transmission means must grant: Integrity and Availability of data.	Medium

5   Conclusions and Future Work

The AmI's applications involve an extensive and invisible integration of computer technologies in people´s daily lives. Ambient Intelligence has potential applications in many areas of life, including home, office, transport, industry, entertainment, tourism, recommender systems, safety systems, healthcare and supported living.

Ambient Intelligence involves all sorts of legal complexities. Hence, it merits further research on how to strengthen existing regulatory safeguards and devise new ones to meet the challenges before us in the world of Ambient Intelligence.

To approach design by privacy, an important challenge to be considered is the development of an architecture that includes the different privacy policies and how can we fusion them in a specific domain. To design by privacy we should identify the design issues that should be addressed for his developing

This paper presents a survey of AmI´s applications based in the domains and technologies involved, in order to provide a conceptual framework that include the different privacy policies that must be considered in the design in AmI´s applications. This architecture should include several levels of privacy about how a specific application in AmI obtains, stores, manages, shares and sends different types of personal dates.

The AmI´s applications offer great opportunities but in many cases, they are too focused on technology and forgot users. The quality of a system should take in regard several non-technical factors that also play crucial roles in the applications, such as affordability, legal, regulatory and ethical issues like privacy. The quality of the privacy protection highly depends on the used policies.

The success and acceptance of AmI by the citizens-consumers will depend on how secure and reliable it is and to what extent it is perceived to allow the protection of the rights and privacy of individuals. In order to enjoy the benefits of AmI, we must considerer a new approach to privacy and data protection, based on control and responsibility rather than on restriction and prohibition.

Our future researches will focus on a methodology to systematically consider privacy issues (PIA, Privacy Impact Assessment) in an AAL System (Ambient Assisted Living) to evaluate its utility. Other lines of research will address privacy enforcement that includes privacy policies in the design by Privacy in Ambient Intelligence. Design by privacy is a step toward proposing design guidelines for the development of AAL Systems that support independent and private living of the people with disabilities can autonomously live in their own home.

Acknowledgements. This work has been supported in part by the projects: CAM "Contexts"(S2009/TIC-1485), MINECO "Falcon" (TEC2011-28626-C02-02), MINECO "Tease" (TEC2012-37832-C02-01).

References

1. ISTAG, Scenarios for ambient intelligence in 2010. European Commission Report (2001), http://www.cordis.lu/ist/istag.html (2010)
2. ISTAG, Strategic orientation & priorities for IST in FP6. European Commission Report (2002), http://www.cordis.europa.eu/fp7/ict/istag/reports_en.html (2010)

3. ISTAG, Ambient intelligence: from vision to reality. European Commission Report (2003), http://www.cordis.europa.eu/fp7/ict/istag/reports_en.html (2010)
4. Weiser, M.: The computer for the twenty-first century. Scientific Am. 265(3), 91–104 (1991)
5. Aarts, E., Marzano: The new everyday: Views of Ambient Intelligence. 010 Publishers, Rotterdam (2003)
6. Gaggioli, A.: Optimal experience in ambient intelligence. In: Riva, G., Vatalaro, F., Davide, F., Alcaniz, M. (eds.) Ambient Intelligence, pp. 35–43. IOS Press, Amsterdam (2005)
7. Aarts, E.: Ambient intelligence: a multimedia perspective. IEEE Intell. Syst. 19(1), 12–19 (2004)
8. Sadri, F.: Ambient Intelligence: A Survey. ACM Computing Surveys 43(4), Article 36 (2011)
9. Geven, A., Strassl, P., Ferro, B., Tscheligi, M., Scwab, H.: Experiencing Real-World Interaction: Results from a NFC User Experience Field Trial. In: Proceedings of the 9th International Conference on Human Computer Interaction with Mobile Devices and Services, HCI 2007 (2007)
10. Belt, S., Greenblatt, D., Häkkilä, J., Mäkelä, K.: User Perceptions on Mobile Interaction with Visual and RFID Tags. In: Proc. of the Workshop on Mobile Interaction with the Real World, Espoo, Finland, pp. 23–26 (2006)
11. Bojen Nielsen, L.: Post Disney experience paradigm? Some implications for the development of content to mobile tourist services. In: Proceedings of the 6th International Conference on Electronic Commerce, ICEC 2004, Delft, The Netherlands (2004)
12. DeVries, P.: The state of RFID for effective baggage tracking in the airline industry. International Journal of Mobile Communications 2008 6(2), 151–164 (2008)
13. Borrego-Jaraba, F., Luque Ruiz, I., Gómez-Nieto, M.Á.: NFC Solution for the Development of Smart Scenarios Supporting Tourism Applications and Surfing in Urban Environments. In: García-Pedrajas, N., Herrera, F., Fyfe, C., Benítez, J.M., Ali, M. (eds.) IEA/AIE 2010, Part III. LNCS, vol. 6098, pp. 229–238. Springer, Heidelberg (2010)
14. Holzinger, A., et al.: Lifelong-learning support by mlearning: Example scenarios. eLearn 11, 2 (2005)
15. Maria, F., Costabile, A., De Angeli, R., Lanzilotti, C., Ardito, P., Buono, T.: Explore! Possibilities and Cahallenges of Mobile Learning. In: CHI 2008 Proceedings-Learning Support. 26th Annual SIGCHI Conference on Human Factors in Computing, Florence (2008)
16. Kanstrup, A.M., Bertelsen, P., Glasemann, M., Boye, N.: Design for More: an Ambient Perspective on Diabetes. In: Proceedings of the 10th Anniversary Conference on Participatory Design, PDC 2008, Bloomington, USA (2008)
17. Heinzelman, W., Murphy, A., Carvalho, H., Perillo, M.: Middleware to support sensor network applications. IEEE Network 18 (2004)
18. Jung, D., Hinze, A.: A mobile alerting system for the support of patients with chronic conditions. In: First European Conference on Mobile Government (EURO mGOV), Brighton, UK, pp. 264–274 (2005)
19. Silva, J.M., Mouttham, A., El Saddik, A.: UbiMeds: A mobile application to improve accessibility and support medication adherence. In: Proceedings of the 1st ACM SIGMM International Workshop on Media Studies and Implementations that Help Improving Access to Disabled Users, Beijing, China (2009)

20. Corchado, J.M., Bajo, J., Abraham, A.: GerAmi: improving healthcare delivery in geriatric residences. J. IEEE Intell. Syst. (Special Issue on Ambient Intelligence) 3(2), 19–25 (2008)
21. Carmichael, A., Rice, M., MacMillan, F., Kirk, A.: Investigating a DTV-based physical activity application to facilitate wellbeing in older adults. In: Proceedings of the 24th BCS Interaction Specialist Group Conference, BCS 2010, Dundee, UK (2010)
22. Doyle, J., Skrba, Z., McDonnell, R., Arent, B.: Designing a touch screen communication device to support social interaction amongst older adults. In: Proceedings of the 24th BCS Interaction Specialist Group Conference, BCS 2010 (2010)
23. De Hert, P., Gutwirth, S., Moscibroda, A., Wright, D., González, G.: Legal safeguards for privacy and data protection in ambient intelligence. Pers. Ubiquit. Comput. 13, 435–444 (2009)
24. Wright, D., Gutwirth, S., Friedewald, M., Punie, Y., Vildjiounaite, E. (eds.): Safeguards in a world of ambient intelligence, p. 291. Springer Press, Dordrecht (2008)
25. Friedewald, M., Da Costa, O., Punie, Y., Alahuhta, P., Heinonen, S.: Perspectives of ambient intelligence in the home environment. Telematics Informatics 22, 221–238 (2005)
26. Bohn, J., Coroama, V., Langheinrich, M., Mattern, F., Rohs, M.: Living in a world of smart everyday objects—Social, economic, and ethical implications. Human Ecol. Risk Assess. 10(5) (2004)
27. Rouvroy, A.: Privacy, data protection, and the unprecedented challenges of ambient intelligence. Studies Ethics, Law, Technol. 2(1), Article 3 (2008)
28. Hong, J.I., Ng, J.D., Lederer, S., Landay, J.: Privacy Risk Models for Designing Privacy-Sensitive Ubiquitous Computing Systems. In: Proceedings of the 5th Conf. on Designing Interactive Systems, DIS 2004, pp. 91–100 (2004), http://dx.doi.org/10.1145/1013115.1013129

High-Level Information Fusion for Risk and Accidents Prevention in Pervasive Oil Industry Environments

Nayat Sanchez-Pi[1], Luis Martí[2], José Manuel Molina[3],
and Ana Cristina Bicharra Garcia[4]

[1] Instituto de Lógica, Filosofia e Teoria da Ciéncia (ILTC), Niterói (RJ) Brazil
`nayat@iltc.br`
[2] Dept. of Electrical Engineering, Pontifícia Universidade Católica do Rio de Janeiro,
Rio de Janeiro (RJ) Brazil
`lmarti@ele.puc-rio.br`
[3] Dept. of Informatics, Universidad Carlos III de Madrid,
Colmenarejo, Madrid, Spain
`molina@ia.uc3m.es`
[4] ADDLabs, Fluminense Federal University, Niterói (RJ) Brazil
`cristina@addlabs.uff.br`

Abstract. Information fusion studies theories and methods to effectively combine data from multiple sensors and related information to achieve more specific inferences that could be achieved by using a single, independent sensor. Information fused from sensors and data mining analysis has recently attracted the attention of the research community for real-world applications. In this sense, the deployment of an Intelligent Offshore Oil Industry Environment will help to figure out a risky scenario based on the events occurred in the past related to anomalies and the profile of the current employee (role, location, etc.). In this paper we propose an information fusion model for an intelligent oil environment in which employees are alerted about possible risk situations while their are moving around their working place. The layered architecture, implements a reasoning engine capable of intelligently filtering the context profile of the employee (role, location) for the feature selection of an inter-transaction mining process. Depending on the employee contextual information he will receive intelligent alerts based on the prediction model that use his role and his current location. This model provides the big picture about risk analysis for that employee at that place in that moment.

Keywords: Information fusion, context, data mining, ontologies, oil industry.

1 Introduction

There is an important effort of oil and gas industry to reduce the number of accidents and incidents. In oil industry exist standards to identify and record workplace accidents and incidents to provide guiding means on prevention efforts, indicating specific failures or reference, means of correction of conditions

J.M. Corchado et al. (Eds.): PAAMS 2014 Workshops, CCIS 430, pp. 202–213, 2014.
© Springer International Publishing Switzerland 2014

or circumstances that culminated in accident. Besides, oil and gas industry is increasingly concerned with achieving and demonstrating good performance of occupational health and safety (OHS), through the control of its OHS risks, which is consistent with its policy and objectives.

OHS continues to be a priority issue for the offshore oil and gas industry and a determining factor in its overall success. Years passed since community takes into account the implications of oil industry to Health, Safety and the Environment but nowadays industries invest a lot of efforts in accidents prevention. With the advances of communication technologies and the novelty researches in Ubiquitous Computing (UC) and Ambient Intelligence (AmI), is almost a fact to think of a Pervasive Offshore Oil Industry Environment.

In this scenario employees are surrounded of intelligent technology capable of not only interacting in an natural way, but also to intelligently reason on the accidents risk picture in order to alert the employees when an risky event is probable to occur in the place where is located. The process of constructing a dynamic risk picture for accident or incident detection and recognition involves contextual reasoning about past events, dynamic context (location, user, profile, etc), as well as relations between them with respect to particular goals,capabilities, and policies of the decision makers.

In this paper we propose an information fusion model for an intelligent oil environment in which employees are alerted about possible risk situations while their are moving around their working place. The layered architecture, implements a reasoning engine capable of intelligently filter the context profile of the employee (role, location) for the feature selection of an inter-transaction mining process. So, depending on the employee contextual information he will receive intelligent alerts based on the prediction model that use his role and his current location.

This model provides the big picture about risk analysis for that employee at that place in that moment. Our contribution is to build a causality model for accidents investigation by means of a well-defined spatio-temporal constraints on offshore oil industry domain. We use ontological constraints in the post-processing mining stage to prune resulting rules.

The paper is organized as follows. After providing an introduction to the HSE problem and the role of information fusion processes in building a risk picture, Section 2 briefly describes the state of the art and some application domains. Section 3 focuses on knowledge retrieval model, its architecture, domain model and reasoning process. Section 4 depicts the formalization of the mining information used by the context based reasoning process for threat detection and recognition. Finally, Section 5 presents some final remarks.

2   Foundations

Ambient Intelligence represents, a new generation of user-centred computing environments aiming to find new ways to obtain a better integration of the information technology in everyday life devices and activities. In order to work efficiently, software running on these devices may have some knowledge about the user, it means that there is an increasing need of improve context awareness and knowledge sharing without interfering with users daily life activities [1].

Techniques for using contextual information in high-level information fusion architectures has been studied at [2].In the context of oil and gas industry is increasingly concerned with achieving and demonstrating good performance of occupational health and safety (OHS), through the control of its OHS risks, which is consistent with its policy and objectives. In oil industry exist standards to identify and record workplace accidents and incidents to provide guiding means on prevention efforts, indicating specific failures or reference, means of correction of conditions or circumstances that culminated in accident. So, events recognition is central to OHS, since the system can selectively start proper prediction services according to the user current situation and past knowledge.

Knowledge discovery (KDD) is the process of extracting and refining useful knowledge from large databases. KDD stages are: inductive learning, deductive verification and human intuition. Data mining can could be applied to any domain where large databases are saved. Some applications are: failure prediction [3], biomedical applications [4], process and quality control [5].

Data mining enables finding interesting patterns in very large databases. It is the most essential part of the knowledge discovery process which combines databases, artificial intelligence, machine learning and statistics techniques. The basic techniques for data mining include: decision tree induction, rule induction, artificial neural network, clustering and association rules.

Association rule learning is a popular and well researched method for discovering interesting relations between variables in large databases. It is intended to identify strong rules discovered in databases using different measures of interestingness. Many algorithms for generating association rules were presented over time. Some well known algorithms are Apriori [6], Eclat [7] and FP-Growth [8], but they only do half the job, since they are algorithms for mining frequent itemsets. Another step needs to be done after to generate rules from frequent itemsets found in a database.

There is a need of a fusion framework to combine data from multiples sources to achieve more specific inferences. A fusion system must satisfy the users functional needs and extend their sensory capabilities.

After years of intensive research that is mainly focused on low-level information fusion (IF), the focus is currently shifting towards high-level information fusion [9]. Compared to the increasingly mature field of low-level IF, theoretical and practical challenges posed by high-level IF are more difficult to handle.

Some of the applications that involve high-level IF are:

- Defense [10–14]
- Computer and Information Security [15, 16]
- Disaster Management [17–20]
- Fault Detection [21–23]
- Environment [24–26]

But these contributions lack of a well-defined spatio-temporal constraints on relevant evidence and suitable models for causality.[27].

Our proposed model provides the big picture about risk analysis for that employee at that place in that moment in a real world environment. Our contribution is to build a causality model for accidents investigation by means of a well-defined spatio-temporal constraints on offshore oil industry domain. We use ontological constraints in the post-processing mining stage to prune resulting rules.

3   Knowledge Retrieval Model

In this section more details about the Knowledge Retrieval Model are provided. First a detailed description of the proposed architecture, domain ontology and reasoning process described by means of inductive learning process.

3.1   Architecture

The architecture of our context-based fusion framework is depicted in Figure 1. The context-aware system developed has a hierarchical architecture with the following layers: Services layer, Context Acquisition layer, Context Representation layer, Context Information Fusion layer and Infrastructure layer. The hierarchical architecture reflects the complex functionality of the system as shown in the following brief description of the functionality of particular layers:

- Infrastructure Layer. The lowest level of the location management architecture is the Sensor Layer which represents the variety of physical and logical location sensor agents producing sensor-specific location information.
- Context Acquisition: The link between sensors (lowest layer) and the representation layer
- Context Representation: This is where the low-level information fusion occurs
- Context Information Fusion layer: This layer takes sensor-specific location information and other contextual information related to the user and transforms it into a standard format. This is where the high-level information fusion occurs. It is here where reasoning about context and events of the past takes place. Extended description is given in next section.
- Services Layer. This layer interacts with the variety of users of the system (employees) and therefore needs to address several issues including access rights to location information (who can access the information and to what degree of accuracy), privacy of location information (how the location information can be used) and security of interactions between users and the system.

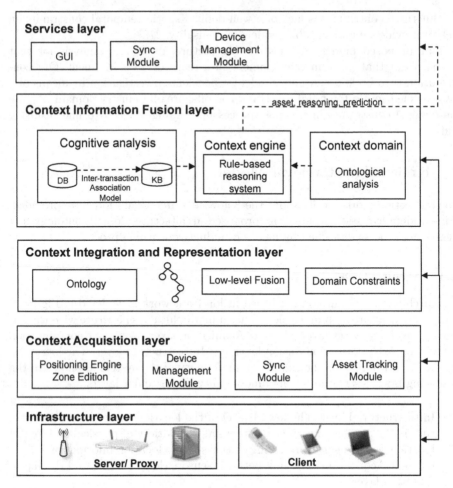

Fig. 1. Architecture

3.2 Ontology

Normally, ontology represents a conceptualization of particular domains. In our case, we will use the ontology for representing the contextual information of the offshore oil industry environment.Ontologies are particularly suitable to project parts of the information describing and being used in our daily life onto a data structure usable by computers.

Using ontologies provides an uniform way for specifying the models core concepts as well as an arbitrary amount of subconcepts and facts, altogether enabling contextual knowledge

An ontology is defined as "an explicit specification of a conceptualization" [28]. An ontology created for a given domain includes a set of concepts as well as relationships connecting them within the domain. Collectively, the concepts and the relationships form a foundation for reasoning about the domain. A comprehensive, well-populated ontology with classes and relationships closely modeling a specific domain represents a vast compendium of knowledge in the domain.

Furthermore, if the concepts in the ontology are organized into hierarchies of higher-level categories, it should be possible to identify the category (or a few categories) that best classify the context of the user. Within the area of computing, the ontological concepts are frequently regarded as classes that are organized into hierarchies. The classes define the types of attributes, or properties common to individual objects within the class. Moreover, classes are interconnected by relationships, indicating their semantic interdependence (relationships are also regarded as attributes).

We built a domain ontology for the Health, Safety and Environment (HSE) of oil and gas domain [29]. We also obtain the inferences that describe the dynamic side and finally we group the inferences sequentially to form tasks. Principal concepts of the ontology are the following:

- Anomaly: Undesirable event or situation which results or may result in damage or faults that affect people, the environment, equity (own or third party), the image of the Petrobras System, products or production processes. This concept includes accidents, illnesses, incidents, deviations and non-conformances.
  - Neglect: Any action or condition that has the potential to lead to, directly or indirectly, damage to people, to property (own or third party) or environmental impact, which is inconsistent with labor standards, procedures, legal or regulatory requirements, requirements management system or practice.
    * Behavioral neglect: Act or omission which, contrary provision of security, may cause or contribute to the occurrence of accidents.
    * Non-behavioral neglect: Environmental condition that can cause an accident or contribute to its occurrence. The environment includes adjective here, everything that relates to the environment, from the atmosphere of the workplace to the facilities, equipment, materials used and methods of working employees who is inconsistent with labor standards, procedures, legal requirements or normative requirements of the management system or practice.
  - Incident: Any evidence, personal occurrence or condition that relates to the environment and / or working conditions, can lead to damage to physical and / or mental.
  - Accident: Occurrence of unexpected and unwelcome, instant or otherwise, related to the exercise of the job, which results or may result in personal injury. The accident includes both events that may be identified in relation to a particular time or occurrences as continuous or intermittent exposure, which can only be identified in terms of time period probable. A personal injury includes both traumatic injuries and illnesses, as damaging effects mental, neurological or systemic, resulting from exposures or circumstances prevailing at the year's work force. In the period for meal or rest, or upon satisfaction of other physiological

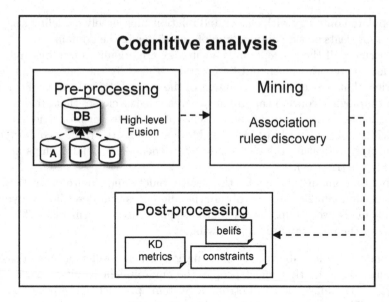

Fig. 2. Cognitive analysis

needs at the workplace or during this, the employee is considered in carrying out the work.

* Accident with injury: It's all an accident in which the employee suffers some kind of injury. Injury: Any damage suffered by a part of the human organism as a consequence of an accident at work.
  · With leave: Personal injury that prevents the injured from returning to work the day after the accident or resulting in permanent disability. This injury can cause total permanent disability, permanent partial disability, total temporary disability or death.
  · Without leave: Personal injury that does not prevent the injured to return to work the day after the accident, since there is no permanent disability. This injury, not resulting in death, permanent total or partial disability or total temporary disability, requires, however, first aid or emergency medical aid. Expressions should be avoided "lost-time accident" and "accident without leave", used improperly to mean, respectively, "with leave injury" and "injury without leave."
* Accident Without Injury: Accident causes no personal injury.

3.3 Reasoning

Standard ontology reasoning procedures can be performed within the ontologies to infer additional knowledge from the explicitly asserted facts. By using an inference engine, tasks such as classification or instance checking can be performed. Figure 2.

Risk prevention is a paradigmatic case of inductive reasoning. Inductive reasoning begins with observations that are specific and limited in scope, and proceeds to a generalized conclusion that is likely, but not certain, in light of accumulated evidence. You could say that inductive reasoning moves from the specific to the general. Much scientific research is carried out by the inductive method: gathering evidence, seeking patterns, and forming a hypothesis or theory to explain what is seen.

In our framework, inductive rules formally represent contextual, heuristic and common sense knowledge to accomplish high-level scene interpretation and low-level location refinement.

Once an employee enters the network, it immediately connects with a local proxy, which evaluates the position of the client device and assign a role to the employee. A pre-processing step begins then filtering the relevant features that are selected to participate in the process of knowledge discovery by type of employee (role). The association rules mining process starts with the selected configuration and the set of resulting rules can be analyzed. Later a post-processing step starts. It is an important component of KDD consisting of many various procedures and methods for pruning and filtering the resulting rules.

The fusion engine implements an association rules model that combines dynamically feature selection based on the role of the user in order to find spacio-temporal patterns between different types of anomalies (or event sequence, ex. neglects, incidents, accidents) that match with the current location of the user.

Two categories of association mining are employed: Intra-anomaly and Inter-anomaly [30]. Intra-transaction associations are the associating among items within the same type of anomaly, where the notion of the transaction could be events where the same user participate. However, Inter-transaction describes relationships among different transactions. That meas between incidents, accidents and neglects. Further details are giving in the next sections.

4   Mining Anomaly Information

As already explained, the task of providing context-based information calls for the processing and extraction of information in the form of rules. One of the possible ways of obtaining those rules is to apply one of the previously described. In this work we employ Aprori and FP-Growth algorithms in parallel in order to mutually validate the results from each other.

As explained in the above section, the fusion engine implements an association rules model that combines dynamically feature selection based on the role of the user in order to find spacio-temporal patterns between different types of anomalies (or event sequence, ex. neglects, incidents, accidents) that match with the current location of the user.

The dataset of anomalies, S, is composed by anomaly instances,

$$S := \{A_1, A_2, \ldots, A_n\}, n \in \mathbb{N}, \tag{1}$$

with the instances defined as

Definition 1 (Anomaly instance). *An anomaly instance can be defined as a tuple,*

$$A := \langle t, c, \mathcal{L}, \mathcal{O}, \mathcal{N}, \mathcal{F} \rangle, \tag{2}$$

that is composed by:

- *t, a time instant that marks when the anomaly took place;*
- *c ∈ {accident, incident, report}, that sets the class of anomaly, and, therefore, its associated gravity;*
- *$\mathcal{L}$, a set of geo-location description attributes, which describe the geographical localization of the anomaly at different levels of accuracy;*
- *$\mathcal{O}$, a set of organizational location attributes that represent where in terms of organization structure the anomaly took place;*
- *$\mathcal{N}$, a group of descriptive nominal attributes that characterize the anomaly with a predefined values, and;*
- *$\mathcal{F}$, a set of free-text attributes that are used to complement or improve the descriptive power reachable with $\mathcal{N}$ attributes.*

In order to make the rules produced interesting for the user the mining dataset, $\mathcal{S}$, must be preprocessed to meet the her/his needs. Using the above described problem ontology, the set of anomalies relevant for mining can be (i) filtered and (ii) its attributed selected.

For the first task we defined a function `filter_anomalies`$(u, \mathcal{S}) \rightarrow \mathcal{S}'$, $\mathcal{S}' \subseteq \mathcal{S}$, which determines the subset, $\mathcal{S}'$, of the anomalies dataset, $\mathcal{S}$, that are of interest for a given user, u. For the second task we created the function `filter_attributes`$(u, \mathcal{S}') \rightarrow \mathcal{S}^*$, where $\forall A' = \in \mathcal{S}'$, $\exists A^* \in \mathcal{S}^*$ such that $t^* = t'$, $c^* = c'$, $\mathcal{L}^* \subseteq \mathcal{L}'$, $\mathcal{O}^* \subseteq \mathcal{O}'$, $\mathcal{N}^* \subseteq \mathcal{N}'$ and $\mathcal{F}^* \subseteq \mathcal{F}'$.

Relying on the $\mathcal{S}^*$ dataset customized to the user profile two classes of data mining operations can be carry out to extract knowledge rules. The first mines for rules regarding the relations of different attribute values in anomalies, and hence was called *intra-anomaly rule mining*. The other, more complex one, mines for relationships between anomalies, that take place in a same location —either geographical or organizational— and in similar dates. Because of that this operation was denominated *spatio-temporal* or *inter-anomaly rule mining*. In the subsequent sections we describe both mining processes.

4.1 Mining for Intra-Anomaly Information

In this case the data pre-processing before mining is pretty straightforward, as the interest is to discover relationships between the values of different attributes and the possible presence of probabilistic implication rules between them. In particular, each anomaly in $\mathcal{S}^*$ is treated as a transaction whose items are the non-null values of the corresponding $\mathcal{N}^*$. The results of applying the rule mining algorithms are post-processed to eliminate cyclic rules and to sort them according to an interestingness criterion.

4.2 Spatio-Temporal Causality Mining

Mining spatio-temporal rules calls for a more complex pre-processing. As the most relevant anomalies are the accidents mining is centered around them. In this case, transactions will be constituted by anomalies that took place in the same location (deduced from the user profile) and with a given amount of time of precedence.

More formally, having the set of all accidents $\Lambda = \{A \in \mathcal{S}^* | A.c = \text{accident}\}$, for each element $\lambda \in \Lambda$, we construct the set of co-occurring anomalies, $\mathcal{C}(\lambda)$ as,

$$\mathcal{C}(\lambda) := \{\lambda\} \cup \{\kappa \in \mathcal{S}^* | \lambda.t - \kappa.t \leq \Delta t; \text{loc}(\lambda, u) = \text{loc}(\kappa, u)\}, \qquad (3)$$

with $\text{loc}(\cdot)$, a function that for a given anomaly an user returns the value of the location attribute of interest for that user according to her/his role, and Δt, a time interval for maximum co-occurrence.

The set of co-occurring anomalies $\{\mathcal{C}(\lambda)|\forall \lambda \in \Lambda\}$ is used as transactions dataset for the mining algorithms. However, anomalies can not be used as-is, as it is necessary to express them in abstract form, in order to achieve sufficient generalization as to yield results that not are excessively particular or refined.

For this task, again depending on the user profile, a group of elements of each $\mathcal{N}^*$ is selected to create the abstract anomaly. This reduced set of attribute values are then used to construct the transactions.

More formally, having the set of all accidents $\Lambda = \{A \in \mathcal{S}^* | A.c = \text{accident}\}$, for each element $\lambda \in \Lambda$, we construct the set of co-occurring anomalies, $\mathcal{C}(\lambda)$ as,

$$\mathcal{C}(\lambda) := \{\lambda\} \cup \{\kappa \in \mathcal{S}^* | \lambda.t - \kappa.t \leq \Delta t; \text{loc}(\lambda, u) = \text{loc}(\kappa, u)\}, \qquad (4)$$

with $\text{loc}(\cdot)$, a function that for a given anomaly an user returns the value of the location attribute of interest for that user according to her/his role, and Δt, a time interval for maximum co-occurrence.

The set of co-occurring anomalies $\{\mathcal{C}(\lambda)|\forall \lambda \in \Lambda\}$ is used as transactions dataset for the mining algorithms. However, anomalies can not be used as-is, as it is necessary to express them in abstract form, in order to achieve sufficient generalization as to yield results that not are excessively particular or refined.

For this task, again depending on the user profile, a group of elements of each $\mathcal{N}^*$ is selected to create the abstract anomaly. This reduced set of attribute values are then used to construct the transactions.

5 Final Remarks

In this work we have discussed an information fusion framework for providing context-aware services related to risk prevention in offshore oil industry environment. We made an innovative use of rule mining for provisioning knowledge for assessing and decision making regarding risk an accidents prevention. The solution presented here is currently deployed and in use by a major oil extraction and processing industrial conglomerate of Brazil. Future work will focus on dealing with uncertainty data and unstructured data

Acknowledgement. This work was partially funded by CNPq BJT Project 407851/2012-7 and CNPq PVE Project 314017/2013-5.

References

1. Sánchez Pi, N.: Intelligent techniques for context-aware systems (2011)
2. Gómez-Romero, J., Garcia, J., Kandefer, M., Llinas, J., Molina, J., Patricio, M., Prentice, M., Shapiro, S.: Strategies and techniques for use and exploitation of contextual information in high-level fusion architectures. In: 2010 13th Conference on Information Fusion (FUSION), pp. 1–8. IEEE (2010)
3. Borrajo, M.L., Baruque, B., Corchado, E., Bajo, J., Corchado, J.M.: Hybrid neural intelligent system to predict business failure in small-to-medium-size enterprises. International Journal of Neural Systems 21(04), 277–296 (2011)
4. De Paz, J.F., Bajo, J., López, V.F., Corchado, J.M.: Biomedic organizations: An intelligent dynamic architecture for kdd. Information Sciences 224, 49–61 (2013)
5. Conti, M., Pietro, R.D., Mancini, L.V., Mei, A.: Distributed data source verification in wireless sensor networks. Information Fusion 10(4), 342–353 (2009)
6. Agrawal, R., Srikant, R., et al.: Fast algorithms for mining association rules. In: Proc. 20th Int. Conf. Very Large Data Bases, VLDB., vol. 1215, pp. 487–499 (1994)
7. Zaki, M.J.: Scalable algorithms for association mining. IEEE Transactions on Knowledge and Data Engineering 12(3), 372–390 (2000)
8. Han, J., Pei, J., Yin, Y.: Mining frequent patterns without candidate generation. ACM SIGMOD Record 29, 1–12 (2000)
9. Blasch, E., Llinas, J., Lambert, D., Valin, P., Das, S., Chong, C., Kokar, M., Shahbazian, E.: High level information fusion developments, issues, and grand challenges: Fusion 2010 panel discussion. In: 2010 13th Conference on Information Fusion (FUSION), pp. 1–8. IEEE (2010)
10. Chong, C.Y., Liggins, M., et al.: Fusion technologies for drug interdiction. In: IEEE International Conference on Multisensor Fusion and Integration for Intelligent Systems, MFI 1994, pp. 435–441. IEEE (1994)
11. Gad, A., Farooq, M.: Data fusion architecture for maritime surveillance. In: Proceedings of the Fifth International Conference on Information Fusion, vol. 1, pp. 448–455. IEEE (2002)
12. Liggins, M.E., Bramson, A., et al.: Off-board augmented fusion for improved target detection and track. In: 1993 Conference Record of The Twenty-Seventh Asilomar Conference on Signals, Systems and Computers, pp. 295–299. IEEE (1993)
13. Ahlberg, S., Hörling, P., Johansson, K., Jöred, K., Kjellström, H., Mårtenson, C., Neider, G., Schubert, J., Svenson, P., Svensson, P., et al.: An information fusion demonstrator for tactical intelligence processing in network-based defense. Information Fusion 8(1), 84–107 (2007)
14. Aldinger, T., Kao, J.: Data fusion and theater undersea warfare-an oceanographer's perspective. In: MTTS/IEEE TECHNO-OCEAN 2004, OCEANS 2004, vol. 4, pp. 2008–2012. IEEE (2004)
15. Corona, I., Giacinto, G., Mazzariello, C., Roli, F., Sansone, C.: Information fusion for computer security: State of the art and open issues. Information Fusion 10(4), 274–284 (2009)
16. Giacinto, G., Roli, F., Sansone, C.: Information fusion in computer security. Information Fusion 10(4), 272–273 (2009)

17. Little, E.G., Rogova, G.L.: Ontology meta-model for building a situational picture of catastrophic events. In: 2005 8th International Conference on Information Fusion, vol. 1, 8 p. IEEE (2005)
18. Llinas, J.: Information fusion for natural and man-made disasters. In: Proceedings of the Fifth International Conference on Information Fusion, vol. 1, pp. 570–576. IEEE (2002)
19. Llinas, J., Moskal, M., McMahon, T.: Information fusion for nuclear, chemical, biological & radiological (ncbr) battle management support/disaster response management support. Center for MultiSource Information Fusion, School of Engineering and Applied Sciences, University of Buffalo, USA (2002)
20. Mattioli, J., Museux, N., Hemaissia, M., Laudy, C.: A crisis response situation model. In: 2007 10th International Conference on Information Fusion, pp. 1–7. IEEE (2007)
21. Bashi, A.: Fault detection for systems with multiple unknown modes and similar units (2010)
22. Bashi, A., Jilkov, V.P., Li, X.R.: Fault detection for systems with multiple unknown modes and similar units-part i. In: 12th International Conference on Information Fusion, FUSION 2009, pp. 732–739. IEEE (2009)
23. Basir, O., Yuan, X.: Engine fault diagnosis based on multi-sensor information fusion using dempster–shafer evidence theory. Information Fusion 8(4), 379–386 (2007)
24. Heiden, U., Segl, K., Roessner, S., Kaufmann, H.: Ecological evaluation of urban biotope types using airborne hyperspectral hymap data. In: 2nd GRSS/ISPRS Joint Workshop on Remote Sensing and Data Fusion over Urban Areas, pp. 18–22. IEEE (2003)
25. Khalil, A., Gill, M.K., McKee, M.: New applications for information fusion and soil moisture forecasting. In: 2005 8th International Conference on Information Fusion, vol. 2, p. 7. IEEE (2005)
26. Hubert-Moy, L., Corgne, S., Mercier, G., Solaiman, B.: Land use and land cover change prediction with the theory of evidence: a case study in an intensive agricultural region of france. In: Proceedings of the Fifth International Conference on Information Fusion, vol. 1, pp. 114–121. IEEE (2002)
27. Blasch, E., Kadar, I., Salerno, J., Kokar, M.M., Das, S., Powell, G.M., Corkill, D.D., Ruspini, E.H.: Issues and challenges of knowledge representation and reasoning methods in situation assessment (level 2 fusion). In: Defense and Security Symposium, International Society for Optics and Photonics, p. 623510 (2006)
28. Gómez-Romero, J., Patricio, M.A., García, J., Molina, J.M.: Ontological representation of context knowledge for visual data fusion. In: 12th International Conference on Information Fusion, FUSION 2009, pp. 2136–2143. IEEE (2009)
29. Sanchez-Pi, N., Martí, L., Garcia, A.C.B.: Text classification techniques in oil industry applications. In: SOCO-CISIS-ICEUTE, pp. 211–220 (2013)
30. Berberidis, C., Angelis, L., Vlahavas, I.: Inter-transaction association rules mining for rare events prediction. In: Proc. 3rd Hellenic Conference on Artificial Intelligence (2004)

An Agent-Based Framework for Aggregation of Manageable Distributed Energy Resources

Anders Clausen[1], Yves Demazeau[2], and Bo Nørregaard Jørgensen[1]

[1] University of Southern Denmark
ancla@mmmi.sdu.dk, bnj@iti.sdu.dk
[2] CNRS, LIG Laboratory
yves.demazeau@imag.fr

Abstract. Distributed energy resources (DER) offer an economically attractive alternative to traditional centralized generation. However, the unpredictable and scattered nature of DER prevents them from replacing traditional centralized generator capacity. Aggregating DER under a virtual power plant (VPP) addresses this issue by exposing the combined capabilities of connected DER as a single controllable entity towards the utility. In this paper we propose an architecture that supports multi-level aggregation of DER under VPPs. In this architecture, DER submit energy profiles to a VPP. The VPP may then control the DER within the boundaries defined in the energy profiles. The proposed architecture is hosted in an agent-based framework, Controleum, and is to be demonstrated at a primary school in Denmark, first quarter 2014.

Keywords: Distributed Energy Resources, Virtual Power Plant, Agent Framework, Load Management, Demand Side Management, Centralized Control, Distributed Control, Multi-Agent Systems.

1 Introduction

Distributed generator capacity, controllable loads and storage collectively known as Distributed Energy Resources (DER) [1] offer an economically attractive alternative to the expansion of centralized generation. In particular, the utilization of DER may postpone investments in grid reinforcement [2]. However, the autonomous and unpredictable behavior of DER and their heterogeneous nature is an obstacle in the integration of DER in grid management tasks [3]. Solving this issue is not trivial. DER-entities often want to preserve local control, in order to fulfill local requirements. At the same time, the utility wants to be able to perform Load Management (LM) of DER. LM falls under the concept of Demand Side Management (DSM) which covers several activities aiming to change the timing and/or amount of electricity used by customers [4]. A Virtual Power Plant (VPP) can be used to facilitate participation of a high number of DER in a LM context [5]. The VPP concept strives to support the integration of DER, by aggregating a portfolio of often diverse DER and representing them as a single entity within the grid [5]. The problem of implementing DER through

J.M. Corchado et al. (Eds.): PAAMS 2014 Workshops, CCIS 430, pp. 214–225, 2014.

a VPP spans several domains. In an energy context, a VPP is comparable to a normal power plant in that it has operating costs and generations limits and schedules [6]. This means that a VPP needs to be able to coordinate consumption and production of connected DER. Further, preferences of the connected DER should be preserved. A DER may have one (or several) preferred consumption or production patterns which it prefers over other, viable patterns. These preferences should not be ignored, when taking decisions at the VPP. Finally, the solution should be robust so that the VPP can run even when one or possibly several DER fail. Naturally, DER should also be able to operate if the VPP fails.

From a modeling perspective, the relation between a VPP and DER is interesting. Often, goals of DER deviate from the goals of a VPP which means that a global optimum may not exist. This problem extends into the local domains of the DER and VPP where contradicting goals may also exist. As an example, a VPP may want to minimize cost of electricity while maximizing satisfaction of connected DER.

Several approaches have been made to implement a VPP ranging from fully distributed control approaches, where each DER act on behalf of local requirements (for example [7]) to fully centralized approaches, where each DER is modeled at a central controlling entity (for example [8]).

We propose an agent-based architecture in which VPPs and DER are represented as agents. The architecture combines centralized and distributed control by enabling a VPP-agent to coordinate consumption and production of connected DER-agents while allowing DER-agents to preserve local preferences. The architecture separates decision-making at the VPP and the DER, allowing DER-agents and VPP-agents to pursue different and possibly conflicting goals. Cooperation between a set of DER-agents and a VPP-agent is enabled through the exchange of energy profiles. These energy profiles are calculated locally by each DER-agent and submitted to the VPP-agent. The VPP-agent may then select an energy profile for each DER-agent based on the local requirements and goals of the VPP-agent.

The proposed architecture has been implemented in our control and decision-making framework - *Controleum*. Controleum is a software framework which was developed based on the results of [9] and [10]. It offers satisfaction-based multi-objective search, which allows a DER-agent or a VPP-agent to include multiple, possibly conflicting goals in their decision-making process. This enables support for non-convex problem solution.

Using Controleum, a subclass of DER, namely flexible consumers, have been implemented as agents. Experiments in spring 2014 are going to demonstrate the ability to aggregate a number of these consumers under a VPP within the framework.

The rest of this paper is organized as follows: In section 2 a summary of related work is presented. Section 3 describes the architecture proposed and section 4 describes the framework used to implement the architecture. In section 5 a case study is presented and finally in section 6 we conclude the paper.

2   Related Work

Previous works have described several possible ways of integrating DER through a VPP. Ruiz et. al. [6] and Mathieu et. al. [8] propose a centralized approach, in which the VPP retains full control over connected DER. However, this approach presents several drawbacks generic to centralized control. The central entity becomes a single point of failure. At the same time, it might pose a bottleneck if many nodes are connected. Thirdly, the controlling entity needs to receive all sensor data from connected nodes [11]. The latter two issues presents an obstacle towards scalability. Distributed control addresses many of these issues by delegating responsibility of control to the individual DER. This approach is taken by Beer and Appelrath [7] who propose an agent-based approach where agents form coalitions in order to create ad hoc VPPs. The agents are however not coordinated, and this requires a new market model. Thus, using this approach a VPP cannot replace traditional generation capacity. Several approaches seek to combine the centralized and distributed approach. Maruf et. al. [12] make a proposal where DER-agents generate cost functions and submit these to a central coordinating agent which maintains communication between agents. Vasirani et. al. [13] propose an approach, where owners of EVs submit schedules where their capacity is available to a coordinating VPP. Halvgaard et. al. [14] seperate a central control problem into smaller subproblems which are distributed among the DER. Militor et. al. [15] suggest solving mixed integer problems at DER before solving a mixed integer problem at aggregation level. These approaches however, all assume convex problems at the DER and the VPP.

3   Architecture for an Agent-Based Virtual Power Plant

The approach proposed in this paper enables central control of DER at the VPP while preserving preferences of individual DER. This is done by having DER calculate viable energy profiles and submit these to the VPP. Within the area defined by these energy profiles, the VPP may control the DER. This isolates the problem domain of the VPP from that of the DER, and enables DER and VPP to aim for goals which may be contradicting. Since the problem domains are isolated, this approach is robust as well, as the VPP and the DER are independent of each other.

Figure 1 illustrates the concept of the VPP where a number of DER are connected to a VPP. Each DER may have different characteristics and requirements which it has to fulfill. An example of a DER is illustrated in figure 2. In this particular example, a *prosumer* is shown. A prosumer may appear as either a producer or consumer depending on local state [16]. Note however, that in principle a VPP could aggregate both DG, storage, flexible consumers and prosumers. We reckon that each DER connected to a VPP must express their energy flexibility. In the architecture, energy flexibility is defined based on goals expressed in DER-agents representing physical DER. Each DER-agent generates a set of viable *energy profiles*. An energy profile describes a load schedule for a given

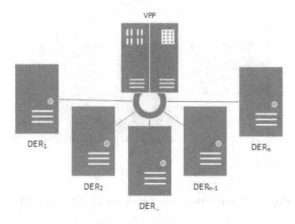

Fig. 1. Conceptual drawing of DER connected to a VPP

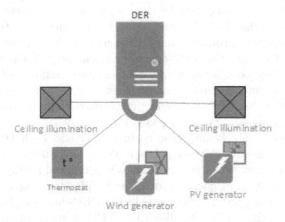

Fig. 2. Example of a DER node containing a wind generator, a photovoltaic generator, two groups of ceiling illumination and a thermostat

DER over a period of time and contains a variable number of fields which each represents a *prosumption level* at a given point in time. The term prosumption level is an abstraction covering the nature of DER; sometimes DER may consume energy, for example when a storage unit is charging or a prosumer is consuming energy. At other times, DER generates energy. This happens, when a distributed generator is running, when a storage unit is discharging or when a prosumer is producing more energy than it consumes. Note that flexible consumers is a special case of prosumers in this context. Since they never actually produce energy, their prosumption level is defined as the difference between the energy allocated for them and their actual consumption. Figure 3 depicts prosumption characteristics of different types of DER. An energy profile then becomes a prediction of anticipated prosumption over a period of time. As control intervals and ability to predict vary between DER-agents, so does the number of fields in their

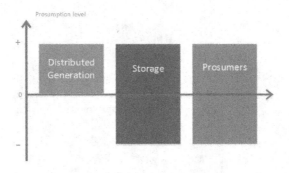

Fig. 3. Prosumption characteristics of different DER

respective energy profiles. Each DER-agent may generate multiple energy profiles, which are all viable considering the current state and goals of the DER-agent. The set of viable energy profiles then, represents the current and predicted future flexibility of the DER. Depending on local preferences, the DER-agent may rank these energy profiles. Each DER-agent sends a set of viable energy profiles to a VPP-agent. The VPP-agent then generates viable energy profiles for the aggregate by combining energy profiles from each of the sets received. When the VPP-agent effectuates one of these energy profiles, based on goals and preferences of the VPP, it is effectively controlling the energy profile of DER-agents while adhering to their goals.

In the collaboration scheme proposed in this article, each DER-agent may submit energy profiles at arbitrary points in time. This allows agents to submit plans only when a new set of energy profiles is generated locally. The intervals between the generation of energy profiles may differ from agent to agent due variance in complexity and requirements in the DER-domains. By pushing new energy profiles to the VPP, this allows the VPP to react to emergent conditions such as emergencies or other abnormalities in DER behavior. If frequent optimization is done at the VPP-agent, this scheme also helps to reduce network overhead, where the VPP-agent polls the same energy profiles multiple times from each DER-agent. The tradeoff of this scheme is induced network overhead if optimization is done frequently at the DER-agents compared to the VPP-agent.

As each DER-agent may resubmit a set of energy profiles at any point in time, the prediction of future prosumption levels may seem like overhead, as the DER-agent does not commit to these predictions. This is however not the case, as the sets of energy profiles allows the VPP-agent to forecast the aggregated prosumption of the connected DER-agents. This enables the VPP-agent to coordinate accordingly. For example the VPP-agent may obtain a generally lower consumption for the aggregate at a later point in time e.g. due to high electricity prices. This is done by selecting energy profiles for each DER-agent which predict a low consumption at that point in time.

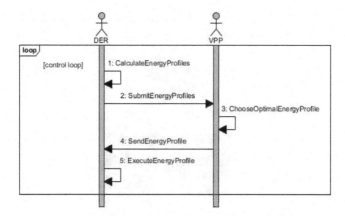

Fig. 4. Cooperation protocol between a DER-agent and a VPP-agent. This protocol is defined between each DER-agent in the aggregate and the VPP-agent.

The sequence diagram in figure 4 depicts the cooperation between a DER-agent and a VPP-agent. In each control loop, the DER-agent initiates the cooperation protocol by calculating a set of energy profiles based on the current state and goals of the particular DER-agent. As the state and goals of each DER-agent vary, the number of energy profiles could differ from one DER-agent to another. Further, as the number of energy profiles generated could depend on a time-varying state, the number of energy profiles a particular DER-agent submits may vary with time as well. The set of energy profiles is then sent from the DER-agent to the VPP-agent. This set represents the flexibility if the particular DER, and thus each of the DER-agents cooperate with the VPP-agent. At some point in time determined by the VPP-agent, an energy profile is chosen for each DER-agent. This choice depends on the goals of the VPP-agent. The chosen energy profile is communicated back to each DER-agent by changing priority ranking of energy profiles at the DER-agent. The DER-agent always executes the energy profile with top priority, and thus, this scheme provides a solution to the case, where the VPP does not respond to the energy profiles submitted. The only change in case of fail-over is, that the ranking of energy profiles at the DER-agent is not changed. In next iteration of the control loop, the cooperation protocol repeats itself, and an updated set of energy profiles is sent to the VPP-agent. As this loop is asynchronous, the VPP-agent assumes that the last set of energy profiles submitted by each DER-agent is always valid. This requires from each of the DER-agents to keep the portfolio of energy profiles updated at the VPP-agent. Multiple VPP-agents may be aggregated by a VPP-agent. This situation arises when solutions found by a VPP-agent is sent to another VPP, following the cooperation protocol described above. This is possible since each VPP-agent generates energy profiles just as the DER-agents. In principle, this

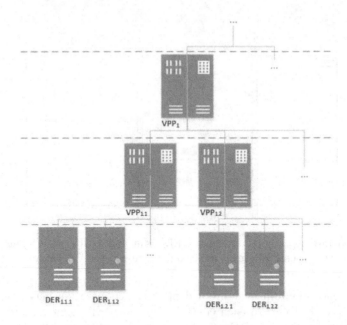

Fig. 5. Aggregation of DER and VPP in the architecture. Dashed lines mark tiers of aggregation.

means that an arbitrary number of aggregation levels may exist. This concept is illustrated in figure 5 where aggregation levels are partitioned by dashed lines. This enhances scalability as the amount of connected DER to a single VPP can be reduced.

Since each VPP-agent may have different goals, the architecture does not dictate the behavior of a VPP-agent instance. This means that multiple types of VPP-agents may be defined within the architecture. In figure 5, $VPP_{1.1}$ and $VPP_{1.2}$ might prefer the most cost effective energy profiles for their aggregates. At the same time, VPP_1 might attempt to adjust real-time prosumption to match a previously defined day-ahead energy profile. In this scenario, VPP_1 could choose the energy profiles for $VPP_{1.1}$ and $VPP_{1.2}$ with the highest priority that satisfies prosumption defined in the day-ahead energy profile.

4   Framework for Cooperative Multi-dimensional Decision-Making

The architecture proposed in this paper has been implemented using Controleum. Controleum is a generic multi-dimensional decision-making framework that is applicable to a broad range of application domains. Decision problems are formulated using the abstractions *Issue, Information, Concern, Decision* and *Consequence*.

An issue describes a social construct or physical phenomenon for which we need to decide a value. The type and range of the value is domain specific. Information is typically user inputs or inputs from sensors and other systems, such as weather forecasts. Concerns represent domain requirements and are implemented as a set of independent agents. Each of these agents attempts to influence the values assigned to the issues it is concerned with. This is done by returning a fitness value to the proposed values of one or more issues. The fitness value is calculated by a model implemented by each agent and may include input from information entities. Note that these agents are not the same agents as the DER-agents or VPP-agents described in section 3. Rather, these agents are contained in a Controleum-instance which may itself be a DER-agent or a VPP-agent.

A decision is a set of values for each of the issues defined. A decision becomes satisfying if it is added to a Pareto-front of decisions. A proposed decision may be added either by replacing an existing satisfying solution or by extending the Pareto-front. A decision replaces a satisfying decision on the Pareto-front if the values it contains improves fitness for one or more agents without deteriorating fitness for any other agents compared to the decision being replaced. A decision extends the Pareto-front if no existing satisfying decisions is able to replace the proposed decision and the proposed decision is unable to replace any current satisfying decisions on the Pareto-front. Each of the satisfying decisions have an associated consequence. A consequence describes the possible outcomes of choosing a given satisfying decision. The concepts and their relations are shown in figure 6.

A Controleum-instance may send a set of consequences associated with a set of satisfying solutions to another Controleum-instance. An issue at the aggregating Controleum-instance may then be assigned values equal to one of the consequences submitted by a Controleum-instance. A Controleum-instance may receive consequences from several Controleum-instances and map them to issues thus becoming an aggregator. By assigning a value from the consequences received to each of these issues, the aggregating Controleum-instance is effectively controlling the aggregated Controleum-instances while adhering to requirements of each aggregated instance. The consequences of each of the satisfying decisions created at the aggregating Controleum-instance are then the accumulated consequences of a specific satisfying decision for each of the aggregated Controleum-instances. As an aggregating Controleum-instance may choose to send consequences to another Controleum-instance as well, multi-level aggregation is enabled as described in the previous section. In this scheme, Controleum-instances acts as agents towards each other. This means that the approach presented in this paper utilizes a compound agent organization [17], where Controleum-instances may encompass several agents in a congregate while the Controleum-instance itself belongs to a hierarchy, holarchy or federation depending on application of the framework.

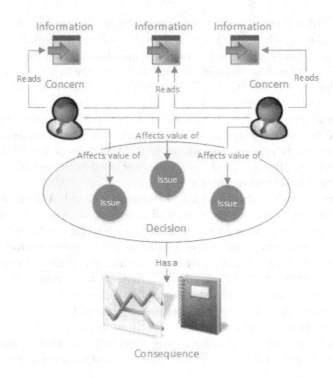

Fig. 6. Illustration of Controleum concepts

5   Case Study

Controleum is used to host the agent-architecture described in section 3. Each Controleum-instance translates to either a DER-agent or a VPP-agent. Note that the framework described in section 4 may be used to implement any kind of DER-agent and VPP-agent. This means that the actual behavior of the DER-agents and the VPP-agents is not determined by the framework. Rather, this is modeled according to local preferences. The case-study presented here is an example of the application of Controleum.

Our case-study includes two classrooms at a public school. We are concerned with control of the light level in each of the classrooms. Each of the classrooms are considered a DER-agent. In the case presented here, the DER-agents are identical, and thus, only one of the DER-agents are described.

The DER-agent contains two issues, three inputs constituting the information and two concerns implemented as agents. Each of the issues map to a controllable light group. The issues may take on values in the form of a 24-hours schedule of light levels at a one hour resolution. Two of the inputs map to lux meters and the last input maps to an external weather forecast, predicting future light levels. Each of the two agents attempts to affect the values of the issues, which in this case means the light schedules of the light groups. One agent attempts to keep the level of light over a certain threshold in time slots where activity is planned in the class rooms. A model, which estimates the light level in the classroom as a function of the time of day, time of year and a weather forecast is used by this agent. The other agent attempts to ensure, that the light level of the light groups between two time slots does not change too quickly, leading to discomfort of the people in the classroom. As values in this context are light schedules for each of the issues, satisfying decisions are the sets of light schedules for each of the controllable light groups that belong to the Pareto-front according to the fitness-values returned by the two agents. The consequence of choosing a specific satisfying decision is an energy profile which determines the resulting predicted energy consumption of the light groups. Each of the consequences then becomes a prediction of the energy consumption associated with a given satisfying decision. The precision of these predictions depends on the precision of the models utilized by the agents. The predictions tend to become more precise when the hour of use is approached. As an example, consider the case where a weather forecast is too optimistic. In this case, the agent ensuring a certain light level in the class room, will make new estimates when the hour of use is approached, which predicts a higher energy consumption, since presumably the weather forecast is updated to reflect actual conditions. As a result, the uncertainty of the predictions does not accumulate. Rather, the predictions of a given time slot tend to become more precise over time as the amount of uncertainty induced by external factors is reduced. This resembles the concept of prediction adopted by Vasirani et. al [13].

Each of the two DER-agents submit their consequences to a VPP-agent. Thus the VPP-agent contains two issues - one for each classroom. Values for these issues then, are the consequences submitted by the classrooms which translates to energy profiles for each of the class rooms. The VPP-agent further contains one input and a concern. The input is an electricity-price signal, which describes electricity prices by hour. The agent implementing the concern tries to affect values of the issues to follow the fluctuations of the price-signal, which means, that the agent tries to achieve a higher consumption when electricity prices are low and vice versa.

In order to validate the approach proposed in this paper, experiments are planned at the public school, Skt. Klemensskolen, in Odense, Denmark. The experiments are to be carried out in the spring 2014.

Experiments will be done in two phases: In the first phase, Controleum will be used to validate that satisfying decisions can be created for the issues of the classrooms. In the second phase, the consequences from each of the class rooms will be included in issues at the VPP-agent. In this phase, the goal is to control light levels of the classrooms based on the consequences calculated for each classroom.

Once these experiments have been carried out, experiments which include a larger and more heterogeneous aggregate of DER may be carried out.

6   Conclusion

This paper addresses the issue of integrating DER into grid management. We propose an architecture which allows DER to be integrated through a VPP which is able to control the consumption of aggregated DER, while preserving requirements and preferences of each DER. This is done by allowing DER to be modeled as agents that submit sets of energy profiles to a VPP-agent. Based on local goals of the VPP-agent an energy profile is chosen for each DER-agent. In this way the VPP-agent is able to control the aggregated energy profile of the connected DER-agents, while adhering to their goals, thus enabling VPP-agents and DER-agents to pursue different and possibly conflicting goals. Further, the architecture enables multi-level aggregation, as a VPP-agent may submit sets of energy profiles to another VPP-agent. Finally, operation in the case of a failure at the VPP-agent is ensured as energy profiles are selected locally, based on priority.

The proposed architecture is hosted in our framework for multi-dimensional decision-making, Controleum. This framework enables DER- and VPP-agents to include multiple, possibly conflicting models thus enabling solution of non-convex problems locally.

The proposed architecture is to be evaluated through experiments at a Danish public school in spring 2014.

References

1. Rahimi, F., Ipakchi, A.: Demand response as a market resource under the smart grid paradigm. IEEE Transactions on Smart Grid 1(1), 82–88 (2010)
2. Mutule, A., Obushevs, A., Lvov, A., Segerberg, H., Shao, N., You, S., Bacher, R., Sauvain, H., Remund, J., Schroder, U., et al.: Efficient identification of opportunities for distributed generation based on smart grid technology. In: 2013 4th IEEE/PES Innovative Smart Grid Technologies Europe (ISGT EUROPE), pp. 1–5. IEEE (2013)
3. Pudjianto, D., Ramsay, C., Strbac, G.: Virtual power plant and system integration of distributed energy resources. Renewable Power Generation, IET 1, 10–16 (2007)
4. Assessment of demand response and advanced metering: 2007. Technical report, Federal Energy Regulatory Commission (FERC) (2007) (accessed December 28, 2013)
5. Pudjianto, D., Ramsay, C., Strbac, G.: Microgrids and virtual power plants: concepts to support the integration of distributed energy resources. Proceedings of the Institution of Mechanical Engineers, Part A: Journal of Power and Energy 222, 731–741 (2008)
6. Ruiz, N., Cobelo, I., Oyarzabal, J.: A direct load control model for virtual power plant management. IEEE Transactions on Power Systems 24, 959–966 (2009)
7. Beer, S., Appelrath, H.J.: A formal model for agent–based coalition formation in electricity markets. In: 4th European Innovative Smart Grid Technologies, ISGT 2013 (2013)
8. Mathieu, S., Ernst, D., Louveaux, Q.: An efficient algorithm for the provision of a day-ahead modulation service by a load aggregator. In: 4th European Innovative Smart Grid Technologies, ISGT 2013 (2013)

9. Sørensen, J.C., Jørgensen, B.N., Klein, M., Demazeau, Y.: An agent-based extensible climate control system for sustainable greenhouse production. In: Kinny, D., Hsu, J.Y.-j., Governatori, G., Ghose, A.K. (eds.) PRIMA 2011. LNCS, vol. 7047, pp. 218–233. Springer, Heidelberg (2011)

10. Rytter, M., Sørensen, J., Jørgensen, B., Körner, O.: Advanced model-based greenhouse climate control using multi-objective optimization. In: IV International Symposium on Models for Plant Growth, Environmental Control and Farm Management in Protected Cultivation, vol. 957, pp. 29–35 (2012)

11. Durfee, E.H., Lesser, V.R.: Partial global planning: A coordination framework for distributed hypothesis formation. IEEE Transactions on Systems, Man and Cybernetics 21, 1167–1183 (1991)

12. Maruf, M., Hortado Munoz, L., Nguyen, P., Lopes Ferreira, H., Kling, W.: An enhancement of agent-based power supply-demand matching by using ann-based forecaster. In: 4th European Innovative Smart Grid Technologies, ISGT 2013 (2013)

13. Vasirani, M., Kota, R., Cavalcante, R.L., Ossowski, S., Jennings, N.R.: An agent-based approach to virtual power plants of wind power generators and electric vehicles. IEEE Transactions on Smart Grid 4, 1314–1322 (2013)

14. Halvgaard, R., Jørgensen, J.B., Poulsen, N.K., Madsen, H., Vandenberghe, L.: Decentralized large-scale power balancing. In: 4th European Innovative Smart Grid Technologies, ISGT 2013 (2013)

15. Molitor, C., Marin, M., Hernández, L., Monti, A.: Decentralized coordination of the operation of residential heating units. In: 4th European Innovative Smart Grid Technologies, ISGT 2013 (2013)

16. Kanchev, H., Lu, D., Colas, F., Lazarov, V., Francois, B.: Energy management and operational planning of a microgrid with a pv-based active generator for smart grid applications. IEEE Transactions on Industrial Electronics 58, 4583–4592 (2011)

17. Horling, B., Lesser, V.: A survey of multi-agent organizational paradigms. The Knowledge Engineering Review 19, 281–316 (2004)

The Proper Role of Agents in Future Resilient Smart Grids

Rune Gustavsson and Shahid Hussain

ICS KTH Sweden
{runeg,shahidh}@ics.kth.se

Abstract. Smart Grids are in focus of several international R&D past and present efforts since at least a decade. Smart Grids is a well-known metaphor for future power grids. However, the meaning, or semantics of the concept has, naturally, changed due to increased understanding of the inherent complexities of the subject matter. The driving forces behind the efforts on Smart Grids include:

- Demands of integrating new energy sources such as Distributed Energy Resources (DER) and Renewable Energy Resources (RES) in a massive way into generation, transmission and distribution of future energy systems.
- Establishment of a de-regulated customer oriented energy markets, including new types of energy based service markets.
- Design and implementation of resilient and trustworthy services coordinating and monitoring use-case dependent sets of stakeholders during operations.

The transition from today's mostly hierarchical power grids towards tomorrow´s Smart Grids poses several challenges to be properly addressed and harnessed. We argue that proper use of agent technologies is a key technology towards this end. Furthermore, we argue that design and implementation of Smart Grids have to be supported by Configurable Experiment Platforms to carter for the under specifications of such systems. Resilience of systems has several aspects. We focus on resilience related to different kinds of cyber attacks and self-healing.

Keywords: Agent based Smart Grids, Resilience, Self healing, Cyber security, Configurable experiments.

1 Background

There are several Architecture Models describing different views of Smart Grids (SGs). For instance, the *Smart Grid Architecture Model (SGAM)*, Figure 1, illustrates the full Smart Grid Architecture Model (SGAM) on top of the Smart Grid Plane.

J.M. Corchado et al. (Eds.): PAAMS 2014 Workshops, CCIS 430, pp. 226–237, 2014.

In effect, Smart Grids will consist of three types of interleaved systems:

- Systems supporting energy management
- Systems supporting information management
- Systems supporting business management

Those systems will demand vertical as well as horizontal information integration in the SGAM cube of Figure 1.

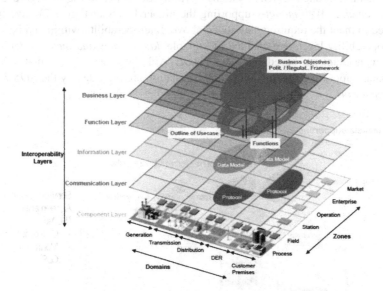

Fig. 1. Layers of SGAM framework

Figure 1 illustrates interconnections of domains often considered in isolation. Smart Control systems will be essential in closing the numerous gaps between those domains and thus realizing the promised benefits of the Smart Grid. From the Architectures above we derive a set of requirements on future Smart Grids.

Firstly, ensure vertical and horizontal interoperability of information flows of Figure 1, taking into account the different sets of protocols and data models of the three interleaved systems mentioned above. Secondly address properly the following three types of constraints:

- Top down constraints derived from different (user-centric) use cases (business based semantics)
- Bottom up constraints derived from physical demands from infrastructures (real-time semantics)
- Constraints related to Trustworthy Coordination and control of tasks performed by different agents at and between different layers of the SGAM model

The following Figure 2 from *GridWise Architecture Council (GWAC)* [2] focuses on the Interoperability Categories of Figure 1 supplemented with Cross-cutting issues. Cross-cutting issues impose performance constraints on the functions of the different categories. The GWAC view has also been adopted by SGAM. Figure 2 highlights the importance of *Service Level Agreements (SLAs)* as a mechanism of coordination between agents and tasks related to a given use case and providing trustworthy interoperability. In Figure 2 the *Footprint* of the involved SLA (Cross-cutting Issues) is also indicated. Furthermore, the importance of *models* supporting data aggregation (top-down and bottom-up) and data handling are stressed. The different data models involved (e.g., *Common Information Model (CIM)* adopted by IEC and supporting electricity transmission and SCADA systems covering the lower levels of Figure 2 and the *W3C Semantic Web models* supporting the higher levels of Figure 2) have to be configured to meet the requirements stated above. Interoperability within and between the interoperability layers are enabled by suitable *data models and meta models* with translation mechanisms based on agent based APIs. We have found that suitable meta models supporting this modeling and translation are provided by the *AOS JACK Agent Framework*.

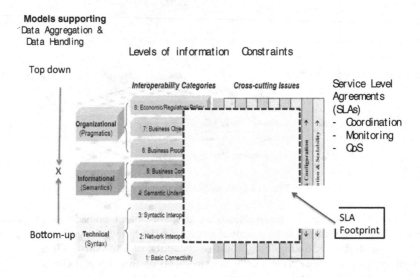

Fig. 2. GWAC Interoperability Framework

The remaining part of the paper is organized as follows. *Section 2 Proposed Solutions* Introduces Service Level Agreements (SLAs) as a mechanism to address the requirements listed above. *Section 3 Setting the Smart Grid Scene* addresses challenges of operating and monitoring Smart Grids. *Section 4 Antagonistic Threats* gives an overview of Persistent Targeting Attacks (PTAs) threatening the resilience of Smart Grids. Some countermeasures are given in *Section 5 Resilient Smart Grids*. *Section 6 Configurable Experiment Platforms* focus on platforms supporting goal oriented verifications and experiments related to resilient Smart Grids. The paper ends with *Section 7 Concluding Remarks* and *Section 8 References*.

2   Proposed Solutions

We propose introduction of *Service-Level Agreements (SLAs)* as a mechanism to address the system challenges listed above. *The SLA components* are derived from a given *Use case* (Business Case) at the Business layer (Figure 1). Projection of the Use case downwards identifies:

Stakeholders and functions related to the Use case:

- *Information structures and formats* related to information exchange related to the different interleaved systems of *Energy Management* (EM), *Information Management* (IM), and *Business Management* (BM)
- *Communication infrastructures* and protocols enabling the intended operations of the Information Infrastructures
- *Components of the Zones and Domains* of the Smart Grid Plane of Figure 1 related to the Use case.

Setting up Service Level Agreements supporting the coordination and monitoring of the tasks performed by the different stakeholders executing the identified use case involves the following steps:

- Identifying and addressing concerns by involved stakeholders related to *functional and non-functional* issues as well as smart system behavior (Figure 1 and Figure 2)
- Specific concerns are identification and monitoring of *Key Performance Indicators (KPIs)*
- Identification of architectures, protocols and standards to be implemented to deliver trustworthy system behavior (e.g., SGAM and GWAC frameworks)

Introduction of 'Smartness' of Smart Grids requires some new views and designs of systems to be implemented in a proper way. Some decades ago classical Power systems were mainly hierarchical stovepipe hardcoded systems with SCADA systems monitoring and controlling the generation, transmission and distribution of energy, of agreed upon Quality of Service (QoS), to the sockets at customer´s premises.

A first step to allow for flexibility across and within stovepipe systems is to decouple classical hierarchical systems into Service- Oriented Systems (SOS) (Figure 1), and to introduce open interfaces between the components (Figure 2). That is, standard interfaces supported by tools and methods to inspect and assess data-flows across those interfaces. Those methods also allow design and implementation of defense-in-depth to carter for increased system - and data security.

A second step is to introduce architectures to bridge the gap between high-level (business) requirements and low-level real time constraints, indicated by a red cross in Figure 2. Our suggested solution is to introduce a *network of high- and/or low level case dependent SLA bundles* supporting Figure 1 and Figure 2. Coordination between SLA bundles is maintained by eventual message exchanges at information level. High-level SLAs are given in [1]. Low level SLAs specifically addressing *Interoperability* and *Cyber security* issues are illustrated in section 6.1 [8, 10, 13, 14].

Arguably, implementation of needed distributed intelligence supporting flexibilities in connectivity as well as loosely coupled coordination patterns enabling detection and sustainable response, requires a careful selection and adaption of agent technologies and configurable infrastructures. Resilience and interoperability are two important systemic properties of Smart Grids that have been assessed and clarified. For instance, self-healing could be addressed and solved in a proper way, provided that a stated invariance relation (KPI) based on resilience and interoperability properties is maintained. Setting up and validating such invariances is dependent on a suitable experimental platform such as the one we are suggest in this paper (Sections 5 and 6).

3   Setting the Smart Grid Scene

The power grid is an interesting critical infrastructure in that its main output, electricity, is crucial in the operation of most other infrastructures and services that the modern society depends on. The complexities involved in operating and maintaining these infrastructures, however, depend on the trustworthy presence of a large assortment of information and communication technologies (ICTs) which in turn relies on electricity from the grid, forming a circular dependency [14].

Other complicating circumstances for operating the grid as an infrastructure include:

- Massive distribution of resources
- Brittle, with a mostly unidirectional structure for generation, transmission and distribution with many "single points of failure" and limited redundancy
- Lacks a safe-state, meaning that the system can not be reverted to a previous known state as an immediate response to a system failure (e.g., a blackout)
- The possibility and outcome from restarting the grid from a de-energized state (black-start) is unverifiable
- Numerous stakeholders with dynamic, and at times conflicting, goals and behavior, e.g., international markets where available supply (approximated) is bought, sold, and traded between actors
- Most protective devices are designed to combat natural disturbances, e.g., weather, rather than antagonistic threats.

Thus, solutions that cater to harness most or all of these caveats are paramount to the success of smart-grid initiatives, hence making *resilience* a key property for future smart-grid deployment. Resilience, in our setting, means systems that have ductile and self-healing properties while maintaining well-formed *Key Performance Indicators* (KPIs). The systems of systems view of Smart Grids entail compositions and coordination of smart software and hardware components into a service oriented system view [13, 14].

In this article we argue that models and mechanisms exploring increased software and communication resilience is a key enabler towards distributed intelligence and therefore towards future Smart Grids. Interoperability Issues are addressed as stated by the GridWise and SGAM frameworks.

3.1   Monitoring Smart Microgrids

A specific vision of one kind of smart grid is the *microgrid*. In microgrids, the topology is a mesh of operationally independent, but interconnected cells. In the EU INTEGRAL [3] project, the following three different *States* of operations for a cell, supporting aggregations of massive amounts of DER / RES, were defined as follows:

- *Normal* operating conditions, showing the potential to reduce grid power imbalances, optimize local power and energy management, minimize cost etc.
- *Critical* operating conditions, showing resilience opportunities also in integrated grids. Resilience could be modeled as detection of a critical state followed by a self-healing action to bring the system back to a normal state.
- *Emergency* operating conditions, showing self healing capabilities.

The practical details of implementing support for such a system restructuring relies heavy on expanding the underlying metering structure, hence the steady introduction of Smart Metering technologies worldwide. The extent of capabilities and regulating policies regarding deployed smart meters vary between countries, and suggestions for their final role range between being additional data-points for increased precision in demand forecasting, to local control-systems in themselves.

In order to identify and monitor the Normal, Critical, and Emergency states with corresponding system hardening [13, 14] to achieve increased resilience, we address in Section 4 *Antagonistic Threats* and in Section 5 *Resilient Smart Grids*. The role of Smart metering systems is covered both as a tool supporting customer empowerment and as a new kind of vulnerability of Smart grids. In *5.1 Towards Comprehensive Resilient Architectures* our analysis of vulnerabilities is summarized in two *principles towards ensuring increased resilience of Smart Grids*:

- Proper *data and meta data models* of components and their interaction in Smart Grids is crucial. Candidates include the standards IEC 61850, IEC 61499, and JACK.
- Proper *Architecture models,* for instance ANSI/ISA-99, supporting network segmentation into security *zones* (DMZ) with information exchange across specified *conduits*.

These principles supports defence in depth strategies based on context dependent intelligent multi agent systems covered in *Section 5.1Towards Comprehensive Resilient Architectures*. Assessment and validation of proposed solutions for critical situations are presented in *Configurable Experiment Platforms*, Section 6. The configurable test bed is supporting fault injection and monitoring at selected interfaces.

4   Antagonistic Threats

Before the advent of cyber security as a central concern, threat and risk management models for the power grid were primarily focused around environmental (weather, component wear), design (deployed structure and restructuring, load balancing, generation, etc.) and challenges inherent to power systems (transients, short circuits, etc.) with related issues in the ICT taking a more distant role. With such a perspective, antagonistic threats (break-ins and physical sabotage, theft of property, etc.) could be dealt with by making sure that the perimeter protection with locks and keys had a corresponding separation within the corporate ICT environment, it is however well-known that this model has, for all intents and purposes failed [4]. Thus, a precondition to all other advanced forms of SG deployment, is that monitoring and protective technologies will effectively cover not only said threats to previous grid structures but also encompass more sophisticated antagonistic threats. We focus on *Sabotage*, *Business intelligence* and *Business sabotage*.

The *Stuxnet* attack [5] provides an interesting perspective on the means and motivation behind sabotage through manipulating parts of a SCADA system, showing that ICT can allow an attacker luxuries that more military intervention cannot.

What distinguishes Stuxnet is thus the *coordination of multiple attacks, both online and offline, to precisely strike at one well-defined target without directly exposing the aggressor.*

Although the shadier side of business intelligence in the sense of data harvesting botnets and other forms of computerized corporate espionage is a notable threat from a generic ICT perspective, they may be even more potent in the more stringent data-models in SCADA. Unfortunately, evidence of such events are scarce at best and it is therefore difficult to get a grasp on how frequent they are and which attack strategies are used. Recently, a few major incidents have been uncovered that shed a little light on the issue, e.g. Night Dragon [6] and ShadyRat [7]. Even though Night Dragon and Stuxnet covers different objectives and work at different levels of technical refinement, they are similar in the sense that the respective attack progression is heterogeneous and iterative; following a broad and generic initial method of attack, they become increasingly domain specific and targeted.

The last case concerns the combination of the two aforementioned threats. Gaming consoles and more recently, smartphones are attractive target for both legitimate and illegitimate forms of tampering and represent advanced computers with heavy restrictions on the level of access that end-users have. The business sabotage case is interesting in a smart-grid context when used as an analog for smart meters in the sense of trusted devices acting as part of the larger monitoring system, placed in an untrusted and possibly hostile environment, illustrating the capacity of antagonistic threats for manipulating and controlling the sensory input for agent- enabled decision making.

5   Resilient Smart Grids

When the presented cases, of Section 4, are combined into a broader picture, the scope of the challenge in defining and protecting the smart grid perimeter from both external and internal threats is clear. While the role of the Smart Meters have been scrutinized in other contexts [8], the threat may well turn out to be *both horizontal* (between prosumers) *and vertical* (between prosumers and utility companies), as shown in Section 4 (cheating between users, piracy between users and distributors) and similar cryptography engineering flaws have already been exposed in key components used by at least one brand of Smart Meters.

If data from these meters are being used as sensory input for agents trading on dynamic markets or acting as decision support for operators attempting to fix a cell in an emergency state, they are very likely targets for attacks similar to the ones described in Section 4, but also, due to the economical incentive, as an aid for manipulating markets. Our suggestion to harness those threats is to aim at *defense-in-depth* solutions based on the identified principles of Section 3.1 as outlined below.

5.1   Towards Comprehensive Resilient Architectures

In the previous sections, the focus has been on illustrating the depth and breadth of current and coming problems of maintaining and securing monitoring and resilience in a smart grid setting: the mere inclusion of quite standard defense-in-depth measures e.g. firewalls, antivirus software, patch management procedures and other 'after the fact' pattern- based approaches will be woefully inadequate against the kind of adversaries now known to be present.

The advantages in defending Smart Grids however, is that there are systemic properties that assist in leveling the playing field; because of the data-driven nature, *the most well-known entity is in fact the data-models on which all components involved indirectly operate.* Even though a great deal of effort have been placed on making sure that sampled data can be retrieved within a set threshold and arrives intact, this is rather within the domains of any modern communication technology. If, however, the actual data-model (e.g. IEC61850/IEC61499 standards) of the governed structure is verified, locked down and integrated into both the processing components and security- centric ones stronger benefits can be reaped alongside possibilities for easier external validation of processing components.

In short, the larger design challenge may not be the mere development of strong protective mechanisms but in *fitting these together into a comprehensive architecture (e.g. ANSI/ISA99)* such that they neither hinder normal operations nor cause incompatibilities, yet still provide necessary protection. Smart Self-healing requires smart monitoring and smart response! That is, basically two types of support tools; firstly *empowerment of operators*, secondly *smarter control and assessment/detection of information exchange across interfaces.* Wee argue that those goals can be approached by identifying the proper roles of agent technologies in future resilient SGs.

6   Configurable Experiment Platforms

We have implemented several agent based configurable platforms at BTH and KTH to support implementation and validation of different mechanisms supporting development of resilient Smart Grids. The BTH based platforms EXPI and EXPII have addressed issues related to software security and resilience [13, 14]. The KTH based platforms have been focused on SLA development [1]. Based on the requirements and problem specifications from *Section 2* and *Section 3*, we have, together with G2EELab/INPG/IDEA in Grenoble, France [9, 10, 11, 12], developed a Test bed structure in accordance with ANSI/ISA-99 (Section 5) aiming at demonstrating agent- enabled self-healing capabilities related to the Smart Grid threats presented in *Section 4 and handling emergency operating conditions of Section 3.1.*

Figure 3 describes the main components of the test bed supporting Demo C of the INTEGRAL project [3].

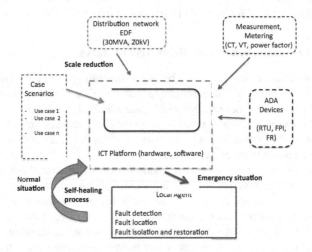

Fig. 3. Configurable distributed platform at Grenoble/BTH supporting resilience remote experiments

The main components are the *Controllers*, one in France (INPG, Grenoble) and one in Sweden (BTH, Karlskrona). The Controllers are remotely connected via a VPN link. The Controllers enable configurations of experimental platforms as well as remote access for monitoring of experiments. The test bed comprise an ICT/monitoring system operating on a scaled down microgrid cell complete with loads, transformers, distribution network and DER/RES. The major components of the SCADA system are a number of *Remote Terminal Units* located in transformer stations which connect to a centralized *Main Terminal Unit* with a database storage (*Historian*) and an operator interface (*Human Machine Interface, HMI*). Further technical detail can be found in [9]. To extend this system with self-healing capabilities, there is an *Agent*, a network of *Fault-Passage Indicators* (FPI) and a *Fault Recorder* (FR). The FPIs are monitoring devices that can approximate the location of a fault. The Fault Recorder subsequently logs sensor data. The Agent is capable of scanning SCADA topology, interpreting FPI data from the Fault Recorder and presenting a suggestion to the operator at the HMI on how the fault could be addressed.

Lastly, the Controller, Control Nodes, VPN and Security Labs in Grenoble and Karlskrona are part of the ICT experimentation setup and its primary role is partitioning the communication network between the Agent, FPIs, Fault Recorder and SCADA into separated networks, with all inter- network communication monitored and controlled. These are further specified by *three modes of operation*:

1. *Local* Operation – The connection between the controllers are severed, and control nodes are only used for their monitoring and traffic shaping abilities.

2. *Remote Monitoring* – All traffic is transparently mirrored to the security lab through an encrypted tunnel.
3. *Remote Tampering* – All traffic is redirected to the Security Lab, manipulated or corrupted, then returned.

These correspond to the *States* defined in Section 3.1 and to the threats in Section 4, with the Security Lab at BTH acting the role of the antagonistic threat. Thus, by alternating between these modes it is possible to play out a number of scenarios based on the aforementioned threats. Unfortunately, the SCADA also exhibits the same properties and vulnerabilities of real-world SCADA systems, in the sense that it is designed to operate in a secure demilitarized zone   (DMZ) with little or no safeguards in place, should the DMZ be breached. Given the sensitive and costly nature of the equipment involved there are several restrictions in play that effectively hinders most scenarios, until several verification and validation steps have been passed at both locations.

6.1   Experiments

The experiments aims at monitoring KPIs related to self-healing and ICT performance. Among the principal goals for experiments on the Test bed are thus validations of (i) agent empowered self-healing, (ii) to support the development of dynamic monitoring and protection mechanisms that harness both *environmental* and *antagonistic* threats, and (iii) to demonstrate the feasibility *of self-healing and monitoring as resilience mechanisms* in smart Microgrid cells facing *critical or emergence situations*. Among supposed key benefits of introducing agents as *complement/support* to operator actions, would be a *decrease in response time* of disturbances reducing it from roughly a *few minutes* down to a *few seconds* (Section 6.2). A prerequisite to achieve this effect is the ability to query a large number of sensors (here represented by the FPIs with the FR acting as their interface), making the reliance of the communication infrastructure a key concern [14]. Thus, there are tree primary areas of interest for a first round of experimentation:

- The first area of interest is *latency*, or how large an effect, introduced delays, will have on the outcome of a self-healing cycle, e.g., if it is possible for an adversary to time an attack in such a way that any self-healing activities are undermined.
- The second area of interest is *data*, in terms of both traffic volumes and actual content. Given the central role of the underlying data models, both in designing more precise monitoring systems, and for tuning protection mechanisms it is interesting to know how well the current Test bed reflects aforementioned standards (e.g. IEC 61850) and how resistant these are with regard to informed manipulations.
- The last area of interest concerns *information-leakage*. There are concerns that the increased precision of Smart Meters can be used to discern otherwise private and sensitive information belonging to individual customers. In this context, we are interested in the reverse, i.e., if unprivileged access can be used to discern sensitive information about the state of the Microgrid as such.

6.2   Results

The main goal of the experiment; our agent based self-healing mechanisms handling disturbances of the distribution grid were successfully validated. The experiments also demonstrated shortcomings of present ICT systems to detect and handle cyber attacks [13, 14]. The results of remote attacks from the BTH controller demonstrated the following communication results. Regarding *latency.* Without any active traffic shaping, was on average about 6 seconds. Activation, corresponding to an attacker redirecting all traffic to a foreign location (stable at a round-trip of 10ms in average between the sites over the course of a month), yielded *no observable* qualitative difference in normal operation of the SCADA, yet increased the completion time for the scenario to 24 seconds. It took extreme network conditions (600ms latency, 40% packet loss) to push the completion time to the upper unassisted operator intervention threshold (2 minutes). Concerning captured *data*, the majority of the traffic was, unsurprisingly, domain specific to the activities at hand, never surpassing 160 KiB/s. However, the public available dissectors at that time (e.g., Modbus/rpc-dom/... in Wireshark) *failed* to detect and decode the majority of the data. This means that any external monitoring (i.e., not part of the SCADA software) would need to be *reverse engineered* to increase performance, a costly and time – consuming operation. Regarding Information leakage. Even lacking detailed domain expertise, the different stages are clearly discernable from those measurements, showing when, for instance, a *Denial of Service attack* (DoS) would be most effective. Common counter-measures, e.g., padding traffic with random noise would be *ill-suited* in this situation due to latency and bandwidth requirements.

7   Concluding Remarks

We have in the paper advocated *Service Level Agreements* (SLAs) as a mechanism to coordinate, monitor and control use cases of future Smart Grids taking into account requirements if interoperability and trustworthiness. We have in the paper also described a Experimental platform and experiments related to system resilience. Specifically we have explored the use of agents in resilient Smart Grids in the following settings:

- A decision support mechanism *complementing*, not replacing, *mandatory and regulated* operator inventions during critical and emergency states
- An *experiment supported tool* for generating and assessing *interaction patterns* as an input for generating data addressing challenges of *under-specified* information processing systems with a strong legacy component

We furthermore suggest a taxonomy of three principal threats, i.e., *Sabotage, Business Intelligence* and *Business Sabotage* illustrating threats with recent real-world incidents. These threats represent a minimal baseline of what any intelligent smart-grid solution will account for. Lastly, we detailed a *distributed Test bed* allowing experts from different domains to collaborate in experimental validation of the aforementioned use of agents. Initial results highlighted exploitable vulnerabilities in the current designs. Future work thus includes addressing those vulnerabilities and introducing refined real-time monitoring in the sense of systemic tracing facilities.

References

1. Gustavsson, R., Hussain, S., Nordström, L.: Engineering of Trustworthy Smart Grids Implementing Service Level Agreements. In: Proceedings of 16th International Conference on Intelligent System, Applications to Power Systems, Greece, September 25-28 (2011)
2. Interoperability Framework, GridWise Architecture Council,
   http://www.gridwiseac.org/about/mission.aspx
3. INTEGRAL, Integrated ICT-platform based Distributed Control in Electricity Grids,
   http://www.integral-eu.com
4. Maynor, D., Graham, R.: SCADA security and terrorism: We're not crying wolf. BlackHat 2006 (2006), http://www.blackhat.com/presentations/bh-federal-06/BH-Fed-06-Maynor-Graham-up.pdf
5. Nicolas, F., Liam, O.M., Eric, C.: W32.Stuxnet Dossier, whitepaper (2011),
   http://www.symantec.com/content/en/us/enterprise/media/security_response/whitepapers/w32_stuxnet_dossier.pdf
6. Global Energy Cyberattacks: Night Dragon, Mcafee (2011),
   http://www.mcafee.com/us/resources/white-papers/wp-global-energy-cyberattacks-night-dragon.pdf
7. Dmitri, A.: Revealed: Operation Shady RAT, Mcafee (2011),
   http://www.mcafee.com/us/resources/white-papers/wp-operation-shady-rat.pdf
8. Gustavsson, R., Ståhl, B.: Self-healing and Resilient Critical Infrastructures. In: Setola, R., Geretshuber, S. (eds.) CRITIS 2008. LNCS, vol. 5508, pp. 84–94. Springer, Heidelberg (2009)
9. Hadjsaid, N., Le-Thanh, L., Caire, R., Raison, B., Blache, F., Ståhl, B., Gustavsson, R.: Integrated ICT framework for distribution network with decentralized energy resources: Prototype, design and development. In: 2010 IEEE Power and Energy Society General Meeting, pp. 1–4 (2010)
10. Ståhl, B., Luong Le, T., Caire, R., Gustavsson, R.: Experimenting with Infrastructures. In: 2010 5th International Conference on Critical Infrastructure (CRIS), September 20-22, pp. 1–7 (2010)
11. Bou, G.B., Ranagnathan, P., Salem, S., Tang, J., Loegering, D., Nygard, K.-E.: Agent-Oriented Designs for a Self Healing Smart Grid. In: Proceedings of First IEEE International Conference on Smart Grid Communications (SmartGridComm 2010) (2010)
12. Pang, Q., Gao, H., Minijiang, X.: Multi-agent based fault location algorithm for smart distribution grid. In: Proceedings of 10th EIT International Conference on Developments in Power System Protection (DDSP 2010). Managing the Change (2010)
13. Mellstrand, P.: Informed System Protection. Blekinge Institute of Technology, Doctoral Dissertation Series No. 2007:10
14. Ståhl, B.: Monitoring Infrastructure Affordances. Blekinge Institute of Technology, Doctoral Thesis Series No 2013:01

Symphony – Agent-Based Platform for Distributed Smart Grid Experiments

Michel A. Oey, Zulkuf Genc, Elizabeth Ogston, and Frances M.T. Brazier

Delft University of Technology, The Netherlands
{M.A.Oey,Z.Genc,E.F.Y.Ogston,F.M.Brazier}@tudelft.nl

Abstract. The electricity networks in many countries are facing a number of challenges due to growth in peak demand, integration of renewable energy sources, increasing security risks and environmental concerns. Smart Grid, as an automated and widely distributed energy network, offers viable solutions to those challenges. Software agents running on customer premises or embedded in appliances and equipment can be used to plan future energy consumption and to shift loads according to pre-defined constraints. However, testing such distributed solutions prior to actual deployment in domestic households is a challenge. Simulations may not capture all the aspects of distributed, large-scale, complex environments, such as one can find in the Smart Grid. This paper presents a distributed Smart Grid simulation/emulation environment called Symphony that allows running real-world experiments within distributed environment with the participation of multiple actors. Symphony is being developed in the context of a European Institute for Innovation and Technology project.

Keywords: multi-agent, smart-grid, distributed, AgentScape, simulation, emulation, Symphony, experiment platform.

1 Introduction

Today's electricity grid was designed to move power from centralised supply sources to consumers according to fairly, predictable loads. However, the transition to renewable energy requires the existing grid to adapt to distributed power generation. These physically distributed generation installations (e.g., gas turbines, micro turbines, fuel cells, solar panels, wind turbines) need to be connected to existing infrastructure.

Management of large-scale, distributed energy networks is a challenge. Techniques such as load balancing, load shifting, demand-response management, demand reduction, etc. need to be implemented. One possible solution is to use a distributed, multi-agent approach to energy resource management [6,14]. The multi-agent-paradigm allows entities, such as energy resources, to be modelled separately as autonomous agents. In practice, software agents run on customer premises or embedded in appliances controlling energy resources. Such agents enable more flexible distributed (self-)management [1,18].

J.M. Corchado et al. (Eds.): PAAMS 2014 Workshops, CCIS 430, pp. 238–249, 2014.

Agents communicate with each other to plan future energy consumption and to shift loads according to constraints placed on the system. Each agent manages local energy demand and production and negotiates with other agents to reach an overall goal [11,15]. For example, agents form partnerships with other agents to form virtual organizations to accomplish higher level goals. On-the-fly negotiation of partnerships between agents allows a system to dynamically adapt, changing how responsibility for a shared goal, like reliability, is divided. This allows individual agents to better meet local constraints, maintaining reliability while making more effective use of available resources. With the addition of multi-agent-based management, small-scale investments in infrastructure made by prosumers complement larger-scale investments by utilities.

The challenge this paper addresses is the design of an architecture, the actions and interactions between agents such that they can effectively and efficiently manage the energy supply and demand within the Smart Grid. In such large-scale distributed environments centralised solutions are less desirable than decentralised ones because of reliability and scalability concerns.

Simulation and emulation are two key phases in the design and development of large-scale, distributed, decentralised multi-agent applications [10]. In simulations designers test multiple configurations of their solutions (algorithms) in a controlled, usually, single machine environment. These tests focus on the functionality of the multi-agent application. In emulation, in contrast, designers test their application in a real, but more-or-less controlled, distributed environment. The importance of emulations is that they include real network characteristics, such as latencies, non-determinism, failures, and concurrency, that determine the correctness, effectiveness, and efficiency of any distributed application. An emulation environment also provides debugging support, such as logs and snapshots. After design and simulation, emulation is necessary before large-scale, distributed applications can be deployed in the real world.

A distributed emulation platform should facilitate setup of distributed experiments with real hardware at different locations to emulate the environment in which the tested solutions are to be deployed. This paper researches the possibility of an open distributed experiment platform within Europe. It describes exploratory research within the context of a European Institute of Innovation and Technology (EIT) [2] project. The result of this research is twofold: (1) the identification of a minimum set of requirements and (2) a design of an open distributed multi-agent experiment platform, called Symphony, that supports joint distributed Smart Grid experiments with real hardware-in-the-loop.

The remainder of this paper is structured as follows. Section 2 briefly elaborates on the identified requirements. Section 3 introduces the architecture of the Symphony platform. Section 4 illustrates a use of the Symphony platform for a simply scenario. Section 5 discusses a number of related simulation platforms. Finally, Section 6 concludes this paper.

2   Requirements

A distributed experiment platform is a useful tool for researchers and energy producers who want to experiment with the Smart Grid. The strength of such a distributed experiment platform is that actual hardware can be in the loop as well as the distributedness of the resources with all its characteristics, making the experiments more realistic. In addition, such a platform can also scale up to larger experiments by adding more hardware resources or adding virtual resources, implemented in software, to add more complexity to the experiment.

Sessions with partners within the EIT project have identified a minimum of requirements for such an open distributed experiment platform as listed below.

Security and Privacy: Large-scale distributed experiments typically run over the internet. If real hardware, such as solar panels, smart-meters, and home appliances, are connected to an experiment platform, access must be secured. Therefore, a distributed experiment platform should provide a secure environment in which access to resources inside the platform must be controllable by the owners of the resources. Furthermore, data communication between nodes inside a distributed platform must be secured, to ensure read confidentiality of information in running experiments. A secure environment requires authentication and authorization facilities [3].

Loosely Coupledness and Openness: One aim of a distributed experiment platform is that a community can share access to hardware and data to run large-scale distributed experiments. However, the autonomy of the participants must be ensured so that they keep in control of their own resources. Furthermore, participants should be able to join and leave the platform independently of others. In short, the distributed experiment platform should be open so that participants can join and leave at will, and be autonomous at all times. In other words, it should be a loosely coupled system.

Scalability: The distributed experiment platform should scale to a large number of nodes. Distributed experiments are usually quite network intensive, therefore, it is important to design a platform to be scalable. Smart grid experiments, for example, can become quite complex and use many resources spread over multiple distributed nodes. An initial requirement is that at least a large number of participants can connect to the distributed platform and join in running experiments. It is the task of the experiment designer to keep the amount of network communication as low as possible.

As mentioned, the requirements form a minimum set of requirements. The following section introduces Symphony, a distributed platform that conforms to this list of minimum requirements.

3   Symphony – Distributed Smart Grid Experiment Platform

Symphony is a distributed experiment platform that enables joint Smart Grid experiments in a distributed way with the involvement of both simulated and real-world actors. Symphony takes care of interconnection and security issues so that actors in different physical locations can safely join distributed experiments. The flexible infrastructure provided by Symphony connects participants to distributed services. These participants can use the platform, for example, to experiment with pricing and load balancing.

Fig. 1 shows a graphical representation of Symphony and a number of labs and institutions that are currently connected to it. There are two types of labs: *Energy Labs* and *Virtual Labs*. An energy lab is a physical location (1) with actual hardware installations that use and/or produce electricity or (2) provides services such as simulations of energy users and/or producers. A virtual lab is a software agent that simulates the behaviour of real labs based on a resource model or historical data. The latter help increase the size of experiments by simulating extra resources to complement the resources of actual labs. In short, Symphony offers the following features.

Fig. 1. Symphony platform with real and virtual labs

Secure Distributed Experiment Platform. The distributed environment of Symphony enables realistic experiments and simulations of interactions between prosumer nodes. Symphony takes care of interconnection and security issues so that labs in different physical locations can safely join distributed experiments. Furthermore, it provides a role-based access mechanism that can be used to control access to resources at participants.

Distributed Services. Symphony provides a flexible infrastructure that allows participants to offer services to other participants in distributed experiments. A service could be anything that can be used in a distributed energy experiment. For example, a service could provide access to actual hardware energy resources (e.g., solar panels or electrical appliances), access to historical (consumer) energy usage data, or access to an energy market where participants can bid for energy.

Dynamic (Re-)Configurations. Symphony allows dynamic experiments where labs can join/leave anytime at will and form various clusters. This provides for an open platform, where the participants are loosely coupled. Furthermore, each participant remains autonomous and remains in control of its own resources through configuration of the resource's access policy.

Scalability. Symphony is built on top of a distributed agent platform called AgentScape [4,13,20]. AgentScape has been designed with scalability and security in mind. As a result, Symphony can benefit from the scalability features of AgentScape and connect many participants in a distributed experiment.

Logging and Visualizations. Symphony also provides logging and visualizations of experimental results. These results can be used to debug and analyze the performance of experiments.

The symphony architecture includes three layers as illustrated in Fig. 2. The bottom layer consists of AgentScape [4,13,20], an agent operating system. AgentScope [12] is located in the middle layer and includes the simulation library. The top layer contains the actual agents and web services of an experiment. All the layers are implemented in Java. A web service interface, based on the IEC 61850 protocol [5], is used to communicate with external components, such as the hardware of research labs.

Experiments are performed by sets of agents that communicate with each other by exchanging messages, and with the outside world through Web Services. Each connected energy lab and virtual lab is an agent. In addition, many more agents can be used in an experiment. These agents can have different purposes such as managing groups of labs or just for debugging/logging purposes.

An experiment consists of distributed protocols that run inside multiple agents. Together these protocols implement the functionality of the experiment that is being tested, e.g., a distributed load-balancing protocol. Agents are experiment specific. Each experiment has its own set of customised agents that exists only for the duration of the experiment. New experiments can be designed by creating new sets of agents. In principle, multiple experiments can run simultaneously.

Agents are programmed in Java and can use the Symphony experiment interface to implement a distributed experiment. Symphony defines a minimal agent interface that allows for the creation of highly-reusable agent components. In addition, it includes interfaces for the measurement of experimental results and for defining the setup of experimental configurations. The layered architecture of Symphony allows customization of an experiment's runtime environment. For example, the bottom layer, which runs the Agent Operating System, can be

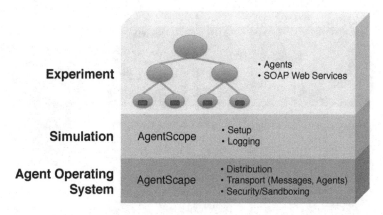

Fig. 2. Symphony architecture

exchanged for a different implementation (backend) with different features or characteristics as described in [10]. For a distributed version, Symphony uses the agent platform AgentScape as its backend. The advantage of this architecture is that running an experiment in a non-distributed environment is in theory a matter of exchanging the backend for a version that runs on a single machine.

In a distributed experiment, the AgentScape agent operating system layer runs the agents and takes care of the core aspects of running a distributed system. It provides a method of sending messages between agents, including maintaining a directory service, and a method of transporting agents between locations including distributing experiment specific code. AgentScape further provides the core security model for the system, including secure communication between locations, sandboxing of agent actions, and access control[1].

Fig. 3 illustrates the distributed nature of the Symphony platform. Partners each have their own location, consisting of their hardware-lab or co-simulation and a computer, or computers, that run AgentScape. The AgentScape platform automatically combines these AgentScape Locations into a single AgentScape World. The AgentScape World runs continuously. To run an experiment, a participant creates a set of agents specific to that experiment and injects it into the AgentScape World. The location at which each agent is to run is specified in the AgentScope experiment configuration. The AgentScape platform takes care of migrating the agents (and their code) and running them on the correct locations. At these locations, agents can access the resources made available by partners at those particular locations in their experiments. During the experiment, AgentScape transports messages between agents, AgentScope runs logs that record local results and gathers logged results to a central location. AgentScope logs can provide local and central user interfaces that display the progress of the experiment. At the end of the experiment the agents are removed from the system and the central logs are returned.

---

[1] Details of AgentScape, including a user manual, are given at
http://www.agentscape.org.

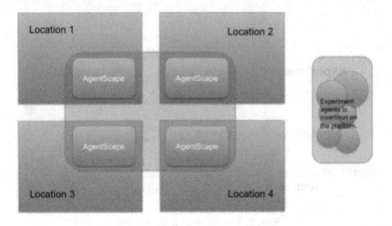

Fig. 3. Distributed AgentScape locations

4   An Example Scenario

This section illustrates the use of Symphony for one simple scenario as shown in Fig. 4. In this scenario, a distributed experiment is run that uses load aggregation and price dissemination. Labs have electrical appliances that have a predicted load. By aggregating the predicted loads of all labs together, a total load can be determined and based on that load an energy price forecast can be made. This price forecast is disseminated back to the labs. The labs can then, based on the future prices, decide to change their plans on how to use the electrical appliances, thereby changing their predicted load. This change, in turn, will change the aggregated total load and lead to price changes again, and so forth. In this experiment, different pricing strategies can be tested to see how they would influence the behaviour of energy consumers.

The agents implement two types of services: a load aggregation service and a price dissemination service. These services are implemented in the protocols that run inside the agents. In a large-scale, distributed environment implementing scalable, efficient load aggregation is not trivial. The scenario uses a tree structure. The agents form themselves into a tree and each agent then informs its parent of the load of the corresponding lab. The parent aggregates the load of its children and forwards it to its parent. In the end, the root node will have the total aggregated (predicted) load of all the labs. The price dissemination uses the same tree to push down the energy price forecast to all the labs. Virtual nodes can be used to increase the aggregate load with historical data for even larger experiments.

The labs themselves are connected to Symphony through proxy nodes and standard web service interfaces. Each proxy node is an AgentScape agent that runs on the lab's location and implements the *meter read web service*. This service provides the methods to join/leave an experiment and to receive the updates of the current load and load predictions from the participating labs as

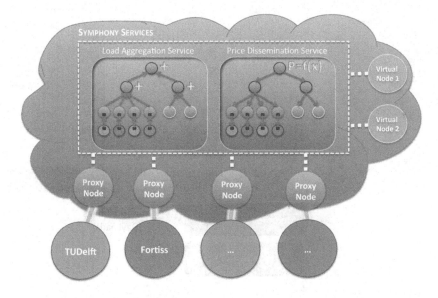

Fig. 4. Symphony load aggregation and price dissemination services

seen in Fig. 5. The labs implement the *price info web service* that provides the method used to receive the pricing information from Symphony. The flow of the experiment can be summarised as follows.

- A lab joins the experiment by invoking the join method of the web service of the proxy node. The URL of the lab's local price info web service is sent to the proxy node as an argument, so that Symphony knows how to contact the lab.
- The lab periodically sends its current load and predicted load (the meter load information) to the proxy node through the meter read web service. The labs can send their meter load at any time. Alternatively, labs can send their data at fixed intervals. The proxy node will send this predicted load information up the tree to create an aggregated predicted load.
- The proxy node, in turn, pushes price forecast information periodically to the lab via the price info web service interface.
- If a lab wants to leave an experiment, it invokes the leave method of the web service of the proxy. From now on, the lab is disconnected from the running experiment and will not receive updated price forecasts anymore. Optionally, the proxy node can pretend to the running experiment that the lab is still connected to the experiment by sending dummy values or use historical data when the experiment determines the aggregated predicted load.

5   Related Work

Much research has been done in the field of Smart Grids and the deregulation of the energy market. The topics range from security to the robustness of smart-grids, and from energy-market dynamics to forming virtual groups for distributed

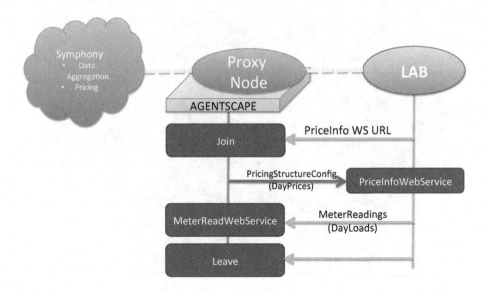

Fig. 5. Implementation of load aggregation and price dissemination services

energy resource management. Many researchers use some type of simulation for testing and validating the research. This section discusses some of the most popular ones.

NetLogo [21,19] is a well-known, generic, agent-based simulation tool. It is used by many educational institutions in their education and research. NetLogo provides a user-friendly programming language, a graphical user-interface, and a library containing many example simulation models, enabling users to quickly create their own agent-based simulation. Another strength of NetLogo is that it visualizes running simulations, so users can quickly see the effects of changing parameters in their model. However, NetLogo is purely a simulator in that it runs on one machine and it does not support hardware-in-the-loop. All entities in the simulation are modelled in software.

Repast [9,16] is another well-known, generic, agent-based simulation tool. It has been in development for over 14 years and has support for different programming languages such as ReLogo, Java, and C++. A high-performance version of Repast enables simulations to be run in parallel on a supercomputer or compute clusters. It supports genetic algorithms, neural networks, and regressions for agents through external (Java) libraries. Similar to NetLogo, Repast is focused on simulations and not emulations. The high-performance versions use parallellism mainly to speed up the calculations, not to represent real-world conditions of distributedness.

Power TAC [8,7] is a competitive simulation of future retail electric power markets. It focuses on simulations of electrical power brokers who compete on buying and selling power from customers and trading on a wholesale energy market. Annually, a Power Trading Agent Competition is held where competing teams can enter with their own broker agent to try to make the most profit in the competition, outperforming the other contestants. The simulation platform uses a client-server architecture where contestants remotely run their agent and compete against other agents by connecting to the central Power TAC simulation server. Power TAC focuses on market simulations in order to gain insights on policy mechanisms for future energy markets. Again, Power TAC focuses on simulations rather than on emulations. The client-server architecture only makes it easier for participants to take part in a simulation (game), but the distributedness is not used in the simulation logic itself. In addition, the energy entities are all modelled in software; hardware is not considered.

Lastly, CASSANDRA [17] is a simulation platform for assessing strategic decisions by energy market stakeholders by modelling several aspects of the demand side. CASSANDRA is developed as part of a European FP7 project which focuses on providing a platform for realistically modelling energy market stakeholders including small-scale consumers. The platform allows users to test and benchmark scenarios and provides methods for aggregating multiple small-scale consumers. Early versions of the platform are currently available. Cassandra too is focused more on simulations than on emulations.

Concluding, every platform has its specific strenghts, and the above mentioned simulators each provides features that are useful in their domains. However, simulations have their limitations in representing the actual characteristics of a distributed environment and real hardware. Symphony does provide the ability to run emulations in addition to simulations. It connects real users and real hardware and allows their input to be used in distributed energy experiments.

6   Summary

This paper has shown that it is possible to create a distributed experiment platform across Europe. It has also shown the added value of having a distributed experiment platform for researching the Smart Grid. It is important to have the ability to run experiments with real hardware in the loop and with all the characteristics of a non-deterministic distributed networked environment. Both simulations and emulations are key phases in the design of distributed solutions for the Smart Grid.

As part of the European EIT project, a number of minimum requirements have been identified for such a distributed experiment platform: security & privacy, loosely coupledness, and scalability. Next, the paper presented Symphony as a distributed experiment platform that fulfills these requirements. Symphony is built on top of AgentScape, a secure, scalable, distributed multi-agent platform. Symphony uses agents to loosely connect research labs and companies into a distributed experiment. Each experiment is implemented by a set of agents that communicate with each other. These agents can locally access the hardware and/or data provided by research labs and use it in their experiments. Symphony provides logging and debugging tools to follow the progress of an experiment.

To illustrate the use of Symphony, a simple load aggregation and price dissemination scenario has been shown. It showed how labs are connected to Symphony and how agents can use messages to process the data from labs together (aggregate the load) and after processing this data, push the result (price forecast) back to the labs. These labs can then use this information to change their behaviour. In short, this experiment tests how pricing can implement energy load balancing.

Symphony is currently under development by the Delft University of Technology and is being used in the European EIT ICT Labs activities, with partners including the Delft University of Technology, Imperial College London, Fortiss, Centrum Wiskunde & Informatica (CWI) Amsterdam, Technische Universität Berlin, Fraunhofer FOKUS, Deutsches Forschungszentrum für Künstliche Intelligenz (DFKI), KTH Royal Institute of Technology, Karlsruhe Institute of Technology (KIT), and many more.

Acknowledgements. The work in this paper has partially been made possible by EIT ICT Labs activities Virtual Labs (11814) and Experience Labs (11831).

References

1. Brazier, F.M., Kephart, J.O., Van Dyke Parunak, H., Huhns, M.N.: Agents and service-oriented computing for autonomic computing: A research agenda. IEEE Internet Computing 13(3), 82–87 (2009)
2. European Union. European Institute of Innovation & Technology, http://eit.europa.eu/
3. Gollmann, D.: Computer Security, 3rd edn. Wiley (2011)
4. IIDS. AgentScape Agent Middleware, http://www.agentscape.org
5. International Electrotechnical Commission. IEC Standards, http://www.iec.ch/smartgrid/standards/
6. James, G., Cohen, D., Dodier, R., Platt, G., Palmer, D.: A deployed multi-agent framework for distributed energy applications. In: Proceedings of the Fifth Int. Joint Conference on Autonomous Agents and Multiagent Systems, AAMAS 2006, pp. 676–678. ACM, New York (2006)
7. Ketter, W.: Power Trading Agent Competition, http://www.powertac.org
8. Ketter, W., Collins, J., Reddy, P.: Power tac: A competitive economic simulation of the smart grid. Energy Economics 39, 262–270 (2013)
9. North, M., Collier, N., Ozik, J., Tatara, E., Macal, C., Bragen, M., Sydelko, P.: Complex adaptive systems modeling with repast simphony. Complex Adaptive Systems Modeling 1(1), 3 (2013)
10. Oey, M.A., van Splunter, S., Ogston, E.F.Y., Warnier, M., Brazier, F.M.T.: A framework for developing agent-based distributed applications. In: Proceedings of the 2010 IEEE/WIC/ACM International Conference on Intelligent Agent Technology (IAT 2010), pp. 470–474. IEEE Press, Washington, DC (2010)
11. Ogston, E., Brazier, F.: Apportionment of control in virtual power stations. In: 2009 Second Int. Conference on Infrastructure Systems and Services: Developing 21st Century Infrastructure Networks (INFRA), pp. 1–6 (December 2009)
12. Ogston, E.F.Y., Brazier, F.M.T.: Agentscope: Multi-agent systems development in focus. In: Tenth Int. Conference on Autonomous Agents and Multi-Agent Systems (AAMAS 2011), Taipei, Taiwan, pp. 389–396. IFAAMAS (May 2011)

13. Overeinder, B.J., Brazier, F.M.T.: Scalable middleware environment for agent-based internet applications. In: Dongarra, J., Madsen, K., Waśniewski, J. (eds.) PARA 2004. LNCS, vol. 3732, pp. 675–679. Springer, Heidelberg (2006)

14. Pipattanasomporn, M., Feroze, H., Rahman, S.: Multi-agent systems in a distributed smart grid: Design and implementation. In: IEEE/PES Power Systems Conference and Exposition, PSCE 2009, pp. 1–8 (March 2009)

15. Pournaras, E., Warnier, M., Brazier, F.M.T.: A distributed agent-based approach to stabilization of global resource utilization. In: The International Conference on Complex, Intelligent and Software Intensive Systems (CISIS 2009). IEEE (March 2009)

16. Repast Development Team. The repast suite, http://repast.sourceforge.net

17. Seventh Framework Research Programme of the European Commission (FP7). CASSANDRA, http://www.cassandra-fp7.eu

18. Tesauro, G., Chess, D.M., Walsh, W.E., Das, R., Segal, A., Whalley, I., Kephart, J.O., White, S.R.: A multi-agent systems approach to autonomic computing. In: Proceedings of the Third Int. Joint Conference on Autonomous Agents and Multi-agent Systems. AAMAS 2004, vol. 1, pp. 464–471. IEEE Computer Society, Washington, DC (2004)

19. Tisue, S., Wilensky, U.: Netlogo: A simple environment for modeling complexity. In: International Conference on Complex Systems, pp. 16–21 (2004)

20. Wijngaards, N.J.E., Overeinder, B.J., van Steen, M., Brazier, F.M.T.: Supporting internet-scale multi-agent systems. Data and Knowledge Engineering 41(2-3), 229–245 (2002)

21. Wilensky, U.: NetLogo and NetLogo User Manual (1999), http://ccl.northwestern.edu/netlogo

Consensus in Smart Grids for Decentralized Energy Management

M. Rebollo, C. Carrascosa, and A. Palomares

Departamento de sistemas informáticos y computación
Universitat Politècnica de València
Camino de Vera S/N 46022 Valencia, Spain
{mrebollo,carrasco,apalomares}@dsic.upv.es

Abstract. This work proposes the use of a combination of gossip and consensus algorithms to allow a power grid to be self-organized by its components, adapting to the changes in the demand and compensating the possible failures that may occur. The Balearic Power Grid has been used to check the validity of the proposal.

1 Introduction

The problem of managing an electrical network has been growing in interest and importance. It represents a meaningful part of the GDP of a country and it is an strategic sector essential for the rest of the economic activities. In this work, we have focused on the demand management. Electrical energy cannot be stored in large quantities, so the amount of energy required must be generated when it is demanded. How can we distribute this demand among the components of the network so this demand is provided? and, how can we overcome failures in any substation so that the rest of the available network can compensate the lost? Those problems are faced in this work with the added difficulty of solving it with only local information.

We have modeled the energy network as a multiagent system, where each substation is modeled as an agent that can communicate only with the agents corresponding to the substations it is directly connected to. This multiagent system uses a consensus process to adjust the provided power to the current demand, whereas a gossip algorithm calculates, at the same time, the current total number of active stations and the required capacity of the network.

As a case study to show the performance of our solution, we have made a demo application that, using the electrical network in Balearic Islands and some historic information of the real demand, shows how the network provides the required demand and how it quickly adapts to failures in power substations.

2 Related Work

In the last years the use of more and more distributed energy resources, for example the new renewable energy systems, is increasing the complexity of the

J.M. Corchado et al. (Eds.): PAAMS 2014 Workshops, CCIS 430, pp. 250–261, 2014.

power distributions systems, not only by the complexity of the network itself but also by the intermittent changes in the capacity of the systems (for example wind and photovoltaic sources). Also the demand of users changes in real time depending of complex factors. For these reasons today centralized control of these networks is being infeasible. Actually distributed algorithms are required in order to control the power distribution systems [4].

Nowadays, power distributions systems are more related to smart grids than centralized control systems. Consensus algorithms are an interesting distributed coordination mechanism for control purposes. So, it is being studied its application to power distributions systems. For instance, [9,10] use a distributed approach, but without being able to adapt to failures in the network as the present approach. Along with these approaches, it can be also found in the literature some work related to managing the power distributions market [11,1]

The theoretical framework for solving consensus problems in dynamic agent networks was formally introduced by Olfati–Saber and Murray[5]. The interaction topology of the agents is represented using directed graphs, and *consensus* means reaching an agreement based on a certain amount of interest that depends on the state of all agents in the network. This value represents the variable of interest in *agreement term* problem, which might be, for example, a physical quantity, a control parameter, or a price.

Let G be a graph of order n with the set of nodes E and where x_i is a real value that is associated with the node E_i. The value of a node might represent physical quantities that are measured in a distributed network of sensors (temperatures, voltages, etc). A consensus algorithm is an interaction rule that specifies the information exchange between the agents. It has been demonstrated that a convergent and distributed consensus algorithm in discrete-time is achieved by:

$$x_i(k+1) = x_i(k) + \varepsilon \sum_{j \in N_i(k)} [x_j(k) - x_i(k))] \tag{1}$$

where $N_i(k)$ denotes the set formed by all nodes connected to the node i (neighbors of i) at iteration k.

Although consensus can be used to calculate the value of different functions (i.e. mean, maximal, or minimal values), there some functions it is not able to calculate. Specifically, consensus cannot make aggregate calculations, as for instance to sum up all the values in a network. To make these calculations, there exist other algorithms that are considered disorganized methods because there is not assumed any control structure ruling the process.

The work of Jesus et al. [2] and Rajagopalan and Varshney [8] thoroughly study and characterize the techniques used for distributed aggregation of data. From all this different kind of algorithms, gossiping ones are the most similar to consensus working. All the gossiping algorithms are inspired or extensions of the original algorithm called Push-Sum [3]. The main idea of this algorithm is to distribute the value of each node with the one of its neighbors. The result is that each node is pushing to the rest of the network part of its accumulated value.

3 Adaptive Consensus-Based Distributed Coordination Algorithm

The proposed mechanism is a combination of two belief propagation methods: Push-Sum algorithm [3] and consensus processes [5].

Push-Sum algorithm is one of the *gossip-based* or *epidemic* protocols that have emerged as a way to share information to make some global calculations in a decentralized way. Each agent i is characterized by a value $s_i(t)$ and a weight $w_i(t)$. These values are divided among the agent and its neighbors and the new values are calculated as:

$$s_i(t+1) = \frac{s_i(t)}{d_i + 1} + \sum_{j \in N_i} \frac{s_j(t)}{d_j + 1}, \qquad w_i(t+1) = \frac{w_i(t)}{d_i + 1} + \sum_{j \in N_i} \frac{w_j(t)}{d_j + 1} \qquad (2)$$

where d_i is the number of neighbors of agent i (degree of i). The quotient $s_i(t)/w_i(t)$ converges to $\lim_{t \to \infty} \frac{s_i(t)}{w_i(t)} = \sum_i s_i(0)$ when $w_i(0) = 1 \; \forall i$. This version of the push-sum algorithm exchanges the information with all the neighbors instead to choose randomly selected one. In this way, the random component of the original method is eliminated and a deterministic method is obtained.

Consensus algorithm allows a faster convergence rate than the push-sum, so it is used to adapt to the demand. In each step, agents exchange their current values with their neighbors. The process converges to the average of the initial values $x_i(0)$ of the agents. The dynamics of the system is modeled as follows:

$$x_i(t+1) = x_i(t) + \frac{\varepsilon}{v_i(t)} \sum_{j \in N_i} [x_j(t) - x_i(t)] \qquad (3)$$

where N_i are the neighbors of agent i, $v_i(t)$ is the weight of agent i, and ε is a constant that defines the learning step. The process converges to $\lim_{t \to \infty} x_i(t) = \frac{\sum_i w_i x_i(0)}{\sum_i w_i}$ under certain conditions [7]. This is a modified version of the original Olfati–Saber & Murray algorithm that includes weights in the network.

The consensus framework offers the possibility of control the complete MAS using a particular, 'leader' agent that evolves independently of the other agents in the network. All the rest of agents converge to the state of the leader as time goes by. This problem is commonly known as 'The Leader-Following Consensus Problem'.

The algorithm proposed in this work combines

- a weighted consensus algorithm as an adaptive coordination mechanism for a MAS;
- a 'follow the leader' mechanism to adapt the convergence values to the dynamics of the environment;
- a gossip method to calculate total aggregated magnitudes (such as the total number of participants), which can change during the process.

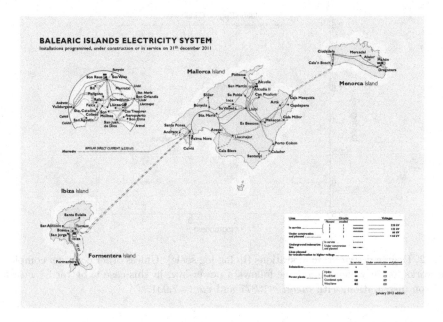

Fig. 1. Electrical network in Balearic Islands

Push-sum algorithm and consensus algorithm run in parallel, so the information required by both processes can be exchanged in one, unique message. The number of exchanged messages are the same used by the consensus process, which belongs to $O(2m)$, where m is the number of links in the network. In complex networks, usually $m \ll n^2$ because the structure of the network is sparse (see the characteristics of the case study network in Section 4). We call this process Adaptive Consensus-based Distributed Coordination Algorithm (ACDCA)

4   Case Study: Balearic Islands Power Grid

The Balearic Islands electricity network is composed of 57 substations and 82 lines from 30 kV to 220 kV. The transmission grid links the four islands that form the archipelago: Mallorca, Menorca, Ibiza and Formentera (see Figure 1). Furthermore, a connection with the Spanish peninsula compensate the negative balance of the demand. For example, during 2013, the net production of the islands was 4,405 GWh, whereas the demand was 5,671 GWh.

The demand is not uniform along the day and a characteristic pattern appears (Figure 3). The data with the real demand can be obtained from *Red Elctrica de Espaa*[1]. This source provides data regarding to programmed generation, actual and forecasted demand and it is updated every ten minutes. This information has

---

[1] http://www.ree.es

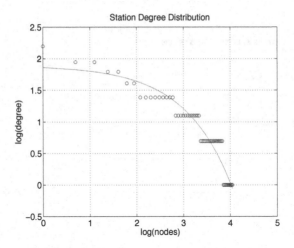

Fig. 2. Degree distribution of stations (in log-log scale). Unless other common complex networks [6], in which the degree follows a power-law, in this case is better fit with a Poisson distribution, with $mean = 2.877$ and $var = 2.931$.

been used in our case to validate the proposal under actual information from the real user's demand in the analyzed period. This time series shows the variation between working days and weekends. The demand shows a smooth change along the day and the week and this tendency is maintained in longer periods. As no abrupt changes have been detected, a short period can be examined and the conclusions extrapolated to the rest.

4.1   Network Characterization

As other artificial networks, and despite its small size, the Balearic power grid presents most of the characteristics of the small-world networks. This structure provides the network with efficiency in the diffusion and robustness to perturbation or damage. The *average degree* indicates that each substation is linked to 2.8 other substations (as average). The total *diameter* of the network is 14. That means that we need 14 steps to transport electricity between the two farthest substations. Nevertheless, the *mean path length* is only 4; which means that, as average, we only need 4 steps to transport energy between any pair of substations. The *clustering coefficient* measures the number of 'triangles' that are in the network; that is, if one substation is connected to other two substations, the clustering measures if these substations are linked together too. The combination of a high clustering and short paths gives the network some properties shared with small-world networks, as it has been observed in other power grids [6].

Nevertheless, there is other characteristic typical in many complex networks: the degree distribution. It measures how the degree (number of neighbors) is distributed along the network. Usually, a power-law distribution appears. That means that there are a few nodes in the network with a exceptionally high degree

Table 1. Importance of the towns depending of different centrality measures: degree, k-core, closeness, betweenness and eigenvector. The same top 5 towns appear in all classifications.

degree		k-core		closeness		betweenness		eigenvector	
town	*value*	*town*	*value*	*town*	*value*	*town*	*value*	*town*	*value*
Son Reus	9	Son Reus	8	Son Reus	0.326	Son Reus	776	Son Reus	0.055
Llubi	7	Llubi	6	Llubi	0.318	Llubi	628	Llubi	0.043
Es Bessons	7	Es Bessons	6	Con Orlandis	0.308	Valldurgent	567	Es Bessons	0.043
Valldurgent	6	Con Orlandis	5	Es Bessons	0.289	Es Bessons	555	Con Orlandis	0.037
Con Orlandis	6	Valldurgent	5	Valldurgent	0.281	Con Orlandis	392	Valldurgent	0.036
Llucmajor	5	Llucmajor	4	Llucmajor	0.280	Santa Ponsa	344	Llucmajor	0.031
Coliseo	5	Coliseo	4	Marratx	0.264	Llucmajor	307	Coliseo	0.030
Rafal	4	Cas Tresorer	3	Can Picafort	0.264	Torrent	301	Ciudadela	0.025
Torrent	4	Ciudadela	3	Coliseo	0.259	Calvi	243	Arenal	0.024
Ibiza	4	San Antonio	3	Ses Veles	0.256	Cala Millor	193	Inca	0.024

(they are called hubs), whereas the majority of the nodes has a low degree. But in the case of the Balearic power grid, we have observed a Poisson probability distribution (see Figure 2). So the studied grid is not a scale-free network and the degree distribution is similar to the distribution of random graphs.

Finally, there are other measures related with the importance of a node inside the network. This concept is know as *centrality*. There are four main measures of centrality: degree, closeness, betweenness and eigenvalue. The degree centrality measures the importance of a node by its degree (number of connections). The closeness centrality determines the distance to the other nodes in the network: the most central node is those with minimal distance to all the rest of the network. The betweenness is related with how many paths pass through a node, which acts as a bridge among many nodes in the network. Finally, eigenvector centrality is a measure of the influence of the node in the network, giving a high score to those nodes connected with other nodes with a high score too. Table 1 shows the values of these centrality measures for the top ten towns. A fifth measure has been added: the k-core, which creates groups of nodes that are linked to other nodes with degree k or greater. In the Balearic network, a group of five substations is clearly identified that systematically obtain the high score in all centrality measures: Son Reus, Llubi, Es Bessons, Valldurgent and Con Orlandis. Furthermore, Son Reus and Llubi substations are critical ones because they are the most central substations independently of the measure taken into account.

4.2   Consensus Process in Balearic Power Grid

To coordinate the network, a decentralized algorithm that combines the two belief propagation methods has been designed.

In each substation, the same information is maintained. To be used for the push-sum algorithm, $s_i(0) = 1$ is the count variable for stations, with $ws_i(0) = 1$ $\forall i$ (indicates to the push-sum algorithm an aggregation of values); $c_i(0)$ is initialized with the capacity of each substation i, with $ws_i(0) = 1$. For the consensus process, x_i is the variable that contains the total demand of the network and v_i is the proportion of the total capacity of the network provided by agent i (the weight for the consensus method). In each iteration, agent i exchanges a tuple

$$\left(\frac{s_i(t)}{d_i+1}, \frac{ws_i(t)}{d_i+1}, \frac{c_i(t)}{d_i+1}, \frac{wc_i(t)}{d_i+1}, x_i(t) \right) \tag{4}$$

with all its neighbors and the values are updated according to the corresponding algorithms.

These two mechanisms are combined in ACDCA as follows. Push-Sum is used to keep the track of current active substations as an aggregate value of the total number of agents $NA(t) = s_i(t)/ws_i(t)$ (which is locally calculated). The total capacity of the network is similarly defined as $NC(t) = c_i(t)/wc_i(t)$. These values are constantly updated. If a change is produced in the network (a failure in the network or a change in the global capacity), it is automatically detected by the neighbors and propagated to the rest of the network.

This information is used by the consensus algorithm to adjust the performance of the individual agents. Each agent has to provide only the proportional part of the whole capacity of the network. Therefore, the weight of station i in the system is obtained as $v_i(t) = c_i(0)/NC(t)$. When all the messages have been received from their neighbors, agents update their values following Equations 2 and 3. After a transient phase, $x_i(t)$ will contain the total demand and, therefore, $v_i(t)x_i(t)$ will be the part of the demand provided by substation i.

We would like to underline that these three values (NA, NC, and x_i) are calculated at the same time, so that any change in the number of agents (some agents leave the system or enter in it during the process) and in the capacity of the network can be detected and the system adapts to them.

A demo application has been modeled, where each one of these substations are agents. One additional agent (the *leader agent*) represents the global demand of the energy network. We have checked how the multi-agent system, following our method ,approaches this demand even when it is changing (following real data of the existing demand happened at the Balearic Islands) as can be seen at Figure 3. This demo shows how the network adapts by its own to changes in the demand and detects and corrects the effects of possible failures. The only condition to reach the exact solution is that the network must remain connected. If some part of the network is isolated from the rest, it still will work, but the values calculated will show some deviation.

4.3   Adaption to the Demand

The convergence of the network is theoretically assured by the algorithm, so it is not relevant for our purpose. Nevertheless, the 'follow the leader' mechanism provide us with an elegant an efficient way to adapt the output of the system to a dynamic, changing demand on real-time.

Lets consider the actual electrical demand of the Balearic islands during two weeks. A fictitious node will model the complete demand, updating its value each 10 minutes (this is the granularity of the real lectures). Therefore, one day is represented by 144 lectures. This node is connected to a selected subset of

Table 2. Differences in the convergence speed related to the granularity of changes, using different rates in the information and power exchange. The demand and information periods (T) are measures in seconds.

model	T elec.	T info	freq. rate	mean	std. dev.
$P = I - \varepsilon L$	600	300	1:2	10.5705	80.1273
$P = I - \varepsilon L$	600	200	1:3	6.3020	57.9475
$P = I - \varepsilon L$	600	150	1:4	6.5643	53.2062
$P = I - \varepsilon L$	600	100	1:5	7.7443	52.9254
$P = I - \varepsilon L$	600	50	1:12	0.0031	0.0516
$P = I - \varepsilon L$	600	10	1:60	-0.5e-04	0.0088
$P = D^{-1}A$	600	600	1:1	1.6e-04	0.0121

substations. With the same frequency, substations executes the ACDCA. The substations connected with the demand node receive the value by a consensus process. From their viewpoint, the demand node is just another substation, so no special behavior has to be implemented. To introduce a fictitious node is equivalent to a gossip process over n aggregated values, but it would introduce unnecessary complication into the model.

To measure the efficiency of the method, an error $e = (\sum_i v_i(t)x_i(t) - D_G)/D_G$ is calculated, where D_G is the global demand and $\sum_i v_i(t)x_i(t)$ is the total power provided by the network. A slow convergence produces a high error in the demand estimation. Table 2 shows the results obtained by two different implementations of the consensus protocol with different update frequencies. The standard consensus is calculated using $P = I - \varepsilon L$. An alternative formulation can be used with $P = D^{-1}A$. The standard consensus algorithm needs to exchange information several times per cycle in order to properly converge to the actual demand (each 10 seconds). On the other hand, the alternative formulation obtains a comparable performance keeping the original information and energy exchange rate. So we have opted for the second version of the algorithm.

Once the proper algorithm has been selected, we have studied how the AD-CDA adapts to the changes in the demand. Figure 3 shows the adaption process. There is a transient phase at the beginning, due to the lack of information until the push-sum algorithm has been executed and the substations have a more precise information about of the total capacity of the network. After 20 or 25 iterations, all the substations have begun to converge to the demand. The zoom provided in the same Figure shows us the differences in the speed of the convergence to the demand. This fact is due to the differences in the network topology and the centrality measures indicate which nodes will adapt faster to the changes.

The evolution of the error is shown in Figure 4. On the top, the error associated to the actual demand is calculated. A regular pattern appears as consequence of the periodicity of the demand. The peaks corresponds to the points with faster changes in the demand. During this period, the networks need to transmit the information and to change the reference values quickly. Whereas in the local maxima and minima the values are quite stable and error tends to zero.

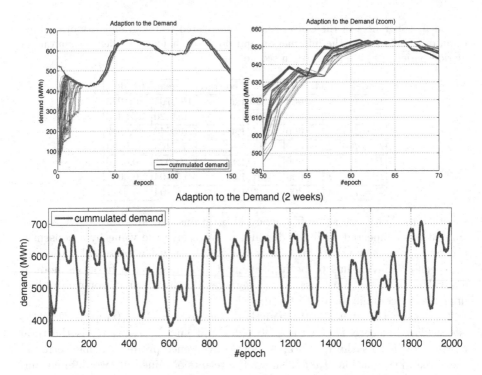

Fig. 3. Adaption to the demand. (Top) Daily evolution (Bottom) 2-weeks evolution. The lines represent the estimation of each one of the stations of the total capacity required by the system. The substation will provide the percentage of this total capacity that corresponds to its weight in the network.

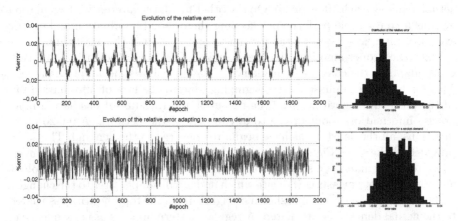

Fig. 4. Relative error evolution. We assume that the information is exchanged at the same frequency than electricity. (Top) Actual demand (Bottom) Randomly generated demand.

To compare the behavior of the algorithm, it has been executed with a random demand. To simulate it, random changes of 200 MWh are introduced in each epoch (10 minutes). We can see that the patter has disappear of the error. Nevertheless, the range of the error is approximately the same. In both cases, the distribution of the error is better adjusted to a bimodal distribution, as a mixture of two gaussian populations. In the case of the adaption to the actual Balearic demand, values of $\mu_1 = -0.0098$ and $\sigma_1 = 0.0069$ are obtained for the mean and the standard deviation for the first population; and $\mu_2 = 0.0027$ and $\sigma_2 = 0.0103$ for the second, with a mixing proportion $= 0.23/0.77$. In the case of a randomly generated demand, $\mu_1 = -0.0103$ and $\sigma_1 = 0.0068$ are the mean and the standard deviation for the first population and $\mu_2 = 0.0084$ and $\sigma_2 = 0.0085$ for the second, with mixing proportion $= 0.49/0.51$.

4.4 Adaption to Failures

The most interesting aspect of ACDCA is the failure tolerance. Besides the robustness of the network, the algorithm must work properly even when a sub-station fails, updating the information so the remaining active substations could assume the load lost by the failure, so the whole demand could be satisfied.

Two deviations from the values are considered to check the behavior of the ACDCA to isolate their effects. The first one is related with the changes in the demand and it is not a failure. This behavior appears each time a new value is obtained for the demand and it is propagated through the network to be adjusted. Figure 5 (left) shows this effect. The global demand descend in 1,000 MWh and the network smoothly converges again to the new reference value in 10 iterations. The second effect is related with the failure of one substation (Llucmajor) and shown in Figure 5 (right). In this case, an oscillation is observed until the networks compensates the power lost by the failed substation.

In both cases, this behavior is performed automatically by the neighbors of the nodes that fail or that detects the change in the demand. No central control nor global information is needed.

Finally, Figure 6 compares the behavior of the network without failures with the effect of the failure in one substation while the demand is being updated, so all the effects are considered at the same time. The red line shows the difference between both errors (with and without failures). As the initial conditions are the same, before the failure in the substation both networks behaves equally. When the substation fails, an oscillation is observed and after, a short transition time, the network seems to adapt to the new situation. Appears a smooth difference between the two networks, due to the change in the topology introduced by the failed substation Llucmajor is one of the most central substations, as appears in Table 1). In epoch 1,600, the substation is reactivated and the network recovers the normal evolution. What is more, it recovers totally from the failure and continues with the normal evolution as if the substation never had failed, as the zero difference between the errors indicates.

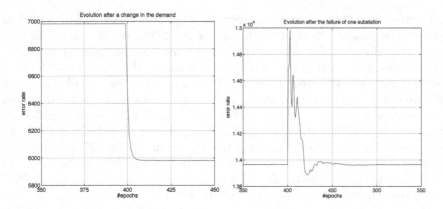

Fig. 5. (Left) Error after a change in the demand. The demand is constant until a descend of 1,000 MWh is produced. (Right) Error after a failure in a substation. The demand remains constant and one substation fails.

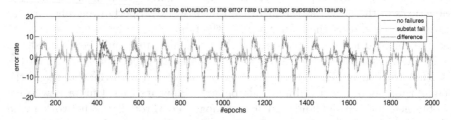

Fig. 6. Relative error evolution after a failure compared with the normal behavior of the network. The red line (color on-line) indicates the difference between both errors. In epoch 1,600, the substation is reactivated and the network recovers its evolution.

5 Conclusions

The application of belief propagation methods to construct a self-adaptive MAS that manages a electrical network formed by a set of substations that distribute the required power has been studied.

A bounded rationality scheme is assumed: nodes of the network are connected to a reduced set of pairs. Information and energy is exchanged with direct neighbors only. The information spreads and each agent is capable of calculating general network properties, such as the number of active substations or the total capacity of the network. These data are calculated and maintained in each node, without central repositories or middle-agents.

Two methods are combined. Push-sum protocol (a gossip method) is used to calculate aggregated values, such as the size of the network and its total capacity. Consensus protocol is used to adapt the current power provided by the network to the current demand. Both methods run in parallel, so the changes in the network can be propagated immediately

The Balearic Islands Electrical Network as been used to test the validity of this approach. It is a relatively small network, with 57 substations and 82 lines, with a capacity varying from 33 kV to 220 kV. The network show some of the characteristics of a small-world structure, which makes it efficient in the propagation and robust under random failures.

The obtained results show that the proposed method has been successful and, after a initial transitory period, the network adapts itself to the dynamic of the demand. Failures in substations are automatically detected and the remaining active substations assume the load of the failed one. Nevertheless, the total demand is overestimated.

Acknowledgments. This work has been funded thanks to the following research projects: CSD2007-00022, TIN2012-36586-C03-01 and PROMETEO.

References

1. Gensollen, N., Gauthier, V., Marot, M., Becker, M.: Modeling and optimizing a distributed power network: A complex system approach of the prosumer management in the smart grid. arXiv preprint arXiv:1305.4096 (2013)
2. Jesus, P., Baquero, C., Almeida, P.S.: A survey of distributed data aggregation algorithms. CoRR, abs/1110.0725 (2011)
3. Kempe, D., Dobra, A., Gehrke, J.: Gossip-based computation of aggregate information. In: Proceedings of the 44th Annual IEEE Symposium on Foundations of Computer Science, FOCS 2003, pp. 482–491 (2003)
4. McMillin, B., Akella, R., Ditch, D., Heydt, G., Zhang, Z., Chow, M.-Y.: Architecture of a smart microgrid distributed operating system. In: 2011 IEEE/PES Power Systems Conference and Exposition (PSCE), pp. 1–5. IEEE (2011)
5. Olfati-Saber, R., Fax, J., Murray, R.: Consensus and cooperation in networked multi-agent systems. Proceedings of the IEEE 95(1), 215–233 (2007)
6. Pagani, G.A., Aiello, M.: The power grid as a complex network: A survey. Physica A: Statistical Mechanics and its Applications 392(11), 2688–2700 (2013)
7. Pedroche, F., Rebollo, M., Carrascosa, C., Palomares, A.: On the convergence of weighted-average consensus. CoRR, abs/1307.7562 (2013)
8. Rajagopalan, R., Varshney, P.: Data-aggregation techniques in sensor networks: a survey. IEEE Communications Surveys Tutorials 8(4), 48–63 (2006)
9. Robbins, B., Dominguez-Garcia, A., Hadjicostis, C.: Control of distributed energy resources for reactive power support. In: 2011 North American Power Symposium (NAPS), pp. 1–5. IEEE (2011)
10. Zhang, M., Xin, H., Lu, Z., Gan, D., Seuss, J.: A real-time power allocation algorithm for dispersed energy storages and its communication network design. In: 2013 IEEE Power and Energy Society General Meeting (PES), pp. 1–5. IEEE (2013)
11. Zhang, Z., Ying, X., Chow, M.-Y.: Decentralizing the economic dispatch problem using a two-level incremental cost consensus algorithm in a smart grid environment. In: 2011 North American Power Symposium (NAPS), pp. 1–7. IEEE (2011)

Elspot: Nord Pool Spot Integration in MASCEM Electricity Market Simulator[*]

Ricardo Fernandes[1], Gabriel Santos[1], Isabel Praça[1], Tiago Pinto[1],
Hugo Morais[2], Ivo F. Pereira[1], and Zita Vale[1]

[1] GECAD – Knowledge Engineering and Decision-Support Research Center,
Institute of Engineering – Politechnic of Porto (ISEP/IPP), Porto, Portugal
{rifer,gajls,icp,tmcfp,ifdsp,zav}@isep.ipp.pt
[2] Automation and Control Group – Technical University of Denmark, Denmark
morais@elektro.dtu.dk

Abstract. The energy sector in industrialized countries has been restructured in the last years, with the purpose of decreasing electricity prices through the increase in competition, and facilitating the integration of distributed energy resources. However, the restructuring process increased the complexity in market players' interactions and generated emerging problems and new issues to be addressed. In order to provide players with competitive advantage in the market, decision support tools that facilitate the study and understanding of these markets become extremely useful. In this context arises MASCEM (Multi-Agent Simulator of Competitive Electricity Markets), a multi-agent based simulator that models real electricity markets. To reinforce MASCEM with the capability of recreating the electricity markets reality in the fullest possible extent, it is crucial to make it able to simulate as many market models and player types as possible. This paper presents a new negotiation model implemented in MASCEM based on the negotiation model used in day-ahead market (Elspot) of Nord Pool. This is a key module to study competitive electricity markets, as it presents well defined and distinct characteristics from the already implemented markets, and it is a reference electricity market in Europe (the one with the larger amount of traded power).

1   Introduction

Over the last few decades the electricity markets (EM) restructuring has been changing the EM paradigm. Some examples of the transformations that have been applied are the privatization, liberalization and international integration of previously nationally owned systems [1].

With this restructuring process several challenges were placed to governments and companies that are involved in the area of generation, transmission and distribution of

[*] This work is supported by FEDER Funds through COMPETE program and by National Funds through FCT under the projects FCOMP-01-0124-FEDER: PEst-OE/EEI/UI0760/2011, PTDC/SEN-ENR/122174/2010 and SFRH/BD/80632/2011 (Tiago Pinto PhD).

J.M. Corchado et al. (Eds.): PAAMS 2014 Workshops, CCIS 430, pp. 262–272, 2014.
© Springer International Publishing Switzerland 2014

electrical energy. To overcome these challenges, it became essential for the professionals to fully understand the principles of the markets, and how to evaluate their investments under such a competitive environment [2].

The need for understanding those mechanisms and how the involved players' interaction affects the outcomes of the markets, contributed to the growth of usage of simulation tools, with the purpose of taking the best possible results out of each market context for each participating entity.

To analyze dynamic and adaptive systems with complex interactions among its constituents, such as electricity markets, multi-agent based software is particularly well fitted. Some relevant modelling tools in the domain of restructured wholesale power markets have emerged, e.g. AMES (Agent-based Modeling of Electricity Systems) [3], EMCAS (Electricity Market Complex Adaptive System) [4], and MASCEM (Multi-Agent System for Competitive Electricity Markets) [5, 6].

The main goal of our research is to explore and study different approaches concerning the electricity markets environment, and power systems generally. For that we use the multi-agent system MASCEM [5, 6]. This system provides us with the realistic simulation of electricity markets, considering all the most relevant entities that take part in such operations, by representing reality in a controlled environment.

This paper presents the implementation and integration of Elspot (Nord Pool day-ahead market) [7] in MASCEM. The Nord Pool Spot is currently the largest energy market in the world, relative to the amount of electricity traded - in 2012 the volume of electricity transacted in this market reached 432 Terawatt-hours (TWh). This market operates in the Nordic and Baltic regions of Europe, accounting for about 70% of traded energy in these regions. *"Nord Pool Spot runs the leading power market in Europe, offering both day-ahead and intraday markets to its customers."* [8]. The countries covered by Nord Pool Spot Market are: Norway, Denmark, Sweden, Finland, Estonia, Latvia and Lithuania. It includes the day-ahead market (Elspot), intraday market (Elbas) and a balancing market [8].

The implementation of Elspot market in MASCEM brings significant added value to the multi-agent platform. The European electricity market is evolving into a continental scale electricity market in day-ahead negotiation. Given the scale of the Elspot market, this market and its players will have great influence in the unified market operation [9]. The enhanced electricity markets simulator resulting from the integration of the Nord Pool in MASCEM provides a solid platform to study and explore the implications and consequences of new and existing approaches for both the scientific community and also for the electricity market involved players, whether market negotiating players, regulators, or operators. It also provides a good tool for power systems students to learn and understand how the market mechanisms work, and how the players' interactions affect the outcomes of the market.

After this introductory section, Section 2 features an overview of the MASCEM simulator. Section 3 presents the Elspot market from Nord Pool Spot, a discussion on its most important characteristics and particularities, and its implementation in MASCEM. A study case demonstrating and analyzing the simulation of Elspot market in MASCEM and its implications is adduced in Section 4. Finally, in Section 5 the most relevant conclusions of this article are exposed.

2   MASCEM Overview

MASCEM is a multi-agent simulator of competitive electricity markets and it was developed with the purpose of studying the complex and restructured electricity markets. It models the main entities involved in the electricity market including their interactions, collecting data in the medium and long term to support the decisions of these entities according to their characteristics and objectives, thus allowing better understanding of the behavior, the development of trade relations and the mechanisms of these markets. The simulator uses game theory, learning techniques, scenario analysis and optimization techniques for modeling and supporting market actors in their decisions [5, 6, 10]. Figure 1 illustrates the multi-agent model and market structure of MASCEM.

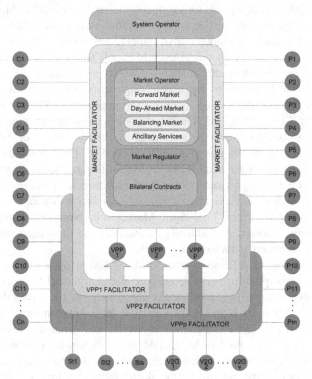

Fig. 1. - MASCEM's structure [10]

MASCEM went through a restructuring processing in which a new framework for developing multi-agent systems was adopted - JADE (Java Agent Development Framework) [11]. JADE is a developing environment for agent-based applications, according to the specifications of FIPA (Foundation for Intelligent Physical Agents) [12] and fully implemented in JAVA programming language. It ensures a standard of interoperability between multi-agent systems through a comprehensive set of system services, which enable communication between agents. All communication between agents is carried out through the exchange of messages [12].

The agents present in MASCEM represent various entities in the electricity market, such as: Producers, Buyers, Brokers, Virtual Power Players (VPPs) Market Operators and System Operators. The user defines the market mechanisms to simulate, the number of agents, the strategy and characteristics of each agent.

Due to its flexibility, MASCEM allows users to have all the autonomy in the definition of scenarios to simulate, allowing indicating the number and characteristics of buyers and electricity suppliers, selecting the trading mechanism of the study and the duration (number of days) of the market analysis.

Currently MASCEM is capable of simulating several real electricity markets, supported by real data concerning the market characteristics and particularities, as well as the information regarding the involved players in each market, and their log of past actions, thus providing a realistic simulation platform to undertake a large variety of studies and experiences.

MASCEM establishes a solid base simulation that allows the study of various models of electric markets and obtaining conclusions extrapolated to reality. After the simulation, it is possible to analyze what is the market price and amount of electricity traded in each trading period. It also allows analyzing the results of the individual agents, representing both buyers and suppliers of electricity, i.e., how the goals of each are met under different simulations circumstances and negotiation contexts.

The MASCEM simulator is additionally integrated with ALBidS (Adaptive Learning for strategic Bidding System), a system equipped with adaptive learning abilities, which endows agents with capabilities to analyze negotiation contexts, such as the day of the week, the period, the particular market in which agents are negotiating, the economic situation and weather conditions. ALBidS thus allows market agents to automatically adapt their strategic behavior according to their current situation. The ALBidS system uses reinforcement learning algorithms to choose the most appropriate from a set of several different strategies according to each context [6]. Figure 2 shows the structure of MASCEM considering the integration of ALBidS.

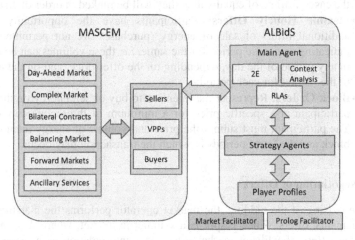

Fig. 2. - MASCEM integration with ALBidS [10]

3   Nord Pool Elspot

The Elspot market works like a stock exchange market that allows its participants to transact energy for the following day. It is also a symmetric market, since it allows offers of sale and purchase of energy by the players participating in the auction. These participants include producers, traders and retailers. Some end users (companies with very high demand consumption) participate directly in the market, rather than obtaining their energy through retailers, as happens with smaller size entities.

The operation of the Elspot market is divided into 4 stages throughout each day [8]: **(i) Until 10h:** the power transmission capabilities for each area of bidding are indicated by each transmission system operator. The bidding areas are used in order to define areas of the transmission grid that avoid congestion situations. **(ii) Up to 12h:** market participants wishing to sell or buy energy place their bids to the auction for a particular area of bidding. **(iii) 12h-13h:** the energy prices for each hour of the following day are calculated based on the transmission capabilities and offers to buy / sell. **(iv) 13h-15h:** established energy transactions are announced.

3.1   Offers

The offers placed in Elspot market should be expressed in a positive volume of energy in case of a purchase and expressed as negative if the volume is available for sale. The offers must still be contained in the price range set by Nord Pool Spot. There are three possible types of offers that can be presented in Elspot [13]:

- **Hourly Orders:** Refers to the intention to buy or sell energy from an agent in the market, in a given area with a given bid price for a particular period. The participant submits a set of pairs composed by the bid price and the amount of energy required for each period. Offers must be sorted by price in ascending order in case of sale or descending order in case of purchase. In the case of offers of equal value, they will be ranked in order of arrival;
- **Flexible Hourly Offers:** Participants have the opportunity to make additional offers of sale of energy (purchases are not permitted) without indicating a specific period for the same, *i.e.* these volumes can be transacted in any period of the day, depending on the offer price, and on the necessities of the market for each period;
- **Block Orders:** Represent the intention to buy or sell energy on the part of a participant at a specific price for a minimum of three consecutive periods. The participant must submit the price and volume of energy intended for the block and the set of periods in which the transaction may occur.

3.2   Negotiation of Offers

After the closing of the bidding, the market operator performs the matching process the participants' offers. Since Elspot is a symmetric market, where there are buying and selling offers, the Elspot market uses linear interpolation as a mean to obtain aggregated curves of selling and buying offers. Figure 3 illustrates the matching mechanism of the symmetric market.

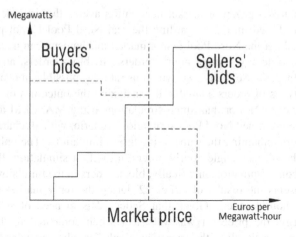

Fig. 3. Symmetrical Pool, adapted from [5]

The intersection point establishes the market price and the volume of electricity for each period. After the market auction is finished, if congestion occurs in a connection point between areas, a *market split* takes place. The *market split* divides the market into two independent ones, one considering the area where the congestion occurs, and the other without that area. Once the division is performed, the market mechanism is run again for each area separately, and in case of congestion occurring once more in other points of the electrical grid, the *market split* process divides the network in more areas, following the same principle as before, repeating the entire process until there are no more congestion problems.

The sale offers with prices below the market price and the purchase offers with prices above the market price will be accepted in the market, and the price at which energy is traded is equal for all offers (unique market price for each period).

For offers of flexible type, trading occurs in the same way, and these deals will apply in the period when its use will maximize the market profit. There are several offers of this kind, they will be ordered by price, with the lowest prices to be more likely to be accepted (always depending on the market price for each period).

In the case of block offers, they will be accepted if the market price of all periods in which the block applies is equal to or higher than the price of the block bid in case of offers for sale; or if the market price of the block periods is equal or less than the price of the block in the case of purchase bids. The acceptance of an offer which is within a block is still dependent on the acceptance of all the other offerings of the same block. This condition is called fill-or-kill [13]

4   Case Study

This case study is based on three scenarios, created using real data extracted from the Nord Pool Elspot market [7]. The three scenarios are set during the summer, on the 25th July, 2013 (Thursday), and were created to represent the Nord Pool reality through a summarized group of market negotiation agents that include 84 seller and 68 buyer players based on data regarding the real Nord Pool Elspot players. These agents, as defined per the Nord Pool Elspot market mechanism, can make use of three distinct types of orders: (i) single hourly orders, (ii) block orders, and (iii) flexible hourly orders. In this case study, we will illustrate the possible impact of using the three different types of orders available by analyzing the outcomes of one particular seller player (Seller 22). For that, three simulations using MASCEM are performed, using the same pre-defined Nord Pool simulation scenario, with all characteristics and players' behaviors remaining the same in the three simulations. The only exception is Seller 22, which will use single hourly orders in the first simulation, flexible hourly orders in the second simulation, and finally, block orders in the third simulation.

Figure 4 presents the results of Seller 22 during the daily market session, using only the single hourly orders. Given that Seller 22 is in need of selling a certain amount of energy, the price set was very low when compared to the established market price. As a result, all of the energy available for sale was indeed negotiated in the market. Analyzing the chart of Figure 4, it is possible to observe that there are no light green bars (meant to indicate the energy not sold during the session).

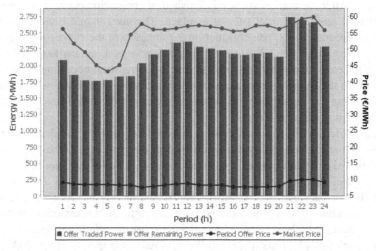

Fig. 4. Market results for agent Seller 22 during the Elspot market on 25-07-2013 using single hourly orders

Figure 5 presents the results of Seller 22 using a different negotiating behavior. In addition to the single hourly orders of the previous scenario, three flexible hourly orders were submitted by our player. These flexible hourly orders (available only to seller agents), allow the players to specify a fixed price and volume. The hour is not specified. The order will be accepted in the hour that optimizes the overall socioeconomic welfare of the market. A maximum of five flexible hourly orders is available per agent during a market session. In this scenario three orders were submitted with the volume of 2000 MWh each, all three at the price of 40 €/MWh.

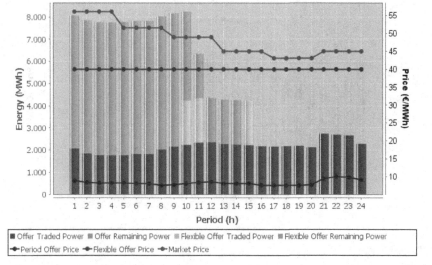

Fig. 5. Market results for the player Seller 22 during the Elspot Market on 25-07-2013 using flexible hourly orders

It is possible to observe from the chart of Figure 5 that during the first nine market periods (hours) none of the orders was accepted in spite of the bid price being below the established market price. The orange bars indicate a total of 6000 MWh of unsold energy during these periods (referring to the total of the three flexible offers, of 2000 MWh each). The flexible hourly orders were accepted in the 10th, 11th and 15th periods. In these three periods the total amount of energy of the order was sold. As can be seen by the graph of Figure 5, since the first flexible offer is accepted in period 10, only 4000 MWh remain to be negotiated in the 11th period. From these, 2000 MWh are accepted, and the remaining 2000 MWh, referring to the third and final flexible offer are negotiated in the following periods, being finally accepted in the 15th period. As mentioned before, the condition for the acceptance of each (or all) flexible offer is not only the proposed bid price, but also the maximization of the overall socioeconomic welfare of the market session, from the market operator's perspective.

Figure 6 presents the market results for Seller 22, this time using block orders. This type of order can be seen as a group of single hourly orders, where each order can have a different amount of energy, but all must obey to the same price. All of the orders comprising the block must belong to three or more consecutive hours. These orders have a fill-or-kill condition, which means that all of the orders comprising the block must be accepted in the market, for the block to be negotiated.

The block order submitted by Seller 22 is comprised of 24 individual orders, one for each of the 24 hourly periods of the market session. The same energy volume was defined for all of the orders (200 MWh). The price set for the block is 44 €/MWh.

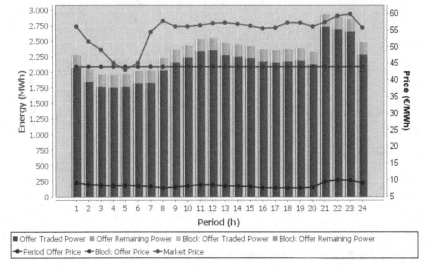

Fig. 6. Market results for player Seller 22 during the Elspot Market on 25-07-2013 using block orders

It is possible to observe in the chart of Figure 6, that the block was not accepted, despite the block price being inferior to the established market price in 23 of the 24 hourly periods of the market. The market price of the 5th period was set at 42 €/MWh, which caused the entire block being refused in the market, after failing the fill-or-kill condition.

When comparing the three studied scenarios, it is possible to observe that it is vital for an agent to have a full understanding of all the different conditions that each market presents. In the Nord Pool Elspot market, the use of flexible and block orders can make a colossal difference both in an individual player's profits, and also in the overall socioeconomic welfare of the market. The flexible orders allow a player to sell an extra volume of energy, at a higher price, in hours when that energy is most demanded. By defining a lower price for a block order, a player can sell a predetermined amount of energy throughout the whole market session. In that case, the risk is not very high. However, if the player tries to maximize its profit, by setting a higher price, such as Seller 22 in the third simulation presented in this case study, the risk of the whole block being rejected increases exponentially because of the fill-or-kill condition.

5   Conclusions

This paper presented the Nord Pool Elspot market integration in the MASCEM Simulator. Being the biggest electricity market in Europe regarding the amount of energy negotiated, and having three different types of orders that market agents can use to define their proposals, this market integration comes to improve MASCEM's capacity to recreate the electricity markets reality in the fullest possible extent. The implementation of the Elspot market proves to be of great added value to understand how the methodologies and strategies of the day-ahead electricity markets behave in Europe, furthermore when the integration of the European electricity markets is fast approaching.

The new enhanced electricity markets simulator resulting from the integration of the Nord Pool in MASCEM provides a solid platform to study and explore the implications and consequences of new and already existing approaches in electricity markets. Tools with this type of capabilities are essential for researchers of the power systems area in order to be prepared to deal with the constant changes in the electricity markets environment. Additionally, market negotiating players, regulators, and operators can fruitfully use the simulation capabilities of MASCEM to test negotiation alternatives in order to maximize their goals.

In the presented case study, it was possibly to observe the particularities of the Nord Pool Elspot market, using three different types of orders, with very different results. Agents may use these orders to their advantage, trying new strategies to better achieve their goals and make the most profits out of the market. That was the case of agent Seller 22 with the use of flexible orders in order to successfully sell an extra amount of energy at higher prices. However, when using block offers, the conclusion is that the approach must be more cautious, as the outcome of one particular negotiation period affects the results of all periods of the block. Moreover, this type of offer is particularly useful for generation units which cannot change their generation drastically from one period to another, or if such change is not economically viable. Therefore, low prices should be practiced, in order to guarantee the successful sale of the entire amount of power, as long as it is high enough to cover the company's generation costs.

Regarding the market operator's perspective, the flexible orders, in particular, present a very important resource to manage the variance in generation and consumption throughout a day. With access to flexible amounts of power that can be assigned to any hour of the day, the market operator is able to balance the needs when it is necessary, avoiding eventual lacks of supply.

These different types of offers, each one with specific rules will allow many further studies, mainly regarding the inclusion of intelligent techniques for supporting the players' actions taking into account this market's characteristics. Taking into account, and acknowledging the differences in different electricity markets operation becomes essential for players to be prepared to deal with different negotiation contexts, mainly with the ongoing unification of the European electricity market, and the consequential changes that it will bring to the electricity negotiation process.

References

1. Shahidehpour, M., et al.: Market Operations in Electric Power Systems: Forecasting, Scheduling, and Risk Management, pp. 233–274. Wiley-IEEE Press (2002)
2. Meeus, L., et al.: Development of the Internal Electricity Market in Europe. The Electricity Journal 18(6), 25–35 (2005)

3. Li, H., Tesfatsion, L.: Development of Open Source Software for Power Market Research: The AMES Test Bed. Journal of Energy Markets 2(2), 111–128 (2009)
4. Koritarov, V.: Real-World Market Representation with Agents: Modeling the Electricity Market as a Complex Adaptive System with an Agent-Based Approach. IEEE Power & Energy Magazine, 39–46 (2004)
5. Praça, I., et al.: MASCEM: A Multi-Agent System that Simulates Competitive Electricity Markets. IEEE Intelligent Systems 18(6), 54–60
6. Vale, Z., et al.: MASCEM - Electricity markets simulation with strategically acting players. IEEE Intelligent Systems 26(2) (2011); Special Issue on AI in Power Systems and Energy Markets
7. Nord Pool Spot website, http://www.nordpoolspot.com/ (accessed on January 2014)
8. Nord Pool Spot, Annual Report, Europe's Leading Power Markets (2013), http://www.nordpoolspot.com/Global/Download%20Center/Annual-report/Nord-Pool-Spot_Europe's-leading-power-markets.pdf (accessed on January 2014)
9. EMCC - European Market Coupling Company, http://www.marketcoupling.com/ (accessed on November 2013)
10. Pinto, T., et al.: A new approach for multi-agent coalition formation and management in the scope of electricity markets. Energy Journal (2011), doi:10.1016/j.energy.2011.05.045
11. JADE - Java Agent DEvelopment Framework, http://jade.tilab.com/ (accessed on October 2013)
12. Foundation for Intelligent Physical Agents (FIPA), Agent Management Specification (2002), http://www.fipa.org/specs/fipa00023/SC00023J.html (accessed on October 2013)
13. Nord Pool Spot, Trading Appendix 2a: Elspot Market Regulations (2011), http://www.nordpoolspot.com/Global/Download%20Center/Rules-and-regulations/Elspot%20Market%20(Regulations%20Effective%20from%207%20January%202014).pdf (accessed on January 2014)

Particle Swarm Optimization of Electricity Market Negotiating Players Portfolio[*]

Tiago Pinto[1], Zita Vale[1], Tiago M. Sousa[1], Tiago Sousa[1],
Hugo Morais[2], and Isabel Praça[1]

[1] GECAD – Knowledge Engineering and Decision-Support Research Center,
Institute of Engineering – Polytechnic of Porto (ISEP/IPP), Porto, Portugal
{tmcfp,zav,tmsbs,tabsa,icp}@isep.ipp.pt
[2] Automation and Control Group – Technical University of Denmark, Denmark
morais@elektro.dtu.dk

Abstract. Energy systems worldwide are complex and challenging environments. Multi-agent based simulation platforms are increasing at a high rate, as they show to be a good option to study many issues related to these systems, as well as the involved players at act in this domain. In this scope the authors' research group has developed a multi-agent system: MASCEM (Multi-Agent System for Competitive Electricity Markets), which performs realistic simulations of the electricity markets. MASCEM is integrated with ALBidS (Adaptive Learning Strategic Bidding System) that works as a decision support system for market players. The ALBidS system allows MASCEM market negotiating players to take the best possible advantages from each market context. However, it is still necessary to adequately optimize the players' portfolio investment. For this purpose, this paper proposes a market portfolio optimization method, based on particle swarm optimization, which provides the best investment profile for a market player, considering different market opportunities (bilateral negotiation, market sessions, and operation in different markets) and the negotiation context such as the peak and off-peak periods of the day, the type of day (business day, weekend, holiday, etc.) and most important, the renewable based distributed generation forecast. The proposed approach is tested and validated using real electricity markets data from the Iberian operator – MIBEL.

1 Introduction

Electricity markets worldwide are complex and challenging environments, involving a considerable number of participating entities, operating dynamically trying to obtain the best possible advantages and profits [1]. The recent restructuring of these markets increased the competitiveness of this sector, leading to relevant changes and new problems to be addressed, namely physical constraints, market operation rules and

---

[*] This work is supported by FEDER Funds through COMPETE program and by National Funds through FCT under the projects FCOMP-01-0124-FEDER: PEst-OE/EEI/UI0760/2011, PTDC/SEN-ENR/122174/2010 and SFRH/BD/80632/2011 (Tiago Pinto PhD).

J.M. Corchado et al. (Eds.): PAAMS 2014 Workshops, CCIS 430, pp. 273–284, 2014.
© Springer International Publishing Switzerland 2014

financial issues [1, 2]. Potential benefits depend on the efficient operation of the market [1]. Market players and regulators are very interested in foreseeing market behavior, as it is essential for them to fully understand the market's principles and learn how to evaluate their investments in such a competitive environment [2].

The development of simulation platforms based in multi-agent systems is increasing as a good option to simulate real systems in which stakeholders have different and often conflicting objectives. These systems allow simulating scenarios and strategies, providing users with decision making according to their profile of activity. Several modeling tools can be fruitfully applied to study and explore restructured power markets, such as "AMES Wholesale Power Market Test Bed" [3] and "EMCAS - Electricity Market Complex Adaptive System" [4].

MASCEM - Multi-Agent Simulator for Electricity Markets [5, 6] is also a modeling tool to study and explore restructured electricity markets. Its purpose is to be able to simulate as many market models and player types as possible, enabling it to be used as a simulation and decision-support tool for short/medium term purposes but also as a tool to support long-term decisions, such as the ones taken by regulators. Agents in MASCEM use several distinct strategies when negotiating in the market and learning mechanisms in order to best fulfill their objectives. The learning process is undertaken using MASCEM's connection with another multi-agent system: ALBidS (Adaptive Learning strategic Bidding System) [6]. ALBidS provides decision support to electricity markets' negotiating players, allowing them to analyze different contexts of negotiation, such as the week day, the period, the particular market in which the player is negotiating, the economic situation and weather conditions, and automatically adapt their strategic behavior according to the current situation. This system implements several negotiation mechanisms and data analysis algorithms, enhancing the strategic behavior of the players.

Despite the continuous development of multiagent software, a gap still exists, regarding the ability of learning and adaptation in order to provide the best possible results. In particular, concerning the automatic and intelligent use of multiple market opportunities as they arise.

This paper presents a portfolio optimization mechanism for electricity market participation. Firstly, a database is created, with the prices expected in each market session of the electricity markets in which the player is registered over the various periods of each day. This database is filled using price forecasts made by trained neural networks with historical data of real electricity markets [7]. The database is used to execute an optimization based on the Particle Swarm Optimization (PSO) [8], to optimize investments in market environment.

2   MASCEM and ALBidS Overview

MASCEM [5, 6] is a simulation platform developed in order to study the electricity markets' restructuring. It creates agents dynamically, including their interactions, information and experience acquirement in long term so it can support players' decisions, according to their own characteristics and goals. The purpose of MASCEM is to be able to simulate the most possible market models and agent types so that it can create in a more realistic way the electrical markets environment. This allows MASCEM to be used as a simulation, and decision-support tool for players.

MASCEM can represent the most important entities involved in electrical markets' negotiations, and their relations. The market operator controls the pool and validates offers to set the price market. The system operator ensures that all conditions are according to regulations and is responsible for the system security. Buyers and sellers are the key players in the market. Buyers represent consumers and distribution companies. Sellers represent electricity producers, competing among themselves to get the highest profit. Moreover, buyers and sellers can cooperate with each other so they can achieve their goals.

MASCEM includes the negotiation mechanisms normally found in electricity markets and it is able to simulate several kinds of market such as day-ahead pool (asymmetric or symmetric, with or without complex conditions), bilateral contracts, balancing market, forward markets and ancillary services.

The different types of trading implemented on MASCEM and the interactions between the participating entities in different situations create the necessity for the use of adaptive learning. Recently, a new system – ALBidS [6] - has been integrated with MASCEM, for that purpose. Fig. 1 presents the integration of these two systems.

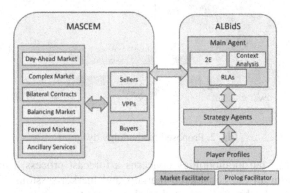

Fig. 1. Integration of MASCEM and ALBidS

ALBidS is an adaptive learning system providing decision support for participants in the electricity markets. This multi-agent system has an agent responsible for performing each distinct trading strategy to support the bidding process. Thus, it prevents the system performance degradation when each agent gets his answer and sends it to the main agent, which allows running parallel algorithms. The main agent uses the distinct acting proposals, provided by each algorithm, and chooses the most appropriate from them through the use of reinforcement learning algorithms (RLA). These RLA are dependent on the context, so that different stats for each algorithm are considered for distinct negotiating contexts.

ALBidS integrates different approaches regarding the market type and respective prices. Each of these approaches is executed independently. In order to choose the best alternative for each moment and context, there is a competitor players' profile mechanism with the purpose of generating suitable profiles for ALBidS strategies usage. There is also a mechanism to manage the system efficiency so that it is able to adapt to different simulations. This way, results quality and execution speed are adequately balanced to meet each simulation's requirements.

3   Particle Swarm Optimization of Electricity Market Players Portfolios

The objective of the proposed methodology is the analysis of the specific characteristics of electricity markets' historical data. This provides the ability to intelligently manage the investments to be made, *i.e.,* based on different markets prices predictions, the amount power that should be negotiated in each context can be optimized. The process of the proposed methodology is presented in Figure 2.

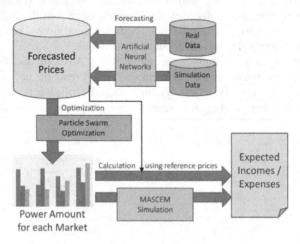

Fig. 2. Proposed methodolgy dyagram

The first step of the methodology concerns a forecast process, using the historic market prices from all the considered markets and market sessions. These forecasts are used to build a database of expected market prices for each market, for each time period of each considered day. Using the market prices forecast database, an optimization process is executed in order to achieve the optimal amount of power that should be negotiated by the supported player in each market type, at each time period (given the total amount the player desired to sell or buy). This optimization process originates a reference value of incomes that should be expected by investing the suggested amounts of power in each market. Finally, realistic market simulations using real data from different electricity markets are used to validate the results, and analyze if the outcomes of the optimization process are in accordance to what can be expected in the reality.

3.1   Data-Base Construction

The first step of the proposed methodology is the creation of a database containing the forecasts of different market prices under different contexts. The output result considers a set of columns for each market type. For each type of market several days are considered, and for each day, there are three forecast values: minimum, medium and maximum. These three values are used for predictions which may have the maximum value that can be attained in a given period of one day from the minimum value that the price can be achieved, and the average expected. These values are intended to be used by the efficiency management mechanism of ALBidS. Regarding the lines, they are divided by quantities of electricity traded. These amounts represent the amount ranges (e.g. from 0 to 50MW, 50 to 100 MW, etc.). For each of these amounts of energy that is a row for each considered negotiating period.

Some markets depend on the amount of negotiated power. Bilateral contracts for instance. This means that even though the optimal solution would be to allocate everything in the market with the higher expectation, the negotiated amount is by itself restrictive, and obligates the solution to disperse the allocation by other markets, depending on the expected prices and on the negotiation amounts. The amount ranges are used to take this into account.

In order to achieve this database, we have identified the following as key steps:

- Generation of dynamic output files depending on input variables, namely: Types of markets; The number of days; The number of periods; The number of value ranges of quantities of energy; Maximum power; Number of balancing market's sessions, if this market is chosen.
- Implementation of artificial neural networks (ANN) [9] trained with the specific real historical data from the Iberian energy market [7]. The forecasts returned from the various ANNs are used to fill the database. The structure of the ANN has been based on previous experiments in forecasting market prices, resulting from the authors' previous works, such as described in [10].

3.2   Optimization Problem

Considering the expected production of one player for each period of each day, the amount of power to be negotiated in each market is optimized to get the maximum profit that can be achieved.

The inputs are:

- the weekday, referred as d in equation (1);
- the number of days, $Nday$;
- the negotiation period, referred as p;
- the number of periods, $Nper$;
- a boolean variable for each distinct market or negotiation platform, indicating if this player can enter it to sell: $Asell_{M1...NumM}$;
- a boolean variable for each session of the balancing market, indicating if this player is allowed to buy in each of them: $Abuy_{S1...NumS}$;
- $M1, M2, ..., NumM$ are the considered markets;
- $S1, S2, ..., NumS$ are the considered balancing market sessions;

The outputs are:

- $Spow_{M1...NumM}$ representing the amount of power to sell in each market;
- $Bpow_{S1...NumS}$ representing the amount of power to buy in each session of the balancing market;

In this formulation $ps_{M,d,p}$ is the expected price for the selling of power, and $pb_{S,d,p}$ the expected price for buying. The objective function is presented in (1).

$$f\left(Spow_{M1...NumM}, Bpow_{S1...NumS}\right) =$$

$$Max \begin{bmatrix} \sum_{M=M1}^{NumM} \left(Spow_{M,d,p} \times ps_{M,d,p} \times Asell_M\right) - \\ \sum_{S=S1}^{NumS} \left(Bpow_S \times pb_{S,d,p} \times Abuy_S\right) \end{bmatrix}, \qquad (1)$$

$$\forall d \in Nday, \forall p \in Nper, Asell_M \in \{0,1\}, Abuy \in \{0,1\}$$

$$ps_{M,d,p} = Value\left(d, p, Spow_M, \text{M}\right)$$

$$pb_{S,d,p} = Value\left(d, p, Bpow_S, \text{S}\right)$$

The Value function returns the expected value of the power for each particular period of each day, and for each market. That also depends on the power amount to trade. When a player tries to establish a bilateral contract, the deals may be highly dependent on the amount of power that is being negotiated. The same fact is verified in other markets, even if not in such a clear way. So, this prediction takes that in consideration too, by applying fuzzy logic on the absolute amount of the power, to classify it in one of the categories defined by a clustering mechanism, which groups the ranges of amounts that present similar prices in each market. The correspondent price is obtained through the Data matrix which stores all the prices. The value function is expressed in (2).

$$Value\left(day, per, Pow, Market\right) = Data\left(fuzzy\left(Pow\right), day, per, Market\right) \qquad (2)$$

This formulation has some constraints that are dependent on the individual characteristics and requirements of each particular market. Other constraints that must be taken into consideration are the ones imposed by the complex conditions that each player can present. These constraints are formulated depending on the set of conditions that the player presents, that also depend on each market that it enters.

The main constraint, which is applied to every situation, is expressed in (3), to impose that the total power reserved to be sold in the set of all markets is never higher than the total expected production (TEP) of the player, plus the power expected to be bought along all sessions of the balancing market.

$$\sum_{M=M1}^{NumM} Spow_M \le TEP + \sum_{S=S1}^{NumS} Bpow_S \qquad (3)$$

This optimization process allows us to:

- Play with the possibility to negotiate with different players in the bilateral contracts, and so having the chance to get higher or lower prices, depending on the circumstances;
- Play with the chance to wait for the later sessions of the balancing market to provide higher amounts of energy, if it is expected for the price to go up;
- Play with the possibility for sellers to buy and buyers to sell in the balancing market, to get good business opportunities:
  - using arbitrage opportunities, buying extra energy when the prices are expected to be lower, and then selling it later when the prices go up; or if the prices show the opposite tendency, offer more energy than the player actually expects to produce, to get greater profit, and then buy that difference in the expected lower prices opportunities.

3.3   Particle Swarm Optimization

PSO is an evolutionary technique developed by James Kennedy and Russell Eberhart [8], which intents to simulate a simplified social system. Initially, the basic idea was to demonstrate the behavior that flocks of birds or shoals of fish take in their local random flight, but globally determined. In a computational way, PSO algorithms appear as an abstraction of natural biological behavior where demand for a better spot is the search for an optimal solution, and the set of particle positions the search space or space of possible solutions. The behavior of each particle is based on its previous experience, and the other particles with which it relates. As in genetic algorithms where the fittest individuals are preserved, the PSO also safeguards the best positions found, which theoretically means the solution found, with the highest quality.

This method is different from other evolutionary techniques, showing encouraging developments. PSO considers N particles, and each particle adjusts its direction based on its experience of flight and the experience of the general population (group of particles). These particles are inserted in the solution space, and are based on deterministic procedures to make the search for the optimal location. Each movement of each particle is based on three parameters: the sociability factor, the factor of individuality, and the maximum speed.

The algorithm combines these parameters together with a random value generated (between 0 and 1), and calculates the next position of the particle, the parameters are:

- Cognitive Factor (C1): determines the attraction of the particle with the best position;
- Social Factor (C2): determines the attraction (convergence) of the particles to the best solution discovered by a member of the group;
- Speed Factor (W): delimits the movement, since this is directional and determined.

In addition to the mentioned factors, it is necessary to specify a few parameters such as the number of particles, their size, and stopping criteria. Each particle is treated as a point in a multidimensional space, so it is necessary to specify the value for that dimension. Each particle stores the positions of their size into data structures. This position is decisive for the calculation of fitness. Typically, in the statement of PSO several notations are used for the representation of variables central to its operation:

- Current position of the particle. Stores the current position of the particles via $Xi = Xi1, Xi2, ..., XiD$, where X represents the position of particle i in dimension D. The position values are changed depending on the change of speed;
- Best local positions. The best positions for found by each particle, i.e. positions which achieved the best calculated fitness to date: $Pi = Pi1, Pi2, ..., PiD$;
- Best overall position: to store the best position, for which the calculation of the fitness reaches the best overall value. At the end of the search space of solutions, the solution found by the algorithm is given by Gd;
- Rate of change of velocity: this value is decisive for the change of position on each particle $Vi = Vi1, Vi2, ..., Vid$. The values for each velocity of the particle i, are calculated using expression (4).

$$Vidt+1 = Wt * Vidt + C1 * R1t * (Pid - Xidt) + C2 * R2t * (Gd - Xidt) \qquad (4)$$

where R1 and R2 are random variables.

Regarding the implementation of the PSO process for the specific problem presented in this paper, the traditional PSO approach, as described in this sub-section, has been used.

4   Case Study

In order to test the proposed methodology for portfolios optimization, the historic of real electricity market prices from the Iberian Market – MIBEL [7] is used, concerning the time range from January, 2002 to October, 2012. This data is used to train the ANNs, providing the forecasts of the price for each market for each circumstance. For this test case, three different types of markets were considered: the day-ahead spot market, the balancing market, and the forwards market. The time scale for this test is of one week (7 days), with 24 hourly periods of negotiation. Table 1 presents the average Mean Absolute Percentage Error (MAPE) values, concerning the forecasts for the three required cases, explained in section 3: minimum, medium and maximum expected prices. This table presents the minimum, average and maximum errors of prediction for the considered days and periods.

Table 1. MAPE forecast error values (%)

Market	Minimum			Average			Maximum		
	Min	Med	Max	Min	Med	Max	Min	Med	Max
Spot	9,3	6,2	12	12,3	8,1	17,6	18,6	11,7	22,3
Balancing	9,8	5,8	7,6	13,2	10,5	12,8	18,2	14,9	16,3
Forward	10,4	8,3	9,8	13,8	11,2	13,2	22,3	16,5	26,1

From Table 1 it is visible that the error values vary from 5% to 26%. Note that a higher error value is not restrictive in using such predictions, since the purpose of these forecasts is to provide a basis price that expected for a certain market, for a certain period of the day. The actual incomes achieved by the player in the market depend on its actual actions in the market after having the notion of which markets are most adequate to invest in at each time.

The most important conclusion to be taken from Table 1 is that the forecasts that present the lower error percentage are the ones corresponding to the medium expected price. This means that this value is the most reliable (the maximum MAPE is of 16%).

With the database built from these predictions, the PSO approach is ran, for a seller player negotiating a fix amount of 50MWh for each period of each considered day. The portfolio optimization approach is executed for three different cases:

- Participation of the player exclusively in the day-ahead spot market – the most commonly used type of market (auction based), which represents the outcomes that should be expectable for a player not using the proposed portfolio optimization approach;
- Participation of the player in the day-ahead spot market, and in balancing market;
- Participation of the player in all three considered market types; day-ahead spot market, balancing market, and forwards market.

For each of the three considered market participation cases, three optimizations are performed, considering the three types of expected prices:

- Player using the proposed approach considering the minimum possible achieved prices in each market;
- Player using the proposed approach considering the medium (most reliable) forecasted prices;
- Player using the proposed approach considering the maximum possible achieved prices in each market.

From these nine optimization processes result the respective optimal negotiation amounts of power in each market, for each case. Additionally, the objective function value represents the total amount of expected incomes of the player.

Finally, in order to validate the optimization results, three simulations using MASCEM are performed, one for each of the player participation cases: only in the day-ahead spot market, participation in the day-ahead spot market and in the balancing market, and finally, considering the participation in all three considered market types. These simulations are performed for the same 24 hourly periods of the 7 days considered in the optimization process, using a realistic scenario, representing the MIBEL electricity market.

The amounts of power that the subject seller player tries to negotiate in each market type are the optimal amounts resulting from the optimization process considering the medium expected prices (the ones with smaller forecast error). From these simulations result the incomes that the player achieves in a realistic and most reliable scenario, which projects the MIBEL market reality. The achieved incomes can then be compared to those resulting from the optimization processes, in order to realize if the optimization expected results are, in fact, reliable or not.

Figure 3 presents the comparison of the objective function value (incomes in €) resulting from the optimization process considering the participation of the subject player in the three distinct combinations of markets, for the three expected prices (minimum, medium, and maximum). Figure 3 also presents the MASCEM simulations results (selling incomes), for the three cases of market participation.

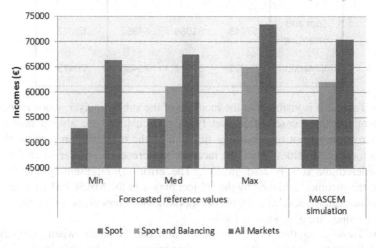

Fig. 3. Incomes of the subject player for each of the considered cases

From Figure 3 it is visible that, in all cases, the participation of the player in a higher number of market types leads to achieving higher incomes. The optimization process using the expected prices in each market at each time, leads to the optimal participation amount of power in each market, which leads to the best achievement of incomes given the negotiation opportunities that the player has. Therefore, the achievement of higher incomes when the number of alternative market types increases is, by its own, a proof of the proposed methodology's utility.

Referring to the use of the minimum, medium, and maximum expected prices for each market, the outcomes, are, as expected, the achievement of higher incomes when the expected prices are higher.

When analyzing the performance of the player in the MIBEL MASCEM simulations, it is visible that the value of the player's incomes are always (in the three considered market participation combinations) higher than the minimum expected incomes, and also smaller than the maximum expected incomes. This validates the usefulness of considering the minimum and maximum expected prices, as reference values for the possible achieved incomes interval.

Another important conclusion to be taken from the graphs of Figure 3 is that the incomes resulting from the simulations in MASCEM are always nearer to the incomes resulting from the optimization processes using the medium expected prices. This conclusion is supported by the income values achieved by the subject player in all cases, presented in Table 2.

Table 2. Incomes of the subject player (in €) resulting from the optimization processes, and from the MASCEM simulations of the MIBEL market

Market	Forecasted reference values			MASCEM simulation
	Min	Med	Max	
Spot	52890	54804	55329	54620
Spot and Balancing	57243	61086	64892	62012
All Markets	66322	67512	73480	70473

From Table 2 it is visible that the incomes of the subject player, when participating in each of the three cases of market types participation, are always nearer to the incomes resulting from the objective function of the optimization process using the medium forecasted values. Also, the incomes' difference is smaller when the number of considered markets is also smaller. The error (ε) representing the difference between the incomes achieved by the subject player in the MASCEM simulations and the income values resulting from the optimization processes using the medium reference values are presented in Table 3.

From Table 2 another important conclusion can be taken when comparing the value of the incomes when the player is participating exclusively in the day-ahead spot market (most common approach by real market players) and when the player participates in all available market types. If analyzing only the most reliable values (results of the MASCEM simulations; and the results of the optimization process using the medium forecasted values) one can see that the exclusive participation in the day-ahead spot market originates, in both cases, incomes around €55000. While, when considering the participation in the three considered market types: day-ahead spot market, balancing market, and forwards market, the player is able to achieve a value of incomes around €70000. The increase in incomes originated by the adequate investment of the optimal amounts of power in each market, at each time, resulting from the proposed methodology, is of about €15000.

Table 3. Error (ε) representing the difference between the results of the MIBEL simulations, and the results of the optimization processes using the medium forecasted values

Spot	Spot and Balancing	All Markets
0,003357419	0,015158956	0,04385887

From Table 3 it is visible that the error value when comparing the incomes achieved by the subject player in the MIBEL simulation, and the expected income values originated by the optimization process with the medium forecasted prices, is very small when considering only the participation in the spot market. The error value increases (although it is still very small) when the number of markets increases. The small error values validate the reliability of the optimization process using the medium values. Regarding the increasing difference as the number of considered markets increases, it is easily explained, since the number of variables increases exponentially, when the number of markets is higher, especially when the considered cases concern several days (one week in this case). Also, the performance (strategic behavior) of the player when actually negotiating can also influence the outcomes of the market. Moreover when participating in several. The use of decision support tools such as ALBidS, which is integrated with MASCEM and supports the player's decisions in the market, contributes to the difference between what could be normally expected, and what can, in fact, be achieved by using adequate strategic behavior directed to each different market type, allied to the understanding of what should be the adequate amounts of power to negotiate in each market type, at each time, as provided by the proposed methodology.

5   Conclusions

Electricity markets are dynamic environments, with a high level of complexity. The number of different market types and models increases, which makes the negotiation process a matter of extreme care from behalf of the involved entities, in order to achieve the best possible results.

This paper presented an optimization mechanism, based on forecasted market prices regarding distinct markets under different contexts. The PSO based approach provides decision support to market negotiating players in what concerns the optimal investment that can be performed when considering a multiple market environment.

Using the proposed approach players are able to adequately choose between business opportunities, taking advantage on the variance of prices from different markets, in different contexts and circumstances.

The presented case study results show that the optimization process enables players to achieve higher profits when acting in the electricity markets. The reliability of the decision support is dependent on the forecasts that are performed to the various markets under distinct situations. Using the most reliable forecasts, the players achieve great benefits. Using the minimum prices predictions for each market, which represent the minimum price that can be achieved, the results are still very favourable, supporting the conclusion that the proposed approach is suitable and advantageous.

The execution of realistic simulations of the MIBEL market, using the MASCEM simulator help validating the optimization results, and comparing the expected incomes, to those that can, in fact, be achieved. The results show that the use of the most reliable forecasts originates income predictions that are very close to those that can be achieved in the market. This supports the competence and advantage of the market investment amounts suggested by the proposed methodology.

References

1. Shahidehpour, M., et al.: Market Operations in Electric Power Systems: Forecasting, Scheduling, and Risk Management, pp. 233–274. Wiley-IEEE Press (2002)
2. Meeus, L., et al.: Development of the Internal Electricity Market in Europe. The Electricity Journal 18(6), 25–35 (2005)
3. Li, H., Tesfatsion, L.: Development of Open Source Software for Power Market Research: The AMES Test Bed. Journal of Energy Markets 2(2), 111–128 (2009)
4. Koritarov, V.: Real-World Market Representation with Agents: Modeling the Electricity Market as a Complex Adaptive System with an Agent-Based Approach. IEEE Power & Energy Magazine, 39–46 (2004)
5. Praça, I., et al.: MASCEM: A Multi-Agent System that Simulates Competitive Electricity Markets. IEEE Intelligent Systems 18(6), 54–60
6. Vale, Z., et al.: MASCEM - Electricity markets simulation with strategically acting players. IEEE Intelligent Systems 26(2) (2011); Special Issue on AI in Power Systems and Energy Markets
7. OMIE – Operador del Mercado Iberico de Energia website, http://www.omie.es/ (acessed on January 2013)
8. AlRashidi, M.R., El-Hawary, M.E.: A Survey of Particle Swarm Optimization Applications in Electric Power Systems. IEEE Transactions on Evolutionary Computation 13, 913–918 (2009)
9. Amjady, N., et al.: Day-ahead electricity price forecasting by modified relief algorithm and hybrid neural network. IET Generation, Transmission & Distribution 4(3), 432–444 (2010)
10. Pinto, T., et al.: A new approach for multi-agent coalition formation and management in the scope of electricity markets. Energy 36(8), 5004–5015 (2011)

Bilateral Contracting in Multi-agent Energy Markets with Demand Response

Fernando Lopes[1,*], Hugo Algarvio[1], and Jorge Sousa[2]

[1] LNEG–National Research Institute, Est. Paço do Lumiar 22, Lisbon, Portugal
{fernando.lopes,hugo.algarvio}@lneg.pt
[2] ISEL–Lisbon Engineering Institute, INESC-ID, Lisbon, Portugal
jsousa@deea.isel.ipl.pt

Abstract. In competitive energy markets (EMs), customers can freely choose their energy suppliers. The electricity trade can be done in organized markets or using forward bilateral contracts. Currently, there are several simulation tools based on multi-agent techniques that allow modeling, partially or globally, competitive EMs. The existing tools allow simulating negotiation prices and volumes through bilateral contracts, transactions in pool markets, etc. However, these tools have some limitations, mainly due to the complexity of the electric system. In this context, this article focuses on bilateral trading and presents the key features of software agents able to negotiate forward bilateral contracts. Special attention is devoted to demand response in bilateral contracting, notably utility functions and trading strategies for promoting demand response. The article also presents a case study on forward bilateral contracting with demand response: a retailer agent and an industrial customer agent negotiate a 24h-rate tariff.

Keywords: Energy markets, multi-agent systems, bilateral contracting, demand response, trading strategies, simulation.

1 Introduction

Traditionally, the organization of the electricity sector was based on vertically integrated electric power companies from production to sale of electricity, which produced, transported and distributed the energy without any competition. The deregulation process began in the earlier nineties and basically separated the functions of electrical generation and retail from the natural monopoly functions of transmission and distribution. This process led to the implementation of a wholesale market, where competing generators offer their energy to retailers, and a retail market, in which retailers ensure delivery to end customers. Customers are able to choose their supplier of electricity depending on the best offers.

* This work was performed under the project MAN-REM: Multi-agent Negotiation and Risk Management in Electricity Markets (FCOMP-01-0124-FEDER-020397), and supported by both FEDER and National funds through the program "COMPETE–Programa Operacional Temático Factores de Competividade".

J.M. Corchado et al. (Eds.): PAAMS 2014 Workshops, CCIS 430, pp. 285–296, 2014.
© Springer International Publishing Switzerland 2014

Due to the complexity and unpredictability of Energy Markets (EMs), decision making becomes increasingly difficult. Thus, the entities involved have been forced to rethink their behavior and market strategies. Recent changes in the electricity sector have come to prove that the demand side may also have a relevant influence on the whole process, especially regarding strategic decision making by end customers. In this new paradigm, customers and buyers of energy can play a much more active role in EMs and, through appropriate strategies, achieve their objectives. Several strategies are associated to consumption efficiency and represent the actions related to the concepts of conservation, management and rational use of energy. One of these actions, that are expected to grow in the scope of EMs, is Demand Response (DR). DR can be defined as the capacity to manage the electricity consumption of end customers and in response provide appropriate conditions, including reducing the price of electricity, improve system reliability and reduce price volatility.

However, the entities of EMs are heterogeneous and autonomous, and follow their own goals and strategies. Usually, the production companies seek to adopt strategies that maximize profit, while costumers adopt strategies that minimize electricity cost. Thus, strategies have as their main objective reaching favourable agreements between the players involved. Strategies can be applied to any type of EMs. Several major markets are often distinguished, notably pools and bilateral contracts [1]. A pool market is defined as a centralized marketplace that clears the market for sellers and buyers. Electric power sellers/buyers submit bids to the pool for the amounts of power that they are willing to trade in the market. The bids are submitted to a market operator, whose function is to coordinate and manage the different transactions between the participants. Bilateral contracts are negotiable agreements on delivery and receipt of power between two traders. These contracts have the advantage of price predictability in comparison of uncertain pool prices.

Multi-agent systems (MAS) are essentially loosely coupled networks of software agents that interact to solve problems that are beyond the individual capabilities of each agent. MAS can deal with complex dynamic interactions and support both artificial intelligence techniques and numerical algorithms. Conceptually, a multi-agent approach is an ideal fit to the naturally distributed domain of a deregulated electricity market.

This article is devoted to demand response in forward bilateral contracting. It presents the key features of software agents able to negotiate forward bilateral contracts, paying special attention to demand response programs, including different utility functions and strategies for promoting DR. It also presents a case study on forward bilateral contracting involving DR management: a retailer agent (a seller) and an industrial customer agent (a buyer) negotiate a 24h-rate tariff. Furthermore, the work presented here refines and extends our previous work in the area of automated negotiation [2,3,4] and bilateral contracting with demand response [6,7]. As stated, it considers demand response into bilateral contracting, focusing on specific utility functions and DR management strategies, and describing a case study involving a 24h-rate tariff.

2   Demand Response in Competitive Energy Markets

Demand response involves changes in electric usage by end-use customers from their normal consumption patterns in response to changes in the price of electricity over time, or to incentive payments designed to induce lower electricity use at times of high wholesale market prices or when system reliability is jeopardized [8]. The principle of DR aims to change the tendency of evolution of the energy consumption of the end customer in order to reduce the operating costs of the system, from the point of view of the producer or customer.

Customers participating in demand response options may adopt one (or more) of three basic load response strategies [9]. Each of these actions involves costs and measures taken by customers. The first option involves reducing the electricity usage by customers at times of high prices without changing the consumption pattern during other periods. For example, a residential customer might turn off lights during an event, or a commercial facility might turn off some office equipment. In both cases, this option results in a temporary loss of comfort. The second option involves rescheduling usage away from times of high prices. For example, a residential customer might put off running a dishwasher until later in the day, or an industrial facility might reschedule a batch production process to the evening hours or the next day. In the third option, customers may respond by using onsite generation to supply some or all of their electricity needs. However, the may experience little change in their electricity usage pattern.

Besides these options, there are different DR programs, such as Priced Based Programs (PBP) and Incentive-Based Programs (IBP). PBP programs refer to changes in usage by customers in response to changes in the prices they pay and include real-time pricing, critical-peak pricing, and time-of-use rates. IPB programs are established by utilities, load-serving entities, or a regional grid operator. These programs give customers load-reduction incentives that are separate from, or additional to, their retail electricity rate, which may be fixed (based on average costs) or time-varying (see, e.g., [8,9]).

The present situation of the DR in the world is presented in [10]. Several implementations of DR in the wholesale market are also occurring in Europe [11], China [12] and in other places around the world [13].

3   Bilateral Contracting with Demand Response

This section describes the process of forward bilateral contracting with demand response, involving a seller agent and a buyer agent. Negotiation includes the determination of prices and quantities of energy, and is executed on a long term, usually six months or more. Special attention is devoted to different utility functions and strategies for promoting demand response. As noted earlier, bilateral contracts are financially safer for market participants, due to the fact that they may guarantee protection against the volatility of high prices of energy markets in real time.

3.1 Pre-negotiation

The pre-negotiation process involves mainly the creation of a well-laid plan specifying the activities that negotiators should attend to before actually starting to negotiate. These activities include [4]:

- Identifying the issues to negotiate;
- Defining limits and priorities for the issues;
- Selecting an appropriate protocol;
- Defining preferences over outcomes.

Let a_s denote the seller agent and a_b the buyer agent. The agents define the negotiation issues, which in this case are the prices and volumes of energy. Let $\left[P^s_{k_{min}}, P^s_{k_{max}}\right]$ ($k = 1..n$) denote the range of values for price that are acceptable to agent a_s. Also, let $\left[P^b_{k_{min}}, P^b_{k_{max}}\right]$ and $\left[V^b_{k_{min}}, V^b_{k_{max}}\right]$ ($i = k..n$) denote the range of values for price and volumes that are acceptable to agent a_b. Priorities are set by ranking-order the issues, i.e., by defining the most important, the second most important, and so on.

A protocol is a set of rules that define how the negotiation process can progress, specifying what actions are allowed and when. We consider an alternating offers negotiation protocol [14]. This protocol models the iterative exchange of offers and counter-offers. At any given period of negotiation, an agent may accept an offer, send a counter-offer, or end the negotiation. If a counter-offer is submitted, the process is repeated until one of the agents accept or abandon the negotiation. Thus, the agents a_s and a_b bargain over the division of the surplus of $n \geq 2$ issues by alternately proposing offers at times in $T = \{1, 2, ...\}$. This means that one offer is made per time period $t \in T$, with an agent offering in odd periods and the other agent offering in even periods. As noted, the agents have the ability to unilaterally opt out of the negotiation when responding to a proposal.

Definition 1 (Proposal). *Let $\mathcal{A}$ be the set of negotiating agents and $\mathcal{I}$ the set of issues at stake in negotiation. Let $\mathcal{T}$ be the set of time periods. A proposal $p^t_{i \rightarrow j}$ submitted by an agent $a_i \in \mathcal{A}$ to an agent $a_j \in \mathcal{A}$ in period $t \in \mathcal{T}$ is a vector of issue values:*

$$p^t_{i \rightarrow j} = (v_1, \ldots, v_n)$$

where v_k, $k = 1, \ldots, n$, is a value of an issue $x_k \in \mathcal{I}$.

Definition 2 (Agreement, Possible Agreements). *. An agreement is a proposal accepted by all the negotiating agents in $\mathcal{A}$. The set of possible agreements is:*

$$\mathcal{S} = \{(v_1, \ldots, v_n) \in \mathbb{R}^n : v_k \in D_k, \text{ for } k = 1, \ldots, n\}$$

where v_k is a value of an issue $x_k \in \mathcal{I}$.

Negotiators should express their own preferences to rate and compare incoming offers and counter-offers. Let $\mathcal{I} = \{x_1, \ldots, x_n\}$ be the agenda and $\mathcal{D} = \{D_1, \ldots, D_n\}$ the set of issue domains. We consider that each agent $a_i \in \mathcal{A}$ has a continuous utility function, denoted as U_i. Accordingly, when the utility for a_i from one outcome is greater than from another outcome, we assume that a_i prefers the first outcome over the second.

Now, the additive model is probably the most widely used in multi-issue negotiation: agents determine weights for the issues at stake, assign scores to the different levels on each issue, and take a weighted sum of them to get an entire offer evaluation (see, e.g., [15]). Typically, each agent a_i defines a partial (or marginal) utility function for each issue at stake in negotiation, $i.e.$, a function that gives the score a_i assigns to a value of an issue x_k. The utility of an offer is then computed by adding the weighted scores together. For convenience, scores are often kept in the interval [0,1].

Definition 3 (Additive Utility Function). *Let $\mathcal{A}$ be the set of negotiating agents and $\mathcal{I}$ the negotiating agenda. The utility function U_i of an agent $a_i \in \mathcal{A}$ to rate offers and counter-offers takes the form:*

$$U_i(x_1, \ldots, x_n) = \sum_{k=1}^{n} w_k V_k(x_k)$$

where:

(i) w_k *is the weight of a_i for an issue $x_k \in \mathcal{I}$;*
(ii) $V_k(x_k)$ *is the (marginal) utility function of a_i for x_k, i.e., the function that gives the score a_i assigns to a value of an issue x_k.*

The additive model is simple and intuitive, but it is not suitable for all circumstances. In particular, the model assumes two types of independence:

1. *additive independence*: the utility of an offer is simply the weighted sum of the scores for all issues at stake;
2. *utility independence*: issue x is utility independent of the other issues on the agenda, if the preference order for outcomes involving only changes in the level of x does not depend on the levels of the remaining issues, provided that these levels are fixed.

The additive independence assumption is usually not acceptable when there are specific interactions among issues. For instance, two or more issues may be complementary, leading to a combined utility for an offer that is greater than the weighted sum of the individual scores. Also, two or more issues may be substitutable, in the sense that they can be substitutes of one another. The multiplicative utility function is the most well-known function handling these types of interactions among issues (see, e.g., [16,17]). It accommodates interdependencies by considering a specific interaction constant and interaction terms involving the multiplication of the weighted scores together. However, for it to be valid, every pair of issues must be utility independent of the remaining issues.

Definition 4 (Multiplicative Utility Function). *Let $\mathcal{A}$ be the set of negotiating agents and $\mathcal{I}$ the negotiating agenda. The multiplicative utility function U_i of an agent $a_i \in \mathcal{A}$ to rate offers and counter-offers takes the form:*

$$U_i(x_1, \ldots, x_n) = \frac{\prod_{k=1}^{n} [1 + w w_k V_k(x_k)] - 1}{w}$$

where:

(i) w_k *is the weight of a_i for an issue $x_k \in \mathcal{I}$;*
(ii) $V_k(x_k)$ *is the (marginal) utility function of a_i for x_k, i.e., the function that gives the score a_i assigns to a value of an issue x_k.*

The question at this stage relates to the degree to which preferences may be sensitive to the use of an additive rather than a multiplicative function. The question has important practical implications, as additive functions are clearly easier to understand and to construct. Reading of the literature suggests that in practice the use of an additive function is likely to be adequate in the vast majority of settings. Also, in practice, there are often many issues under consideration, but only a few are interdependent. Certainly, in complex negotiation settings where the additive function may be considered inappropriate, agents should use the multiplicative function. This seems to be the case of the present work, since agents negotiate prices and volumes of energy, variables that are interdependent.

3.2   Actual Negotiation and Strategies for Promoting DR

The actual negotiation process involves basically an iterative exchange or offers and counter-offers. The negotiation protocol marks branching points at which agents have to make decisions according to their strategies. In this work, we consider strategies for promoting demand response. The two agents have similar structure, but opposite preferences. Thus, the seller agent is equipped with a strategic behaviour that maximizes its benefit, while the end customer (buyer) is equipped with a strategic behavior that allows to minimize its cost, through DR actions.

Seller Strategy: Price Management. This strategy aims to maximize the benefit of a_s. The objective problem includes the price (P_k^s) proposed by a_s, the volume (V_k^b) proposed by a_b, and the cost of production (C_k). The mathematical formulation of the objective problem is as follows:

$$Maximize\ B^s = \sum_{k=1}^{n} (P_k^s - C_k) \times V_k^b \tag{1}$$

Subject to

$$P_k^s \geq C_k \tag{2}$$

The constraint expressed by (2) has the main goal of guaranteeing that the cost of production does not exceed the price of energy of a_s.

Buyer Strategy: Volume Management. This strategy was developed with the aim of enabling the end users of energy having a more active involvement in EMs. Specifically, the "Volume Management" strategy has the main goal of minimizing the energy cost of customers through DR actions. Thus, through this type of actions, customers can manage their energy consumption in response to high prices for different periods of the day.

Generally speaking, DR actions refer to the end-user customers participation in the EM and are seen as a response, from them, to the price variations of electrical energy over time. We consider that customers can respond to the variations of retailers' prices by transferring volume quantities from the periods when the prices proposed by a retail agent are high to the remaining hours.

Thus, this strategy consists in determining the prices and volumes of a_b. The volumes are determined through an optimization problem that aims to minimize the cost of a_b, including the prices (P_k^s) proposed by a_s, and the volumes (V_k^b) proposed by a_b. The mathematical formulation of the objective problem is as follows:

$$Minimize \ C^b = \sum_{k=1}^{n} P_k^s \times V_k^b \tag{3}$$

Subject to

$$V_{k_{min}}^b \leq V_k^b \leq V_{k_{max}}^b \tag{4}$$

$$\sum_{k=1}^{n} V_k^b = V_{tot}^b \tag{5}$$

The constraint expressed by (4) has the main goal of guaranteeing that the quantity of volume offered by a_b is in the range of its acceptable values. Also, the constraint (5) guarantees that the total quantity of energy (V_{tot}^b) remains unchanged, or in a range close to the initial value.

The optimization problem is resolved through a linear programming method called simplex using lp_solve, a Mixed Integer Linear Programming (MILP) solver.[1] lp_solve is a free linear (integer) programming solver based on the revised simplex method and the Branch-and-bound method for the integers. lp_solve solves pure linear, (mixed) integer/binary, semi-continuous and special ordered sets (SOS) models. Via the Branch-and-bound algorithm, it can handle integer variables, semi-continuous variables and SOS.

Beyond the volumes of energy, the customer also negotiates prices. The prices offered in a new proposal are obtained by the following formula:

$$P_{k_{new}}^b = P_{k_{previous}}^b + Ct \times P_{k_{previous}}^b, \ k = 1..n \tag{6}$$

where $P_{k_{new}}^b$ is the new price to send by a_b, $P_{k_{previous}}^b$ is the previous price sent by a_b, and Ct is a constant.

---

[1] `lpsolve.sourceforge.net`

4   A Case Study on Bilateral Contracting with DR

David Colburn, representing N2K Power (a retailer or seller agent), and Tom Britton, representing SCO Corporation (a customer agent), negotiate a 24-rate tariff in a multi-agent electricity market. Table 4 shows the initial offers and the price limits for the two negotiating agents, and also the load profile of the customer agent. Some values were selected by looking up to real trading prices associated with a pool market in an attempt to approximate the case study to the real-world. In particular, market reference prices were obtained by analysing the Iberian Electricity Market.[2] The minimum seller prices, i.e. the limits, were then set to these reference prices. Also, some energy quantities were based on consumer load profiles provided by the New York State Electric & Gas.[3]

Negotiation involves an iterative exchange of offers and counter-offers. We consider the following:

- Priorities are (indirectly) set for the prices of a_s and the volumes of a_b (higher values mean greater importance);
- Preferences are specified by using the multiplicative model;
- The customer submits the load profile;
- After receiving the load profile, the retailer submits the first proposal;
- The agents are allowed to propose only strictly monotonically—the customer's offers increase monotonically and the retailer's offers decrease monotonically;
- The acceptability of a proposal is determined by a negotiation threshold—an agent $a_i \in \mathcal{A}$ accepts a proposal $p_{j \to i}^{t-1}$, submitted by $a_j \in \mathcal{A}$ at $t-1$, when the difference between the benefit provided by the proposal $p_{i \to j}^{t}$ that a_i is ready to send in the next time period t is lower than or equal to the negotiation threshold;
- The agents are allowed to exchange only a maximum number of proposals, denoted by max_p.

Figure 1 and tables 2 and 3 summarize the results obtained. The results show that the agents reach agreement before the maximum limit of proposals, namely after the seller and the buyer agents sending six proposals (three proposals each). During the course of negotiation, the buyer agent adjusts the load profile using the "Volume Management" strategy, in response to the prices submitted by the seller agent, and simultaneously defines new values for the prices. Also, the seller agent adjusts the prices using the "Price Management" strategy (and accepts the load profile proposed by the buyer). Figure 1 shows the variation of both prices and volumes, considering the first proposal submitted and the final proposal accepted. Table 2 shows the cost values of the received and ready to send proposals of the buyer agent. Table 3 shows the agreed prices and the final load profile.

---

[2] www.mibel.com
[3] www.nyseg.com

Table 1. Initial offers and price limits for the negotiating parties

	Consumer			Retailer	
Hour	Price (€/MWh)	Limit (€/MWh)	Energy (MWh)	Price (€/MWh)	Limit (€/MWh)
1	45.26	49.69	16.77	51.18	43.23
2	34.85	39.52	13.56	40.45	34.72
3	33.49	37.76	7.65	39.61	32.20
4	33.45	38.70	5.96	39.55	32.15
5	33.15	37.32	5.89	39.15	32.82
6	33.45	38.70	6.02	39.55	32.15
7	40.36	44.64	25.63	46.90	40.87
8	47.51	53.89	55.92	55.57	48.86
9	45.52	50.32	77.20	53.88	45.64
10	47.51	52.89	66.08	55.57	47.86
11	49.44	55.39	82.68	58.18	50.02
12	46.51	52.89	74.30	55.57	47.86
13	46.56	52.96	44.03	55.64	47.92
14	46.51	52.89	76.91	55.57	47.86
15	44.54	49.06	74.00	51.56	44.55
16	43.65	48.90	53.88	50.35	43.55
17	36.31	41.41	17.20	42.43	36.35
18	34.47	49.02	15.41	40.93	35.29
19	32.08	37.23	15.44	38.06	33.74
20	36.00	41.00	16.21	42.00	35.00
21	44.26	49.69	16.34	51.18	43.23
22	46.22	52.52	16.50	55.18	47.54
23	46.31	52.63	16.66	55.30	48.64
24	44.03	50.68	16.49	52.21	45.09

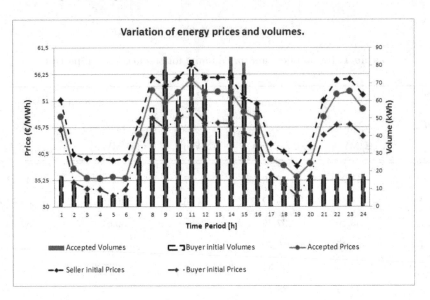

Fig. 1. Variation of energy prices and volumes

It is also important to mention, from the results, that the customer agent transferred quantities of energy from the market peak periods of greater importance, notably the periods 8, 10, 11, 12, and 13, to some periods for which the prices of the retailer agent are lower (see Figure 1). The cost of energy has proven to be minimal for the distribution of the volumes of the final proposal accepted. Furthermore, the retailer agent manages its prices by slightly reducing the price for the periods in which it has transferred a greater amount of energy. Accordingly to the results of the simulation, the negotiation ended when the retailer agent accepted the third proposal sent by customer, i.e. when the value of the buyers' Utility to send (U_{cmp}) showed to be greater than the value of the cost in the received proposal (U_{rcv}).

Table 2. Cost values of the received and new proposals of the customer

Cost (€)	1st Proposal	2nd Proposal	3rd Proposal
Received proposal	215,00	205,00	201,00
Ready to send proposal	179,00	195,00	200,00

Table 3. Case-Study final results

Hour	Price (€/MWh)	Energy (€/MWh)	Hour (MWh)	Price (€/MWh)	Energy (€/MWh)
1	47.87	17.61	13	52.72	37.43
2	37.61	14.24	14	52.65	84.6
3	35.65	8.03	15	48.75	81.40
4	35.60	6.26	16	47.57	59.27
5	35.85	6.18	17	39.48	18.92
6	35.60	6.32	18	38.13	16.95
7	44.28	28.19	19	35.86	16.98
8	53.08	28.19	20	35.86	16.98
9	50.64	84.92	21	47.87	17.97
10	52.65	58.05	22	52.29	18.15
11	55.20	70.28	23	52.83	18.33
12	52.65	63.15	24	49.36	18.14

5 Conclusion

This paper has presented several key features of agents with DR competence operating in a multi-agent electricity market. In particular, it has described a model for bilateral contracting with demand response, incorporating two negotiation strategies for DR management: a "Volume Management" strategy for a buyer agent and a "Price Management" for a seller or retailer agent. It has also presented the additive and multiplicative models for specifying the preferences of the agents over the negotiation outcomes. Furthermore, it has presented a case study on bilateral contracts involving a retailer and a customer of energy negotiating a 24h-rate tariff.

The simulation results, obtained with the new strategies and the multiplicative model, support the belief that the behavior of market participants is as expected in managing energy prices and volumes. They also confirm the belief that the simulation tool currently being developed can be important to help the decision process of the two parties during the negotiation of bilateral contracts in competitive EMs with demand response. In the future, we intend to perform a number of inter-related experiments to empirically evaluate the key components of the bilateral contracting model, notably the DR management strategies.

References

1. Shahidehpour, M., Yamin, H., Li, Z.: Market Operations in Electric Power Systems. John Wiley & Sons, Chicester (2002)
2. Lopes, F., Mamede, N., Novais, A.Q., Coelho, H.: A Negotiation Model for Autonomous Computational Agents: Formal Description and Empirical Evaluation. Journal of Intelligent & Fuzzy Systems 12, 195–212 (2002)
3. Lopes, F., Mamede, N., Novais, A.Q., Coelho, H.: Negotiation Strategies for Autonomous Computational Agents. In: ECAI 2004, pp. 38–42. IOS Press (2004)
4. Lopes, F., Wooldridge, M., Novais, A.Q.: Negotiation Among Autonomous Computational Agents: Principles, Analysis and Challenges. Artificial Intelligence Review 29, 1–44 (2008)
5. Lopes, F., Coelho, H.: Concession Strategies for Negotiating Bilateral Contracts in Multi-agent Electricity Markets. In: IATEM-12 Workshop and DEXA-12 Event, pp. 321–325. IEEE Computer Society Press (2012)
6. Lopes, F., Ilco, C., Sousa, J.: Bilateral Negotiation in Energy Markets: Strategies for Promoting Demand Response. In: International Conference on the European Energy Market (EEEM 2013). IEEE Computer Society Press (2013)
7. Lopes, F., Algarvio, H., Ilco, C., Sousa, J.: Agent-Based Simulation of Retail Electricity Markets: Bilateral Contracting with Demand Response. In: IATEM 2013 Workshop and DEXA 2013 Event, pp. 194–198. IEEE Computer Society Press (2013)
8. Benefits of demand response in electricity markets and recommendations for achieving them. Report to the United States Congress, US Department of Energy (February 2006)
9. Albadi, M., El-Saadany, E.: A summary of demand response in electricity markets. Electric Power Systems Research 78, 1989–1996 (2008)
10. Woo, C., Greening, L.: Guest editors' introduction. Energy 35, 1515–1517 (2010)
11. Torriti, J., Hassan, M., Leach, M.: Demand response experience in Europe: policies, programmes and implementation. Energy (2009)
12. Wang, J., Bloyd, C., Hu, Z., Tan, Z.: Demand response in China. Energy 35, 1592–1597 (2010)
13. Charles River Associates: Primer on demand-side management with an emphasis on price-responsive programs. Report prepared for The World Bank, Washington, DC (2005)
14. Osborne, M., Rubinstein, A.: Bargaining and Markets. Academic Press, London (1990)
15. Raiffa, H.: The Art and Science of Negotiation. Harvard University Press, Cambridge (1982)
16. Bodily, S.: Modern Decision Making. McGraw Hill, New York (1985)
17. Keeney, R.: Value-Focused Thinking: A Path to Creative Decision Making. Harvard University Press, Cambridge (1992)

Risk Management and Bilateral Contracts in Multi-agent Electricity Markets

Hugo Algarvio and Fernando Lopes*

LNEG—National Research Institute, Est. Paço do Lumiar 22, Lisbon, Portugal
{hugo.algarvio,fernando.lopes}@lneg.pt

Abstract. In competitive energy markets, customers can freely choose their energy suppliers. The electricity trade can be done in organized markets or using bilateral contracts between customers and suppliers. In the latter case, market participants set the terms and conditions of agreements independent of the market operator. They often enter into bilateral contracts to hedge against pool price volatility. Furthermore, these contracts are very flexible since the negotiating parties can specify their own contract terms. This article focuses on bilateral trading and presents the key features of software agents able to negotiate forward bilateral contracts. Special attention is devoted to risk management in bilateral contracting, notably utility functions and trading strategies for dealing with risk. The article also presents a case study on forward bilateral contracting involving risk management: a retailer agent and an industrial customer agent negotiate a 24h-rate tariff.

Keywords: Energy markets, multi-agent systems, bilateral contracting, risk management, trading strategies, simulation.

1 Introduction

The electricity industry throughout the world, which has long been dominated by vertically integrated utilities, has experienced major changes. In particular, liberalization has led to the establishment of a wholesale market for electricity generation and a retail market for electricity retailing. Market forces drive now the price of electricity and reduce the net cost through increased competition.

Several major market models have been considered, including electricity pools and bilateral transactions. A pool, or market exchange, involves basically a specific form of auction, where participants send bids to sell and buy electricity, for a certain period of time. Bilateral contracts consist essentially in direct negotiations of energy prices, volumes, time of delivery, duration, among other possible issues, between two traders. Market participants set the terms and conditions of agreements independent of a market operator.

* This work was performed under the project MAN-REM: Multi-agent Negotiation and Risk Management in Electricity Markets (FCOMP-01-0124-FEDER-020397), and supported by both FEDER and National funds through the program "COMPETE—Programa Operacional Temático Factores de Competividade".

J.M. Corchado et al. (Eds.): PAAMS 2014 Workshops, CCIS 430, pp. 297–308, 2014.
© Springer International Publishing Switzerland 2014

Bilateral contracts can take several forms, including future and forward contracts. Future contracts are generally traded in an exchange, and can be traded continuously up until their time of delivery [1]. Forward contracts are typically negotiated directly between the load and the generator with the terms of the contract remaining fixed until the time of delivery. Also, bilateral contracts can be either physical or financial. A physical contract means that all the power transacted bilaterally must be self-generated and self-consumed at a pair of specified network buses. In comparison, a contract is financial if the power transacted need not be self-generated and self-consumed but could be transferred up to the short-term market-clearing time to another entity such as the pool. This kind of contract can be understood as a contract for differences that simply guarantees the difference between the contract price and the pool price and has no direct physical transmission implications.

Bilateral contracts are commonly used in electricity markets to hedge against pool price volatility. However, if inappropriately chosen, a bilateral contract may actually worsen the benefit, since the eventual random spot price at market-clearing time may end up being either too high or too low compared to the contract price. Beyond spot price volatility, there exist other sources of risk associated with engaging in bilateral contracting, principally random generator, and network forced outages , load forecast errors, and fuel price uncertainty [2]. Risk sharing can be useful to decrease these risks, with or without direct association to the spot price. The negotiation of a bilateral contract will therefore converge only if both sides can find a pool/bilateral mix that provide an acceptable compromise between risk and benefit.

This article is devoted to risk management in forward bilateral contracting. It presents several key features of software agents able to negotiate forward bilateral contracts, paying special attention to risk management, notably utility functions and strategies for dealing with risk. It also presents a case study on forward bilateral contracting involving risk management. Furthermore, the work presented here refines and extends our previous work in the area of automated negotiation [3,4,5] and bilateral contracting in electricity markets [6,7,8]. In particular, it introduces risk into bilateral contracting and describes a case study involving risk management in the negotiation of a 24h-rate tariff.

2   Bilateral Contracts

Either physical or financial, a bilateral contract is typically negotiated weeks or months prior to its delivery and can include the following specifications: 1) starting date and time, 2) ending date and time, 3) price per hour (€/MWh) over the length of the contract (GD), 4) variable megawatt (MW) amount over the length of the contract, and 5) range of hours when the contract is to be delivered. In a more general form, the MW amount, GD and price could be time-varying over the contract duration. This generalization is, however, not followed in this work, where we consider a 24h-rate tariff, equal over the whole contract duration.

A bilateral transaction involves only two parties: a buyer and a seller. Depending on the amount of time available and the quantities to be traded, buyers and sellers will resort to the following forms of bilateral trading [9]: customized long-term contracts, trading "over the counter" and electronic trading.

2.1 Types of Bilateral Contracts

Bilateral contracts are often negotiated in the Forward/Derivatives Market. The transactions in the Forward Market are performed assuming their liquidation, i.e., the seller deliver the product and the buyer pays the product price, in a future date. The description of several important types of contracts follows.

1. *Forward Contracts.* Contracts to purchase and sale a given amount and quality of an asset (financial or otherwise), in a specific future date, at a price set in the present, and negotiated bilaterally (outside the Stock Exchange). The buyer is bound to pay the agreed price and the seller is linked to the delivery of the asset under agreed conditions. These contracts may be subject to physical settlement (where the seller delivers the goods sold) or financial settlement (in which there is no physical delivery of the goods, but only a reckoning due to the market price of asset on the settlement date). Unlike future contracts, which are contracts traded multilaterally (in a Stock Exchange) and subject to a high degree of standardization, forward contracts are likely to be drawn freely according to the will of the parties.

2. *Future Contracts.* Standardized contracts, reversible, buying and selling a given quantity and quality of an asset, at a future date, with a price fixed in the present. The buyer is bound to pay the agreed price and the seller to deliver the active under the agreed conditions. These contracts may also be subject to physical or financial settlement. Unlike forward contracts, which are negotiated outside the Stock Exchange, and can be drawn on the basis of the will of both parties, future contracts are fully standardized, meaning that the price is the only variable allowed to be negotiated. Future contracts allow the parties to reverse their contractual, by doing an operation opposite to the initial, i.e., by either selling contracts of the same series initially purchased or buying contracts of the same series originally sold.

3. *Option Contracts.* Contracts that give the right to purchase (call option) or to sold (put option) an asset at a given price (exercise price). The seller assumes the obligation to sell (option to purchase) or to buy (option to sell) the asset. The buyer has the right, but not the obligation to buy (option to purchase) or to sell (option to sell) the asset. The right can be done at the deadline (European style options) or throughout the period (American style options). Options may be settled physically (in which the seller delivers the goods sold) or subject to settlement (in which there is no physical delivery of the goods, but only a reckoning due to the market price of the asset on the date of settlement). Option contracts allow each party to reverse its contract by doing an operation opposite to the initial.

4. *Contracts for Difference (CfDs)*. Differential contracts between two parties, which state that the seller pays to the buyer the difference (if positive) between the market value of an asset (e.g. stocks) on the closing date of the position taken, and its market value on the opening date of the position taken (the buyer protects itself, due to the possibility of price increases). If this difference is negative (i.e., the price falls), the buyer will pay to the seller (so this protects it from fall prices). CfDs enable investors to gain financial exposure leveraged to variation in the price of an asset without detention, obtaining benefits or suffering losses resulting from the rising prices of the underlying asset (long positions) or of its descent (short positions). The counterparty of the investors, who assumes a CfD position, is usually the financial intermediary that provides the trading platform for this type of derivatives. CfDs do not confer rights inherent to the underlying asset (e.g., vote right), while reflecting events or performance of the asset, such as the dividends distribution.

3   Forward Bilateral Contracting and Risk Management

Forward bilateral contracts can be considered a form of hedging, as described in the previous section. Now, in order to effectively manage the risk, it is important to understand several factors and processes associated with the potential risks that each stakeholder can be exposed in a transaction.

In a systematic way, risk management can be divided into three phases:

1. Identification of risk factors, namely in terms of modeling. It involves mainly the identification of deterministic and stochastic variables.
2. Measuring or assessing risk. Several different methods can be used. The most common and accepted in financial markets is the VaR: Value at Risk method, also used in electricity markets. Another complementary concept, not so used in markets, is CVaR: Conditional Value at Risk. The main difference between these two methods is related to the conclusions that can be drawn. Specifically, VaR measures the potential loss of the investor to a certain degree of confidence in a given time interval. A limitation of this method is the failure to know the potential loss that may exist above the value of VaR. In this way, the method CVaR tries to complements this gap. This method is based on the weighted average of losses with probability higher than the one that is defined in VaR. If the VaR and CVaR account for possible losses, methods based on variance account to the scatter of values, not only losses but also possible gains.
3. Mitigation or hedging, which is the product application in the portfolio that allows reducing the risk to which the investor is subject to, such as forwards, futures or CfDs, under products that are assumed as random or stochastic variables in the input of the system.

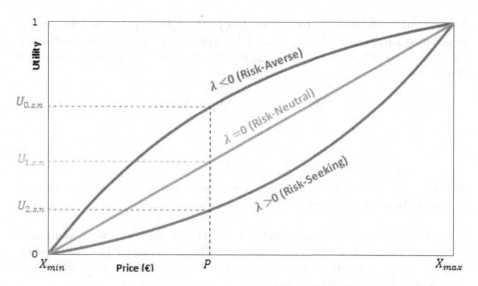

Fig. 1. Increasing Utility Function for Risk-Averse, Risk-Neutral, and Risk-Seeking Agents

3.1   Agent Decision Functions

In this work, the agents' risk preferences are broadly classified into risk-averse ($\lambda < 0$), risk neutral ($\lambda = 0$), and risk-seeking ($\lambda > 0$), where λ is a risk preference constant.

For illustrative purposes, we present next a simple example describing how a seller agent can trade energy in a liberalized market.

Example. Consider a seller agent a_s selling power either through bilateral contracts or from the day-ahead pool market. One of the objectives of the agent is to maximize the benefit. The utility increases for increasing values of the benefit. For a given price, say P, the utility of a risk-averse agent is higher than the one of a risk-seeking agent (see Figure 1). If the energy cost C of a_s is lower than its selling price P, then for higher values of P the agent a_s will obtain higher benefits and consequently higher values of the utility. Hence, under similar circumstances, a risk-averse agent may not change its strategy to sell energy either through bilateral contracts or the pool market, while a risk-seeking agent may not be satisfied with the a value of the utility and may try to increase it by shifting some quantity of energy from the bilateral market to the pool market.

The agents are equipped with different multi-objective utility functions, notably the well-known additive function and a risk management (RM) marginal utility function.

Definition 1 (Additive function [10]). *Let $\mathcal{A}=\{a_s, a_b\}$ be the set of negotiating agents and $\mathcal{I}=\{x_1, \ldots, x_n\}$ the negotiating agenda. The multi-issue additive function U_i of an agent $a_i \in \mathcal{A}$ to rate offers and counter-offers takes the form:*

$$U_i(x_1, \ldots, x_n) = \sum_{k=1}^{n} w_k V_k(x_k)$$

where:

(i) w_k *is the weight of a_i for an issue $x_k \in \mathcal{I}$;*
(ii) $V_k(x_k)$ *is the (marginal) utility function of a_i for x_k, i.e., the function that gives the score a_i assigns to a value of an issue x_k.*

Risk preferences are also modeled by the well-known von Neumann-Morgenstern expected utility functions [11]. Now, to model the risk sharing between the two negotiating agents, denoted by a parameter β, we define the following RM marginal utility functions.

Definition 2 (RM marginal utility functions). *The marginal function $V_{s,k}$ of a seller agent $a_s \in \mathcal{A}$ for a generic issue, say price p_k, takes the form:*

$$V_{s,k}(p_k, \beta) = \begin{cases} \dfrac{1 - \left(\lambda \times \frac{(p_k - lim_k) - (1-\beta)\sigma_{C_k}}{(P_{k,ref} - lim_k) - (1-\beta)\sigma_{C_k}}\right)}{1 - e^\lambda}, & \text{for } \lambda \neq 0 \\[3mm] \dfrac{(p_k - lim_k) - (1-\beta)\sigma_{C_k}}{(P_{k,ref} - lim_k) - (1-\beta)\sigma_{C_k}}, & \text{for } \lambda = 0 \end{cases}$$

Similarly, the marginal utility function for the buyer agent $a_b \in \mathcal{A}$ is defined as follows:

$$V_{b,k}(p_k, \beta) = \begin{cases} \dfrac{1 - \left(\lambda \times \frac{lim_k - (p_k + \beta\sigma_{C_k})}{lim_k - (P_{k,ref} + \beta\sigma_{C_k})}\right)}{1 - e^\lambda}, & \text{for } \lambda \neq 0 \\[3mm] \dfrac{lim_k - (p_k + \beta\sigma_{C_k})}{lim_k - (P_{k,ref} + \beta\sigma_{C_k})}, & \text{for } \lambda = 0 \end{cases}$$

where:

(i) p_k *is the price to offer;*
(ii) $\beta \in [0, 1]$ *is the risk sharing parameter (negotiated between the agents);*
(iii) λ *is a risk preference constant;*
(iv) $P_{k,ref}$ *is the reference price;*
(v) lim_k *is the limit for price p_k;*
(vi) σ_{C_k} *is the uncertainty related to the energy cost.*

The behaviour of these utility functions is similar to the behaviour of the aforementioned von Neumann-Morgenstern utility functions. However, for the reasons mentioned above, they suit better our purposes and thus were considered in this work. Also, they will be tested in a case study (but see section 4).

3.2   Agent Strategies for Price Negotiation

The agents interact and trade according to a specific protocol—that is, a set of rules that define how negotiation proceeds, specifying what actions are allowed and when. In this work, we consider an alternating offers protocol [12]. Two agents bargain over the division of the surplus of $n \geq 2$ issues by alternately submitting offers at times in $\mathcal{T} = \{1, 2, \ldots\}$. This means that one offer is made per time period $t \in \mathcal{T}$, with an agent offering in odd periods and the other agent offering in even periods. An offer (or proposal) is a vector specifying a division of the surplus of all the issues. After receiving an offer, an agent can either accept it, reject it and opt out of the negotiation, or reject it and continue bargaining. In the first two cases, negotiation ends. In the last case, negotiation proceeds to the next time period, in which the other agent makes a counter-proposal. The tasks just described are then repeated.

The agents pursue negotiation strategies that model typical patterns of concessions. Generally speaking, concession making involves reducing negotiators' demands to (partially) accommodate the opponent. This behaviour can take several different forms and a representative example follows. Negotiators sometimes start with ambitious demands, well in excess of limits and aspirations, and concede slowly. High demands and slow concessions, also referred to as starting high and conceding slowly, are often motivated by concern about position loss and image loss [13].

A formal definition of a negotiation strategy that models these and other existing forms of concession making follows. For a given time period $t > 1$ of negotiation, the strategy specifies the concession tactics to be used in preparing counter-offers. It also states whether bargaining should continue or terminate.

Definition 3 (Concession Strategy [6]). *Let $\mathcal{A}$ be the set of negotiating agents, $\mathcal{I}$ the negotiating agenda, $\mathcal{T}$ the set of time periods, and $\mathcal{S}$ the set of possible agreements. Let $a_i \in \mathcal{A}$ be a negotiating agent and T_i its set of tactics. Let $a_j \in \mathcal{A}$ be the other negotiating agent and $p_{j \to i}^{t-1}$ the offer that a_j has just proposed to a_i in period $t-1$. A concession strategy $C_i : \mathcal{T} \to \mathcal{S} \cup \{\text{Yes}, \text{No}, \text{Opt}\}$ for a_i is a function with the following general form:*

$$C_i = \begin{cases} \begin{array}{l} \text{apply } Y_i \text{ and prepare } p_{i \to j}^t \\ \text{if } \triangle U_i \geq 0 \text{ accept } p_{j \to i}^{t-1} \text{ else reject,} \end{array} & \text{if } a_j\text{'s turn and } U_i(p_{j \to i}^{t-1}) \geq U_i(\hat{s}_i) \\ \text{reject } p_{j \to i}^{t-1} \text{ and quit,} & \text{if } a_j\text{'s turn and } U_i(p_{j \to i}^{t-1}) < U_i(\hat{s}_i) \\ \text{offer compromise } p_{i \to j}^t, & \text{if } a_i\text{'s turn (time period } t) \end{cases}$$

where:

(i) Y_i is a concession tactic (see below);
(ii) $p_{i \to j}^t$ is the offer of a_i for period t of negotiation;
(iii) $\triangle U_i = U_i(p_{j \to i}^{t-1}) - U_i(p_{i \to j}^t)$;
(iv) $U_i(\hat{s}_i)$ is the utility of the least-acceptable agreement for a_i, i.e., the worst (but still acceptable) agreement for a_i.

Concession tactics are functions that model the concessions to be made throughout negotiation. A formal definition of a generic concession tactic follows (without loss of generality, we consider that a negotiating agent $a_i \in \mathcal{A}$ wants to maximize an issue $x_k \in \mathcal{I}$).

Definition 4 (Concession Tactic [6]). *Let* $\mathcal{A} = \{a_1, a_2\}$ *be the set of negotiating agents,* $\mathcal{I} = \{x_1, \ldots, x_n\}$ *the negotiating agenda, and* $\mathcal{D} = \{D_1, \ldots, D_n\}$ *the set of issue domains. A concession tactic* $Y_i : D_k \times [0,1] \to D_k$ *of an agent* $a_i \in \mathcal{A}$ *for an issue* $x_k \in \mathcal{I}$ *is a function with the following general form:*

$$Y_i(x_k, f_k) = x_k - f_k(x_k - lim_k)$$

where:

(i) $f_k \in [0,1]$ *is the concession factor of* a_i *for* x_k;
(ii) lim_k *is the limit of* a_i *for* x_k.

The following three levels of concession magnitude are commonly discussed in the negotiation literature [14]: large, substantial, and small. To this we would add two other levels: null and complete. Accordingly, we consider the following five concession tactics: (i) stalemate (models a null concession on an issue x_k at stake), tough (models a small concession on x_k), moderate (models a substantial concession on x_k), soft (models a large concession on x_k), and accommodate (models a complete concession on x_k). These and other similar tactics can be defined by considering specific values for the concession factor f_k.

Now, concession tactics can generate new values for each issue at stake by considering specific criteria. Typical criteria include the time elapsed since the beginning of negotiation, the quantity of resources available, the previous behavior of the opponent, and the total concession made on each issue throughout negotiation (see, e.g., [3,15]). In bilateral contracting in electricity markets, sellers face typically greater risks than buyers, since energy costs involve frequently several uncertanties. Accordingly, in this work we consider a different criterion: the sharing of risk between agents (see next definition).

Definition 5 (Risk sharing concession factor). *The price is controlled by a concession factor,* f_k, *defined by the following equations:*

$$f_k(\beta) = \begin{cases} k \times \beta, & \text{for seller} \\ k \times (1 - \beta), & \text{for buyer} \end{cases}$$

where:

(i) $f_k \in [0,1]$ *is the concession factor of* a_i *for* x_k;
(ii) β *is the risk sharing parameter.*

Now, a concession tactic for negotiating the risk sharing parameter β follows.

Definition 6 (Risk Sharing Tactic).
A risk sharing tactic R_i of an agent $a_i \in \mathcal{A}$ for computing new values for β during the course of negotiation is a function with the following general form:

$$R_i(\beta, f_k) = \begin{cases} \beta - f_k(\beta - \beta_{lim}), & \text{for } \lambda \neq 0 \\ \beta - f_k(\beta_{lim} - \beta), & \text{for } \lambda = 0 \end{cases}$$

where:

(i) $f_k \in [0, 1]$ is the concession factor of a_i;
(ii) β is the risk sharing parameter;
(iii) β_{lim} is the limit for the risk sharing parameter.

4   A Case-Study on Forward Bilateral Contracts

David Colburn, representing N2K Power (seller agent), and Tom Britton, representing SCO Corporation (customer agent), negotiate a 24-rate DSM tariff. Table 4 shows the initial offers and the price limits for both agents, and also the load profile of the customer. Some values were selected by looking up to real trading prices associated with a pool market in an attempt to approximate the case study to the real-world. In particular, market reference prices were obtained by analyzing the Iberian Electricity Market.[1] The minimum seller prices were then set to these reference prices. Also, some energy quantities were based on consumer load profiles provided by the New York State Electric & Gas.[2] Negotiation involves an iterative exchange of offers and counter-offers. We consider the following:

- The customer submits the load profile and then the retailer submits the first proposal; the agents are allowed to propose only strictly monotonically—the customer's offers increase monotonically and the retailer's offers decrease monotonically;
- The acceptability of a proposal is determined by a negotiation threshold— an agent $a_i \in \mathcal{A}$ accepts a proposal $p_{j \to i}^{t-1}$, submitted by $a_j \in \mathcal{A}$ at $t-1$, when the difference between the benefit provided by the proposal $p_{i \to j}^t$ that a_i is ready to send at t is lower than or equal to the negotiation threshold;
- The agents can exchange only a maximum number of proposals (max_p).

Both agents are risk-averse and pursue a starting reasonable and conceding moderately strategy. The benefit score of each agent is calculated by using the MAN-REM utility functions. Concession rate is set to 10%.

The agents are allowed to negotiate the risk sharing parameter. To this end, the seller agent can start by proposing 90% of risk sharing to the customer, who can reply by submitting only 10% of the total risk.

---

[1] www.mibel.com
[2] www.nyseg.com

Table 1. Initial offers and price limits for the negotiating parties

Hour	Consumer			Retailer	
	Price (€/MWh)	Limit (€/MWh)	Energy (MWh)	Price (€/MWh)	Limit (€/MWh)
1	47.81	50.54	16.77	48.59	45.34
2	36.62	39.29	13.56	37.56	35.25
3	36.14	37.66	7.65	36.96	33.79
4	36.10	37.61	5.96	36.91	33.74
5	36.10	37.26	5.89	36.56	33.43
6	35.78	37.61	6.02	36.91	33.74
7	43.58	45.87	25.63	44.01	41.16
8	48.33	54.42	55.92	50.40	48.83
9	48.18	52.04	77.20	49.07	46.69
10	49.33	54.42	66.08	51.40	48.83
11	50.43	56.73	82.68	52.67	50.90
12	49.33	54.42	74.30	50.40	48.83
13	49.39	54.48	44.03	50.47	48.88
14	49.33	54.42	76.91	50.40	48.83
15	47.12	50.88	74.00	47.93	45.65
16	45.15	49.81	53.88	46.88	44.69
17	39.20	41.03	17.20	40.27	36.82
18	36.20	38.83	15.41	37.10	34.84
19	35.70	37.17	15.44	36.48	33.35
20	38.86	40.66	16.21	39.90	36.48
21	47.81	50.54	16.34	49.59	45.34
22	51.02	54.08	16.50	52.07	48.52
23	51.12	54.18	16.66	52.17	48.61
24	48.65	51.46	16.49	50.49	46.17

Table 2. Case-Study final results

Hour	Price (€/MWh)	Energy (€/MWh)	Hour (MWh)	Price (€/MWh)	Energy (€/MWh)
1	47.73	16.77	13	50.11	44.03
2	37.03	13.56	14	50.05	76.91
3	36.24	7.65	15	47.41	74.00
4	36.19	5.96	16	46.38	53.88
5	35.85	5.89	17	39.49	17.20
6	36.19	6.02	18	36.59	15.41
7	43.37	25.63	19	35.77	15.44
8	50.04	55.92	20	39.13	16.21
9	48.53	77.20	21	48.63	16.34
10	50.82	66.08	22	51.27	16.50
11	50.27	82.68	23	51.36	16.66
12	50.04	74.30	24	49.51	16.49

Table 3. Case-Study final results

Consumer			Retailer		
Proposals	Benefit	β	Proposals	Benefit	β
4	0.63	50%	3	0.67	50%

Tables 2 and 3 summarize the results obtained. The agents reach an agreement after the seller agent sending 4 proposals and the buyer agent submitting 3 proposals. Both agents agree with an equal share of the price risk (50% to each). The results allow us to conclude that the mutual benefit of both agents is higher than in other case-studies [7,8], where risk management and sharing were not considered.

5   Conclusion

This paper has presented several key features of software agents able to negotiate bilateral contracts in energy markets, paying special attention to risk management. In particular, it has described two utility functions and strategies for risk management and risk sharing. Instead of spot price volatility, risk sharing should be directly associated with several other risks, such as fuel price uncertainty, in order to avoid considering forward contracts as CfDs. Furthermore, the paper has also presented a case study on forward bilateral contracts involving a seller and a customer negotiating a 24h-rate tariff. The simulation results support the belief that the behavior of market participants is as expected in managing price risk.

References

1. Hull, J.C.: Options, Futures, and Other Derivatives, pp. 1–15. Prentice-Hall, Englewood Cliffs (1997)
2. Das, D., Wollenberg, B.: Risk assessment of generators bidding in day-ahead market. IEEE Trans. Power Syst. 20(1), 416–424 (2005)
3. Lopes, F., Mamede, N., Novais, A.Q., Coelho, H.: A Negotiation Model for Autonomous Computational Agents: Formal Description and Empirical Evaluation. Journal of Intelligent & Fuzzy Systems 12, 195–212 (2002)
4. Lopes, F., Mamede, N., Novais, A.Q., Coelho, H.: Negotiation Strategies for Autonomous Computational Agents. In: ECAI 2004, pp. 38–42. IOS Press (2004)
5. Lopes, F., Wooldridge, M., Novais, A.Q.: Negotiation Among Autonomous Computational Agents: Principles, Analysis and Challenges. Artificial Intelligence Review 29, 1–44 (2008)
6. Lopes, F., Coelho, H.: Concession Strategies for Negotiating Bilateral Contracts in Multi-agent Electricity Markets. In: IATEM 2012 Workshop and DEXA 2012 Event, pp. 321–325. IEEE Computer Society Press (2012)
7. Lopes, F., Algarvio, H., Coelho, H.: Bilateral Contracting in Multi-agent Electricity Markets: Negotiation Strategies and a Case Study. In: International Conference on the European Energy Market (EEM 2013). IEEE Computer Society Press (2013)
8. Lopes, F., Algarvio, H., Coelho, H.: Negotiating Hour-Wise Tariffs in Multi-Agent Electricity Markets. In: Mařík, V., Lastra, J.L.M., Skobelev, P. (eds.) HoloMAS 2013. LNCS, vol. 8062, pp. 246–256. Springer, Heidelberg (2013)
9. Kirschen, D., Strbac, G.: Fundamentals of Power System Economics. Wiley, Chichester (2004)
10. Raiffa, H.: The Art and Science of Negotiation. Harvard University Press, Cambridge (1982)
11. Von Neumann, J., Morgenstern, O.: The Theory of Games and Economic Behavior. Princeton University Press (1944)
12. Osborne, M., Rubinstein, A.: Bargaining and Markets. Academic Press, London (1990)
13. Pruitt, D.: Negotiation Behavior. Academic Press, New York (1981)
14. Lewicki, R., Barry, B., Saunders, D.: Negotiation. McGraw Hill, New York (2010)
15. Faratin, P., Sierra, C., Jennings, N.: Negotiation Decision Functions for Autonomous Agents. Robotics and Autonomous Systems 24, 59–182 (1998)

Artificial Neural Networks in the Detection of Known and Unknown DDoS Attacks: Proof-of-Concept

Alan Saied, Richard E. Overill, and Tomasz Radzik

Department of Informatics, King's College London, Strand, WC2R 2LS, UK
{alan.saied,richard.overill,tomasz.radzik}@kcl.ac.uk

Abstract. A Distributed Denial of Service attack (DDoS) is designed to overload a target device and its networks with packets to damage its resources or services. This paper proposes an Artificial Neural Network (ANN) detection engine to flag known and unknown attacks from genuine traffic. Based on experiments and data analysis, specific patterns are selected to separate genuine from DDoS packets, thus allowing normal traffic to reach its destination. The mitigation process is triggered when the detection system identifies attacks based on the known characteristic features (patterns) that were fed to the ANN during the training process. Such characteristic patterns separate attacks from normal traffic. We have evaluated our solution against related work based on accuracy, sensitivity, specificity and precision.

Keywords: ANN, Snort-AI, forged packets, characteristic features (patterns), training process, known and unknown DDoS attacks.

1   Introduction and Background

The key objective of a DDoS attack is to compile multiple systems across the Internet with infected zombies/agents [1] and form botnets of networks. Such zombies are designed to attack a particular target or network with different types of packets. The infected systems are either remotely controlled by an attacker or by self-installed Trojans (e.g. roj/Flood-IM) [2] that are programed to launch packet floods. Authors in [3] have explained different DDoS architectural structures used by DDoS engineers to launch successful attacks.

A DDoS attack is a serious security issue that costs organisations and individuals a great deal of time, money and reputation, yet it does not usually result in the compromise of either credentials or data loss. It can damage one or a group of devices and their resources. A DDoS attack slows or halts communications between devices as well as the victim machine. It introduces loss of Internet services like email, online applications or program performance. Within this context, the purpose of our work is to detect and mitigate known and unknown DDoS attacks in real time.

Attacks that are not detected by existing available detection solutions are called unknown (zero-day) attacks. We have chosen Artificial Neural Network (ANN) [4] to detect specific characteristic features (patterns) that separate attacks from genuine traffic. We have intensively trained the algorithm with real life cases and attacking

J.M. Corchado et al. (Eds.): PAAMS 2014 Workshops, CCIS 430, pp. 309–320, 2014.

scenarios (patterns) based on the existing DDoS tools. The more we train the algorithm with up-to-date patterns (latest known attacks), the further we increase the chances of detecting unknown attacks, considering that over training is avoided. This is because ANN algorithm learns from scenarios and detects zero-day patterns that are similar to what it was trained with.   In its yearly reports (2010 to 2013), Prolexic, the world´s largest DDoS mitigation service, has stated that TCP, UDP and ICMP are the most used protocols to launch DDoS attacks [5].

This paper is organised as follows: Section 2 addresses approaches related to this work. Section 3 explains the aims and objectives of our work. Section 4 identifies the mechanisms and approaches used to achieve the aims and objectives. Section 5 describes the design of our solution, while section 6 evaluates our solution in comparison with with other related work.

2   Related Work

Various methodologies and techniques for reducing the effects of DDoS attacks in different network environments have been proposed and evaluated. Jie-Hao, Ming and Jie-Hao [27] have used ANN to detect DDoS attacks where they compared the detection outcome with decision tree, ANN, entropy and Bayesian. The authors identified users request or demand to a specific resource and their communicative data. Then samples of such requests are sent to the detection systems to be judged for abnormalities. Also, Li, Liu and Gu have used Learning Vector Quantisation (LVQ) neural networks to detect attacks [6]. This is a supervised version of quantisation, which can be used for pattern recognition, multi-class classification and data compression tasks. The datasets used in the experiments were converted into numerical form and given as inputs to the neural network. Akilandeswari and Shalinie [7] have introduced a Probabilistic Neural Network Based Attack Traffic Classification to detect different DDoS attacks. However, the authors focused on separating Flash Crowd Event from Denial of Service Attacks. As part of their research, they used Bayes decision rule for Bayes inferences coupled with Radial Basis Function Neural Network (RBFNN) for classifying DDoS attack traffic and normal traffic. Siaterlis & Maglaris [8] have experimented with single sets of network characteristics to detect attacks. They use Multi-Layer Perceptron (MLP) as a data fusion algorithm where the inputs are metrics coming from different passive measurements that are available in a network and then coupled this with traffic that was generated by the experimenters themselves. Gupta, Joshi and Misra [9] have used a neural network to detect the number of zombies that have been involved in DDoS attacks. The objective of their work is to identify the relationship between the zombies and in sample entropy. The process workload is based on prediction using a feed-forward neural network.

Another line of research is to use infrastructure for detecting and mitigating DDoS attack. Badishi, Keidar & Yachin [10] have used authentication and cryptographic approaches to protect network services from DDoS attacks. Similar approach has been introduced by Shi, Stoica and Anderson [11], but instead puzzling mechanism is used to detect DDoS attacks before reaching the target. Hwang and Ku [12] have developed a distributed mechanism to combat DDoS. Their architecture, called Distributed Change-point Detection (DCD), is designed to reduce. The authors adopt the non-parametric CUSUM (Cumulative Sum) algorithm to describe any changes in the network traffic. Some research focused on the source of the attack for the purpose of detection. The authors of [13][14][15] have used packet-marking mechanism and entropy to identify the source of the packet considering that each packet is marked on each router that passes through.

Some of the above approaches used ANN or infrastructure to detect known DDoS attacks while others focused on source of the attack (traceability). However, the above authors have not covered unknown (zero-day) high and/or low rate DDoS attack detection in their approaches. Detecting unknown DDoS attacks is one of the vital objectives that distinguish our work from the works of [6][7][8][9] (see section 3).

3   Aims and Objectives

Our primary aim is to combine detection of known and unknown DDoS attacks followed by a defence mechanism that prevents forged packets from reaching the victim, but allows genuine packets to pass through. Furthermore we aim to observe ANNs behaviour towards unknown DDoS detection when trained with old and up-to-date datasets[1]. One can summarise the objectives of our research in the following points:

- Detection of known and unknown DDoS attacks (high and low rates) as opposed to detecting known attacks in real time only.
- Prevent attacking (forged) packets from reaching the target while allowing genuine packets to get through.
- Train, deploy and test the solution in a physical environment as opposed to s imulators.
- Reduce the strength of the attack before it reaches the victim as opposed to nearby detection systems.
- Evaluate our approach using old and up to date datasets with relevant works based on accuracy, sensitivity, specificity and precision (Section 6).

The effectiveness of this work can be measured if the end product is evaluated under realistic traffic conditions where both known and unknown attacks are detected

4   Theoretical and Conceptual Framework

The strength of the attack can be minimised if multiple effective DDoS detectors are deployed across the network. These detectors analyse the network for abnormalities and prevent them from reaching the victim when detected. It is important to allow genuine traffic flows pass through the detectors and reach their destinations. Thus, it is vital for the detection process to be accurate and tested against all possible existing

---

[1] Old datasets are datasets with old known attack patterns while up-to-date datasets are datasets with latest known attack patterns.

use-cases and patterns. Due to ease of implementation, practicality and online documentations, TCP, UDP and ICMP [16] are commonly used. Most DDoS designers manipulate such protocols to launch their attacks as explained in Prolexic yearly reports [5]. Our detection mechanism is based on ANN (Back-proportion and sigmoid [4]) where its accuracy primarily relies on how well the algorithm is trained with relevant datasets. The patterns used for training purposes are entities of packet headers, which include source addresses; ID and sequence numbers coupled with source destination port numbers. Based on our experiments and analysis, most installed zombies use their built-in libraries as opposed to operating system libraries to generate packets. This is to assist the attacker manipulate and forge the packets during the attack. Therefore, one can study the characteristic features of genuine packets that are generated by genuine applications and compare them with forged packets that are generated by the attacking tools and present them as input variables to train the ANN.

Selecting the patterns to be our inputs began by building new network infrastructures in corporative and isolated environments with different types of DDoS attacks launched at different levels (high and low rates). The results were carefully studied, compared and cross-matched with genuine traffic to verify the characteristic patterns that separate genuine from attack traffic. This part of the process required intensive understanding of how different protocols exchange and communicate with each other. The datasets are organised and structured to accommodate genuine and attack patterns in a qualified format that Java Neural Network Simulator (JNNS) [17] accepts. However, 80% of the datasets is used to train the algorithm and 20% of it to validate the learning process. Before training the algorithm using JNNS, the input values are normalised to maximise the performance in sensitive applications like ours where accurate detection is vital. If the input values are not normalised and applied directly, then large values may lead to suppress the influence of smaller values [18]. Jayalakshmi, Santhakumaran, Zhang and Sun have also explained the positive effect of normalization on ANN performance and training process [19][20].

A typical ANN consists of input, hidden and output layers where the patterns are fed to the learning algorithm via the input nodes. The input values represent the characteristic patterns that separate attacks from genuine traffic. Then we selected three topological ANN structures, each with three layers (input, hidden and output layers). The number of nodes in each topological structure is different - for example, the ICMP topological structure consists of three inputs and four hidden nodes, the TCP topological structure consists of five input and four hidden nodes, and the UDP topological structure consists of four input and three hidden nodes. Hidden nodes, however, deal with the computation process with respect to input and output nodes.

The output layer consists of one node to represent 1 (attack) or 0 (normal traffic). Figure 1, 2 and 3 respectively represent TCP, ICMP and UDP topological structure. Choosing relevant learning algorithm or the number of hidden nodes and activation function was based on initial experiments where sigmoid and Back-Propagation provided most accurate results. The comparison was between QuickProp, Backpropagation, Backprop Weight Decay, Backprop thru time while sigmoid, Elliott, SoftMax, BAM are used as functions [4][18][19]. Our experiments show that Back-Propagation coupled with sigmoid activation function and chosen topological structure can provide up to 98.6% accuracy (see Table 1)

Table 1. Combined results of learning algorithms, activation functions and hidden layers

Protocol	Learning algorithms	Activation functions	Number of hidden nodes.	Detection accuracy and CPU usage	Best results.
ICMP	Back-propagation	Sigmoid, Elliott ,BAM, SoftMax	One or more hidden nodes.	98.5% 70% (CPU Utilization)	Best recorded with 4 hidden nodes using Sigmoid.
UDP	Back-propagation	Sigmoid, Elliott BAM, SoftMax	One or more hidden nodes	98.6% 69% (CPU Utilization)	Best recorded with 3 hidden nodes using Sigmoid.
TCP	Back-propagation	Sigmoid, Elliott, BAM, SoftMax	One or more hidden nodes	98.6% 66% (CPU Utilization)	Best recorded with 4 hidden nodes using Sigmoid.

In Figure 1, the input layer of TCP topological structure consists of five nodes that accommodate TCP sequence, flags, source and destination port numbers and source IP addresses. In Figure 2 represents an ICMP topological design where the input nodes are source IP address, ICMP sequence number and ICMP-ID. Meanwhile in Figure 3 the UDP topological the input values are source IP address, packet length, and UDP source and destination port.

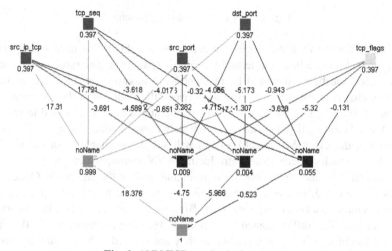

Fig. 1. ANN TCP topological structure

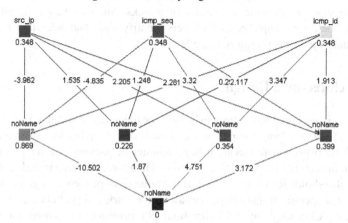

Fig. 2. ANN ICMP topological structure

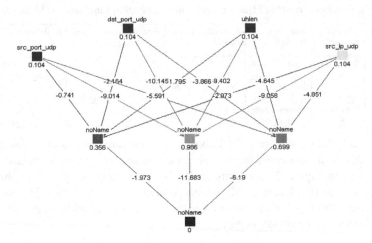

Fig. 3. ANN UDP topological structure

The numbers between the nodes represent the weight that is used by supervised Back-Propagation to adjust and learn by example (patterns). The more new examples one provides, the better it would be in identifying unknown attacks. The algorithm does it by changing the network weights between the nodes until the required output is obtained (0 or 1). Integrating all ANNs as one application as opposed to instances can lack availabilities if the system is technically down. If one instance is down (e.g. instance that detects ICMP attack), others will still be available to detect UDP and TCP related attacks. Meanwhile, introducing ANN instances per protocol provides better maintenance and further control to train and analyse the algorithm. Once forged packets are detected, the defence mechanism is activated to drop the packets while allowing genuine packets to pass through. Blocked packets are unblocked as soon as the system flags the traffic flagged to be normal. However, genuine traffic flowing to the target machine will not be disturbed as they are flagged to be genuine by our proposed solution. Furthermore, the detectors communicate with each other via encrypted messages to provide awareness of attacks. Such exchange of information between the detectors helps security officers identify abnormal behaviour and further deploy countermeasures if required (see Section 5).

5   Architectural Design

Our solution is designed to continuously monitor the network for abnormal behaviour by retrieving packets from the network and analysing their header information using trained ANN. However, retrieving a huge amount of packets in a busy network requires high processing rates and is expensive. Therefore, we have introduced individual packet thresholds for each protocol. If the number of packets in a given network is greater than a specific threshold per protocol, the retrieved packets are subjected to investigation. Choosing the right threshold per protocol was based on real time experiments by calculating the number of packets per unit time (using IPTraf [21]) in different network environments, where the threshold values are configurable. Once the packets are separated and prepared for examination, our proposed solution pipes the patterns (variables) into ANN codes to decide upon the legitimacy of the retrieved traffic (packets). Our design is illustrated in Figure 4, where each network is installed with one DDoS detector that communicates with others via encrypted messages.

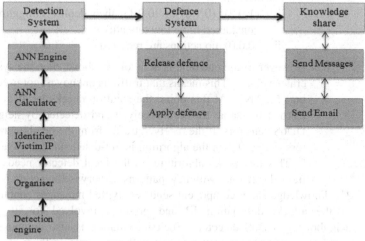

Fig. 4. -Detection, Defence and Cooperative mechanism

Figure 4 can be explained as follows:

1. DDoS detectors are installed on different networks.
2. Each detector registers the IP address of all neighbouring DDoS detectors to inform and send encrypted message when attack are detected.
3. Detectors must continuously monitor their networks for abnormalities.
4. Abnormalities are flagged when the number of passing packets is greater than thresholds.
5. If the number of packets is greater than the thresholds, then:
   a. The organiser organises the packets accordingly and removes unwanted characters.
   b. IP identifier identifies victim IP addresses.
   c. ANN calculator, calculates retrieved patterns and prepare them for ANN engine
   d. The trained ANN engine takes them as inputs and produces one output (1-attack or 0-normal).
   e. Before activating the Defence system, the above steps in point 5 are repeated two more times, producing a total of 3 outputs.
6. Then the Defence system receives the outputs from the detection component and
   a. If the outputs are (0,0,0), then no action is required by the defence system, as the traffic is clean.

b. If outputs are (1,1,1), (1,1,0), (1,0,1) or (0,1,1), then activate defence and stop the attack while allowing genuine traffic to pass through.

c. If outputs are (1,0,0), (0,1,0) or (0,0,1), then the solution repeats point 5 and if outcomes of the new retrieved traffic are:

   i.   (1,1,1), (1,1,0), (1,0,1) or (0,1,1), then activate defence system.

   ii. (1,0,0), (0,1,0) or (0,0,1), then deploy mitigation as this considered to be low rate attack

   iii. (0,0,0), no actions are required.

d. However, if the outcome is none of the above, then the system generates value 2. This means that traffic is unknown (not used in training) by ANN. At this point, the solution checks its local record to learn if the same traffic is received and detected by neighbouring DDoS detectors. If the received traffic from the neighbouring detectors is 1 or 0 then the algorithm is out-dated since its detection was 2. This means the algorithm on the local detector needs to be retrained (off-line) with new patterns. Otherwise no action is taken.

7. The knowledge share component sends encrypted messages containing type of the attack; destination IP and protocol involved to all registered neighbouring DDoS detectors. Such information is also composed by the email element and sent to the security offices to inform them about the attacks for the purpose of logistics.

The outcome of the detection process is 2 when the algorithm is trained with old datasets and lacking in new patterns. ANN has the ability to detect unknown patterns if the attack is similar to what the algorithm was trained with. However, our experiments show that the algorithm fails to detect unknown patterns if trained with old datasets. We identified that up-to-date patterns can detect known and most unknown attacks (see section 6) while trained algorithm with old patterns failed to do so. At this point the ANN of the DDoS detector that has previously trained with old datasets and failed to detect attacks while other detectors detect the same attack must be retrained (off-line). The training process must be done offline as this is a supervised process and patterns must be introduced or reintroduced when desired. Therefore, sharing knowledge between the detectors can provide extra assistant to make further decision when the learning algorithm is not up-to-date. Meanwhile each detector sends a composed email to the security officer with a complete report of all occurred DDoS attacks. One may compare this approach with having one common central server to collect all the attack and send it as one email. However, if the central point is down, then information cannot be sent to the security officer. Consequently no extra countermeasures are deployed if required. Each DDoS detector is designed to function as a standalone component or distributed detector that sends encrypted messages to many registered detectors located in different networks. The solution is not restricted to limited number of detectors to send or receive encrypted messages from. Therefore, if one DDoS detector is not functional or down, other detectors still receive and send messages making the overall solution to be resilient and immune to individual DDoS detector or system failure.

To implement our solution mechanism, we have developed our detection system as plugins and integrated it with Snort-AI (Artificial Intelligence [22]). Snort-AI is based on Snort signature Intrusion Detection System project [23] and one of the authors of this report is an active contributor to Snort-AI by providing plugins and other integration processes. The output of the detection system is coupled with the destination IP address to command iptables [24] to mitigate forged packets while allowing genuine traffic to pass through. We have also used RSA encryption mechanism to encrypt the messages over TCP connection where each detector acts as a sender and a receiver.

6   Quantitative Evaluation

We have evaluated our solution based on accuracy, sensitivity (ability to identify positive results) and specificity (ability to identify negative results). The results are presented in Table 2 and compared with a signature-based solution (Snort) and four other approaches [6][7][25][26] for which quantitative evaluations are reported. The tests were conducted in a controlled, isolated network environment where genuine and DDoS attack flows (high and low-rate) are deployed. During the experiments known and unknown DDoS attacks were launched each with 80 to 90 zombies forming a total of 60 rounds of TCP, UDP and ICMP DDoS attacks on a destination target, together with 60 rounds of normal traffic. The zombies were installed and attacked from virtual platforms on VMware boxes where the boxes were connected to physical devices (victims) via virtual routers. The DDoS detectors/Snorts were deployed between the virtual routers and the victims where they analyse the traffic for abnormalities.

Based on our test experiments our approach provides a high response to detection, accuracy, sensitivity and specificity compared to Snort when both tools are deployed in the same environment and the same attacks are launched at the same time. In [7], the authors deployed their approach (Probabilistic Neural Network) over two periods (attack and normal traffic profiles) accuracy was measured at 92% (period one) and 97% (period two). In [6] the authors compared two different learning approaches, Back-Propagation (BP) and Learning Vector Quantization (LVQ). Our comparison is with BP algorithm since our approach is based on BP, which indicates good performance and accuracy. However, [25] used a statistical approach while [26] used Kernel

Table 2. Comparison between our approach and other work

Approach	Accuracy (%)	Sensitivity (%)	Specificity (%)	Precision (%)
Our approach	98	96	100	100
Snort	93	90	97	96
PNN [7]	92 (P1); 97 (P2)	NA	NA	NA
BP [6]	90 (BP)	NA	NA	NA
Chi-square [25]	94	92	NA	NA
K-PCA-PSO-SVM [26]	NA	96	NA	NA

Principle Component Analysis (KPCA) and Particle Swarm Optimization (PSO)-Support Vector Machine (SVM) to detect DDoS attacks. KPCA is used to remove redundant features and PSO is used to optimize SVM. The detection accuracy of our solution was 98% where 50% represents known attack detection and 48% represent unknown DDoS attacks detection. After that, we further evaluated the detection accuracy of our approach when tested against low and high-rate DDoS attacks. Based on our experiments, our solution detection response was 98% for high-rate DDoS attack while 97.4% for low-rate DDoS attacks. However, Snort responded 93% for high-rate DDoS attack and 92% for low-rate DDoS attacks. Furthermore, we trained our solution with old and up-to-date datasets and deployed different DDoS attacks (known/unknown). The results of the experiment are recorded in Table 3.

Table 3. Our approach with respect to old and new datasets

Our approach	Accuracy (%)	Sensitivity (%)	Specificity (%)	Precision (%)
Old datasets	92	88	96	96
New datasets	98	96	100	100

As shown in Table 3, our approach poorly responded (92% total detection) to unknown (32% detection) and known (60% detection) DDoS attacks when we trained our solution with old datasets. When we trained ANN with up-to-date datasets, the solution was able to detect known and unknown attacks that are similar to what it was trained with (50% known detection, 48% unknown detection). This means, the more and up-to-date patterns we use to train ANN, the better the solution responds to unknown DDoS attacks detection.

7   Summary and Conclusions

For the purpose of this research, we have used a trained Artificial Neural Network algorithm to detect TCP; UDP and ICMP attacks based on characteristic patterns that separate genuine traffic from DDoS attacks. The learning process started by reproducing a network environment that is a mirror image of a real life environment. Different DDoS attacks were launched while normal traffic was flowing through the network. The datasets were pre-processed and prepared to train the algorithm using JNNS. The detection mechanism was then integrated with Snort-AI where it was tested against known and unknown attacks. We have evaluated our solution with signature based and against other related research. Our solution is designed to mitigate this based on preventing forged packets from reaching the victim while allowing genuine packets to pass through. We further evaluated our approach by training with old and up-to-date datasets (patterns) and our solution managed to detect known and unknown DDoS attacks that are similar to what it was trained with (up-to-date patterns). However, when trained with old data patterns, our solution did not detect some unknown DDoS attacks. This means that improper training or old patterns can result in poor detection while a variety of DDoS cases can lead to better detection. This is due to the fact that the algorithm detects on the basis of scenarios; so more scenarios assist the ANN to understand the nature of DDoS attacks. A limitation of our solution is that it cannot handle attacks that are encrypted (encrypted headers). Detecting encrypted DDoS attacks is an interesting and challenging topic for future research.

References

1. Reed, M.: Denial of Service attacks and mitigation techniques: Real time implementation with detailed analysis. SANS Institute InfoSec Reading Room (2011),
   http://www.sans.org/reading-room/whitepapers/detection
2. Troj/Flood-IM. Backdoor DDoS Trojan. Detected by Sophas,
   https://secure2.sophos.com/
3. Alomari, E., Gupta, B.B., Karuppayah, S.: Botnet-based Distributed Denial of Service (DDoS) Attacks on Web Servers: Classification and Art. International Journal of Computer Applications 2012, 24–32 (2012)
4. Mitchell, T.M.: Machine Learning, 1st edn., ch. 3,4,6,7, pp. 52–78, 81–117, 128–145, 157–198. McGraw-Hill Science/Engineering/Math., New York (1997)
5. Prolexic, Global Leader in DDoS Protection and Mitigation. (2003),
   http://www.prolexic.com
6. Li, J., Liu, Y., Gu, L.: DDoS attack detection based on neural network. In: 2nd International Symposium on Aware Computing (ISAC), Tainan, November 1-4, pp. 196–199 (2010)
7. Akilandeswari, V., Shalinie, S.M.: Probabilistic Neural Network based attack traffic classification. In: Fourth International Conference on Advanced Computing (ICoAC), Chennai, December 13-15, pp. 1–8 (2012)
8. Siaterlis, C., Maglaris, V.: Detecting incoming and outgoing DDoS attacks at the edge using a single set of network characteristics. In: Proceedings of the 10th IEEE Symposium. on Computers and Communications (ISCC), June 27-30, pp. 469–475 (2005)
9. Gupta, B.B., Joshi, C., Misra, M.: ANN Based Scheme to Predict Number of Zombies in a DDoS Attack. International Journal of Network Security 13(3), 216–225 (2011)
10. Badishi, G., Keidar, I., Romanov, O., Yachin, A.: Denial of Service? Leave it to Beaver. Project supported by Israeli Ministry of Science, pp. 3–14 (2006)
11. Shi, E., Stoica, I., Andersen, D., Perrig, D.: OverDoSe: A Generic DDoS Protection Service Using an Overlay Network. Technical report CMU-CS-06-114, pp. 2–12 (2006),
    http://www.cs.umd.edu/~elaine/docs/overdose.ps
12. Chen, Y., Hwang, K., Ku, W.: Collaborative Detection of DDoS Attacks over Multiple Network Domains. IEEE Transactions on Parallel and Distributed Systems 18(12), 1649–1662 (2007)
13. Al-Duwairi, B., Manimaran, G.: A novel packet marking scheme for IP traceback. In: Proceedings of the Tenth International Conference on Parallel and Distributed Systems (ICPADS), July 7-9, pp. 195–202 (2004)
14. Gong, C., Sarac, K.: A More Practical Approach for Single-Packet IP Traceback using Packet Logging and Marking. IEEE Trans. on Parallel and Distributed System 19(10), 1310–1324 (2008)
15. Yu, S., Zhou, W., Doss, R., Jia, W.: Traceback of DDoS Attacks Using Entropy Variations. Transactions on Parallel and Distributed Systems 22(3), 412–425 (2011)
16. Novak, J., Northcutt, S.: Network Intrusion Detection, 3rd edn. Sams, pp. 8–30 (2002)
17. Stuttgart Neural Network Simulator, University of Stuttgart (Version 4.1) (1995),
    http://www.nada.kth.se/~orre/snns-manual/

18. Pino, M.: A Theoretical & Practical Introduction to Self Organization using JNNS. University of Applied Sciences Brandenburg (September 2005)
19. Jayalakshmi, T., Santhakumaran, A.: Statistical Normalization and Back Propagation for Classification. International Journal of Computer Theory and Engineering 3(1), 89–93 (2011)
20. Zhang, Q., Sun, S.: Weighted Data Normalization Based on Eigenvalues for Artificial Neural Network Classification. In: Leung, C.S., Lee, M., Chan, J.H. (eds.) ICONIP 2009, Part I. LNCS, vol. 5863, pp. 349–356. Springer, Heidelberg (2009)
21. Wallen, J.: IPTraf (Version 3.0) "Open Source project" (September 2005),
    http://iptraf.seul.org
22. Bedón, C., Saied, A.: Snort-AI (Version 2.4.3) "Open Source project" (January 2009),
    http://snort-ai.sourceforge.net/index.php
23. Roesch, M.: Snort (Version 2.9) "Open Source Project" (1998),
    http://www.snort.org
24. Russell, R.: iptables (Version 1.4.21) "Open Source project" (1998),
    http://ipset.netfilter.org/iptables.man.html
25. Leu, F., Pai, C.: Detecting DoS and DDoS Attacks Using Chi-Square. In: Fifth International Conference on Information Assurance and Security (IAS 2009), Xian, August 18-20, pp. 225–258 (2010)
26. Xu, X., Wei, D., Zhang, Y.: Improved Detection Approach for Distributed Denial of Service Attack Based on SVM. In: 2011 Third Pacific-Asia Conference on Circuits, Communications and Systems (PACCS), Wuhan, July 17-18, pp. 1–3 (2011)
27. Jie-Hao, C., Feng-Jiao, C., Zhang: DDoS defense system with test and neural network. In: IEEE International Conference on Granular Computing (GrC), Hangzhou, China, August 11-13, pp. 38–43 (2012)

A Multiagent Self-healing System against Security Incidents in MANETs

Roberto Magán-Carrión, José Camacho-Páez, and Pedro García-Teodoro

Department of Signal Theory, Telematics and Communications
Faculty of Computer Science - CITIC
University of Granada
{rmagan,josecamacho,pgteodor}@ugr.es

Abstract. Few proposals exist in the literature where security in networks and communications is studied from a pro-active perspective. One of them is MARS, a self-healing system intended to mitigate the malicious effects of common threats in MANETs. MARS makes use of special agent nodes to recover the loss of connectivity due to the operation of malicious nodes in the environment. Despite the general good performance of MARS, this paper shows some situations in which it does not work properly. This is caused by an inappropriate behavior of the optimization objective function considered in MARS. To overcome this limitation, a couple of alternative functions are designed and evaluated. The effectiveness of the new proposals is validated through extensive experiments. The new optimization functions lead to an increase in the resilience and tolerance of the network against security threats, improving network survivability.

Keywords: Agent, connectivity, malicious behavior, MANET, optimization, response, security threat, self-healing, survivability, tolerance.

1 Introduction

MANETs constitute an increasing communication paradigm nowadays. Some possible MANET applications include military scenarios (e.g. soldier communications in the battlefield), emergency rescue (e.g. earthquakes) or fire disasters management when the fixed communication infrastructure is no longer available. The MANETs present a number of inherent special features, namely: there does not exist a predefined communication infrastructure so that end-to-end communications are usually based on multi-hop transmissions, the network topology is variable due to the mobility of the nodes, the communication capacities are limited by resource constraints like energy consumption, and security is a critical aspect due to the implicit wireless open medium nature of the medium [1].

Regarding this last issue, security, MANETs are more insecure than traditional wired networks. Several reasons exist for that: open transmissions make eavesdropping easier, energy restrictions avoid deploying robust complex security solutions, and the distributed nature of the environment and the implicit

J.M. Corchado et al. (Eds.): PAAMS 2014 Workshops, CCIS 430, pp. 321–332, 2014.
© Springer International Publishing Switzerland 2014

mobility of the nodes make this kind of networks much more vulnerable. Attacks like *blackhole, sinkhole, dropping* or malicious behaviors as *selfish,* are specially critical for MANETs [2]. They have a severe impact on the network performance since nodes need to send information through intermediate neighbors that can act maliciously as attackers [3]. Thus, specific security mechanisms to strengthen the services provided in such environments are needed. Deploying efficient security schemes to reduce risks and threats while maximizing the network performance is also desirable. This will raise the network survivability, which is defined as *"the ability of a system to fulfill its mission, in a timely manner, in the presence of attacks, failures or accidents"* [4].

Providing resilience and survivability is not an easy task, it being an open challenge at present [5][6]. In this line, Magán-Carrión et al. introduce in [7] a multiagent response system, MARS, which is intended to mitigate the pernicious effects of common threats on the network connectivity in MANETs. Relying on the detection of malicious behaviors, MARS deploys several smart nodes, called *agent nodes,* which are in charge of restoring and even improving the loss of connectivity when an active attacker (e.g. packet dropper) is detected. This is performed by locating the agents in optimal positions to maximize the overall network connectivity. Although this approach constitutes a novel and useful security response technique, it has some flaws and, thus, it is susceptible to be improved. This is the main aim of the present work, where some alternative solutions for the agents positioning are proposed. These are shown to overcome the original solution by means of extensive experiments with both static and mobility related scenarios.

The rest of the paper is organized as follows. Section 2 presents some relevant literature about multiagent systems in general, and connectivity management and security oriented in particular. Section 3 introduces the multiagent response system proposed in [7], MARS, which is the focus of the current work. Some flaws of the system are also highlighted in this section. Section 4 illustrates how to improve MARS performance by introducing two alternative criteria to lead the deployment of the agents around the environment. A thorough discussion is included to select the best criterion. In Section 5 the connectivity evolution is evaluated through several experiments considering both static and dynamic scenarios. Finally, Section 6 summarizes the principal conclusions and future research directions.

2   Related Work

Traditional agent-based applications are conceived for the industrial field and some of them are deployed in logistics, manufacturing control, automotive, among others. Fields like traffic control, energy and smart grids, buildings and home automation, military and defense and network security are key domain applications in which the employment of agent and multiagent systems will become relevant technologies in a near future [8].

Employing multiagent-based approaches to maintain, recover or even improve network connectivity is an important and recurrent topic in ad hoc networks.

For example, in [9] the location of a number of agent nodes is optimized by means of a particle swarm optimization (PSO) algorithm to maximize the connectivity between user nodes and a control node. A PSO algorithm is enhanced with a model predictive control (MPC) in [10], with the aim of maximizing the connectivity and flow transmission (throughput) in MANETs. In military scenarios, a mobile agent trajectory is optimized according to the deployed positions of the user nodes in [11], maximizing the connectivity between the control node and the arranged user nodes. Authors in [12] present a fault-tolerance system against node failures in MESH networks. The system is conceived to maximize the MESH clients coverage and the overall network connectivity over the time. This is carried out by optimizing several mobile MESH router locations supported by an underlying PSO-based optimization.

Despite the current relevance of security in networks and communications, just a few works exist to address this topic in the context of muliagent systems. In [13] a software agent is created and sent through a suspicious node. If the agent never comes back to the sender node, the suspicious node is concluded to be a *grayhole* or a *blackhole* node. In [14] an agent records the amount of packets received and forwarded by each node along the path. If the agent detects that the forwarded and received packets ratio of a node is under a fixed threshold, the node is labeled as malicious.

A scheme mimicking the human immune system is proposed in [15]. In it, there exists an immune agent (IA) that is distributed through the network. The IA is in charge of detecting, classifying, isolating, and recovering malicious behaviors. A node that exceeds a certain number of malicious actions will be isolated. In [16], a mobile agent trust model based on direct and indirect network observations is proposed. Firstly, several (software) agents are deployed on several network nodes. Each agent moves throughout the network to visit other nodes and share its own trust experience. These are referred to as direct observations. The network nodes also broadcast their own trust perception gathered from the network. Data collected that way are referred to as indirect observations. Combining both direct and indirect observations each node is able to determine the potential existence of malicious nodes. Those nodes with a low level of reputation are gradually isolated from the network.

In this context, a multiagent response system named MARS was proposed in [7] by authors. It consists of a security tolerance approach to fight against common MANET threats: *dropping* or *selfish* behaviors. MARS mitigates the effects of these threats by applying PSO. For that, once an attacker is detected (by some outside way) MARS deploys several agents nodes throughout the environment, that are located at optimal positions to recover or even improve the overall connectivity.

3 MARS: Pros and Cons

MARS is intended to provide resilience and tolerance against several threats with severe effects on the network performance, specially for MANETs. The operation basis relies on deploying a number of agent nodes (ANs) to some optimal locations to improve the loss of connectivity between legitimate user nodes (UNs) due to the action of the malicious nodes (MNs).

The core of MARS is a PSO module. PSO is devised to decide, at each time step, which is the optimal position of each agent by spreading several particles (problem solutions) throughout the optimization space. PSO selects the best particle from the evaluation of several objective functions. Two of them have a especial influence on the connectivity: O_1 and O_3. O_1 specifies the overall network connectivity at a given instant and is always considered in the optimization function in PSO. O_1 is described as:

$$O_{1t} = \frac{2 \times \displaystyle\sum_{i,j \in UN:j>i} Z_{ij}}{UN \times (UN - 1)} \tag{1}$$

where UN is the set of user nodes and $Z_{ij} = 1$ if there exists an available (either single or multi-hop) path connecting the i-th and the j-th UNs. Otherwise, $Z_{ij} = 0$.

Instead, O_3 is evaluated only when the network is partitioned, that is when there exists some nodes which are inaccessible from the rest. Function O_3 measures the minimum distance between the agent nodes and the imaginary middle points between partitions in the network, which are called attraction points (APs):

$$O_3 = \min_{i \in AN, j \in AP} \left\{ \sqrt{(x_i - x_j)^2 + (y_i - y_j)^2} \right\} \tag{2}$$

where AN_i is the i-th agent node and the AP_j is the j-th attraction point. This way, O_3 is optimized by moving the ANs towards the APs, with the expectation of connecting the partitions, and thus improving the global connectivity.

In summary, the PSO procedure considered in MARS, mainly operates as follows:

1. The O_1 function is tried to be improved by positioning the ANs in some strategic positions. This way, the solution with the best O_1 value is selected at each time step.
2. If there exist two solutions with the same O_1 value and both correspond with partitioned networks, the solution with lower O_3 value is then selected.

For more information about MARS see [7].

3.1   Limitations of MARS

Although MARS has demonstrated to have a high performance in recovering the connectivity of the environment when malicious behaviors are taking place, it has a main limitation: O_3 is aimed at attracting the agents to the attraction points to recover the overall connectivity, but it does not work correctly when

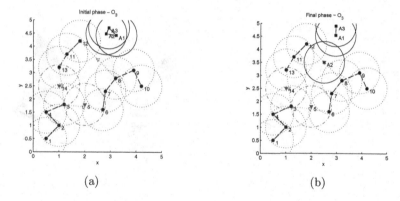

Fig. 1. Experiment 1: AN positioning over time. (a) Locations of the UNs (1-4 and 6-13, filled dots) and the MNs (5 and 14, inverted filled triangles) after the attack of the last ones, and the three APs among the resulting partitions (inverted empty triangles near nodes 5 and 14, and between nodes 8 and 12); also, the initial positions of the ANs are specified (A1-A3, filled squares). (b) Final locations of the ANs obtained from the original O_3 function in [7].

several agents are considered. In order to clarify and illustrate this undesirable behavior, two separated experiments are devised. The first experiment is shown in Figure 1(a). There are 12 legitimate UNs (1-4 and 6-13, filled dots) distributed around the area, 2 MNs (5 and 14, filled inverted triangles) that interrupt the normal network operation, and 3 ANs (A1-A3, filled squares) intended to recover and maximize the connectivity. Initially the network is totally connected. Then, when the attack occurs the network is partitioned in three disconnected regions: nodes 1-4, nodes 6-10, and nodes 11-13, with the corresponding attraction points between each partition (see the inverted empty triangles near nodes 5 and 14, and between nodes 8 and 12 in Figure 1(a)).

The inadequate behavior of the original O_3 function is illustrated in Figure 1(b). It is expected to position each AN just at the AP or in a close area. However, it can be seen that by minimizing the minimum distance between ANs and APs through (2) only A2 agent is correctly positioned, as shown in Figure 1(b).

A second experimentation is carried out to corroborate the incorrect behavior of O_3. Through it, the optimality surface for O_3 is obtained. For that, the static scenario with 10 UNs, 2 ANs and 2APs shown in Figure 2(a) is employed. The ANs A1 and A2 are moved along the diagonal line from the lower right corner to the upper left corner. To obtain a 2D surface we get the O_3 values for each pair of AN1-AN2 positions along the whole diagonal. The resulting surface is represented in Figure 2(b). The ill-definition of O_3 can be concluded from the inspection of this surface. For a correct behavior two minimum points are expected, which should be obtained by positioning each of the ANs at the APs in either order. However, the surface shows a regular shape with four minimum lines, each two crossing the others. These lines represent the fact that provided that one AN is positioned at one AP, whatever the location of the other AN,

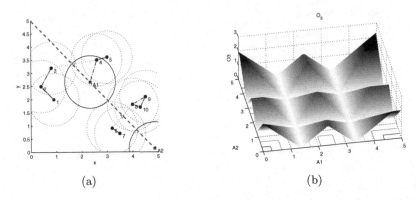

(a)   (b)

Fig. 2. Experiment 2: optimality surface of O_3. (a) Experimental scenario for obtaining such an optimality surface, where A1 and A2 are moved over the diagonal line to try to recover the overall connectivity among UNs 1-10. (b) Optimality surface resulting for O_3, where Z axis represents the function values corresponding to each pair (A1,A2) position solution.

the connectivity is not modified. Also, four minimum lines are obtained as the possible combinations of the two ANs positioned at any of the two APs.

4   Improving Connectivity through Enhanced O_3 Functions

As commented before, O_3 presents an undesirable behavior when more than one agent in the system are considered. Unfortunately, O_3 is often evaluated because the network is partitioned most of the time. This is motivated by the inherent mobility of nodes in MANETs. For this reason, a correct O_3 definition would have a direct impact over the connectivity achieved. Thus, to solve the ill-definition of O_3 and so to improve the network connectivity, two alternative O_3 functions are proposed here.

The first variant, named O_{3a}, is expressed as follows:

$$O_{3a} = \sum_{i=1}^{AN}\sum_{j=1}^{AP} d_{ij} - \sum_{i,j\in AN:j>i} f_{ij} \tag{3}$$

where d_{ij} is the Euclidean distance between the j-th AP and the i-th AN; f_{ij} is the Euclidean distance between the i-th and the j-th ANs. Function O_{3a} subtracts the sum of the distances between pairs of ANs from the sum of the distances between the ANs and the APs. In other words, O_{3a} tries to move the ANs to the APs while maintaining the former separated.

Figure 3(a) shows the final positions reached by the ANs driven by O_{3a} in the example of Figure 1(a). As shown, the agents are located close to each attraction point, what in fact allows to recover the loss of connectivity and improve the

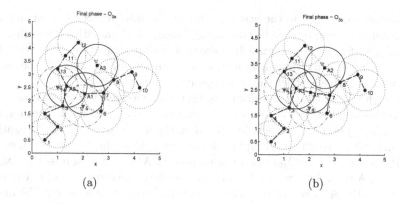

Fig. 3. Experiment 1: AN positions over time applying O_{3a} (a) and O_{3b} (b)

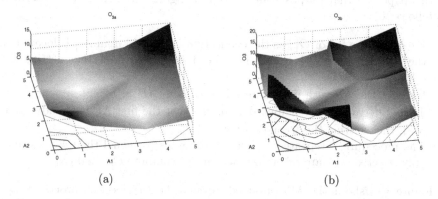

Fig. 4. Experiment 2: optimality surface for functions O_{3a} (a) and O_{3b} (b). As in Figure 2(b), A1 and A2 represent the location of the agents over the diagonal line for the scenario in Figure 2(a), while the Z axis represents the function values obtained for each pair (A1,A2) position solution.

results provided by the original O_3 shown in Figure 1(b). Figure 4(a) shows the optimality surface obtained by O_{3a} in the experiment of Figure 2(a). The surface shows the announced two minimum points corresponding to the positioning of the ANs at the APs in either order.

Alternatively, a second optimization function, O_{3b}, is defined here. This function iteratively associates each AN to a different AP. The optimization function is defined as:

$$O_{3b} = \sum_k \min_{i \in AN, j \in AP} \left(\frac{d_{ij}}{O_{1j}} \right) \quad (4)$$

where O_{1j} is the connectivity obtained if an AN is located at the j-th AP; and $k = \min(\#ANs, \#APs)$. O_{3b} makes an implicit and optimal selection of the APs by dividing the distance d_{ij} by the associated O_{1j}. This function is shown to similar results to O_{3a} in the first experiment. Both solutions get total network connectivity as it can be seen by comparing Figures 3(a) and 3(b). Regarding the optimality surface of O_{3a}, Figure 4(a) shows a similar shape than that exhibited by O_{3b} in Figure 4(b), though some abrupt changes can be found in the latter which may negatively affect the convergence of the optimizer.

Although O_{3a} and O_{3b} outperform O_3, their behavior gets worse as the number of attraction points increases beyond a given value. In O_{3a}, when this occurs, the first term in (3) becomes more influential than the second one in the optimization procedure, which results in grouping the agents around the "center of mass" of the APs. In the case of O_{3b}, when the number of APs grows there is the risk of moving the ANs to APs, which do not increase the connectivity to a large extent just because the ANs are initially closer to them. To overcome these problems, it is desirable to take into account in the optimization only those APs for which the connectivity associated is maximum. The pseudocode of the procedure suggested in this paper for that purpose can be seen in Algorithm 1. Also, it is described as follows:

- We define the factor O_{1j}^k as the connectivity obtained if an AN is located at the j-th AP after $(k-1)$ APs have been already covered, thus getting the selected AP, AP_j^k
- Initially, the AP with maximum O_{1j}^1 is chosen, AP_j^1.
- Then, O_{1j}^2 values are computed assuming that the first AP is already occupied, thus getting the second best AP, AP_j^2.
- The procedure is repeated k times, k being less or equal than $\#ANs$, and only selected APs are taken into account to compute O_{3a} and O_{3b}.

Figure 5(b) shows the APs obtained through the AP selection procedure applied to a highly partitioned network composed of 15 legitimate UNs (6-20, filled dots) and 5 MNs (1-5, filled inverted triangles) randomly distributed throughout

---

Algorithm 1. AP selection procedure

Data: The total number of APs, AP
Result: The selected APs, $AP_{selected}$

for $k = \min(\#ANs, \#APs)$ **do**
    for $j = \#APs$ **do**
        $network \leftarrow addNodes(network, AP_{selected}, AP(j))$;
        $O_{1j} \leftarrow getO1(network)$;
        $O_1(j) \leftarrow O_{1j}$;
    end
    $O_{1j}^k \leftarrow getBestO1(O_1(j))$;
    $AP_j^k \leftarrow getAP(O_1(j), O_{1j}^k, AP)$;
    $AP_{selected}(k) \leftarrow AP_j^k$;
    $AP \leftarrow removeAP(AP_j^k, AP)$;
end

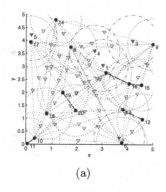
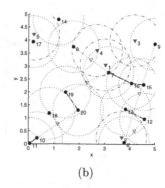

(a)   (b)

Fig. 5. Example of the AP selection procedure considering a highly partitioned network composed of 15 legitimate UNs (6-20, filled dots) and 5 MNs (1-5, filled inverted triangles) randomly distributed throughout the area. (a) Partitioned network with more than 40 APs. (b) Partitioned network when the AP selection procedure is applied, where the number of APs considered is reduced to 5.

the area (see Figure 5(a)). As shown, the method selects those APs providing higher connectivity results, while the rest of them are avoided in optimization.

5   Validation Results

The performance of different optimization functions has been previously discussed from a behavioral point of view. They all try to position the ANs through a compromised environment in order to recover the loss of connectivity among legitimate UNs due to the action of MNs. Now, this section presents further experimentation to corroborate with connectivity values the goodness of O_{3a} and O_{3b}. For that, a scenario composed of 5 ANs, 20 UNs and 5 MNs is simulated with Matlab.

Figure 6 shows the connectivity evolution of O_{3a} and O_{3b} in comparison with that of O_3 when static and dynamic conditions are imposed for the UNs in the environment. Each connectivity value in the figure corresponds to the average of 25 simulation instances as described in [7].

Figure 6(a) shows the connectivity evolution when a static scenario is used. In that situation, the new proposals outperform O_3. Function O_{3a} improves the results of O_{3b} in this specific scenario. Nevertheless, when a dynamic scenario is used (see Figure 6(b)), the three functions obtain similar results. This behavior is motivated by the high number of APs (see the discussion at the end of Section 4) and the node mobility capacity. In a dynamically changing scenario new partitions are continuously appearing and so does the number of APs. This makes the performance of O_{3a} and O_{3b} fall even below that of O_3.

To overcome these problems the procedure proposed in Section 4 to select those most promising APs is employed previously to the location of the ANs.

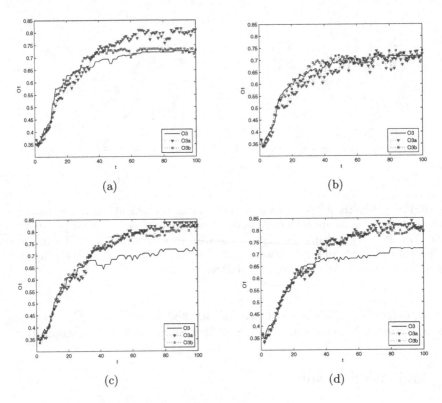

Fig. 6. Connectivity evolution provided by each of the alternative O_3 functions with AN=5, UN=20, and MN=5: when the suggested selection of APs procedure is not used, both in static (a) and in mobile scenarios (b); and when the selection of APs procedure is used, both in static (c) and in mobile (d) scenarios

Figures 6(c) and 6(d) show the connectivity evolution of O_{3a} and O_{3b} in comparison with O_3 for a static and a dynamic scenarios, respectively, when such a selection procedure is employed. The achieved connectivity is higher than when no previous AP selection procedure is made. As shown, this provides better significant performance for O_{3a} and O_{3b} in comparison with the original O_3 function, specially in dynamic scenarios. A remarkable fact is that the method is able to maintain same connectivity levels in dynamic scenarios as well as static ones. This corroborates the system resilience in highly changing environments such as MANETs.

6   Conclusions and Future Work

This paper introduces some improvements on MARS, a technique to mitigate the malicious effects of common threats in MANETs like packet dropping or selfishness. This kind of attacks have a relevant impact on network connectivity and so on network performance. Although MARS performs well in recovering connectivity, there are situations where the approach does not work properly. To fix such undesirable limitations, new alternative objective functions are studied to position the agent nodes in a more intelligent way. The experimental results show the suitability of the improvements proposed.

Further work can be performed to strengthen the current proposal. Firstly, more complete, multi-level objective functions should be studied to deploy the agents throughout the network. Secondly, the optimal positioning of the agent nodes might depend on the particular type of attack detected. For instance, the response to packet dropping may not be the same that those applied to jamming attacks. This should also be addressed in the future. Finally, another important issue is the attraction point location used to position the agents. Improvements in the attraction points location would in turn improve the system efficiency and velocity in recovering the loss of connectivity.

Acknowledgment. This work has been partially supported by Spanish MICINN through project TEC2011-22579 and by the FPU P6A grants program of the University of Granada.

References

1. Lakhtaria, K.I., Lakhtaria, K.I.: Technological Advancements and Applications in Mobile Ad-Hoc Networks: Research Trends, 1st edn. IGI Global, Hershey (2012)
2. Ehsan, H., Khan, F.: Malicious AODV: implementation and analysis of routing attacks in MANETs. In: 2012 IEEE 11th International Conference on Trust, Security and Privacy in Computing and Communications (TrustCom), pp. 1181–1187 (2012)
3. Kanthe, A., Simunic, D., Prasad, R.: Effects of malicious attacks in mobile ad-hoc networks. In: 2012 IEEE International Conference on Computational Intelligence Computing Research (ICCIC), pp. 1–5 (2012)
4. Lima, M., dos Santos, A., Pujolle, G.: A survey of survivability in mobile ad hoc networks. IEEE Communications Surveys & Tutorials 11, 66–77 (2009)
5. Malik, N., Ahmed, A.H.A.: A survey of MANET survivability routing techniques. International Journal of Communications, Network and System Sciences 06(04), 176–185 (2013)
6. Zhang, G., Zhang, H., Zhou, Z., Wang, C.: Research on the survivability based on the algorithms of the key point detection and compensation in ad hoc networks. In: 2013 6th International Conference on Information Management, Innovation Management and Industrial Engineering (ICIII), vol. 1, pp. 493–496 (2013)
7. Magán-Carrión, R., Camacho-Páez, J., García-Teodoro, P.: A security response approach based on the deployment of mobile agents. In: Demazeau, Y., Ishida, T., Corchado, J.M., Bajo, J. (eds.) PAAMS 2013. LNCS, vol. 7879, pp. 182–191. Springer, Heidelberg (2013)
8. Leitao, P., Marik, V., Vrba, P.: Past, present, and future of industrial agent applications. IEEE Transactions on Industrial Informatics 9(4), 2360–2372 (2013)
9. Cho, Y., Smith, J., Smith, A.: Optimizing tactical military MANETs with a specialized PSO. In: 2010 IEEE Congress on Evolutionary Computation (CEC), pp. 1–6 (July 2010)

10. Dengiz, O., Konak, A., Smith, A.E.: Connectivity management in mobile ad hoc networks using particle swarm optimization. Ad Hoc Networks 9(7), 1312–1326 (2011)
11. Miles, J., Kamath, G., Muknahallipatna, S., Stefanovic, M., Kubichek, R.: Optimal trajectory determination of a single moving beacon for efficient localization in a mobile ad-hoc network. Ad Hoc Networks (2012)
12. Lin, C.C.: Dynamic router node placement in wireless mesh networks: A PSO approach with constriction coefficient and its convergence analysis. Information Sciences 232, 294–308 (2013)
13. Taggu, A., Taggu, A.: TraceGray: an application-layer scheme for intrusion detection in MANET using mobile agents. In: 2011 Third International Conference on Communication Systems and Networks (COMSNETS), pp. 1–4 (January 2011)
14. Roy, D.B., Chaki, R.: Detection of denial of service attack due to selfish node in MANET by mobile agent. In: Özcan, A., Zizka, J., Nagamalai, D. (eds.) WiMo/CoNeCo 2011. CCIS, vol. 162, pp. 14–23. Springer, Heidelberg (2011)
15. Mohamed, Y., Abdullah, A.: Immune-inspired framework for securing hybrid MANET. In: IEEE Symposium on Industrial Electronics Applications, ISIEA 2009, vol. 1, pp. 301–306 (October 2009)
16. Chowdhury, C., Neogy, S.: Mobile agent security in MANET using reputation. In: Nagamalai, D., Renault, E., Dhanuskodi, M. (eds.) PDCTA 2011. CCIS, vol. 203, pp. 158–168. Springer, Heidelberg (2011)

An Agent-Based Cloud Platform for Security Services

Fernando De la Prieta[1,*], Luis Enrique Corredera[2], Antonio J. Sánchez-Martin[1],
and Yves Demazeau[3]

[1] University of Salamanca, Department of Computer Science and Automation Control, Plaza de
la Merced s/n, 37007, Salamanca, Spain
{fer,anto}@usal.es
[2] Flag Solutions S.L., C/Bientocadas 12, 37002, Salamanca, Spain
luisenrique@flagsolutions.net
[3] National Center for Scientific Research, Laboratory of Computer Science of Grenoble,
Maison Jeat Kuntzmann – 110 av. De la Chimie, Gregoble, France
yves.demazeau@imag.fr

Abstract. There are many trials where electronic evidences are not digitally
signed. This problem requires the validation of the veracity of these digital resources, thus causing delays in the verdict and increase the price of the process.
The digital signature solves partially the problem because it provides the characteristics of authentication, integrity and non-repudiation; but it has weakness
such as availability, confidentiality and changes control, besides the complexity
on its usage. This paper presents the project DoyFE.es that is an agent-based
platform deployed over a cloud system that provided cloud-based services
to guarantee the veracity of the communications (email, web content and
photographs).

Keywords: Multiagent systems, cloud computing, security, privacy.

1 Introduction

Nowadays, there are many trials where the evidences are based on electronic documents (files, information, emails, photographs, etc.). The majority of these documents
have not been digitally signed, so it is difficult to validate their truthfulness. In these
cases, it is necessary to validate the veracity of these evidences by means of forensic
computer science techniques [3]. This process not only delays the trials, but also increases considerably their costs.

These problems can be *partially* addressed by the users through the use of the digital signature. Besides the electronic communications advantages, digital signed
documents have many advantages facing to non-electronic one (i.e. authentication,
integrity and non repudiation). But the problem is that the process of signing requires
some configurations in the computers of the end-users that are complex for common
users without a specific technical profile. This issue and the lack of awareness about
digital signature advantages constitute an entrance barrier for this technology.

J.M. Corchado et al. (Eds.): PAAMS 2014 Workshops, CCIS 430, pp. 333–343, 2014.

Although the European Commission is boosting the usage of the digital signature, its implantation is still limited[1]. For example, in Spain there is a Law of Digital Signature[2] from 2003 that establishes different levels of digital signature and its legal equivalence with the traditional signature. However, the implantation of the digital signature is limited, following the statistical data of the Spanish Institute of Statistical[3], as shown in Table 1 only the 24,36 % of the Spanish population have some methods of digital signature. In other words, only 11,5 millions of the 47 millions of Spanish have digital signature. But, the percentage of usage is even smaller, because, taking into account only the people that have these methods, only 4,7% use it in the case of eID and 13% in the case of other methods of signing.

Table 1. Usage of digital signature in Spain

	Have digital signature	Use eID	User other methods
Total	24,36 %	4,7 %	13,0 %
Men	52,17 %	5,1 %	14,3 %
Women	47,83 %	4,2 %	11,6 %

As we said, the digital signature deals partially with the problem, but there still are some weaknesses such as (i) *Availability*, it depends directly on the end-users because they are on charge of the backup of the signed document along the time; (ii) *Confidentiality*, it is not possible to monitor access to the signed files, so everyone would be able to see their content; and finally (iii), the Change Control, because when a signed document is changed, it is not possible to know what have been the changes.

This study presents the platform DoyFe.es[4] that tries to solve these open issues. Not only those that are covered by the digital signature, but also the previously presented weaknesses (availability, confidentiality and change control). To do so, DoyFe.es platform exposes three cloud-based services for secure communication in order to ensure the tracking and secure storage of information exchanges and electronic transactions (procurements, shopping, etc.) in order to use this tracking information as evidence in a trial.DoyFe.es platform is based on Cloud Computing paradigm. Concretely, it is developed under +Cloud platform [6][11][8]. Thanks to that, it is possible to deal with the computational requirements and it also facilitates the commercialization following a payment model based on the usage (pay-as-you-go) [2]. The core of DoyFe.es is a multiagent system (MAS) based on virtual organization (VO)[17][7] that allows the interaction both with the underlying cloud platform and with the end-user.

This work is organized as follow, next section present the state of the art of the applications of agents under the frame of security and privacy. Then, Section 3 shows the three main developed services, while section 4 is focused the integration with the

---

[1] http://ec.europa.eu/digital-agenda/en/trust-services-and-eid
[2] Spanish Law 59/2003 –
    http://www.boe.es/boe/dias/2003/12/20/pdfs/A45329-45343.pdf
[3] http://www.ine.es
[4] http://www.doyfe.es/

cloud platform and the MAS. Finally, last section contains the preliminary evaluation and conclusions.

2   Security Services in the Frame of Cloud Computing

Historically, the term Cloud Computing was first used by Professor Rammath. However [4], the concept was becoming popular through Salesforce.com, a company that focused its market strategy to offer software as a service (SaaS) to big companies. However, IBM was the first company to detail the specific terms of the guidelines of this technology (auto-configuration, auto-monitorization, auto-optimization) in the document Autonomic Computing Manifesto [12]. By 2007, Google, IBM and others had joined together to form a research consortium which resulted in the birth of this technology as we know it today [15]. For the large companies, knowledge about this technology is a competitive advantage. First of all, the Cloud provider can offer its services through a pay-as-you-go model following the guidelines proposed by Utility computing. Additionally, the Cloud user does not have to be concerned with demand peaks, transforming passive investments in operational expenses [2].

There are only a limited number of studies in the state of the art that relate Cloud Computing and agent technology [19]. However, some of them are related with security and privacy, these examples can seen from two perspectives: (i) internal to cloud platform, in which they try to ensure the security of the underlying technology; and (ii) external, with examples that try to securize the communication links between the consumers and providers.

At external level, the studies are mainly related with the authentication of the stakeholders in a cloud platform. For example, the ABAC Project [22], or the client-side authentication model [10], as well as the work propose by Habiba et al. [9] in which a MAS uses different policies for grant privileges over the information. At internal level, the studies are focus in guarantee the privacy of the data [5], the monitoring of the system, [16] the security of the infrastructure (real/virtual) [14] and, finally, some works related with the safe storage such as CloudZone [20], Prometheus methodology [21], multilayer security model [13] and so on.

In the state-of-the-art it is not possible to find relevant works about cloud-based services focus on the tracking of the communications in order to use this log as evidence within a trial.

3   Cloud-Based Security Services

Under the frame of DoyFe.es project a set of services has been developed in order to guarantee the authentication, integrity and non-repudiation, but also other open issues such as availability, confidentiality and change control. To do so, three main services has been created: (i) and embedded web browser (*browser-in-a-browser*) focuses on providing of third-party guarantee about transactions and communications done in Internet; (ii) mobile application to take and certify the veracity photographs (iOS and Android); and (iii) an email active gateway to certify the exchange of this kind of communications. The main advantage of these services is their simplicity because the user does not have to install nothing or to set up complex configurations.

The main aim of these services is to track all the communication and store it in order to use them when the end-user needs them. This tracking can be use as evidence in a trial with a third-party certification of its truthfulness. All the information about these services and the evidences is available to the end users in a web application. It makes possible the commercialization of the evidences (web content, photographs and emails) following a usage-based pay model.

Fig. 1. Right: Browser in a browser; Left: Mobile application

3.1   Transmission and Signed Backup of Emails

Figure 1 shows an overview of transmission and receipt of emails within DoyFE.es. An active inbox model is used to facilitate the usability of the system. The process is very easy, because the end-user sends the email normally and only has to put in copy a special email of the platform (doyfe@doyfe.es). With this email in copy the platform also receives it in order to process it. The processing includes the signing, time-stamped and the storage of the data this email (content, dates, addresses, headers, etc.). After that, DoyFe.es sends a proof of the evidence to the sender and recipients.

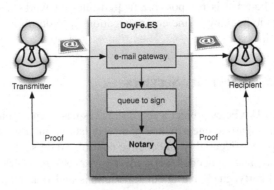

Fig. 2. Transmission and receipt of emails

3.2   Transmission and Signed Backup of Web Content

The process of tracking (signing and storage) of web content is more complex because the web pages usually include related contents (i.e. images, style sheets, javascript, etc.). So, it is needed not only to process the main content (usually pages written in HTML), but also al related content and all exchanges of request and responses.

The process is similar to the email but due the large amount of files and contents it requires more time of processing. Finally, DoyFe.es takes a screenshot of the full webpage in order to avoid the different visualizations that depend on the specific browser.

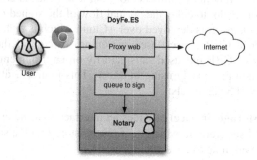

Fig. 3. Process of taking evidences in web browsing

3.3   Signed of Photographs

The process of tracking photographs is different because it is not only necessary to sign the taken photography by a mobile phone, but also geolocalize it. Also, a second photography with the frontal camera is taken in order to know who is the person that takes the photography. This second evidence completes the information related with the electronic evidence.

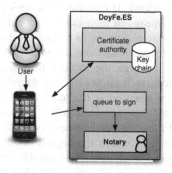

Fig. 4. Process of sign images and their information

In previous services the files are signed within the cloud platform, but in this case they are signed into the mobile phone. To do so, it is necessary to exchange information between the cloud platform and the phone about the security certificate. Once the mobile phone has a valid certificate, the process of sign is similar to the previous ones and then the signed documents are uploaded on the platform.

4   DoyFE Platform

Once the communication services have been presented, there is no doubt that their nature requires large computational resources (CPU and persistence). DoyFE.es not only has to store large amount of information, but also it needs computational power to sign the files in order not to delay the normal flow of the signed resources.

Thus, DoyFe.es platform is deployed over +Cloud which is a cloud-based platform [6][11][8] that used a CBR (Case-Based reasoning) to control the elasticity of the services, the model of CBR has used satisfactorily on environments with uncertainty [1][18]. The CBR is a previously using in uncer. This platform allows offering services at the PaaS and SaaS levels:

- The **FSS (File Storage Service)** provides an interface to a file container, emulating a directory-based structure, in which the files are stored with a set of metadata thus facilitating retrieval, indexing, searching, etc.
- The **OSS (Object Storage Service)** is a document-oriented and schemaless database service, which provides both ease of use and flexibility. In this context, a document is a set of keyword-value pairs where the values can also be documents (is a nested model), or references to other documents (with very weak integrity enforcement).

Both services are presented in the form of stateless web services (REST in API format). The data format used for communication is JSON, which is more easily readable tan XML and includes enough expression capability for the present case.

The internal layer is used to deploy all management and general-purpose applications, in addition to the all services at the platform layer, such as the services offered by DoyFE.es. This layer provides a virtual hosting service with automatic scaling and functions for balancing workload. It consists of a set of physical machines which contribute to the system by means of their computational resources. Abstractions are performed over these hardware resources, as virtual machines, which allows the easy and dynamic management of computational resources. +Cloud platform uses virtual organizations of agents to manage the system resources. MAS can be perfectly adapted to solve this problem, as it allows making decisions in an open environment where the availability of information is limited and agents are thereby required to make decisions, amidst great uncertainty, that affect the entire system.

Under de frame of DoyFE.es, the persistence services at PaaS level (FSS and OSS) represent the *Digital Repository* where the signed documents are stored. But also, +Cloud provides a deployment environment where the computational power (needed for signing) is taken from the virtual machines where each service is deployed. DoyFE.es is also based of VO of MAS that controls the task, signed process, interactions among components, as well as the interaction with +Cloud in order to control the resources requested by the platform.

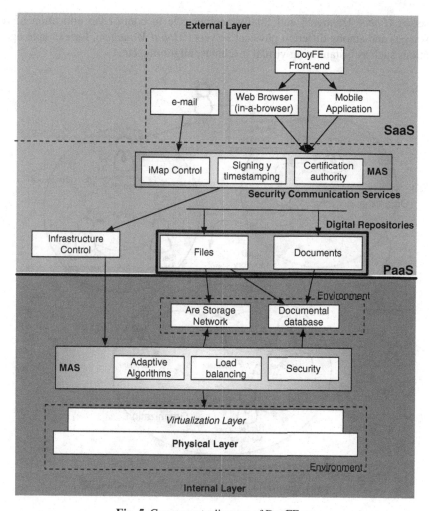

Fig. 5. Components diagram of DoyFE.es

4.1   The Core: A Multiagent System Based on Virtual Organizations

As it is explained in [6], the core of +Cloud is based on two virtual organizations as follow:

- **Resource Organization.** This agent organization is charge of managing both the physical and virtual system resources. The agents are distributed throughout the hardware elements of the Cloud environment. Their main goal is to maximize the use of resources. It is intended that there are no active resources that are underutilized, which implies that there must be the smallest possible number of active physical machines to satisfy the current demand. To do that there is a role to monitor each physical server (*Local Monitor*), a role to control each physical server (*Local Manager*) and finally another role to control the allocation of resources and among different physical servers (*Global Manager*), for example operations such as instantiating virtual machines, migrating, etc.

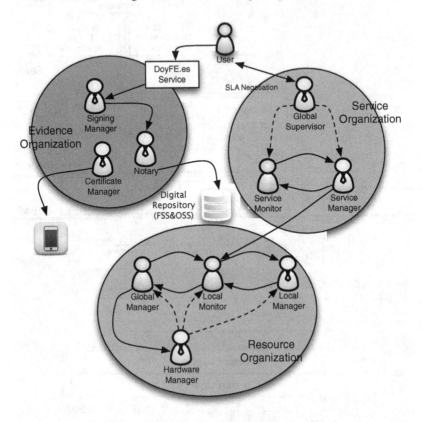

Fig. 6. Organizations of agents in DoyFe.es y +Cloud

- **Consumer Organization.** At the technological level this organization deploys over the computational resources offered by the organization described in the previous section. The services encompassed by this organization will, therefore use the system resources according to existing demand. Its main goal is to maximize the quality of service, which requires monitoring each service individually, keeping in mind that each service will be deployed simultaneously on various virtual machines located in different physical services. The roles within this organizations are the following: the (i) *Service Monitor* that balances between the virtual machines the load and it also monitors each service in terms of quality, the (ii) *Service Manager* that controls each services and alerts to Local Manager when the quality of the services is not enough. These two services take care of all deployed services over +cloud, including the specific communication services at PaaS and SaaS level developed under the frame of DoyFe.Es. Additionally, there is another role, (iii) *Global Supervisor* that takes care about the negotiation of SLA (Service Level Agreement) and their surveillance of those reached with the end-users in order to fulfill with them.

DoyFe.ES incorporates an additional organization in order to manage the evidences, this organization include three main roles:

- **Signing manager.** It is in charge of gather the information for signing, converts it into the appropriate format and sends it to the Notary for signing. It also tests that the information fulfills with the requirements that are need to be signed. Once the Notary signs the information, this role checks that the signing process has been done correctly and then it stores the information in the Cloud.
- **Certificates manager.** It manages the creation, store and revocation of digital certificates. There are two types of certificates: for the mobile clients (to use them in the mobiles phones), and for the notary agents (to use them within the platform).
- **Notary.** It is the role that sign the documents received from the Signing manager, using the keys provided by the Certificate manager.

The main advantage is the combination of both platforms because they are based on MAS and it is easy to exchange of information between DoyFE.es and +Cloud. While the user negotiates the SLA directly with +Cloud, DoyFe can send alerts about the performance of the signing process.

5   Preliminary Evaluation and Conclusions

Once the DoyFE.es and its integration with +cloud are presented, this section focuses on the preliminary evaluation of the overall system. Firstly, the first test is oriented to evaluate the performance of DoyFE.es (without +Cloud). The system has to produce signed files without delaying the normal usage from the user point of view. Following we presented a test that was performed to the heaviest service which is the service oriented to track the web content navigation. The test consists in the comparison of the time load of 60 websites, randomly chosen, using the tool GNU WGET[5]. As it shown in Table 2, the load time using the solution of DoyFE.es, which is a browser in a browser, is acceptable because the process of signing only delays the navigation around a 20% over the normal use.

Table 2. Average of website load with and without (DoyFe.es)

Size	Normal load	Load with DoyFE.es
< 1 Mb	2,42 s	3,13 s
1-3 Mb	4,05 s	5,20 s
> 3	7,08 s	8,62 s

The main advantage of DoyFE.es is to be deployed over a Cloud Computing environment and the easiness of the exchange information between both systems. Moreover, the end user has a perspective of a single system, however, the reality is that the

---

[5] http://www.gnu.org/software/wget/

users make use of the services of DoyFE.es and the computational power of +Cloud, besides the negotiation of SLA are managed directly with the cloud platform. To validate the integration, tests to measure the performance of the DoyFe.es' services after the integration. Table 3 shows the load time average of reference website (http://bisite.usal.es) using the browser-in-a-browser service of DoyFe.es with and without its integration in +Cloud. As this table shows the average are better using +cloud, as expected.

Table 3. Comparison between DoyFE.es and its deployment in +Cloud

Current users	DoyFE.es	DoyFE.es in +Cloud
100	4,81 s	4,02 s
1000	7,40 s	4,84 s
10000	19,54 s	5,52 s

During this study we have demonstrated not only the correct operation of DoyFE.es platform, but also its possible application with the legal frame in order to validate the genuineness of the electronic evidences by a third party using an innovative perspective and traditional tools such as digital signature and service. However if we think beyond, the integration of this system within a cloud computing platform increases notably the performance of the communication services.

We are also demonstrating that the development of an agent-based cloud computing platform has many advantages because it makes easy the interaction with the environment (deployed services, users, other clouds, etc.) in order to give better services to the end-user. In this sense, our open lines are focused on this interaction between both systems, combining the usage information of services (PaaS and SaaS) with their requested resources, in order to achieve the goal of efficiency within the cloud platforms paradigm.

Acknowledgements. This research has been partially supported by Spanish Centre for Industrial Technological Development (CDTI) through the project DoyFE.es (ID-20120798)

References

1. Bajo, J., Corchado, J.M.: Evaluation and monitoring of the air-sea interaction using a CBR-agents approach. In: Muñoz-Ávila, H., Ricci, F. (eds.) ICCBR 2005. LNCS (LNAI), vol. 3620, pp. 50–62. Springer, Heidelberg (2005)
2. Buyya, R.: Market-Oriented Cloud Computing: Vision, Hype, and Reality for Delivering IT Services as Computing Utilities. In: 10th IEEE International Conference on High Performance Computing and Communications, HPCC 2008, pp. 5–13 (2008)
3. Casey, E.: Digital evidence and computer crime: Forensic science, computers, and the internet. Access Online via Elsevier (2011)
4. Chellappa, R.: Intermediaries in cloud-computing: A new computing paradigm. In: INFORMS Dallas 1997 Cluster: Electronic Commerce, Dallas, Texas (1997)

5. Damiani, E., Pagano, F.: Handling confidential data on the untrusted cloud: an agent-based approach. arXiv preprint arXiv:1012.0759 (2010)
6. De la Prieta, F., Rodríguez, S., Bajo, J., Corchado, J.M.: A Multiagent System for Resource Distribution into a Cloud Computing Environment. In: Demazeau, Y., Ishida, T., Corchado, J.M., Bajo, J. (eds.) PAAMS 2013. LNCS, vol. 7879, pp. 37–48. Springer, Heidelberg (2013)
7. Gómez-Sanz, J.J., Pavón, J., Garijo, F.: Meta-models for building multi-agent systems. In: Proceedings of the 2002 ACM Symposium on Applied Computing, pp. 37–41 (2002)
8. González, R., Hernández, D., De la Prieta, F., Gil, A.B.: +Cloud: An Agent-Based Cloud Computing Platform. In: Omatu, S., Neves, J., Rodriguez, J.M.C., Paz Santana, J.F., Gonzalez, S.R. (eds.) Distrib. Computing & Artificial Intelligence. AISC, vol. 217, pp. 377–384. Springer, Heidelberg (2013)
9. Habiba, M., Islam, M., Ali, A.B.M.: Access Control Management for Cloud. In: 2013 12th IEEE International Conference on Trust, Security and Privacy in Computing and Communications (TrustCom), pp. 485–492. IEEE (July 2013)
10. Hajivali, M., Fatemi Moghaddam, F., Alrashdan, M.T., Alothmani, A.Z.: Applying an agent-based user authentication and access control model for cloud servers. In: 2013 International Conference on ICT Convergence (ICTC), pp. 807–812. IEEE (October 2013)
11. Heras, S., De la Prieta, F., Julian, V., Rodríguez, S., Botti, V., Bajo, J., Corchado, J.M.: Agreement technologies and their use in cloud computing environments. Progress in Artificial Intelligence 1(4), 277–290 (2012)
12. Horn, P.: Autonomic Computing: IBM's perspective on the State of Information Technology. IBM Manifesto (October 2001), http://www.research.ibm.com/autonomic/manifesto/autonomic_computing.pdf (last visited: January 2014)
13. Islam, R., Habiba, M.: Collaborative swarm intelligence based Trusted Computing. In: 2012 International Conference on Informatics, Electronics & Vision (ICIEV), pp. 1–6. IEEE (May 2012)
14. Li, Z., Chen, C., Wang, K.: Cloud computing for agent-based urban transportation systems. IEEE Intelligent Systems 26(1), 73–79 (2011)
15. Lohr, S.: Google and ibm join in cloud computing research. New York Times (October 2007), RI: http://www.nytimes.com/2007/10/08/technology/08cloud.html?_r=0
16. Pal, S., Khatua, S., Chaki, N., Sanyal, S.: A new trusted and collaborative agent based approach for ensuring cloud security. arXiv preprint arXiv:1108.4100 (2011)
17. Rodríguez, S., de Paz, Y., Bajo, J., Corchado, J.: Social-based planning model for multiagent systems. Expert Systems with Applications 38(10), 13005–13023 (2011)
18. Sánchez-Pi, N., Carbó, J., Molina, J.M.: A Knowledge-Based System Approach for a Context-Aware System. Knowledge-Based Systems 27, 1–17 (2012)
19. Talia, D.: Clouds meet agents: Toward intelligent cloud services. IEEE Internet Computing 16(2), 78–81 (2012)
20. Talib, A.M., Atan, R., Abdullah, R., Murad, A.: Security framework of cloud data storage based on Multi Agent system architecture-A pilot study. In: 2012 International Conference on Information Retrieval & Knowledge Management (CAMP), pp. 54–59. IEEE (March 2012)
21. Talib, A.M., Atan, R., Abdullah, R., Murad, M.A.A.: Multi Agent System Architecture Oriented Prometheus Methodology Design to Facilitate Security of Cloud Data Storage. Journal of Software Engineering 5(3), 21 (2011)
22. Venkataramana, K., Padmavathamma, M.: Agent Based approach for Authentication in Cloud. IRACST-International Journal of Computer Science and Information Technology & Security 2(3), 598–603 (2012)

An Architecture Proposal for Human-Agent Societies

Holger Billhardt[1], Vicente Julián[2], Juan Manuel Corchado[3], and Alberto Fernández[1]

[1] CETINIA, Universidad Rey Juan Carlos, Spain
{holger.billhardt,alberto.fernandez}@urjc.es
[2] DSIC, Universidad Politécnica de Valencia, Valencia, Spain
vinglada@dsic.upv.es
[3] BISITE, Universidad de Salamanca, Salamanca, Spain
corchado@usal.es

Abstract. Agreement technologies have settled the basis for creating systems that operate on the basis of agreements in societies of independent, autonomous computational entities (agents). However, nowadays more and more systems of such kind rely on a seamless interaction of software agents with humans. Humans work in partnership (directly or indirectly) or closely related with agents that are able to act autonomously and intelligently. Specifically, humans and agents have the ability to establish a series of relationships/collaborative interactions with each other, forming what might be called human-agent teams to meet their individual or collective goals within an organisation or social structure. Systems in which people and agents operate on a large scale offer an enormous potential but also require the consideration of additional issues. In this paper we analyse the open issues that may be addressed for researches in order to develop open human-agent systems. We present a real-world case study and an abstract architecture proposal for such systems.

Keywords: Multi-agent systems, Human-agent societies, Service-oriented multi-agent systems.

1 Introduction

Nowadays more and more humans work in partnership (directly or indirectly) or closely related with computational entities (agents) that are able to act autonomously and intelligently. Considering systems of people and agents operating on a large scale offers an enormous potential and, if performed properly, it will help tackle complex social applications.

As intelligent computational systems pervade the human space, they dramatically change the ways in which human users interact with technological systems. Rather than performing tasks in an isolated and subordinate fashion, computational agents are involved in an increasing range of collaborative relationships with humans, where negotiation and task delegation occur along the agent-agent axis as well as along the human-agent one. Due to its social ground, agreement technologies can be the basic driver to smooth the boundary between the human space and the computational space so as to create cooperative social ensembles of humans and agents that work in strict

J.M. Corchado et al. (Eds.): PAAMS 2014 Workshops, CCIS 430, pp. 344–357, 2014.

partnership to accomplish their individual or collective goals. However, they have to be enhanced in order to take into account the particular requirements that arise when considering interactions among computational agents and humans. Adaptation of the normative context, adjustable and limited autonomy and recognition of user's intentions are some of the characteristics that have to be covered. Semantics, norms, negotiation, learning, context awareness, behavioural modelling and human-agent collaboration will be the building blocks for the specification of such systems.

We call such systems human-agent societies and the research questions to be solved in order to create such systems are: What type of environment or technological platform is appropriate for enabling a computing ecosystem of that kind? What type of services, standards, methods and tools are needed to generate such environment in a way that both, computational agents and humans can seamlessly interact with each other, each of which solving its individual objectives?

The view of human-agent societies also reflects the technological evolution in the areas of Computer Technology and Communications (Internet, WWW, e-commerce, wireless connectivity, etc.). Computation has become an inherently social activity that occurs by means of and through communication among entities (agents or humans) and takes place in our daily lives when and wherever it is needed. Applications are no longer monolithic or distributed applications managed by only one organisation, but rather societies of actors that provide and consume services. Even the notion of application is losing its importance. Instead, computing is something that is enabled by an environment – a virtual ecosystem of intelligent components – in which we are immersed and where complex behaviour is created on the fly. The concepts of "service oriented computing", "computing by interaction and agreement", "cloud computing", the "internet of things" or "social computing" are closely related for such systems, but they have to be enhanced to make computing a truly seamless experience of immersion in such an environment. Possible scenarios of such systems are virtual marketplaces where either agents or humans interact, simulation and training environments (possibly in 3D), the area of health and medical applications, home automation, etc.

In this context, we need to define platforms, as well as development methods and tools that support the creation, operation and evolution of such an ecosystem and allow for a seamless and integrated interoperability of agents, services and humans. This paper presents an analysis of the main open issues related with such systems and which we belief must be taken into account in the research in this area. The analysis is supported by the study of a real-world case: a tourism scenario. Based on this analysis a proposal for an abstract architecture for human-agent societies is presented.

The rest of the paper is structured as follows: section 2 defines human-agent societies; section 3 presents the analysis of a case study: a tourism scenario; section 4 enumerates open issues for research in the field; section 5 proposes an abstract architecture for human-agent societies and, finally, section 6 gives some conclusions.

2 Human-Agent Societies

With the term human-agent society we refer to a computing paradigm in which the traditional notion of application disappears. Rather than developing software applications that accomplish computational tasks for specific purposes, this paradigm is based on an immersion of the users in an environment that enables computation. The environment itself is populated by computational entities with different capacities and intellectual properties, ranging from simple devices that offer specific capacities or rudimentary information, like screens or sensors, to autonomous artificial agents that provide high level services and are able to engage in complex interaction protocols.

Humans participate in this society either through some personal assistance agent or just through some graphical interface on different computing devices. From the point of view of the inside of the society, humans participate just like any other agent, trying to fulfil their individual goals and objectives. From the point of view of the humans, the interactions follow the principles of ubiquitous computing. That is, humans have the perception to interact with objects they are used to and that recognize their contexts and personal needs and preferences. In this way, the immersion of humans in the system is maximized, minimizing at the same time the difficulties of interaction.

Human-agent societies are intrinsically open; participant can enter and leave the system at any time and there is no direct control over the behaviour of the participating components. Computation in such societies is not predefined. Instead it takes place as a consequence of the fact that autonomous agents try to meet their objectives. In order to do this, they interact with others, establishing relations of different kind and different temporal duration; from the simple provisioning of a piece of information, to long lasting collaborations in some business scenario, or connections based on friendship.

In our vision, human-agent societies are an evolution and integration of different paradigms and technologies that have appeared in the last decades.

In the first place, they are an evolution of multi-agent systems (MAS). In the last years, the research on MAS has been centred primarily on open system [1]; systems that are populated by heterogeneous agents that can dynamically enter and leave the system at any time. They are characterized by their limited confidence, possibly conflicting individual goals and a great probability of non-accordance with specifications [2]. All these characteristics are also present in our vision of human-agent societies. In particular, research in open MAS has concentrated on methods for regulating the interactions among the agents. In order to assure that a system with an a priori unknown population of agents will behave according to some global objectives and preferences, researchers have studied the regulation of artificial agent societies upon the contractual and normative relations found in human social interactions and the concept of organisation has become very important [3]. This concept changes the focus in the design of MAS from an agent-centred approach to an organisation-oriented approach where the problem consists in designing the rules of the game rather than the individual components. A wide variety of more or less flexible meta models for specifying virtual organisations have been proposed. Some examples are AGR [3], MESSAGE [4], GAIA and Roadmap [1,5], Electronic Institutions [6,7], OMNI [8], MOISE+ [9], GORMAS [10] and THOMAS[11] or the model proposed in [12]. Other approaches propose to regulate open MAS through more lightweight coordination mechanisms or artifacts that can be embedded in the environment [13-16].

In recent years, the development of agreement technologies has settled the basis for a paradigm of "computing by agreement", where intelligent computational agents autonomously operate and interact among them in a sophisticated way, and whose higher level of intelligence permits to delegate more and more complex tasks [17]. Semantics, norms, organisations, negotiation, argumentation, coordination and trust have been identified as the enabling technologies for such systems. We belief that these are also some of the building blocks for human-agent societies, but they have to be enhanced beyond the computational space for the development of socially acceptable systems in which humans represent just another component.

In the second place, human-agent societies are based on the developments in the field of service oriented computing (SOC) and semantic technologies. Service oriented computing is a field that has evolved in the past in parallel to MAS, but both have a principal aspect in common: the idea of computing by delegation; of creating complex behaviour by composing capacities (services) or information provided by different independent and possibly heterogeneous entities. However, whereas MAS has more concentrated on the autonomy and intelligent behaviour of the components, research in SOC has been rather concentrated on appropriate descriptions that facilitate and enable interoperability, service discovery and service composition. All these issues are relevant for human-agent societies. Thus, the languages and methods that have been developed in this field can provide a starting point for the description of capacities of the different components. Especially of interest are languages for semantic descriptions of web services like OWL-S [18] or WSMO [19], or the more lightweight approaches like SAWSDL [20], SA-REST [21] and WSMO-Lite [22]. However, such languages have to be extended in two ways. First, it is not only necessary to describe the services any component is able to provide to others, but also their intellectual and social capacities – their abilities to negotiate, argue and establish agreements, their social constrains and relationships and their preferences and contextual situations. Some approaches in this sense have already been proposed in the context of Service Oriented Multi-Agent Systems (e.g., [23, 24]. The second necessary extension of current semantic service description languages is related to interoperability. It is necessary to find mechanisms for a transparent access of humans and artificial agents to other components. This implies the need for bridging the gap between ontology based descriptions and easily understandable representations for humans. Some initial ideas in this sense have been proposed for service search and discovery based on key words or tag clouds (e.g., [25, 26]).

Human-agent societies do not only rely on the use of services or capacities other provide, but also on the transparent and integrated access to the available information regardless the location of the actual information sources or the representational structure of information pieces. Semantic technologies have been used in recent years to link data and information sources, both at the instance and the meta level. From these efforts emerges the Linked Data[1] initiative whose objective is to share and interconnect structural data in Internet. The integration of data and information from different possibly heterogeneous sources require the alignment of different languages and

---

[1] http://linkeddata.org

vocabularies used to describe the data schemata and the fusion of data at the instance level. RDF Schema and OWL provide mechanisms to define relationships among different vocabularies and that allow transformations between schemata in an easy way. The openness of the envisioned systems however, requires methods that allow obtaining such alignments in an automatic manner (e.g., [27, 28]).

Finally, the third pillar for constructing human-agent societies arises from the field of ambient intelligence and context aware systems. Ambient intelligence has the same perspective of an environment of computational devices that support humans and in which humans are immersed in their daily lives [29]. Such an environment should be able to perceive and respond to the presence of individuals in a simple, non-intrusive and often invisible manner [30]. Ambient intelligence is closely related to ubiquitous computing, a concept that has been introduced in the 90th [31], and that describes a world where different computational objects communicate and interact with the aim to support the daily activities of humans. Research in this field has concentrated on the following issues [32], all of which are also relevant for human-agent societies: i) the technologies should be transparent for users, ii) service provision should adapt to the context and preferences of users, and iii) the systems have to provide user friendly interfaces. Intelligent systems and Multi-agent technologies are considered to play a fundamental role in meeting these requirements [33].

The concept of context based systems, introduced by Want et al. [34], deals with the issue of adapting the provision of services to the context of users. Context aware applications been created in many different domains (e.g., [35-39]). In most of those applications, however, the definition of context is restricted to some particular attributes. Context should be something that is not predefined. What should be considered as context depends on the interaction a component is carrying out in a particular moment. We belief that the use of agents with higher intellectual capacities (e.g., adaptation, learning, etc.) as core components in human-agents societies will facilitate the creation of systems with a higher degree of context awareness. Moreover, this will also make possible to provide and obtain additional contextual information, like social relationships, or social and institutional roles, for example.

3   Case Study Analysis

A case study of a tourism market is used to illustrate the research requirements of human-agent societies. However, it is important to point out that the requirements identified are independent of the domain of the example. A tourism market can be viewed as a large dynamic problem that interconnects clients (individuals) and suppliers – a huge number of public and private institutions (companies, travel agencies, hotel chains, individual hotels, airlines, ...) – of tourism services. Nowadays, many of such services include additional context-based facilities to adapt to the age, genre, acquisition capacity and interest of users and, thus, to fulfil the final users needs.

In a concrete situation, let's suppose a group of friends wants to organize a holiday trip together. As a group, they have to negotiate with several service providers (e.g., for accommodation, travel arrangements, leisure activities) to get a travel package for the group. But at the same time they need to deal with possible conflicts of interest since each member of the group will have his/her own desires and preferences. Thus, they have to agree upon a package that would somehow satisfy all members of the group. Considering human negotiation, such a task cannot be done without a great deal of effort. It would be time consuming and, context related issues, like geographical distance, different time schedules or idiomatic barriers would complicate the required negotiation and argumentation processes.

Now let's suppose that this problem is solved in a human-agent society, in which each friend of the group would be represented by his/her electronic assistant agent (EAA) that will act in the society on behalf of its user. Moreover, bigger tourist companies will have software agents that offer their products and smaller providers (e.g., small hotels) may also be represented by assistant agents. The assistant agents should be aware of the personal preferences of their users regarding booking conditions. Furthermore, they should also be able to recognize certain context parameters of their users that might be of interest (for instance, one of the friend may have his birthday during the trip). In a first stage, the EAAs would need to create a team whose aim is to collaboratively solve the problem at hand. The system requires mechanisms for searching for different tourist services, hiding away any barriers regarding possible heterogeneous descriptions of such services. In an open system as the one described here, there exist an intrinsic uncertainty about the reliability of service providers, and trust and reputation mechanisms may play an important role in order to assure successful interactions. In our case, a particular hotels may be discarded by the group because one of the members has had a bad experience in this hotel in a previous trip.

The society should provide facilities that allow the EAAs to negotiate, to argue and to establish agreements/contracts with agents that offer tourist services. It should also facilitate the set up of some type or organisational structure that defines the role of each EAA in the group, as well as certain norms or protocols that regulate the negotiation and argumentation process among the EAA within the group in an efficient way. Such norms and protocols should assure the best possible outcome, e.g., a tourist package with which all group members will be happy. Re-organisation should be possible, that is, the system should be adaptable, for instance, if another friend wants to join the trip or if a new offers is available. The society should allow or even may require the human intervention in different moments. Some of the friend may relay totally on the autonomy of their EAAs, but others may want to participate in certain decisions, or may want to be informed on the decision progress. The society should be able to deal with such situations, adapting its operation to the different intervention requirements of the human participants. It should allow the participation of humans through different devices and interfaces and provide the required information to human agents in a human-readable manner.

4 Open Issues

Extending current technologies in order to develop a computational ecosystem that allows for a seamless integration of humans, artificial agents and other computation components poses several challenging problems. As we have tried to demonstrate in section 3, the complexity of such systems is high and there are several open issues for research that should be tackled. In this section we try to identify such issues.

Human-agent collaboration, adjustable and limited autonomy.
In order to obtain a true benefit of the collaboration of humans and computational agents, it is necessary to understand the capabilities and capacities of both components and how these capacities can complement each other in computational systems. Collaborative problem solving and decision-making through collective intelligence and crowdsourcing is an issue to be studied. We need to focus on how humans and computational agents define the agreement space that permits them to collaborate to solve complex problems. Human-agent planning, negotiation, argumentation, mixed-initiatives, teamwork and team monitoring are key technologies that are required.

Within this issue, the concept of adjustable autonomy is of importance, as a way for agents to decide whether to take a decision autonomously or to delegate it to a human user [40,41]. But this concept needs to be extended to what could be called limited autonomy, integrating the fact that humans might want to have the final say on certain operations and decisions made by intelligent agents. Computational agents must be provided with effective protocols that allow them to interact in the system without surpassing the limits of autonomy and authorization that have been imposed on them. This, on the other hand, will require the adaptation of the (normative or organizational) contexts under which interactions take place.

Semantics and information.
The basis of effective and smooth partnership between human and computational agents depends on the transmission of information and knowledge across the boundary between the computational space and the human space. Semantics, knowledge representation and argumentation are the basis of the mutual understanding and knowledge exchange. The development of mechanisms to reliably blend information generated by users and computational agents running on dispersed digital devices and sensors is a topic that has to be analysed and studied. Means are required to transparently provide information and knowledge in a way understandable for each participating entity in the system. Semantic alignment techniques, as proposed for agent-agent interactions [42, 43] and approaches of explaining information that is passed to other entities [44, 45] can provide a basis but have to be extended to provide support for human-agent interactions.

Context awareness and user preferences.
Conveying the information related to human preferences, contexts and objectives, and understanding these pieces of knowledge by computational agents is essential for creating socially acceptable systems in which humans participate in a transparent way. In human-agent societies, where the interactions take place between components that are unknown "a priori" there is a need for creating an infrastructure that allows to obtain any contextual information regarding a given interaction "on the fly". Such an

infrastructure should allow any component to declare/publish contextual information and also to search for contextual information in a transparent manner.

Context-aware system uses contextual information to modify their behaviour to meet user needs better. Although current techniques provide a solid foundation to model and interpret the context, there are aspects that have not been covered completely. In particular, due to the huge quantity of information that is generated continuously, new data fusion algorithms and mechanism are required that are able to filter and process this information, and to generate knowledge.

Normative contexts, regulation and trust.
Systems where different autonomous entities, with possibly different individual objects coexist, require normative contexts or other regulation mechanisms that rule the interactions between the entities. Such context may specify the norms and protocols that should be followed in a particular interaction scenario of a limited duration. But they may also be used to set up long-term relationships between components in the sense of virtual organisations or electronic institutions. The enabling infrastructure for human-agent societies should facilitate the creation of normative contexts for both, short-term interactions and long-term organisations. Due to the intrinsic openness of the envisioned systems (e.g., participants in the society can't be controlled directly), especial importance should be given to the development of "soft" regulation mechanisms (incentives, penalties, social acceptance, etc.). In many situations, such mechanisms may be the way to drive the evolution of the system behaviour towards a desirable global outcome, coping at the same time with individual objectives of humans and computational agents.

Also the concepts of trust and reputation as a means for self-regulation and security in open systems are important. Different trust mechanisms have been proposed in the agent community but it is necessary to adapt such methods to situations where both, humans and agents are involved. Humans are not always rational and often establish trust based on their social relationships. In order to employ reliable trust and reputation mechanisms, the underlying computational infrastructure has to provide means to identify individuals in the system regardless the device or interface they are using.

Adaptation and reorganisation.
The world that surrounds us always changes and evolves. Computational human-agent societies, in order to be socially accepted and to persist in time, have to adapt their behaviour to such changes in a natural way.

At the micro level, computational agents should be able to anticipate and adapt to the context of the world outside the computational scope, as well as to the goals and intentions of human user. Learning by human feedback, intention recognition and behavioural pattern classification are some of the topics that should be studied.

At the macro level, reorganisation at the group or society level, allows to cope with environmental changes. That is, the normative contexts and the organisational structures that govern the interactions among entities should evolve in order to adapt the behaviour of a system to a dynamic environment. Key issues to be studied here are the factors that should trigger reorganization (when), and which changes in the organisational structures will have the desired effect on the adaptation of the system's behaviour (how). Furthermore, reorganisation should take place dynamically, with minimal interference and smooth transitions, and without sacrificing efficiency.

Discovery and composition.
Participants in human-agent societies use the services and capacities that others provide. In this regard, the envisioned ecosystem has to provide means to adequately describe, locate, use and compose services or capacities. Much work in this regard has been done in the Web services community. However, these approaches are not directly transferable to human-agent societies. In service-oriented computing the core component, in general, is the service, and not the service provider. In human-agent societies, individuals should be the core component for description and location. Apart from providing certain services, each individual is characterized by other factors, like its social relationships, roles, reliability, objectives, preferences, etc. and all these characteristics will have to be taken into account when interacting with others. Research should be carried out to define new methods for describing, locating individuals and the services they provide as well as new methods for composing the services provided by several agents or humans. Furthermore, the infrastructure for searching and locating individuals should be decentralized to cope with scalability issues and it should be accessible from different devices with different capacities.

Computational platform.
Human-agent societies rely on the seamless interactions of humans and computational entities based on network connections through physical devices with different computational capacities. A computational platform is needed to cope with this situation. Such a platform should be scalable, facilitating the connection to the society through the network and regardless the devices or interfaces used. Furthermore, it should facilitate the participation of entities (humans or software agents) in a transparent manner, making the development, publication, provision and usage of services an easy and transparent task. From the outside, the platform should provide "universal" computational power, hiding away any problems related to physical restrictions of devices. We believe that such a platform has to be decentralized. It should rely on possibly many computational resources that distribute computation tasks among themselves in a decentralized way and based on parameters like workload, importance, etc.

5   Abstract Architecture for Human-Agent Societies

According to the previous analysis, we propose an abstract architecture for human-agent societies, called iHAS (intelligent Human-Agent Societies). The architecture intents to tackle all the above-mentioned open issues. A general view is shown in Figure 1.

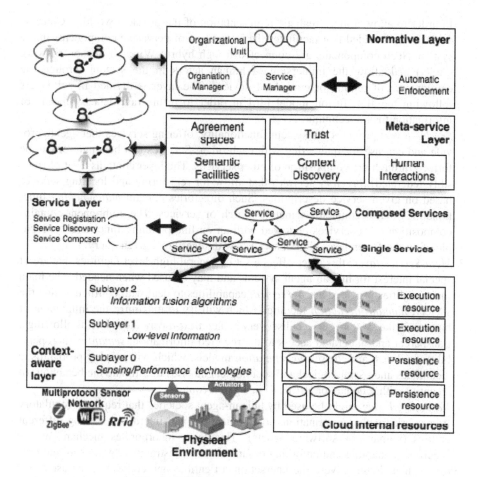

Fig. 1. iHAS abstract architecture proposal

The iHAS framework is organised as a set of layers, which offers Agents or Human access to the iHAS infrastructure. We envision the service as the basic computational unit for interaction. Artificial and human agents may provide services for others and interact with each other through the execution of services. On the lower level, a cloud-like computational platform, enhanced with context aware facilities, enables a transparent deployment of services. On top, a variety of high-level facilities are offered through the Normative and Meta-service layers which might be used by agents in order to set up more complex societies possibly stable in time. In the following we give a detailed description of each layer:

1. *Low-level layers*: it is formed by the *Cloud internal resources*, where services are deployed providing a virtual hosting service with automatic scaling according with reached service level agreements (SLA) and functions for balancing workload. This layer is internal to the system and is formed by the physical resources, which allows the abstraction of these resources shaped as virtual machines (VM).

In order to allow a more realistic representation of the physical world, a Context-aware layer is added that facilitates the integration of pervasive components in the system. Such components are connected trough hybrid Wireless Sensor Network (WSN) and allow the immersion of human actors in the system through the employment of mobile or embedded devices. The layer is divided in sub-layers following the JDL fusion model [46] in order to refine raw data by means of information fusion techniques.

2. *Service layer:* provides the system functionality, offering services that agents provide and can use for interacting with each other. Services can be single or can be formed through the composition of other services. The layer contains a set of (possibly federated) *directory services* that allow for registering and locating services based on given service descriptions. Such directories contain *matchmaking* functionalities that account for semantic search of services. The component contains composition meta-services endowed with an on-line planning functionality, capable of on-the-fly orchestration of services with regard to a given query.

3. *Meta-Service layer:* this layer offers a set of general high-level facilities that are of special interest for human-agent systems and may be used when needed. The main functionalities provided are *agreement* capabilities to deal with conflicts inside the society; *human interaction* facilities which will try to maximize the immersion of humans in the system; service discovery and *context-aware* mechanisms allowing a transparent and integrated access to the required information; *semantic* interoperability facilities; and, *trust and reputation* models, which will employ probabilistic techniques and psychological and sociological theories to estimate the behaviour of an entity (either human or artificial) in a given context.

4. *Normative layer:* might be used by human-agent societies that require a regulatory framework for the coordination, communication, and interaction among different entities (humans or software agents). This layer incorporates mechanisms for specifying, adapting and enforcing organizational constraints (e.g., norms and protocols) that should govern the interactions of entities and coordinate the use of resources. From a technical view, these functionalities can be obtained using the THOMAS platform [11], which consists basically of a set of modular services that enable the development of agent-based organisations in open environments.

6   Conclusions

In this paper an analysis of the main open issues related with human-agent societies is presented. These systems are based on a new paradigm where the key is the immersion of the users in a complex environment that enables computation.

These kinds of systems can be supported by existing platforms, development methods and tools that are appropriated for open systems, which are populated by heterogeneous agents that can dynamically enter and leave the system at any time. But beyond these, it is essential to evolve them and enable the interoperability of agents, services and humans, all the entities together as a unique ecosystem.

In a first place, the essential parts that compose and give sense to these societies must be improved, such as semantics, norms, negotiation, reorganisation, argumentation, delegation and other concepts already mentioned. Moreover, SOC technologies should be easily integrated, creating complex behaviours by composing capacities modelled as services or information provided by different independent and possibly heterogeneous entities. Another challenge is to achieve a complete human-agent society that could be able to perceive and respond to the presence of individuals in a simple, non-intrusive and often invisible manner. Advanced data fusion algorithms and context aware system techniques will be an important area of work to reach such requirements.

It is important to highlight that the final goal is obtaining an intelligent computational system in which, when pervading the human space, computational agents and human users interact and coexist successfully. As presented in this paper, our proposal is a framework called iHAS. This framework offers a variety of facilities to satisfy all the special requirements of human-agent societies and to guide designers of such systems though the integral development of them.

Acknowledgments. Work partially supported by the Spanish Government through the projects OVAMAH (grant TIN2009-13839-C03-02; co-funded by Plan E), AT (grant CSD2007-0022; CONSOLIDER-INGENIO 2010) and iHAS (grant TIN2012-36586-C01/C02/C03).

References

1. Zambonelli, F., Jennings, N., Wooldridge, M.: Developing multiagent systems: The GAIA methodology. ACM Trans. on Soft. Eng. and Methodology 12, 317–370 (2003)
2. Argente, E., Julian, V., Botti, V.: Multi-Agent System Development based on Organizations. Electronic Notes in Theoretical Computer Science 150(3), 55–71 (2006)
3. Ferber, J., Gutknecht, O., Michel, F.: From Agents to Organizations: An Organizational View of Multi-agent Systems. In: Giorgini, P., Müller, J.P., Odell, J. (eds.) AOSE 2003. LNCS, vol. 2935, pp. 214–230. Springer, Heidelberg (2004)
4. Caire, G., et al.: Agent Oriented Analysis Using Message/UML. In: Wooldridge, M.J., Weiß, G., Ciancarini, P. (eds.) AOSE 2001. LNCS, vol. 2222, p. 119. Springer, Heidelberg (2002)
5. Juan, T., Pierce, A., Sterling, L.: Roadmap: Extending the Gaia methodology for complex open systems. In: Proc. AAMAS 2002, pp. 3–10 (2002)
6. Esteva, M., Rodríguez-Aguilar, J.-A., Sierra, C., Garcia, P., Arcos, J.L.: On the Formal Specification of Electronic Institutions. In: Sierra, C., Dignum, F.P.M. (eds.) AgentLink 2000. LNCS (LNAI), vol. 1991, pp. 126–147. Springer, Heidelberg (2001)
7. Noriega, P., Sierra, C.: Electronic institutions: Future trends and challenges. In: Klusch, M., Ossowski, S., Shehory, O. (eds.) CIA 2002. LNCS (LNAI), vol. 2446, pp. 14–17. Springer, Heidelberg (2002)
8. Dignum, V., Vázquez-Salceda, J., Dignum, F.: OMNI: Introducing Social Structure, Norms and Ontologies into Agent Organizations. In: Bordini, R.H., Dastani, M., Dix, J., El Fallah Seghrouchni, A. (eds.) PROMAS 2004. LNCS (LNAI), vol. 3346, pp. 181–198. Springer, Heidelberg (2005)

9. Hübner, J., Sichman, J., Boissier, O.: MOISE+: Towards a Structural, Functional and De-ontic Model for MAS Organizations. In: Proc. AAMAS, pp. 501–502 (2002)
10. Argente, E., Botti, V., Julian, V.: GORMAS: An organizational-oriented methodological guideline for open MAS. In: Gleizes, M.-P., Gomez-Sanz, J.J. (eds.) AOSE 2009. LNCS, vol. 6038, pp. 32–47. Springer, Heidelberg (2011)
11. Argente, E., Botti, V., Carrascosa, C., Giret, A., Julian, V., Rebollo, M.: An Abstract Ar-chitecture for Virtual Organizations: The THOMAS approach. Knowledge and Informa-tion Systems 29, 379–403 (2011)
12. Deloach, S.A., Oyenan, W.H., Matson, E.T.: A capabilities-based model for adaptive or-ganizations. Autonomous Agents and Multi-Agent Systems 16(1), 13–56 (2008)
13. Omicini, A., Ricci, A., Viroli, M.: Artifacts in the a&a meta-model for multi-agent sys-tems. Autonomous Agents and Multi-Agent Systems 17(3), 432–456 (2008)
14. Lopes Cardoso, H., Oliveira, E.: Social control in a normative framework: An adaptive de-terrence approach. Web Intelligence and Agent Systems 9, 363–375 (2011)
15. Centeno, R., Billhardt, H., Hermoso, R.: Persuading agents to act in the right way: An in-centive-based approach. Engineering Applications of Artificial Intelligence 26(1), 198–210 (2013)
16. Centeno, R., Billhardt, H., Hermoso, R., Ossowski, S.: Organising MAS: a formal model based on organisational mechanisms. In: Proceedings of the 2009 ACM symposium on Applied Computing, pp. 740–746 (2009)
17. Ossowski, S. (ed.): Agreement Technologies. Low, Governance and Technologies Series, vol. 8. Springer (2013)
18. Martin, D., et al.: OWL-S: Semantic Markup for Web Services, W3C Member Submission (2004), http://www.w3.org/Submission/OWL-S/
19. Roman, D., Lausen, H., Keller, U. (eds.): Web Service Modeling Ontology (WSMO). Technical report, WSMO Final Draft (2005), http://www.wsmo.org/TR/d2/v1.2/
20. Kopecky, J., Vitvar, T., Bournez, C., Farrell, J.: SAWSDL: Semantic Annotations for WSDL and XML Schema. IEEE Internet Computing 11(6) (2007)
21. Sheth, A., Gomadam, K., Lathem, J.: SA-REST: Semantically Interoperable and Easier-to-Use Services and Mashups. IEEE Internet Computing 11(6), 91–94 (2007)
22. Kopecky, J., Vitvar, Zaremba, M., Fensel, D.: WSMO-Lite: Lightweight Semantic De-scriptions for Services on the Web Full. In: Proceedings of 5th ECOWS, pp. 77–86 (2007)
23. Huhns, M., Singh, M., Burstein, M., Decker, K., Durfee, E., Finin, T., Gasser, L., Goradia, H., Jennings, N.R., Lakartaju, K., Nakashima, H., Parunak, V., Rosenschein, J., Ruvinsky, A., Sukthankar, G., Swarup, S., Sycara, K., Tambe, M., Wagner, T., Zavala, L.: Research directions for service-oriented multiagent systems. IEEE Internet Computing 9(6), 69–70 (2005)
24. Fernández, A., Ossowski, S.: A multiagent approach to the dynamic enactment of semantic transportation services. IEEE Transactions on Intelligent Transportation Systems 12(2), 333–342 (2011)
25. Fernández, A., Hayes, C., Loutas, N., Peristeras, V., Polleres, A., Tarabanis, K.: Closing the Service Discovery Gap by Collaborative Tagging and Clustering Techniques. In: 2nd International Joint Workshop on Service Matchmaking and Resource Retrieval in the Se-mantic Web (SMR2), Karlsruhe, Alemania (2008)
26. Cong, Z., Fernández, A.: Enabling Web Service Discovery in Heterogeneous Environ-ments. International Journal of Metadata, Semantics and Ontologies (in press)
27. Ehrig, M.: Ontology Alignment: Bridging the Semantic Gap. Springer, Heidelberg (2007)
28. Euzenat, J., Shvaiko, P.: Ontology matching. Springer, Heidelberg (2007)

29. Augusto, J.C.: Ambient Intelligence: the Confluence of Ubiquitous/Pervasive Computing and Artificial Intelligence. In: Schuster, A. (ed.) Intelligent Computing Everywhere. Springer (2007)

30. IST Advisory Group. The European Union report: Scenarios for Ambient Intelligence in 2010 (2001), `ftp://ftp.cordis.europa.eu/pub/ist/docs/istagscenarios2010.pdf`

31. Weiser, M.: The Computer for the 21st Century. Scientific American 265, 94–104 (1991)

32. Satyanarayanan, M.: Pervasive Computing: Vision and Challenges. IEEE Personal Communications 8(4), 10–17 (2001)

33. Ramos, C., Augusto, J.C., Shapiro, D.: Ambient Intelligence—the Next Step for Artificial Intelligence. IEEE Intelligent Systems 23, 15–18 (2008)

34. Want, R., Hopper, A., Falcao, V., Gibbons, J.: The Active Badge Location System. ACM Transactions on Information Systems 10(1), 91–102 (1992)

35. Skov, M., Hoegh, R.: Supporting information access in a hospital ward by a context-aware mobile electronic patient record. Journal of Perv. and Ubiq. Computing 10, 205–214 (2006)

36. Park, D., Hwang, S., Kim, A., Chang, B.: A Context-Aware Smart Tourist Guide Application for an Old Palace. In: Proc. of the 3rd International Conference on Convergence Information Technology, pp. 89–94 (2007)

37. Gu, T., Pung, H.K., Zhang, D.Q.: Towards an osgibased infrastructure for context-aware applications in smart homes. IEEE Pervasive Computing, 66–74 (2004)

38. Holvoet, T., Valckenaers, P.: Beliefs, desires and intentions through the environment. In: Proceedings of AAMAS 2006, pp. 1052–1054 (2006)

39. Schilit, B., Theimer, M.: Disseminating active map information to mobile hosts. IEEE Network 8(5), 22–32 (1994)

40. Pynadath, D.V., Scerri, P., Tambe, M.: Towards Adjustable Autonomy for the Real World. Journal of Artificial Intelligence Research 17, 171–228 (2002)

41. Dorais, G., Bonasso, R.P., Kortenkamp, D., Pell, B., Schreckenghost, D.: Adjustable autonomy for human-centered autonomous systems. Working notes of the Sixteenth International Joint Conference on Artificial Intelligence, Workshop on Adjustable Autonomy Systems, pp. 16–35 (1999)

42. Atencia, M., Schorlemmer, M.: An interaction-based approach to semantic alignment. Web Semantics: Science, Services and Agents on the World Wide Web 12-13, 131–147 (2012)

43. Tordai, A.: On Combining Alignment Techniques. Editorial Vrije Universiteit, Amsterdam (2012)

44. Koster, A., Schorlemmer, M., Sabater-Mir, J.: Engineering trust alignment: Theory, method and experimentation. Journal of Human-Computer Studies 70(6), 450–473 (2012)

45. Koster, A., Sabater-Mir, J., Schorlemmer, M.: Trust Alignment: A Sine Qua Non of Open Multi-agent Systems. In: Meersman, R., et al. (eds.) OTM 2011, Part I. LNCS, vol. 7044, pp. 182–199. Springer, Heidelberg (2011)

46. Abras, S., Ploix, S., Pesty, S., Jacomino, M.: A multi-agent home automation system for power management. In: Cetto, J.A., Ferrier, J.-L., Pereira, J.D., Filipe, J. (eds.) Informatics in Control Automation and Robotics. LNEE, vol. 15, pp. 59–68. Springer, Heidelberg (2008)

Using Natural Interfaces for Human-Agent Immersion

Angel Sanchis[1], Vicente Julián[1], Juan M. Corchado[2],
Holger Billhardt[3], and Carlos Carrascosa[1]

[1] Departamento de Sistemas Informáticos y Computación
Universitat Politècnica de València, Spain
[2] Department of Computer Science, University of Salamanca, Spain
[3] CETINIA, Universidad Rey Juan Carlos, Spain
angel2esoc@hotmail.com, {vinglada,carrasco}@dsic.upv.es,
corchado@usal.es, holger.billhardt@urjc.es

Abstract. Multi-agent technology allows the development of current AmI applications. Specifically, a multi-agent system allows the formation and management of applications where the main components can be humans and software agents interact and communicate with humans in order to help them in their daily activities. This kind of applications are what we call a *Human-Agent Society*, where agents provide services to humans or to other agents in an environment of whole integration. This paper presents a solution for the problem of human immersion presented in this kind of systems, providing the use of natural interfaces for the interaction among humans and software agents.

Keywords: Virtual Agents, Human-Agent Societies.

1 Introduction

Ambient Intelligence (AmI) imagines a future where technology surrounds the users [1], and helps them in their daily lives. The AmI scenarios described by the Information Society Technologies Advisory Group (ISTAG) have intelligent environments capable of recognizing and responding to the presence of different individuals in a simple, unobtrusive and often invisible way [5]. AmI is heavily based on the concept of Ubiquitous Computing (UC), introduced by Weiss in the 90s, which describes a world where a multitude of computational objects interact and communicate in order to help humans in daily activities [10]. The main goal of AmI systems is to be invisible, but very useful. This raises some requirements for AmI -based [9] systems. The technology must be transparent to users, services must be adapted to the context and user preferences and the applications must provide intuitive interfaces and must be friendly to users. This situation attributes to Intelligent Systems (IS) a key role in achieving the AmI goals [8]. AmI provides distributed complex problems by applying methodologies inspired by human techniques for solving problems. That is, to provide machine learning procedures, interaction protocols, distributed communication, coordination

J.M. Corchado et al. (Eds.): PAAMS 2014 Workshops, CCIS 430, pp. 358–367, 2014.
© Springer International Publishing Switzerland 2014

and cooperation and adaptive behavior models to the knowledge representation formalisms of AmI.

Recent trends in AmI, based on intelligent systems, have not had much success. There are two main reasons as the cause of this failure. For one side, intelligent systems have not reached the maturity level of other information technologies, and for a long time, they have forgotten traditional industry [6]. On the other hand, it is required an interdisciplinary perspective, which is difficult, since a considerable amount of resources (scientific, economic and human) would be required.

Agent technology, although still immature in some ways, allows the development of systems that support the requirements of AmI applications. Specifically it allows the formation and management of systems where the main components can be humans and software agents providing services to humans or other agents in an environment of whole integration. This kind of applications are what we call a *Human-Agent Society*, which can be defined as a computing paradigm in which the traditional notion of application disappears. Rather than developing software applications that accomplish computational tasks for specific purposes, this paradigm is based on an immersion of the users in a complex environment that enables computation.

This paper deeps in the immersion problem of this kind of systems providing the use of natural interfaces for the interaction among humans and software agents. When a human is completely immersed into a system of this kind, the human can interact with the system using natural gestures. Moreover, agents inserted in the system can learn about human actions adapting its behaviors and taking decisions about future situations. Examples of these systems can be domotic scenarios, production lines in an industry, entertainment industry, ... where humans interact with the rest of components only moving, for example, their arms or hands. In order to show this, the paper presents a proof of concept of this kind of immersion.

The rest of the document is structured as follows. Section 2 describes what we have called *Human-Agent Societies*. Next, in Section 3, we describe JGOMAS, a framework for 3D simulated worlds where we situate our proposal. After that, Section 4 presents the proposal we have made for a *Human-Agent Society* proof of concept. Finally, the conclusions of this paper are commented in Section 5.

2   Human-Agent Societies

With the term Human-Agent Society (HAS) we refer to a computing paradigm in which the traditional notion of application disappears. Rather than developing software applications that accomplish computational tasks for specific purposes, this paradigm is based on an immersion of the users in a complex environment that enables computation. The environment itself is populated by computational entities with different capacities and intellectual properties, ranging from simple devices that offer specific capacities or rudimentary information, like screens or sensors, to autonomous artificial agents that provide high level services and are able to engage in complex interaction protocols. This view of a system is closely related with the development of AmI applications.

When defining a HAS, it can be seen as the next evolution of Multi-agent Systems, where there is an immersion at two levels of agents and humans respectively. Thus, in the MAS level, humans are situated and integrated into the system in such a way that they appear as agents for the other agents. Whereas in the human level (from the perspective of humans) interaction is performed with objects and actions a person is accustomed. This is because the MAS is modeled as an ubiquitous system. Thus, integration of both types of features is achieved allowing a maximum level of immersion of users in the MAS, minimizing the level of difficulty of the interaction. Moreover, considering all this, the satisfaction level of the user is maximized.

The overall objective of this work is to deep in the development of Human-Agent Societies through the use of natural interfaces that allow immersion in the two previously mentioned levels.

The ability of a *Human-Agent Society* to establish connecting links and achieve goals together in a dynamic environment, allows to develop flexible and dynamic systems where individuals, by themselves, are unable to achieve the goals that emerge in a society. It is necessary to provide mechanisms and interfaces for such double immersion at MAS. To achieve this extension is necessary to have information based on the context that allows to perform a more realistic integration of the human situation, including possible actions and behaviors that are part of a human society. Furthermore, at human level, extension mechanisms should be raised allowing access to agent-based systems in an ubiquitous way.

3   JGOMAS

JGOMAS[1] [2] [4] (acronym for *Game Oriented Multi-Agent System* based on *JADE*) is a framework that develops and executes agents in 3D simulated worlds. In this framework, the social interaction to simulate is based on the rules of a "Capture the Flag" type of game: agents belong to one of two teams that compete to capture the opponent's flag. This game modality has become a standard that is included in almost all multiplayer games that have appeared since Quake.

It is very easy and intuitive to apply MAS to games of this type because each soldier can be viewed as an agent. Moreover, agents on a team must cooperate with each other to achieve the team's objective, thus competing with the other team. In fact, it is not uncommon to find applications of agent technology to the game field in general (e.g., the board game developed by Offerman et al. [7]) and to Capture the Flag in particular.

The framework allows designers to incorporate intelligence in agents that interact in a VE and to follow the evolution of these agents through an unlimited number of visualization modules in a distributed fashion.

In summary, JGOMAS is composed of two subsystems (see Figure 1):

---

[1] http://jgomas.gti-ia.dsic.upv.es

- JGOMAS MAS: This subsystem works on a JADE[2] platform. There are two different kinds of agents: Manager Agents (that control the game's logic, and interface with visualizers) and Player Agents (one for each member of each team). Player Agents can play one of three roles: soldier, medic or field operations, each of which is provided with a set of basic behaviors. JGOMAS supports interactions between Manager Agents (virtual world) and Player Agents, so that it abstracts these peculiarities to the users.
- Render Engine (RE): The RE is a 3D multi-platform graphic engine that allows users to view the evolution of JGOMAS agents in the VE, to observe how the components of each team behave and the outcome of the game. More specifically, each RE provides a single window to observe the VE containing the agents. It is also possible to have different RE configurations to satisfy different visualization needs, as explained in [3].

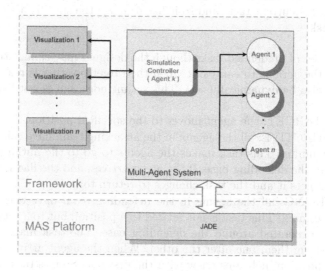

Fig. 1. JGOMAS architecture overview

3.1 Multi-agent System

There exists two main classes of agents defined in JGOMAS: the *simulation controller* and *inhabitant agents* (as *player* agents).

Simulation controller, that is also called *Manager Agent*, is in charge of keeping the virtual environment's data, maintaining the consistency at any time, along with controlling the rules of the game. On the other hand, the *inhabitant agents* simulate players (humans, animals, etc.) situated in the virtual world. These agents are moving, looking, hearing, etc... in the virtual scenario. Furthermore, they can comunicate each other in order to achieve their goals. Thus, an *inhabitant agent* interacts with other *inhabitant agents* and with the scenario. As a

---

[2] http://jade.tilab.com/

result, the virtual world can be changed. And the *simulation controller* generate events for those *inhabitant agents* involved in the changes.

The way an *inhabitant agent* achieves a goal is carrying out tasks. A *Task* is defined as something to carry out in an specific position in the virtual environment. So, the three main states of an *inhabitant agent* are:

- Standing: the agent has no current task to do, so he is waiting to do something.
- Go To Target: the agent has one current task that has been selected from its task list (according to tasks priority). This task has to be carried out in a different position to the one the agent is in, so it is moving to this place. While the agent is moving, it may encounter enemy agents, and react to them (aiming and shooting them).
- Perform Target Reached: the agent has reached the position where he has to carry out his current task, and so it has to make the specific actions related to the task.

There is a set of predefined tasks though the designer may change this set and / or change the actions to carry out when the target position is reached (tasks priority can also be dynamically set). This set includes, but is not limited to:

- GO TO TARGET: the agent moves to the specified position.
- GET OBJECTIVE: all the agents in the attacking team have this task since game beginning. This task makes the agents to go to the initial position of the flag in the defending base. If the agent arrives, and the flag is still there, the agent gets it and the task changes to return to base.
- PATROLLING: all the agents in the defending team have this task since game beginning. This task is not related to a position but to a set of random positions generated around the defending base. The task makes the agent to go visiting them one after the other. When the agent arrives to the last random position, it begins anew with the first one. So this task never ends, and the agent is patrolling defending its base and the flag.

There is also some tasks related to the special abilities of some of the roles agents may play in the game.

There are three different roles for *inhabitant agents* (though the user may add more if he wants it): medic, fieldops and soldier. The medic can create *medic packs* that allow to recuperate health to any *inhabitant agent* by consuming them. In the same way, the fieldops can create *ammo packs* that allow to recuperate ammo to any *inhabitant agent* by consuming them. The special ability of the soldier is that he is very skilled at shooting and he makes more damage than the rest. Any agent registers a service to offer to the other agents in his team his abilities. And each one of these abilities have a task related to carry them out. So, there exist a *GIVE MEDIC PACKS* task, a *GIVE AMMO PACKS* task and a *GIVE BACKUP* task (this last one for the soldier, to go to help their teammates).

The JGOMAS package includes the multi-agent platform, the RE, maps, documentation and a sample that is ready to use. Fig. 2 shows an execution example of this package, with JADE GUI, text console, and some instances of the RE.

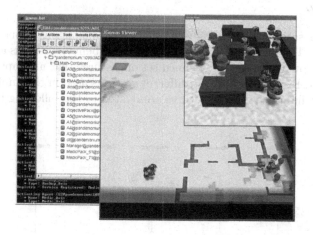

Fig. 2. JGOMAS execution example

4   HAS Case Study

4.1   Design

The present proposal supposes a proof of concept about a *Human-Agent Society*, that is, a system with a double immersion in it. The user is immersed in the system interacting with it by means of a natural interface, and the agents in the system see the user as one of them, interacting with him in the same way.

So, we have added a user to the JGOMAS system as one more of the agents that interacts with the rest of the system (environment –Manager Agent–, and the rest of agents –of their same team and of the other team–).

To have the human user immersed in the multi-agent system we have used a natural interface that allows the user to easily interact with the system. This natural interface is provided through the *Kinect*[3] sensor device.

The Kinect sensor is composed of the following elements:

- an IR emitter and an IR depth sensor: The first one emits a pattern of points over the elements in front of the sensor through a laser diode. The reflex pattern is captured by the IR depth sensor and it is sent to an inner chip to be compared with an original pattern. The result of this comparison is the depth information.
- A color sensor: It is a RGB camera with a resolution of 640x480 px at 30fps.

---

[3] Kinect For Windows: http://www.microsoft.com/en-us/kinectforwindows/

– An inclination motor: It allows an inclination of 27 degrees (positive or negative) with respect to the horizontal.
– A multi-array microphone: It is a set of four microphones allowing the sensor to capture audio and to localize the sound sources. It generates 16 bit audio to 16 khz.

The user is seen in the MAS as any other agent, belonging to one of the competing teams. The user may change the predefined behaviour of his avatar in the virtual world by means of a pre-defined set of gestures that are captured by the Kinect sensor. Figure 3 details the different gestures used in the implementation of the Kinect interface. These gestures are related to the following behaviours:

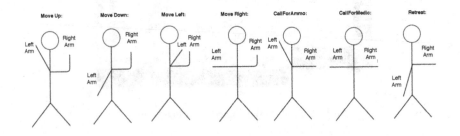

Fig. 3. Kindle gestures used

– Move Up: the user agent is moved up in the virtual environment map.
– Move Down: the user agent is moved down in the virtual environment map.
– Move Left: the user agent is moved left in the virtual environment map.
– Move Right: the user agent is moved right in the virtual environment map.
– CallForAmmo: the user agent sends a message to all living agents in his team playing the field operations rol asking for ammo packs.
– CallForMedic: the user agent sends a message to all living agents in his team playing the medic rol asking for medic packs.
– Retreat: the user agent sends a message to all living agents in his team ordering them to retreat to their base.

Figure 4 shows how the JGOMAS architecture is left now, where the *User Agent* represents the agent that is able to receive orders from the user, having as an input mechanism the *Kinect*.

User gestures are translated into messages sent through a TCP-IP connection to the *User Agent*. These messages are the most prioritary messages that this agent may receive. *User Agent* translates them to tasks and messages to other agents. Move Up, Move Down, Move Left and Move Right orders provoke the user agent to add a priority *Go To Target* task with the corresponding position. The rest of the orders, as have been commented above, provoke the agent to send different messages to their teammates.

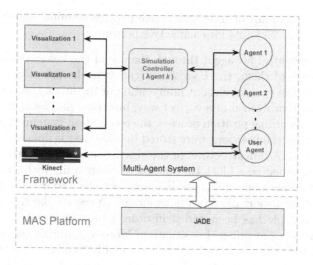

Fig. 4. JGOMAS extended architecture

4.2 Evaluation

The proposal has been implemented over an scenario example in order to validate the whole immersion of the users and software agents. To do this, the scenario is formed by two human players which are located in different rooms playing the same JGOMAS game each one in a different team. Moreover, the game includes nine more software agents playing in each team. These agents have been implemented in JADE (see figure 5).

As before commented, each human player interacts with the system through a Kinect sensor and a JADE agent (User Agent) which represents the human in the virtual scenario. The Kinect sensor is controlled through a driver implemented in C# that must take into account the main technical limitations of the sensor, which are:

- The Horizontal field of view is only a maximum of 57 degrees.
- The Vertical field of view is a maximum of 43 degrees.
- There is a low resolution in the image depth. The detection of small elements is worse when increasing distance.
- There is a range of + - 27 degrees of vertical tilt .
- Regarding depth sensitivity there are two operating modes:

  - In normal mode, the range of distances for the optimal operation of the sensor varies from 0.8m to 4m , and in the range of 4 -8m its performance degrades. Beyond 8m and closer than 0.4m the data has no validity.
  - In the operating mode called *near*, the distance for an optimum performance is reduced to 0.4 m, having an optimal range of 0.4- 3m, being unreliable data for 3 -8m and without any validity in 0-0.4m and beyond 8m.

– It is able to monitor at most two active persons simultaneously, being able to follow up to 20 joints for each active person.

Humans can control his agent through the use of the before commented gestures. In absence of them, the User Agent can take the initiative and interact with the rest of the system without intervention of the human. After several executions the system worked in a correct way, but some problems were detected. Regarding the recording position process, the recognition system which has been used requires that the positions were stored in a file that is uploaded to a serializable classes in a certain structure. In the absence of any tool to record gestures it has been implemented a block that allows to create a file with the gestures to be recognized for each one of the possible actions to be performed. Occasionally, the system suffered short disconnections forcing to restart the Kinect driver. A reconnection module has been added in order to automatically manage these short disconnections avoiding this situation. Moreover, during the development was observed that the number of events launched by the Kinect sensor was too low to properly recognize gestures. To solve this problem different versions of the Kinect for Windows controller were tested over different platforms without getting improvements. Finally, it was decided to limit the number of actions taken by the Kinect taking into account at any time only one active sensor (voice, rgb, or depth).

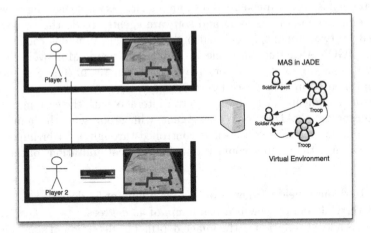

Fig. 5. Real implementation test

5   Conclusions

This work presents the problem of the double immersion in Human-Agent Societies, where human and agents must coexist in a framework of maximum integration. In order to achieve this kind of immersion, a case study has been developed over the JGOMAS framework using natural interfaces allowing an easy integration of the human in the MAS. Future work in this research area will focus on developing a learning module which will allow to modelize the human behavior. This learning mechanism can be seen as a training process allowing software agents to anticipate to human actions. This will allow humans to minimize the number of gestures needed to react in front of typical situations.

Acknowledgments. This work was supported by the Spanish government grant MINECO/FEDER TIN2012-36586-C03-01,

References

1. Augusto, J.: Ambient Intelligence: the Confluence of Ubiquitous/Pervasive Computing and Artificial Intelligence. Intelligent Computing Everywhere (2007)
2. Barella, A., Carrascosa, C., Botti, V.: Agent Architectures for Intelligent Virtual Environments. In: 2007 IEEE/WIC/ACM International Conference on Intelligent Agent Technology, pp. 532–535. IEEE (2007)
3. Barella, A., Mart, M., Carrascosa, C., Botti, V.: Multi-Agent Systems applied to Virtual Environments: a Case Study. In: ACM Symposium on Virtual Reality Software and Technology, pp. 237–238. ACM SIGGRAPH (2007)
4. Barella, A., Valero, S., Carrascosa, C.: JGOMAS: New Approach to AI Teaching. IEEE Transactions on Education 52(2), 228–235 (2009)
5. Group, I.A.: The European Union report: Scenarios for Ambient Intelligence in 2010 (2001),
   ftp://ftp.cordis.europa.eu/pub/ist/docs/istagscenarios2010.pdf
6. Hendler, J.: Where Are All the Intelligent Agents? IEEE Intelligent Systems 22, 2–3 (2007)
7. Offermann, S., Ortmann, J., Reese, C.: Agent based settler game (2005),
   http://x-opennet.org/netdemo/Demos2005/aamas2005/_netdemo/_settler.pdf,
   part of NETDEMO, demonstration at the international conference on Autonomous Agents and Multi Agent Systems, AAMAS 2005
8. Ramos, C., Augusto, J., Shapiro, D.: Ambient Intelligence?the Next Step for Artificial Intelligence. IEEE Intelligent Systems 23, 15–18 (2008)
9. Satyanarayanan, M.: Pervasive Computing: Vision and Challenges. IEEE Personal Communications 8(4), 10–17 (2001)
10. Weiser, M.: The Computer for the 21st Century. Scientific American 265, 94–104 (1991)

Understanding Decision Quality through Satisfaction

João Carneiro[1], Ricardo Santos[1,2], Goreti Marreiros[1], and Paulo Novais[3]

[1] GECAD – Knowledge Engineering and Decision Support Group, Institute of Engineering – Polytechnic of Porto, Porto, Portugal
{jomrc,mgt}@isep.ipp.pt
[2] CIICESI, School of Technology and Management of Felgueiras – Polytechnic of Porto, Felgueiras, Portugal
rjs@estgf.ipp.pt
[3] CCTC – Computer Science and Technology Center, at University of Minho, Braga, Portugal
pjon@di.uminho.pt

Abstract. One of the most important factors to determine the success of an organization is the quality of decisions made. In order to improve the decisions taken and to strengthen the competitiveness of organizations, systems such as Group Decision Support Systems (GDSSs) have been strongly developed and studied in recent decades. The amount of GDSSs incorporating automatic negotiation mechanisms, such as argumentation, is increasing nowadays. The evaluation of these mechanisms and the understanding of their real benefits for the organizations is still a hard challenge. In this article, we propose a model that allows a GDSS to measure the participant's satisfaction with the decision, considering aspects such as problem evaluation, personality, emotions and expectations. This model is intended to enable the understanding of the decision's quality achieved with an argumentation system and to evaluate its capability to potentiate the decision's quality. The proposed model validates all the assumptions found in the literature regarding the participant's satisfaction.

Keywords: Decision Satisfaction, Group Decision Support Systems, Outcomes, Affective Computing, Automatic Negotiation, Argumentation.

1 Introduction

Nowadays the decisions made by managers and executives are mostly performed in groups. Thereby, group decision-making is a process in which a group of people, called participants, act collectively analyzing a set of variables, considering and evaluating the available alternatives in order to select one or more solutions. The number of participants involved in the process is variable and all of them may be either at the same place at the same time or geographically dispersed at different times [1].

It is a known fact that the amount of hours a decision-maker spends in a meeting is not mostly used to make decisions. The time spent on things like social issues, is responsible for consuming the majority of the time of a process [2-4].

Aiming to improve the decision quality and to facilitate its making in certain scenarios GDSSs have been subject of studies in the last decades. One of the great

J.M. Corchado et al. (Eds.): PAAMS 2014 Workshops, CCIS 430, pp. 368–377, 2014.

problems associated to the use of GDSSs is the difficulty to understand the decision makers' satisfaction with the decision made, problem that also exists in decision processes that do not use a GDSS. Being satisfaction a strong indicator of the taken decision quality in the perspective of each participant, its study is very relevant. Higgins [5] says that "a good decision has high outcome benefits (it is worthwhile) and low outcome costs (it is worth it)", and that "independent of outcomes or value from worth, people experience a regulatory fit when they use goal pursuit means that fit their regulatory orientation, and this regulatory fit increases the value of what they are doing". With this, it is possible to understand that the decision quality in the perspective of each participant is related to what he considers relevant. Satisfaction is therefore a strong indicator, not only of the results, but also of the whole decision process. When someone is questioned about the quality of a decision, the answer does not reflect only the assessment of outcomes, but also, even unconsciously; it includes the evaluation process necessary to reach the decision. To understand how suitable a decision is, it is necessary to understand and analyze the means to reach that decision [6][7]. Thus, one should give prominence to the process, when drawing conclusions about the results.

There is a great variety of factors responsible for affecting the satisfaction of a decision-making element with the decision made in a meeting: emotional variables (affective components) [8-10], the process [11][12], the outcomes [5], the factors that affect the situation [13] and expectations [14][15].

Briggs et al. [16] presented a theory of meeting satisfaction, which explains the causes of conflicting research results on meeting satisfaction, as these results have never been fully explained in the Group Support Systems literature. The authors proposed and tested the Satisfaction Attainment Theory (SAT) – a causal model of meeting satisfaction.

Tian et al. [17] conducted a study on how to measure satisfaction based on the emotional space. The results of satisfaction obtained sought to understand the users' acceptance for a product by testing usability.

In their work, Souren et al. [18] explore how the performance of a GDSS affects the different dimensions of satisfaction. They focus on three indicators of group performance, namely: the decision time, the efficiency in decision-making and the number of iterations in the group decision-making process.

The goal of this paper is enable the understanding of the decision's quality achieved with an argumentation system and to evaluate its capability to potentiate the decision's quality. Aiming to contemplate different approaches from researchers of a wide range of areas in this thematic (computer sciences, psychology, economy, etc.), a theoretical-based model is presented, seeking to include in the satisfaction analysis all the necessary variables.

The rest of the paper is organized as follows: in the next section is discussed the decision satisfaction thematic and how satisfaction emerges and is related in a decision environment. Section 3 presents the proposed model. Section 4 discusses the relationship between all the points that compose the model and how they measure the participant's satisfaction with the decision. Finally, some conclusions are taken in section 5, along with the work to be done hereafter.

2   Decision Satisfaction

The satisfaction with a decision resulting from a decision process is something that needs a complex analysis and involves multiple variables. Obviously the satisfaction is related to what we think a good decision is. But what is a good decision? As previously referred, in the common sense a decision is considered good because of the analogy made with the obtained results.

Assumption 1: Decision satisfaction is related with the decision results.

However, psychologically, the results are not enough to make a participant consider a decision as good. Higgins [5] says that "psychologically, then, a decision is perceived as good when its expected value or utility of outcomes is judged to be more beneficial than the alternatives."

Assumption 2: Evaluation of each alternative and comparison between them influences satisfaction.

"The costs of attaining the outcomes can also influence whether a decision is perceived as good. The outcome benefits have to be weighed against the costs of attaining the outcomes. The costs include not only the goods or services one must give in exchange for receiving the benefits but also the costs of the decision-making process itself. The decision-making process that would optimize outcomes might not be used because the costs in cognitive effort or time are too high" [5].

Assumption 3: The process necessary to reach a decision influences satisfaction.

Therefore, it is clear that there is much more than knowing whether the chosen alternative was the participant's favorite in order to evaluate his satisfaction with the decision. It has been suggested that a purely cognitive approach may be inadequate in modeling satisfaction ratings, so it is particularly important to include emotional variables [8-10]. The research that has been made in the field of satisfaction has recognized that there is a need to incorporate the emotional and affective components in regulating consumer's satisfaction [19].

Assumption 4: Emotional and affective components should be included to understand real satisfaction with the decision.

Therefore, it is not only the final results or the decisions made that determine the quality and the satisfaction of the decision. In his work, Higgins says: "We are all familiar with the idea expressed in the maxim of the late-19th-century British statesman John Morley, "It is not enough to do good; one must do it the right way," or the coaching classic, "What counts is not whether you win or lose but how you play the game." Such maxims reflect a moral position: Achievements should be evaluated not only in terms of outcomes but also in terms of the means by which they were attained.

"The ends do not justify the means.""" [5]. Using the reasoning present in this approach and the moral objective of these famous maxims, the relevance of the process in performing a certain action is easily understood. We can also conclude that the impact of the decision-making process can drastically change the participant's satisfaction regardless of the results. Higgins also refers that "this insight concerns how the goodness of a decision depends not only on its relation to ends or outcomes but also on whether the means used to make it were suitable. Suitability here refers only to what is morally proper. By considering proper the more general meaning of suitable as "fit", a new perspective on what makes good decisions good is possible" [5].

Consciously or not, people create expectations on (almost) everything. The relationship between expectations and the satisfaction is rather obvious. For instance, if someone's life goal is to have a yacht, but the expectations on the possibility to get it are extremely low, the fact of not getting the yacht will never have a notorious negative impact. But if someone has the objective to go on vacations next year and if the expectations for that to happen are really high, if that does not happen there will be a very strong negative impact. The same happens in opposite situations. According to assimilation theory [14], consumers experience a psychological conflict if they perceive a discrepancy between their expectations and their perception of the consumption experience [15]. Moreover, the nature of the expectation-satisfaction relationship may depend on several contextual and behavioral factors. So, users' expectations may have a different impact on the satisfaction formation within particular contexts. Expectations may even be more important when they are unambiguous [20], the product performance is ambiguous [21][22] and/or the consumer is well experienced [23].

Assumption 5: Decision makers create expectations. The expectations are created about everything that is undefined or is going to happen (process that leads to a decision and outcomes).

The consideration of several factors is therefore necessary to obtain a correct approach in the satisfaction analysis of a decision-maker regarding the decision made. The studies addressed in this section show the importance of analyzing the whole decision-making process, and the whole set of actions that involve and influence the participant during the process. We also verified that it is necessary to analyze a set of emotional factors in that process, and that emotional changes mean situations that affect the participant. It is obvious that this brings new challenges, such as to better know the participant to better understand the impact of each situation in each kind of person.

3   Proposed Model

In this section, we explain the proposed model and how all the points of the model are connected. Furthermore, while we are explaining the model we do the bridge between the points of the model and the assumptions defined before.

Knowing the importance of the process in the satisfaction analysis, all the analysis that purely stress the analysis of the results fall down. In addition, to study the process we cannot focus only on a cognitive approach. Bailey and Pearson [13] agreed that satisfaction in a given situation is the sum of one's feelings or attitudes toward a variety of factors affecting that situation. By creating this model we tried to find the points that can help measure satisfaction without the need to use the final questionnaires the participants usually have to answer. Our goal is to manipulate certain data, which at the end allows the system itself to evaluate the status of the participants' satisfaction with the decision. Therefore, to analyze the participants' satisfaction with the decision it is important to consider the chosen alternative, his expectations related to the decision and to the process, his personality, and his emotional changes.

3.1   Point 1 – Satisfaction Concerning the Chosen Alternative

According to the literature the perception of the decisions' quality is related to the advantages that the participant identifies in that alternative, comparing it against the others. Thus, whereas the preferred alternative is the best in the participants' perspective, the distance between the preferred alternative and the chosen one means a loss of the participants' satisfaction regarding the decision. The loss of satisfaction comprises the difference in the assessment made by the participant for each of the alternatives, as well as what the participant did not achieve with the final decision.

There are five different scenarios that may occur in a meeting, affecting the satisfaction differently:

1. The alternative chosen by the decision-makers is the one chosen as the preferred by the participant. At this point, his satisfaction is related to the assessment he makes on this alternative (Do not forget that it may be the preferred one and not being in anyway the alternative he finds brilliant. The preferred alternative may be one that was not even an option to choose from).
2. The participant starts the meeting with a preference of an alternative, he does not change his opinion during the process, but at the end the chosen alternative will always be one he never took into consideration.
3. The participant may start the meeting with a preference on an alternative and later switch to another one. However, the alternative chosen by the decision-makers ends up being the one he initially chose.
4. The participant may start the meeting with a preference on an alternative and later switch it to another one that eventually will be chosen.
5. The participant starts the meeting with a preference on an alternative, he changes his mind during the process, but at the end the chosen alternative will always be one that he never took into consideration.

This first point of the model intends to satisfy the argument presented in assumption number 2. The usual approach in this situation is taking only into consideration the evaluation done by the participant (decision maker) to the alternative chosen by the group, but as we could verify in the literature this isn't enough. The idea of this point is to understand the satisfaction in terms of alternatives evaluation but also to contemplate a little bit of the assumption number 3. First, it is important the participant evaluates all the alternatives so we can "evaluate each alternative and compare them" (assumption 2), second, it is also very important to understand in what terms the evaluation occurred (assumption 3).

3.2   Point 2 – Participants' Expectations According to the Decision and Process

As we verified in assumption 5 is important to know the participants' expectations according to some issues, in order to have a more accurate perception of the satisfaction, so we think it is important to study the participants' expectations on the following topics:

6. Complexity of the meeting: The participant should be questioned about how he thinks the meeting will be held, in order to reflect on whether he thinks it will have many conflicts and if the understanding among the participants will be problematic. And so, the following question can be asked: "Will this meeting be problematic?"

1. Probability of the participant's preferred alternative to be chosen: Understanding the expectations regarding the probability of the participant's preferred alternative to be chosen. "How likely you think your preferred alternative will be chosen?"

These two topics are the ones we consider most relevant for analyzing the expectations due to the impact the process and the results have on the participant, as previously stated. Besides that, these two topics are easier for the participant to classify regarding its expectations.

There are three different types of impact on satisfaction for each suggested topic:

- Positive Impact: When the final results exceed the expectations.
- Negative Impact: When the expectations are higher than the results achieved.
- Without Impact: When the expectations are achieved.

3.3   Point 3 – Factor Concerning the Personality

The personality is a concept that cannot be briefly defined, because it has a different meaning according to some psychologists who study it. Although most of them would agree that the field of personality is the study of how individuals differ from each other, psychologists would differ about the best way to conceptualize these types of differences [24]. The fact that people differ in their ideas and attitudes, makes them react differently to the factors they are exposed to. Recently, satisfaction is being studied regarding the most different scenarios according to the persons' personality. For instance, Shiammack et al. [25] conducted a study on two factors of The Big Five that contribute to life satisfaction: the Neuroticism and the Extraversion. Another study was conducted by Timothy et al. [26], where they tried to establish a correlation between the values of each type of personality of The Big Five and Job satisfaction.

Knowing that the personality of each one of us influences satisfaction, we think it is relevant to take into account the personality on our analytical model of satisfaction. At this point, we can't do any kind of considerations on how each personality type lives the satisfaction in this context. Anyway, this point remains open because we find it relevant. This point also will helps in work better the assumption 4.

3.4   Point 4 – Emotional Changes

Knowing the importance of the decision-making process, and to make conclusions about the participants' satisfaction regarding decision-making, it is necessary to understand what happens during the process. As mentioned before, it is important to include in the satisfaction analysis affective and emotional components [8-10][19].

Having said this, we want to include, at this point, the analysis of generated emotions and to know how they can change the participants' mood. There are two important points to be studied:

1. The sum of emotional spaces that exceed positively or negatively the participant's normal state: it is thus possible to measure the emotional cost that the meeting had on the participant;
2. The participant's mood at the end of the meeting.

4   Measure the Result of the Satisfaction Using the Model

To measure the output of each one of the points in the model we must define how they are related. It is considered that the first issue of Point 2 (complexity of the meeting) is strongly related to Point 4 (emotional changes), while the second issue of Point 2 (probability of the participant's preferred alternative to be chosen) is strongly related to Point 1 (satisfaction with the alternative chosen by the group). So the Point 2 (expectations) will not work isolated, but it will influence the results of the other two points.

The expectations will change the values for Point 1 and Point 4 through a particular impact. The impact causes an expectation that is obviously not always the same. Even knowing the impact that causes the expectation is positive, negative or neutral, it is necessary to quantify that impact.

Beyond expectations, Points 3 and 4 will also have an impact on Point 1. This is because it is considered that the satisfaction about something always gets related to the evaluation made (the choice of the service, product, etc.). After this evaluation, there are other factors, such as expectations and the process, that change satisfaction. Thus, in this case, the Point 1 will be the analysis performed by a human being, while the other points, according to the context, will affect or not (positively or negatively) the satisfaction.

To make this clearer, Fig. 1 illustrates the impact of each point of the model in the process of measuring satisfaction. At the moment this is a preliminary process that intends to show how everything fits together from a theoretical point of view.

Initially, satisfaction is calculated taking into account the alternative chosen by the group (Point 1) and the emotional changes (Point 4) with the impacts caused by the expectations. After the values of these two points have been recalculated, the final values for each point are obtained for the calculation of satisfaction. Emotional changes, as well as personality, will also have an impact on the participant's satisfaction with the option chosen by the group.

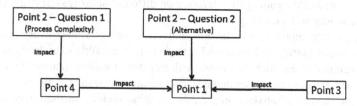

Fig. 1. Impact caused by each of the points of the model

The use of the personality in the final calculation may not exist directly. This happens for example when we are dealing with a multi-agent system in which the arguments used by the agents are according to the identified personalities. This will generate emotions and the change of mood regarding the personality. Thus, Point 3 is not covered in the final formula despite being covered by the system indirectly.

The Fig. 2 shows how every points fix to each other and how they work together to turn this model possible.

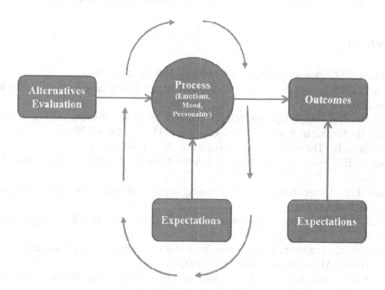

Fig. 2. Proposed Model

5 Conclusions and Future Work

Several concepts of satisfaction and the existing models to assess satisfaction were presented. Furthermore, this paper proposed a whole new model which pretends the assessment of the participants' satisfaction in a meeting, supported by a GDSS. We believe that the proposed model allows the attainment of a large amount of useful and valuable information. The points presented in proposed model try to cover every assumption created after reading the literature on different areas (psychology, computer science, economy and sociology).

This is the first model of satisfaction analysis, which considers every point found as relevant in the literature. This model intends to turn possible to understand how the different automatic negotiation models enhance the decision quality. Through this model it will be possible to evaluate and compare the results between the several models, and maximize satisfaction, i.e., the decision quality, in the future automatic negotiation models, as the most important point in the context of group decision.

As future work, first we will turn this (preliminary) model mathematical and after we will conduct a case study with real people, in partnership with psychologists. With that work, we also intend to make the model assertive by the possible improvements that might result after analyzing and studying the collected data.

Acknowledgements. This work is supported by FEDER Funds through the "Programa Operacional Factores de Competitividade - COMPETE" program and by National Funds through FCT "Fundação para a Ciência e a Tecnologia" under the project: FCOMP-01-0124-FEDER-PEst-OE/EEI/UI0760/2011 and SFRH/BD/89697/2012.

References

1. Luthans, F.: Organizational behavior. McGraw-Hill, Boston (2005)
2. Argyris, C., Schon, D.A.: Theory in practice: Increasing professional effectiveness. Jossey-Bass (1974)
3. Hoffman, L.R.: Applying experimental research on group problem solving to organizations. The Journal of Applied Behavioral Science 15, 375–391 (1979)
4. Mintzberg, H.: The nature of managerial work, New York (1973)
5. Higgins, E.T.: Making a good decision: value from fit. American Psychologist 55, 1217 (2000)
6. Beach, L.R.: Image theory: Decision making in personal and organizational contexts. Wiley, Chichester (1990)
7. March, J.G.: Primer on decision making: How decisions happen. SimonandSchuster. com (1994)
8. Liljander, V., Strandvik, T.: Emotions in service satisfaction. International Journal of Service Industry Management 8, 148–169 (1997)
9. Oliver, R.L., Rust, R.T., Varki, S.: Customer delight: foundations, findings, and managerial insight. Journal of Retailing 73, 311–336 (1997)

10. Wirtz, J., Bateson, J.E.: Consumer satisfaction with services: integrating the environment perspective in services marketing into the traditional disconfirmation paradigm. Journal of Business Research 44, 55–66 (1999)
11. Simon, H.A.: A behavioral model of rational choice. The Quarterly Journal of Economics 69, 99–118 (1955)
12. Simon, H.A.: Motivational and emotional controls of cognition. Psychological Review 74, 29 (1967)
13. Bailey, J.E., Pearson, S.W.: Development of a tool for measuring and analyzing computer user satisfaction. Management Science 29, 530–545 (1983)
14. Sherif, M., Hovland, C.I.: Social judgment: Assimilation and contrast effects in communication and attitude change (1961)
15. Rodríguez del Bosque, I.A., San Martín, H., Collado, J.: The role of expectations in the consumer satisfaction formation process: Empirical evidence in the travel agency sector. Tourism Management 27, 410–419 (2006)
16. Briggs, R.O., de Vreede, G.-J., Reinig, B.A.: A theory and measurement of meeting satisfaction. In: Proceedings of the 36th Annual Hawaii International Conference on System Sciences, p. 8. IEEE (2003)
17. Tian, X., Hou, W., Yuan, K.: A study on the method of satisfaction measurement based on emotion space. In: 9th International Conference on Computer-Aided Industrial Design and Conceptual Design, CAID/CD 2008, pp. 39–43. IEEE (2008)
18. Paul, S., Seetharaman, P., Ramamurthy, K.: User satisfaction with system, decision process, and outcome in GDSS based meeting: an experimental investigation. In: Proceedings of the 37th Annual Hawaii International Conference on System Sciences (HICSS 2004)-Track 1, vol. 1, pp. 10037–10032. IEEE Computer Society (2004)
19. Wirtz, J., Mattila, A.S., Tan, R.L.: The moderating role of target-arousal on the impact of affect on satisfaction—an examination in the context of service experiences. Journal of Retailing 76, 347–365 (2000)
20. Nyer, P.U.: The Determinants of Satisfaction: An Experimental Verification of the Moderating Role of Ambiguity. Advances in Consumer Research 23 (1996)
21. Yi, Y.: The determinants of consumer satisfaction: the moderating role of ambiguity. Advances in Consumer Research 20, 502–506 (1993)
22. Oliver, R.L.: Satisfaction: A behavioral perspective on the consumer. ME Sharpe (2010)
23. Söderlund, M.: Customer familiarity and its effects on satisfaction and behavioral intentions. Psychology & Marketing 19, 861–879 (2002)
24. Santos, R., Marreiros, G., Ramos, C., Neves, J., Bulas-Cruz, J.: Personality, emotion, and mood in agent-based group decision making (2011)
25. Schimmack, U., Oishi, S., Furr, R.M., Funder, D.C.: Personality and life satisfaction: A facet-level analysis. Personality and Social Psychology Bulletin 30, 1062–1075 (2004)
26. Judge, T.A., Heller, D., Mount, M.K.: Five-factor model of personality and job satisfaction: a meta-analysis. Journal of Applied Psychology 87, 530 (2002)

Improving Intelligent Systems: Specialization

Jesús A. Román, Sara Rodríguez, and Juan M. Corchado

Departamento Informática y Automática. Universidad de Salamanca
Plaza de la Merced s/n, 37008, Salamanca, Spain
{zjarg,srg,corchado}@usal.es

Abstract. The specialization exists in biological systems and in human organizations, as a methodology to improve processes and optimize their aims. This specialization in artificial intelligent systems such as multi-agent systems, can improve their aims, depending on the type of specialization and the goals which they need to achieve. The enterprise networks are a collaboration model between companies which we can apply over these intelligent systems, so that, these systems can achieve more complex aims. Therefore, in this collaboration type, is necessary to consider their specialization type, and how they could collaborate to achieve aims, that by themselves would not be possible.

Keywords: multi-agent systems, intelligent systems, specialization, intelligent communities.

1   Introduction

Many of the artificial intelligent systems try to emulate the operation of biological systems, which evolve to achieve their goals in the most efficient possible way (1) (2) (3). The human organizations within enterprise environments (4) (5) (6)are a type of biological systems, which pursue to maximize their benefits through organizational and specialization techniques, and through partnerships with other business environments. The assimilation of these organizational policies over artificial systems improves their efficiency with the introduction of features as specialization and collaboration between different systems which collaborate allowing achieve goals that, in an independent way, would be not possible. This methodology has been applied to improve the operation of a logistic system in a real company which works with two different type of software, and can not communicate between them. To do this, we have based in a previous works where Specialized Intelligent Communities are used. This paper is organized as follows. In section 2 the state of the art is introduced and the related work in biological and artificial systems. Section 3 analyzes the specialization in artificial systems. Section 4 introduces the case of study where the concepts of specialization and cooperation in intelligent systems are applied. Finally, in section 5, are presented the conclusions.

2   Related Work

Specialization can be defined as the particular characteristic of an individual within a group. This specialization is present in all kinds of areas, from biological systems (1)

J.M. Corchado et al. (Eds.): PAAMS 2014 Workshops, CCIS 430, pp. 378–385, 2014.

(2) (3), to enterprise production systems(6), if it is taken as a mechanism to achieve greater efficiency, in the common aims of the group.

The specialization in biological systems has been taken as a reference in human organizations to improve their aims. According to R. Melinkoff the principle of specialization begins when the activities of each of the members of an organized group should be confined, as far as possible, to the execution of a single task (4). In human organizations, specialization is a feature relative to the workstation, internally (4), or the final product or service offered by that organization. This specialization aims to achieve greater efficiency in the products or services offered by the organization. However, productivity increases when there are synergies between different specialized organizations that collaborate to obtain an optimal yield on common production processes, such as the enterprise networks (12)

In collaborative artificial systems, such as social multi-agent systems (13) (14) (15) (16) (8) (17) (18) (19) (20) (21), the specialization is an issue dealt with by several authors in works such as (22)among others . This specialization aims to provide greater efficiency for the artificial system, so that there is an improvement in the achievement of its overall aims.

The idea of apply the specialization of human organizations to intelligent systems, such as multi-agent systems, through business networks methodology, would improve the efficiency of the system units, the aims of the system, and possible goals that would have to be achieved in collaboration with other systems. To achieve this adaptation are used Specialized Intelligent Communities (SIC)(10) as a basis for the development of multi-agent systems, and distributed intelligent systems. These Intelligent Communities present the specialization as an internal feature to their constitution, being this feature very interesting in achieving our aims.

3   Specialization in Intelligent Systems

A complete classification of the types of specialization in cooperative artificial systems, and therefore in multi-agent systems, is given in (28), which suggests that the study of specialization in collaborative artificial systems has been approached from different perspectives depending on the approach that the authors have given their research. Example of these works are(26), among others.

Several authors in the literature, agree that the division of the objectives pursued by a group into specialized subtasks benefits the achieving these goals(35). However, the extrapolation of this specialization, from a point of view of a group of agents that collaborate atomically, in achieving broader goals is not still well defined.

The concept of enterprise network applied on artificial systems is introduced like Specialized Intelligent Communities(10). This type of systems are based in organizations and are fully autonomous. Among their features, they should be specialized, and they should have the ability to interact with each other to achieve overall objectives more complex, without losing their independence, being these features very important to achieve our aims.

4   Development of a Logistic System Based on an Enterprise Network

Often, computer systems which own businesses are generalists and do not allow to fully develop their business processes as they really are. Other times, exist custom developments which implement these business processes perfectly, however, the cost of these computer programs increases due to the time required to develop it. In both cases usually be the communications with other systems already running, a weak point, when is necessary to exchange data or extend functionalities.

In this case, there are no communications between two computer programs which belong to a real enterprise environment, therefore the principal aim is the development of this communication as a new functionality. This environment has the following characteristics:

The customer has two geographically separated locations, where in each one, are implemented different services. In the first one, are performed labors of production of livestock feed, and in the other one, is managed the logistic task. Both sites have a specific software to perform their activities, however the communication between them is not possible, and the management of logistics production is realized via phone and through emails and fax.

The proposed problem is the development of the data communications, from production site to logistics site because the time spent in this task is excessive. In addition, considering that there are several types of products, and in many cases, the final data are not correct because there are errors in shipping or in reception. Thus, is given the possibility that the correct information, is not delivered to the person responsible to perform the planning.

To solve this problem it is proposed a middleware system based on the architecture presented in the Specialized Intelligent Communities (SIC) (10). These SIC are composed by a fixed structure composed by three entities, a coordinator, a planner and an executor, which they are assigned specific and specialized tasks, that working independently and they can collaborate as an enterprise network. This system consists of three SIC which are described below:

Specialized Intelligent Community in Data Capture: This SIC runs itself independently, and their work consists in receiving production data. To achieve this, it is accessed to the production database periodically, checking if there are new products ready for shipment from the factory. If so, the data is extracted and encoded into a JSON format(36) as shown in table 1, to be sent later to the SIC responsible of logistic.

Specialized Intelligent Community in Logistic: Once received the notification and is verified the data integrity, a notification is send to the SIC of data capture. Subsequently, an analysis of these data is performed, and depending on the type of product and quantity, is loaded the information into the database of the software that manages the logistics, due to these features are considered for the distribution. For the estimation of priority to distribute the shipments, is used the expression given in 1.

$$P_{i=}Now(t) - T_R T_C \tag{1}$$

Table 1. Example of JSON data request

JSON request
{"date": "25/11/2013","time": "09:27","typeProducts":"A", "products": [{"name": "Product A","format":"packet 25 kg","lot": "154952013","quantity":30},{"name": "Product A","format":"packet 10 kg","lot": "154872013","quantity":100},{"name": "Product B","format":"packet 25 kg","lot": "284952013","quantity":50}]}

Where P_i is the order priority, Now(t) is the current date and time, T_R is the moment when the order is placed by the end customer and T_C is the type of client, that will change the weight of the order with values between 0 and 1. Through this priority, is the software of logistic which automatically calculates the available vehicles in the selected route, and their size.

Specialized Intelligent Community in Incident Management: The SIC is responsible for managing incidents that may occur during the process of communication between them. In case there is no successful communication, the data will be processed again for a set period of attempts, and if not possible this transmission, it will generate an incidence and will notify via email to the responsible for the administration of the information systems, finally will paralyze sending information until the incidence is not solved. All transactions are recorded in a file in order to determine the fails that could have occurred.

Having described the functions of each SIC individually, the collaboration of these, determines the true objective pursued. Through this assimilation to a vertical enterprise network (6), in which each SIC provides its services, is achieved the final purpose, which is the communication between two independent applications. Asynchronously, can be requested the services of each SIC to obtain reports, highlighting they are distributed so that the computational resources required are reduced. As shown in figure 1, is the SIC of data capture which checks the database of the application of production to check for new products. From this moment the production data are sent in a JSON format that travels through HTTP + SSL to the SIC responsible of logistic which manage the load orders as efficiently as possible and automatically, decrementing considerably the processing time of the orders.

The benefit provided by the specialization in this problem is the simplicity of each component of the intelligent system and the future extensions which can be needed, can be easily implemented in the system. In addition, the services provided by the SIC can be requested by any device and from any programming language, which gives even more versatility in its performance.

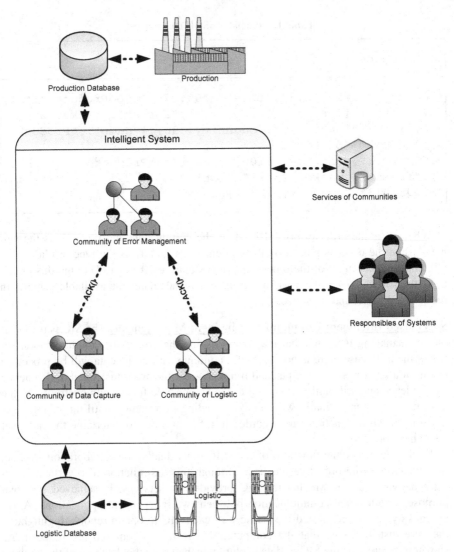

Fig. 1. Complete diagram of the system

The results obtained with the implementation of the system are completely satisfactory, having in account that the legacy system can not be replaced by a new system, because the system can reduce an important amount of time to specific jobs in
the two sites of the company, and therefore use this time to improve the processing of
orders. Another important feature is that the errors in the orders have been reduced
significantly because the generation of orders are made by our system automatically
with realtime data from the production system. Next, table 2 shows a summary of the
results obtained with the implementation of the intelligent system.

Table 2. Benefits of the intelligent system

Without Middleware	With Middleware
Long time to process orders	Important reduction of time process orders
Need several people to attend the orders	Automatic system to process orders
Problems with the quantity of products	No errors in quantity of products
Error control over the process	System to manage error control
No information in real time	Information in real time

5   Conclusions

We are aware that in large companies, the specialization in the jobs are an important feature(11)(37) (5), due to increases the productivity according specialization of workers. In an organization, the maximizing of their benefits due to the collaboration with other companies in the same field or complementary areas is a reality with the implementation of the enterprise networks(6)(12). In artificial systems is important to know and measure the type of specialization that have intelligent systems in order to optimize their performance. In addition, the assimilation of enterprise networks as a model of collaboration between companies, to intelligent systems, has allowed us to determine the possibility to fix more complicated goals that require a set of systems to complete their achievement.

The development of an intelligent system using Specialized Intelligent Communities as a basis for its development, allows the inclusion of specialization within the sys-tem, as an inherent feature of these entities, and their collaboration as enterprise net-works allows to reach more complex targets. If we have in account that the computer programs, used by the company, can not be replaced, the result of the implementation of the communication on the system has been completely satisfactory because there is a significant savings in the time taken to process the information, from production management to logistic management. The reduction of errors in receiving process of products has been improved significantly due to its automation and data extraction directly from the production database. However, the overall system operation is not completely correct, because that the communications fail repeatedly due to the location of the sites and the signal provided by the companies providing Internet. This aspect can be improved because in any distributed system is necessary that the communications run properly in terms of availability and speed.

Acknowledgements. This work has been carried out by the project Sociedades Humano-Agente: Inmersión, Adaptación y Simulación. TIN2012-36586-C03-03. Ministerio de Economía y Competitividad (Spain). Project co-financed with FEDER funds.

References

1. Wenseleers, T., Ratnieks, F., Billen, J.: Caste fate conflict in swarm-founding social hymenoptera: an inclusive fitness analysis. Evolutionary Biology 16(1), 647–658 (2003)
2. Bonabeau, E., Theraulaz, G.: Role and variability of response thresholds in the regulation of division of labour in insect societies. In: Deneubourg, J., Pasteels, J. (eds.) Information Processing in Social Insects, pp. 141–163. Springer, s.l. (1999)

3. Noirot, C., Pasteels, J.: Ontogenetic development and the evolution of the worker caste in termites. Experientia 43(1), 851–860 (1987)
4. Melinkoff, R.V.: La Estructura de la Organización. Universidad de Venezuela, s.l. (1969)
5. Borisov, E.F., Zhamin, V.A., Makarova, M.F.: Diccionario de Economía Política. España, Barcelona (1975)
6. Beccera, F.: Las redes empresariales y la dinámica de la empresa: aproximación teórica. INNOVAR. Revista de Ciencias Administrativas y Sociales 18(32), 27–45 (2008) 0121-5051
7. Sánchez, N., Fuentes, V., Carbó, J., Molina, J.M.: Knowledge-based system to define context in commercial applications. In: 8th ACIS International Conference on Software Engineering, Artificial Intelligence, Networking, and Parallel/Distributed Computing (SNPD 2007) and 3rd ACIS International Workshop on Self-Assembling Wireless Networks (SAWN 2007), pp. 694–699. s.n., Qingdao (2007)
8. Garijo, F., Gómes-Sanz, J.J., Pavón, J., Massonet, P.: Multi-agent system organization: An engineering perspective. Pre-Proceeding of the 10th European Workshop on Modeling Autonomous Agents in a Multi-Agent World, MAAMAW 2001 (2001)
9. Román, J.Á., Rodríguez, S., Corchado, J.M.: Distributed and Specialized Agent Communities. In: Pérez, J.B., et al. (eds.) Trends in Pract. Appl. of Agents & Multiagent Syst. AISC, vol. 221, pp. 33–40. Springer, Heidelberg (2013)
10. Román, J.A., Tapia, D.I., Corchado, J.M.: SCODA para el Desarrollo de Sistemas Multiagente. Revista Ibérica de Sistemas y Tecnologías de Información 8, 25–38 (2011)
11. Rusu, M.: Smart Specialization a Possible Solution to the New Global Challenges. Procedia Economics and Finance 6, 128–136 (2013)
12. Baum, H., Schütze, J.: An Organizational Concept for Collaborative Enterprise Networks. Procedia CIRP 7, 55–60 (2013)
13. Rodríguez, S., de Paz, Y., Bajo, J., Corchado, J.M.: Social-based planning model for multiagent systems. Expert Systems with Applications 38(10), 13005–13023 (2011)
14. Pinzón, C.I., Bajo, J., De Paz, J.F., Corchado, J.M.: S-MAS: An adaptive hierarchical distributed multi-agent architecture for blocking malicious SOAP messages within Web Services environments. Expert Systems with Applications 38(5), 5486–5499
15. Tapia, D.I., Abraham, A., Corchado, J.M., Alonso, R.S.: Agents and ambient intelligence: case studies. Journal of Ambient Intelligence and Humanized Computing 1(2), 85–93 (2010)
16. Tapia, D.I., De Paz, J.F., Rodríguez, S., Bajo, J., Corchado, J.M.: Multi-agent system for security control on industrial environments. International Transactions on System Science and Applications Journal 4(3), 222–226 (2008)
17. Bajo, J., De Paz, J.F., Rodríguez, S., González, A.: Multi-agent system to monitor oceanic environments. Integrated Computer-Aided Engineering 17(2), 131–144 (2010)
18. Bajo, J., Corchado, J.M.: Evaluation and monitoring of the air-sea interaction using a CBR-Agents approach. In: Muñoz-Ávila, H., Ricci, F. (eds.) ICCBR 2005. LNCS (LNAI), vol. 3620, pp. 50–62. Springer, Heidelberg (2005)
19. Rodríguez, S., Pérez-Lancho, B., De Paz, J.F., Bajo, J., Corchado, J.M.: Ovamah: Multiagent-based adaptive virtual organizations. In: 12th International Conference on Information Fusion, FUSION 2009, pp. 990–997 (2009)
20. Rodríguez, S., de Paz, Y., Bajo, J., Corchado, J.M.: Social-based planning model for multiagent systems. Expert Systems with Applications 38(10), 13005–13023 (2011)
21. Corchado, J.M., Bajo, J., De Paz, J.F., Rodríguez, S.: An execution time neural-CBR guidance assistant. Neurocomputing 72(13), 2743–2753 (2009)

22. Murciano, A., Millan, J.: Learning signaling behaviours and specialization in cooperative agents. Adaptative Behaviour 5(1), 5–28 (1997)
23. Li, L., Martinoli, A., Abu-Mostafa, Y.S.: Emergent specialization in swarm systems. In: Yin, H., Allinson, N.M., Freeman, R., Keane, J.A., Hubbard, S. (eds.) IDEAL 2002. LNCS, vol. 2412, pp. 261–266. Springer, Heidelberg (2002)
24. Chai, L., Chen, J., Han, Z., Di, Z., Fan, Y.: Emergence of Specialization from Global Optimizing Evolution in a Multi-agent Systems. In: Shi, Y., van Albada, G.D., Dongarra, J., Sloot, P.M.A. (eds.) ICCS 2007, Part IV. LNCS, vol. 4490, pp. 98–105. Springer, Heidelberg (2007)
25. Okamoto, S., Scerri, P., Sycara, K.: The Impact of Vertical Specialization on Hierarchical Multi-Agent Systems. In: Proceedings of the Twenty-Third AAAI Conference on Artificial Intelligence (2008)
26. Trueba, P., et al.: Specialization analysis of embodied evolution for robotic collective tasks. Robotics and Autonomous Systems 61, 682–693 (2013)
27. Brutschy, A., et al.: Costs and benefits of behavioral specialization. Robotics and Autonomous Systems 60, 1408–1420 (2012)
28. Nitschke, G., Schut, M., Eiben, A.: Emergent specialization in biologically inspired collective behavior systems. Intelligent Complex Adaptive Systems, 100–140 (2007)
29. Bongard, J.C.: The legion system: A novel approach to evolving heterogeneity for collective problem solving. In: Poli, R., Banzhaf, W., Langdon, W.B., Miller, J., Nordin, P., Fogarty, T.C. (eds.) EuroGP 2000. LNCS, vol. 1802, pp. 16–28. Springer, Heidelberg (2000)
30. Stone, P., Veloso, M.: Towards collaborative and adversarial learning: A case study in robotic soccer. Evolution and Learning in Multi-Agent Systems 48(1), 83–104 (2002)
31. Whiteson, S., et al.: Evolving keep-away soccer players through task decomposition. In: Proceeding of the Genetic and Evolutionary Computation Conference, pp. 356–368. AAAI Press, Chicago (2003)
32. Blumenthal, J., Parker, G.: Competing sample sizes for the co-evolution of heterogeneous agents. In: Proceedings of the 2004 IEEE/RSJ International Conference on Intelligent Robots and Systems, pp. 1438–1443. IEEE Press, Sendai (2004)
33. Arkin, R.: Behavior based robotics. MIT Press, Cambridge (1998)
34. Arkin, R., Balch, T.: Behavior-based formation control for multi-robot teams. IEEE Transactions on Robotics and Automation 14(6), 926–939 (1999)
35. Balch, T.: Measuring robot group diversity. In: Balch, T., Parker, E. (eds.) Robot Teams: From Diversity to Polymorphism, Natick, pp. 93–135 (2002)
36. ecma. The JSON Data Interchange Format. Starndard ecma-404 (2013)
37. Arruñada, B.: Economía de la Empresa: Un enfoque contractual. Ariel, Barcelona (1990)

Retraction Note to: HomeCare, Elder People Monitoring System and TV Communication

Victor Parra, Vivian López, and Mohd Saberi Mohamad

Retraction Note to:
Chapter 11 in: J.M. Corchado et al. (Eds.): PAAMS 2014
Workshops, CCIS 430, pp. 111–120, 2014.
https://10.1007/978-3-319-07767-3_11

The Series Editor and the publisher have retracted this chapter. An investigation by the publisher found that a number of chapters, including this one, from multiple conference proceedings raise various concerns, including but not limited to compromised editorial handling, inappropriate or unusual citation behavior and undisclosed competing interests. Based on the findings of the investigation, the Series Editor and the publisher no longer have confidence in the results and conclusions of this chapter.

Author Mohd Saberi Mohamad disagree with this retraction. Authors Victor Parra and Vivian López have not responded to correspondence regarding this retraction.

The retracted version of this chapter can be found at
https://10.1007/978-3-319-07767-3_11

J.M. Corchado et al. (Eds.): PAAMS 2014 Workshops, CCIS 430, p. C1, 2024.
© Springer International Publishing Switzerland 2024
https://doi.org/10.1007/978-3-319-07767-3_35

Author Index

Adam, Carole   66
Algarvio, Hugo   285, 297

Baskar, Jayalakshmi   89
Beltaief, Olfa   179
Bicharra Garcia, Ana Cristina   202
Billhardt, Holger   344, 358
Borucki, Jakub   133
Brazier, Frances M.T.   238
Budaev, Denis   1

Camacho-Páez, José   321
Carbo, Javier   191
Carneiro, João   368
Carrasco, Sergio   22
Carrascosa, Carlos   250, 358
Chowanski, Wojciech   133
Clausen, Anders   214
Corchado, Juan Manuel   54, 344, 358, 378
Corredera, Luis Enrique   333
Costa, Angelo   101

De la Prieta, Fernando   333
Demazeau, Yves   79, 214, 333
Dossou, Paul-Eric   156
Dugdale, Julie   13

El Hadouaj, Sameh   179

Fernandes, Ricardo   262
Fernández, Alberto   344

Gama, Oscar   101
García-Herrero, Jesús   167
García-Teodoro, Pedro   321
Genc, Zulkuf   238
Genthial, Damien   44
Ghazi, Sabri   13
Ghedira, Khaled   179
Griol, David   167
Grzybowska, Katarzyna   121
Gustavsson, Rune   226

Hallenborg, Kasper   79
Hoffa, Patycja   144
Hussain, Shahid   226

Jørgensen, Daniel   79
Julián, Vicente   344, 358

Khadir, Tarek   13
Kimura, Kenta   54

Laruhin, Vladimir   1
Levin, Evgeny   1
Lindgren, Helena   89
Lopes, Fernando   285, 297
Lopez, Mar   191
López, Vivian   111
Lorini, Emiliano   66

Magán-Carrión, Roberto   321
Marreiros, Goreti   368
Martí, Luis   202
Martin, Jorge   22
Matsui, Kenji   54
Mayorov, Igor   1
Mercier, Annabelle   44
Mitchell, Philip   156
Molina, Jose M.   191
Molina, José Manuel   167, 202
Molina, Martin   22
Morais, Hugo   262, 273

Nørregaard Jørgensen, Bo   214
Novais, Paulo   101, 368

Occello, Michel   44
Oey, Michel A.   238
Ogston, Elizabeth   238
Overill, Richard E.   309

Palomares, Alberto   250
Parra, Victor   111
Pawlewski, Pawel   133, 144, 156
Pedraza, Juanita   191
Pereira, Ivo F.   262
Pérez, Alberto   54
Pinto, Tiago   262, 273
Praça, Isabel   262, 273

Radzik, Tomasz   309
Raïevsky, Clément   44
Rebollo, Miguel   250
Rodríguez, Sara   54, 378
Román, Jesús A.   378

Saberi Mohamad, Mohd   111
Saied, Alan   309
Sánchez-Martin, Antonio J.   333
Sanchez-Pi, Nayat   202
Sanchis, Angel   358
Santos, Gabriel   262
Santos, Ricardo   368

Simoes, Ricardo   101
Sitek, Paweł   121
Skobelev, Petr   1
Sousa, Jorge   285
Sousa, Tiago M.   273

Taillandier, Franck   34
Taillandier, Patrick   34

Vale, Zita   262, 273

Wikarek, Jarosław   121

Printed in the United States
by Baker & Taylor Publisher Services